BRIGHT ALLIANCE

Advanced Praise for "Education in a Time Between Worlds"

Dr. Stein is right, schooling needs to change radically—and virtually every change that our worldwide culture needs at this time depends upon education itself. So there literally isn't a more important topic anywhere, which is what makes this book so incredibly significant. Education in a Time Between Worlds touches on all sorts of deeply important and urgent issues, takes a fair and judicious stand on virtually everything it discusses, and opens many areas too little discussed but too important to miss. This work stands on that extraordinary edge of history in which we all find ourselves moving and breathing, and the ways that it handles this staggeringly crucial topic are profound, inclusive, brilliant, and urgently needed.

—Ken Wilber, Founder of Integral Institute, author of over twenty books, including *Trump and a Post-Truth World*

Education is the cornerstone of democracy, not because it produces human capital, but because it enables participatory citizenship and the full actualization of self. During a time of global educational and humanitarian crisis, Stein's essays argue brilliantly for a vision of education that transcends reductive measurement tactics and genuinely empowers the world's youngest citizens, and the teachers to whom they are entrusted, to learn and live well.

—Mary Helen Immordino-Yang Ed.D. Associate Professor of Education, Psychology & Neuroscience, Brain & Creativity Institute; Rossier School of Education, University of Southern California

As is our education, so will be our civilization. Yet with innumerable factors shaping education today, to envision an appropriate education system for our time we need an encompassing framework and a big picture view. Education in a Time Between Worlds offers this and more: a vast integral view, a brilliant, incisive, and far-reaching analysis of the many factors misshaping education and society today, and a vision of what education and society could be tomorrow.

—Roger Walsh MD, Ph.D. Professor of Psychiatry, Philosophy and Anthropology, University of California, Irvine

Dr. Stein has given us a set of essays on education during the opening decades of the 21st century that soon escape their boundaries and overflow into the fabric of the entire culture. Not since William Irwin Thompson have we experienced such penetrating and richly engaging landscapes of cultural criticism.

—Allan Combs, Ph.D. Professor and Director of the Center for Consciousness Studies, California Institute of Integral Studies

Not since John Dewey has the world seen a thinker with the perspective, knowledge, and foresight of Zachary Stein. There are few books that can be described as truly transformative, in the sense of immediately altering our perspective and action in this world—Stein's book is one of those few. Education in a Time Between Worlds is a timely masterpiece—it illustrates to the reader both where we stand in the history of our cultural evolution and how design decisions in the field of education will be instrumental in shaping our future. Every school and university administrator, every government official, every teacher and every student of education should read this book, deliberate over its contents and work together with passion, perspective, knowledge, and foresight to transform the way we learn together in the future.

—Mike Hogan, Ph.D. Senior Lecture in Psychology, National University of Ireland, Galway

Zachary Stein is a new kind of thinker, merging head and heart, and seeking to find a place for emergent forms of spirituality and religion in tomorrow's educational systems. This book sets the standard for integral scholarship and shows the power of truly comprehensive frameworks for thinking about global futures.

—Marc Gafni, Ph.D. Co-founder & President, Center for Integral Wisdom, Author, *A Return to Eros*

Education in a Time Between Worlds is a highly innovative and challenging analysis of the human condition.... The critical dialectics of this book are illuminating; while at the same time the positive contributions regarding pedagogy, philosophy, psychology, and emancipatory politics are breathtaking.

—Hans G. Despain, Ph.D. Professor and Department Chair of Economics, Nichol College, USA and Visiting Professor of Economics and Finance, University of Saint Joseph, Macau, China

Zak Stein is emerging as one of the most refined planetary thinkers of our age—this book is a must read not only for those concerned with educational reform but for those looking for ways out from the false postmodern impasses that block the exercise of the critical-integral imagination so vital to planetary well-being.

—Michael Schwartz, Ph.D. Columbia University, Professor in the Department of Art and Design, Augusta University, and Co-Founding Executive Director of the International Comparative and Continental Philosophy Circle

Dr. Stein's engaging and provocative volume sits at the nexus of meta-theories, political action, educational reform, and human development. The assessment of how the crisis in education is part of the larger global meta-crisis is astute and psychoactive...In a refreshing concrete utopian style Stein paints a vivid picture of what actually is possible. This volume has given me hope and a grounded sense of how we might together create an education-centric planetary society.

—Sean Esbjörn-Hargens, Ph.D. Founder of MetaIntegral and co-editor of *Metatheory for the Twenty-First Century*

Education in a Time Between Worlds

Essays on the Future of Schools, Technology, & Society

Zachary Stein

BRIGHT
ALLIANCE

Education in a Time Between Worlds

Published by Bright Alliance

First Edition

ISBN 978-0-9862826-7-6

BrightAlliance.org

Book layout and design: Brad Reynolds
integralartandstudies.com

Printed and Bound in the United States

For Meghan, again.
My truest inspiration and greatest teacher.

Dr. Zachary Stein is a writer, speaker, and transformative educator working to bring a greater sense of justice and sanity to education. Zak was educated at Hampshire College and Harvard University, during which time he co-founded Lectica, a non-profit organization dedicated to redesigning standardized testing infrastructures. He has taught classes at Harvard University and Meridian University, and has been invited to speak at a wide range of venues, from the National Security Agency to off-the-grid spiritual retreat centers. Zak currently serves as the academic director for the Center for Integral Wisdom, and offers human development and learning science consultations to schools, organizations, and educational technology companies. He lives with his wife Meghan in Vermont.

Table of Contents

Preface
Integral *Paideia*

PAIDEIA is a Greek word with wide-ranging connotations. It is broadly about the raising of younger members of society in the context of a *polity*, or political community.[1] The creation of a collective paideia was believed to transcend and include the creation of a polity. A well-functioning paideia is a community drawn together by commitment to an explicit philosophy of the good life and a related praxis of education. A paideia is a community that is focused on the creation of a certain kind of virtuous human, a community in which economics and politics are subordinate to an explicitly educational vision. This is a society in which life itself is understood as a process of deliberate cultural and ethical aspiration across generations. According to this way of thinking when new forms of social life are created, when new polities are founded, when revolutions are undertaken and sustained, they require more than legislating new laws and transferring property and sovereignty. Remaking society requires remaking education—instituting a new vision of the paideia. Groups can change society by establishing alternate modes of education; new modes of education shape the future of all political and economic life because they involve the creation of a new kind of human.

The creation of the United States is a case in point. From the first Puritans to arrive in what would become the Massachusetts Bay Colony, to the founding fathers who would wage a revolutionary war, the ancient Greek notion of the paideia explicitly shaped the visions of emerging community life in the young nation. It was very clear that the creation of a new kind of society would require the creation of a new kind of human. The American Revolution was as much an educational venture as a political or economic one.

The American (educational) Revolution followed a pattern discussed in the first chapter. It was preceded and enabled by a revolution in educational technologies: "North America was colonized during the first phase of Europe's age of print, the initial two-hundred-year period after Gutenberg, when a reading public gradually came into being that for the first time in history was not confined to the clerisy or the aristocracy.... The colonists brought books."[2] They also brought printing presses (even when cargo space on ships was precious) and printed their own textbooks, which they understood as essential goods in the creation and perpetuation of a new civilization. New technologies (printing) made possible new forms of education (pamphlets and textbooks), which enabled the new forms of socialization that eventually created profoundly revolutionary sentiments and capacities. The *American paideia* would display what I discuss below as the *contradictory* nature of education: it was both liberating and oppressive. The United States would eventually assume leadership in spreading the *modern-capitalist paideia*. Public schools in the image of what first emerged in the revolutionary Massachusetts Bay Colony would shape education throughout the world-system for over two centuries.

In this book I claim that humanity is on the verge of another revolution in the foundations of our collective paideia. A new society is coming into being, which will entail educational configurations of unprecedented size, scope, and complexity. We live in a time of global transformation, when major social and natural systems are in transition, and our only hope of survival is to find ways to support future generations in their development and learning. Educational configurations in the twenty-first century must provide for the proliferation of different and better capabilities than we now possess, new and better identities than we now live with—nothing less than a new and better humanity is needed. Human identities will need to be world-centric, capable of dealing with complexity, cultural difference, and dynamic ethical realities. This describes a level of human consciousness and capability sometimes described as *integral*, because it is self-consciously motivated to integrate or include as much of reality as possible. Integral consciousness is motivated to always learn, grow, and develop. Our goal then must be to initiate the emergent, decentralized, and democratic adoption of integral educational practices across the globe. This is one of the few sane catalysts for a world-system pivot, one of the few ways left open to us that might usher in an epoch of plenitude, justice, and ecological responsibility. The most ambitious vision for actually accomplishing this would be a *planetary integral paideia.* Creating such an education-centric society would take a miracle. Thirteen of them in fact, which I discuss in Chapter 3.

Integral education is humanity's best hope for the future, or so I argue in about a dozen different ways in the essays that follow. The term *integral* is used deliberately and with reference to a particular body of thought and practice; it is contrasted throughout with the mainstream *human capital theory* of education that dominates reform in most places. This book is the climax of over a decade of engagement with the integral meta-theory of philosopher Ken Wilber. I can say of Wilber what John Dewey once said of Hegel: that he "left a permanent deposit in my thinking." Of course, just as Dewey was no Hegelian, I am no Wilberian. Wilber's model is one of many that I work with, from Rawls to Habermas, Bhaskar to Peirce. As I explain in the Introduction, philosophy is a pragmatic and problem-focused affair and I take what I need from a repertoire of theories. Thing is: Wilber's work has been able to give what I need more frequently than most. This is why I have been so actively working with it for close to fifteen years.

As the essays here demonstrate, in my hands Wilber's integral meta-theory is not a proprietary language for use by experts, nor is it an invention of one man's mind. It is not a Cartesian instrument of theoretical colonization, nor is it a judgmental method for ranking and categorizing people and cultures.[3] Integral theory is a tool, like a map or compass. It orients us to reality, but is not itself reality. Integral theory, also like a map or compass, tells us only what we already know or could come to find out for ourselves. The map reveals territory we could go checkout for ourselves, just as the compass reveals the direction of the pole, which we could also triangulate from the stars. Integral theory is not attempting to tell you something you can't find out any other way, but rather inviting you to see and understand what you already know in a new way. It is my hope that even those who are constitutionally opposed to things like "meta-theory" and "integral" will be drawn into the analysis and vision it allows me to articulate here.

Ken Wilber's work appears at the confluence of several complex cultural trends, both in the academy and in the broader marketplace of ideas that constitutes our postmodern public sphere and civil society. In the 1990s a polycentric movement began to emerge, catalyzed by Wilber's ever-expanding theoretical models and voluminous writings. Integral theory has been on the fringes of the academy, but has also gained the respect of certain key individuals near the academy's heart.[4] It has been dismissed as New Age spirituality, and cult-like, while also influencing high-level decision-makers in US politics and the United Nations. Generally speaking, the influence of Wilber's work is hard to characterize because of its heterogeneity and the various decentralized modes of cultural production and activism it has spawned. However, one thing they all have in common is their frequent and significant use of the term *integral.*

The term is magical in some user's mouths, containing richly numinous and almost religious semantic potentials. This is in large part because the brief history of the term includes thinkers of a deeply religious bent. The great Indian freedom fighter and sage Sri Aurobindo, the visionary philosopher and psychologist James Mark Baldwin, the cryptic cultural seer and historian Jean Gebser. Wilber himself has documented his life as a religious adept, practitioner, and controversial public pundit.[5] So association of the term *integral* with terms from religious discourse is often warranted. In the final essay of this book I explore the forms of education that can emerge when we use a definition of *integral* that includes the validity and value of specific forms of religious and spiritual experiences and discourses.

It should also be noted that unlike much integral theorizing, mine is politically radical. I use integral theory to critique existing systems and to explore the need for and possibility of a radically different social world. This makes some of the arguments intensely personal and intentionally politically provocative. This personal and political edge is potent in part because this book was written during a period of profound personal tragedy and pain, brought on by the debilitating iatrogenic illness of my wife, Meghan (an iatrogenic illness is one that results *from* medical treatment; in Meghan's case, it was a prescription drug, taken as prescribed, that resulted in significant brain damage). I have been serving her as a caregiver intensively for five years. The whole heart-wrenching experience is slowly drawing to an end as Meghan continues her brave and inspiring recovery. Over the past year Meghan helped with crucial edits on this book and is one of my closest thought partners. However, the injustice of her situation and the situations of the millions of people like her cannot be understood without grasping how *the health care industry is being systematically distorted by the profit motive*. Malpractice is too weak a word when what has happened involves the knowing collusion of entire industries in the suppression of research and the perpetuation of profitable deceptions. This experience radicalized me politically and brought home what were once only theoretical ideas about the nature of the capitalist world-system.

The experience of being a caregiver has also rearranged the relationship between my heart and my head. John Rawls, the great theorist of social justice, always maintained that we must judge a society first and foremost by how it treats its most vulnerable members. The sick, the young, the poor, the refugee, the so-called "wretched of the earth"—it is they who should be at the center of our concerns about the social world. It is not the powers and lives of the privileged few that signify the extent of human progress. It is the positions and lives of the least well off that are the true indicators of our progress as a civilization. Look around and tell me that we cannot do better to protect and care for those who need it most.

A Word on the Essays

I have prefaced each essay with a preamble that positions it in relation to the other essays and explains the quirks of how, when, and why it was written. The theme of the integral paideia is used to weave the essays together. Each offers a vision of a new future for education based on the orienting generalizations of integral meta-theory.

This is a long and complex book, for which I do not apologize. I intend for it to feel a bit out of control, like it is a bit too much. This is because I want to transform readers. This book is written to function like a psychoactive agent or learning catalyst. My goal has been to make it both interesting and readable, while also remaining challenging and informative. This is one reason the book is divided into essays. Each is a stand-alone chapter containing subsections that can be read in one sitting. The endnotes also serve this end of scaffolding the reader, allowing one to get a deeper story if desired, or to stay with the main text and worry about the endnoted details later. Some endnotes are short essays in themselves; these are noted in the table of contents. While the Introduction and Chapter 1 set the tone for the book, it is certainly possible to jump around as interests dictate. My hope is that each reader can find their own unique way to engage with the overarching themes that weave a larger constellational unity, holding the essays together. These themes point the way toward a saner and more just planetary society. Here is a partial list of these themes, which I elaborate below to conclude this preface:

- The central importance of education as an aspect of the global meta-crisis.
- The inadequacy of approaches to education based on reductive human capital theory.
- The interdependence between educational organizations, teacherly practice, and the rest of society and culture.
- The potentially revolutionary impact of computer technologies on educational practices.
- The importance of retheorizing teacherly authority in contemporary educational configurations.
- The need to revisit the role of religiosity and spirituality as an aspect of human development and education.
- The value of concrete utopian theorizing in a time of planetary transformation.

The future depends on the articulation of a new vision of humanity and a new sense of what is possible for the planet and everyone on it. These essays are fumbling attempts to forge an emergent meta-theory that is suitable for framing a planetary meta-ethics that can justify and motivate the truly revolutionary changes that are necessary if generations to come are to have anything like a life worth living. One of the guiding themes of this book is *the central importance of education as an aspect of the global meta-crisis*. I repeatedly discuss the importance of educational activism and innovation as a political instantiation of emancipatory philosophy. The idea that oppressive and unjust educational systems can undermine the very possibility of humanity's continued existence is urgent. Disempowerment, distortions of personality, and the forfeiture of self-actualization must all be explicitly seen for what they are, while the structures that perpetuate them must be undone and redesigned. We can no longer assume (if we ever could) the unproblematic intergenerational transmission of essential human capacities for reasoning and reflection. These have always been hard-won developmental achievements that are contingent upon the availability and utilization of educational resources.

In this book I hope I have clarified the importance of education in the project of human emancipation, while also clarifying some of the impediments to revolutionary educational movements in contemporary society. The educational resources needed to enable maturity and autonomy are becoming increasingly scarce due to the continued push of neoliberal and neoconservative political agendas. The *contradictory* nature of education as a social practice becomes apparent in light of the dynamics of capitalism's ceaseless occupation of the schools. Education can be a source of oppression or a source of liberation; we can be educated toward greater freedoms or away from them.

This brings us to *the inadequacy of approaches to education based on reductive human capital theory*. As discussed at length in the Introduction and Chapter 2, human capital theory frames education in terms of economic realities, where students are understood as being prepared primarily for entry into the wage labor system. The schools have "succeeded" when they have contributed to economic growth. This leads to a kind of instrumental logic that distorts the relationships between teachers, students, parents, administrators and others with a stake in the outcomes of schooling. What I have called the logic of the *education commodity proposition* makes learning into a measurable commodity and the student into an object to be designed for optimal social efficiency. This is a way of thinking exemplified by the bad symbiosis between standardized testing, ADHD diagnoses, and stimulant prescriptions, discussed further in Chapter 2.

This is why another theme tracked throughout the book is the *interdependence between educational organizations, teacherly practice, and the rest of society and culture.* The social miracles discussed in Chapter 4 get to the heart of this. Imagine how different education would be if there was a basic income guarantee. Imagine the dynamics of teacherly authority about religious topics in schools after there is widespread acceptance of the unity of all religions and their compatibility with the scientific method and evolutionary thinking. Schools have always been nested within the other basic structures of the social system, from the economy, culture, and food systems, to the roads and buses. This means that reforming education does not need to start with schools. The priorities of education and learning can drive policy reform in sectors other than education. Education could be revolutionized by new technologies (such as augmented reality) or currencies (such as Illich's edu-credit card, discussed in Chapter 1), for example.

This meshwork between the education system and all other social systems brings us to another theme, which is *the potentially revolutionary impact of computer technologies on educational practices.* So far the potentials of educational technologies far exceed their accomplishments. The seemingly miraculous educational powers of the Internet have been harnessed by the state or simply bought. In Chapter 1, I propose some abstract design parameters for integral educational technologies and envision their potential future creation and use. Importantly, I proceed assuming that new educational technologies will eventually be so powerful as to make obsolete the institutional forms that characterize what we now call schooling. These kinds of technologies will need to lead us out of the fragmentation and spectacle of the contemporary new media. What now passes as "educational technology" is too often uninformed by the sciences of learning. It offers a depoliticized pedagogy of streaming video, didactic instruction, and mouse-and-click test prep. Lessons about the consumption of web-based content learned in school are taken home by students, where they consume hours of streaming video a day, clicking through an endless variety of claims, answers, and "facts," careening through a cultural techno-info-dreamscape.

The dangers and inadequacies of the new media as an educational environment lead to the next major theme of the book: *the importance of retheorizing teacherly authority and responsibility in contemporary educational configurations.* How do we decide who is the teacher and who is the student? What is to be taught? How should it be taught? And taught according to whose authority? All kinds of authority are now being contested in postmodern culture, and teacherly authority is without a doubt one kind of authority that has both healthy and unhealthy aspects. I examine the dynamics of teacherly authority and how they relate to levels of development in the Introduction and throughout. Teacherly authority is an essential aspect of meaningful educational relationships. This authority has for too long been in the hands of the state and church. In tomorrow's educational landscapes teacherly authority will be distributed and dynamic. Recognizing the teacherly authority of others (that is, choosing the role of student) is also an essential aspect of all meaningful educational configurations. The role of student is currently at risk of being distorted as educational goods are increasingly subject to market transaction—a part of the commodification of education—where the student as *customer* is beginning to replace the student as *learner*. Tomorrow's educational systems will need to re-imagine the relationships between teacher and student beyond the hierarchal authorities of state and church, as well as beyond the new authoritarianism of corporate-backed educational reform, as discussed in Chapter 2.

In the domains of religion and spirituality, teacherly authority is at its most powerful and most contested. This brings us to the penultimate theme woven through the final two chapters: *the need to revisit the role of religiosity and spirituality as an aspect of human development and education.* To be clear: I am not arguing that Ken Wilber and Marc Gafni ought to constitute the cannon of tomorrow's integral paideia. They are discussed as interesting examples—ones somewhat close to me personally—representing the emergent forms of spiritual and intellectual teacherly authority that are arising as postmodern culture continues to expand, fracture, and encircle the planet. The new public intellectual, the new spiritual teacher, and the new education go together, especially as the walls of the schools begin to come down and information begins to flow freely through a vast and technologically sophisticated network of localized educational hubs, as envisioned in Chapter 1.

This vision of replacing schools with a decentralized network of educational hubs demonstrates the final major theme of this book: *the value of concrete utopian theorizing in a time of planetary transformation.* Dystopian predictions and conspiracy theories are all too easy to come by these days (I even offer a few in these pages). What is harder to do is to articulate a positive future that is both possible and clearly preferable to the social world we are taught to accept. Critique is an important and necessary first step, but reconstruction and new creation comes next, which requires vision and action. In this book I discuss social miracles, educational hub networks, new-paradigm measurement infrastructures, emergent educational technologies, and new forms of spirituality and activism—these are all guesses at the riddle of our preferable futures. The value of the concrete utopian is as a catalyst for the social imagination, which is one of our scarcest and most important resources during this time of planetary transformation.

The arguments in the essays here provide elements for a *revolutionary educational politics*, guided by the vision of a *planetary integral paideia*. I seek to disclose the reality of universal human emancipation that is always already immanent as a possibility latent in human social structures. The pulse of freedom, as it were, is irrepressible, ubiquitous, and indefatigable. These essays contain a view of social justice in which human liberation catalyzes *the rational directionality of geo-history* toward universal human flourishing. The planetary transition we are riding out provides us with an opportunity to transform into an education-centric society in which the free development of each individual is the condition for the free development of all. Still open to us is this possibility of a planet-wide refocusing of resources toward educational praxis. Seizing this opportunity requires a new and profound vision of what education is for and how it can be institutionalized as a basic structure of society.

Zak Stein
Burlington, Vermont
July, 2018

---

1. Etymologically the word *paideia* is related to the root of the suffix *–pedia*, as in encyclo*pedia* or Wiki*pedia*.

2. Cremin (1970, pp. 27-28).

3. There is a large and contentious literature on Wilber's work consisting mostly of self-published online articles and a couple book-length critiques, all of which I largely avoid discussing here. I've spent a great deal of time with a great deal of this literature, which ranges from essential criticisms of Wilber's blind spots to caustic *ad-hominem* attacks bordering on emotional outbursts. Similarly, there is a great deal of writing published online by the so-called "integral community" consisting of individuals who have been influenced by Wilber's writings, and who consume and/or produce workshops, media, and conferences related to it. This has led to the commodification of integral approaches, concerns about the "integral brand," brand purity, and brand loyalty. Which is to say, the so-called "integral movement" has succumbed to the logic of the postmodern educational marketplace, fracturing and splintering into a bunch of different competing initiatives, each predicated on proving its own authenticity and originality and in turn the illegitimacy of others.

4. When I was in graduate school at Harvard there were over half a dozen key faculty who all said to me that they admired Wilber's work. And yet none encouraged me to use it in my dissertation, nor did any cite him themselves. It is interesting to see that there are certain subjects (such as religious and spiritual experiences, or going beyond biological reductionism in the human sciences) which are taboo to discuss in polite academic company.

5. See: *One Taste* (1999), where Wilber relates his religious and spiritual practices and beliefs, mostly of Buddhist lineage. Other contemporaries using the term *integral* with religious or spiritual connotations include: Thompson (2004); Laszlo (2004); Esbjörn-Hargens & Zimmerman (2009).

Introduction
Theorizing Education at the Edge of History

> Humanity will need to realize now that neither religions, nation-states, nor machines can serve any longer as the appropriate vehicles for human cultural evolution. Each of the mentalities of the past has had its appropriate educational institution to bring forth the new mentality, from the temple to the Pythagorean Academy to the House of Wisdom in Al Kwarizmi's Baghdad to the modern scientific and technical university. Now a new institution will have to be created to embody and foster the new planetary civilization. My generation did what it could within the political limitations imposed by the commercial materialism, academic nihilism, and religious fanaticism of our time; but the countercultural [educational] institutions... were more like crocuses signaling a change of season in early March than they were the hardy trees that could withstand a blizzard in April or a new climate.
>
> —William Irwin Thompson[1]

This book brings together six essays about the future of education. Each essay takes a different view of the same problem: *what should education look like in the twenty-first century?* This question involves many other questions. Where is the place of schools in this age of online education marketplaces? How useful are existing curricula in a new world where climatological chaos will usher in the end of capitalism? Who still reads

.oks or cares about moral wisdom in an era when commoditized screen cultures spawn fractured and disembodied identities? Do we really know what kinds of skills are needed in perpetually volatile labor markets and technology intensive workplaces? Who are we to tell future generations what to think, feel, or do with this world we are leaving them? Despite some superficial answers from corporate think tanks and academics: *twenty-first century education is an unknown entity*. It is still a future unrealized. Twenty-first century education is beyond what anyone can yet imagine, let alone implement.

Education is happening in unprecedented contexts as new technologies are propelling mass-education beyond schooling. The world will transform in the coming decades and humanity's survival will require people with unprecedented skills and capacities—people with fundamentally new kinds of identities. Under this pressure to learn humanity will utilize any and all methods and tools to educate and train future generations. This urgency is double-edged. There are dystopian visions in which the temptation to *design* future generations creates a preference for instrumental logic: students become objects to be worked upon by a crisis-ridden corporate garrison state, drugged and tested and inundated with images on screens for hours a day.

These essays forecast *positive alternatives* to what are very real and dire possible futures for educational systems. I outline a variety of pathways toward a more positive—even utopian—future for education in the twenty-first century. The field of educational futures is inherently complex and transdisciplinary, involving concerns about the nature of human learning, economics, and ethics. In each essay that follows I attempt to articulate an integral view of education: a view that captures as comprehensive a picture as possible, putting all of what is educationally relevant under one umbrella. Education is perhaps the most important area to engage in the practice of concrete utopian theorizing during our current historical juncture.[2] We must find a way to break open into a new civilization based on new frontiers of human potential.

Education and the Frontier of Human Potential

> The future is a race between catastrophe and education.
>
> —H.G. Wells

Several historians have suggested that with the closing of the American West early in the twentieth century, education became the new frontier. Education came to be invested with the ameliorative and utopian (and opportunistic and exploitative) energies that once characterized westward expansion.[3] During the nineteenth century the Western frontier exemplified the possibilities of American democracy and before that the American continent itself was seen as the great frontier—the New World. Its vast expanses and resources were understood as indispensable enablers of a future full of opportunity, freedom, and equality. In the nineteenth century, the "problems" of immigration and labor, of urban crime and poverty, of anomie and economic stagnation—these could all be solved by heading West, it was said, where the future of America was being forged, where everyone looked out toward an open horizon. Since the early twentieth century, so the argument goes, these same ideals and energies have been tied to the possibilities of education. Just as the West was once thought to make all things possible, so now education is saddled with the burdens of accomplishing democracy. Just as the opening of the West once held off social collapse, conflict, and stagnation, today educational opportunities are the repository of our hopes for a better social world. Now more than ever we find truth in the wisdom of H. G. Wells quoted above: "the future is a race between catastrophe and education."

In this book I argue that *education is the new planetary frontier*. Preferable futures for our species now require the discovery and exploration of unimagined potentials within humanity itself. Notice that I said "exploration" and not "exploitation." Looking at the history of the frontiers of our civilization teaches that the discovery of a new frontier is typically followed quickly by its exploitation. The perpetual colonization of new *commodity frontiers* is part of what has allowed for the resolution of the recurring crises of our capitalist world-system, as I explain in the first chapter. Education is a frontier. And it can be treated like a commodity.[4] Some venture capitalists are already seeing the privatization of educational systems as an Information Age gold rush.[5] This book is in part about rolling back the commodification of educational experience. This book is also about what it will take to liberate and democratize the wide-open frontiers of human potential, which represent the last great hope for our species. I am especially interested in the forms of social organization, technology, and theoretically guided practice that have the potential to profoundly expand the horizons of educational opportunity, impact, and innovation.

I offer these ideas in the context of a multi-decade global expansion of certain specific techno-economic structures and related political organizations, which have made it so that the rule of law and democratic governance processes are increasingly jeopardized in societies worldwide. Climatological chaos is adding fuel to this fire. It is not a coincidence that this is unfolding during what appears to be the climax of free market capitalism and the massive industries it has spawned, built around scientific and technological innovation. As diverse and geographically distant markets and cultures have become irreversibly interconnected through increasingly complex communication networks, all the nations in the world have come to share a common historical trajectory. Since the end of colonialism and the failure of the Soviet experiment there has appeared to be no alternative to the dominant modes of political and economic organization. This means that those major shifts in the trajectory of the world-system, such as those needed to handle climate change and terrorism, are likely to be seen as impossible and out of the question. The possibility of creating a radically new social world has become difficult to even speak about, so weak is our social imagination. Yet we face a pressing need for truly deep social transformation—literally a need to re-imagine humanity. Profound changes in educational systems worldwide must take place in order to secure a just and sustainable global future.

Importantly, *education* as I use the term here signifies more than what happens in schools. Indeed, a large part of what follows is an argument in favor of redesigning schools down to their foundation. *Schooling,* as we have known it, is just one form of education—albeit a particularly important and powerful form. But recent educational configurations have also involved the rise of publishing industries, television, film, and Internet content providers. All have educational affordances and represent some of the most expansive possibilities on the current educational frontier. I argue here that all these new mediums of modern education must be transcended and included within a new kind of educational system. The chapters that follow sketch the shape of this emergent educational system, as well as the kinds of social and cultural changes that would be needed to make it a reality.

My argument is that education, thus broadly defined, and thus fundamentally reconceived, serves a unique and powerful function in the emerging global civilization that surrounds us today. There are no major global challenges that do not have critical educational dimensions. Many key challenges are primarily educational in nature. This is just another way of saying that changing the trajectory of the world-system requires changing how people think and act, which can only be done by finding ways to affect valued and needed transformations of human capabilities. Human development and education are often the elephant in the room when it comes to calls for system-level change.

My line of thought suggests that the climate crisis is actually a crisis of human decision-making, and that educational initiatives are as important, if not more, than legal and economic ones. If the demands of building sustainable systems and lifestyles are more complex than the capabilities of those asked to do so, which I argue is the case today on a massive scale, then no matter how much funding we throw at sustainability technologies our efforts will fail. Building a "smarter planet" through technology and policy is necessary (à la IBM), but *smarter people* are a basic and primary prerequisite. Wilber suggested as much over two decades ago when he noted that the greatest threat to the biosphere is not industrial pollutants but the low level of human capability with regard to relevant decision-making domains.[6] The current crisis in the human-biosphere relationship is only one example. We are "in over our heads" across the board. What we need to understand and do in order to survive seems to be continually outstripping our abilities.[7]

This reading of the climate crisis clarifies what is actually a general trend in contemporary society—a trend toward *educational crises* of increasing prevalence and intensity. Figure 1 displays the general structure of an educational crisis. The mismatch between the demands made on us by the world and the capabilities we have to work with is the great meta-crisis of our time, characterizing the struggles of individuals, organizations, and nation-states.

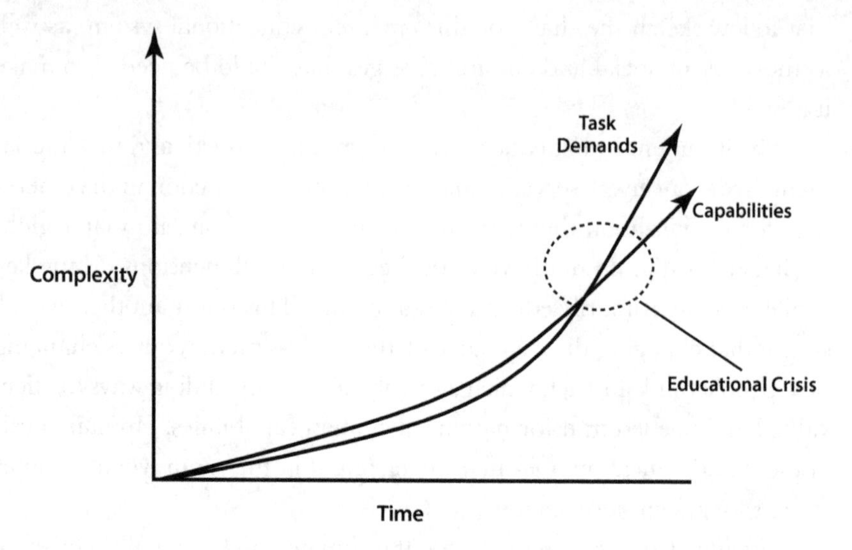

Figure 1: An educational crisis occurs when the complexity (diversity, quality) of task demands outstrips the available capabilities. This can happen to both individuals and societies. Based on a comparable figure rendered by Carreira (2009).

The task demands of work and life outstrip individual capabilities on multiple fronts. It is often said that rapid technological change will lead to a "learning society" that has educational practices and opportunities hard-wired into its institutional DNA.[8] But our individual lives are shaped by more than new technologies and the new demands they make of us at our jobs. Unprecedented forms and amounts of debt put economic pressures on families that profoundly shape life histories, disrupting socialization patterns while generating chronic deficits in mental and physical health. Meanwhile, advances in biomedical technology and an increasingly unwieldy health care system put unprecedented decision-making demands on already sick individuals, who must navigate ever-shifting diagnostic categories, treatment options, and the complexity of the insurance industries, not to mention the new and overwhelming universe of medical information on the Internet. Communications technologies enable expansive social networking opportunities that profoundly alter identity formation and decision-making patterns. New computer technologies are fueling expansions in bureaucratic apparatuses and measurement infrastructures, such as standardized tests, tax forms, and Facebook accounts, which are fragmenting our identities and leaving us overwhelmed, self-consciously surveilled, and confused about what is true and who to trust. Simply put, the construction of a continuous and coherent life-project is more demanding than it has ever been.[9]

Education is a growth market. From self-help books, life coaches, and online universities, to ADHD medication, the blogosphere, and Google, large swaths of society are groping for ways to cope with the mounting complexities of the historical moment. Demand for effective education far exceeds supply. There appears to be a *scarcity* of educational opportunities. We think there is not enough education to go around, and right when we all feel we need it so desperately.[10] This is a kind of artificial scarcity similar to the artificial scarcities created around energy, food, and money, which I discuss in Chapter 4. Education, learning, and human potential are infinite resources.[11] Learning is, in fact, an activity much like breathing or digestion, a natural process that the human organism engages in by its very nature, spontaneously. As the discussion of learning theory and human development in this Introduction will show, *humans are built to learn.* The all too common idea that learning is something that requires professional guidance and state-sanctioned materials is profoundly misguided. Every child learns to walk, speak, eat, and to do any number of other things through educational interactions that are unforced, easy, involve no expertise or commodities, and are often quite joyful. Your mind does not need to be coerced to learn—learning is its natural state. Schooling, on the other hand, is quite unnatural, and that is why all known public school systems have required some forms of coercion, a point to which I will return. My goal here is simply to clarify the fact that there is a false sense of scarcity surrounding human potential, learning, and education. We are scrambling for solutions to an educational crisis involving profound inequalities of learning opportunity between the haves and have-nots, based entirely on the idea that there is only so much education to go around, only so many opportunities to learn. There must therefore be competition for opportunity, as if education is a zero-sum game and more learning for you means less for me.

This perceived sense of scarcity allows snake oil salesmen to successfully sell so-called "brain-based" educational approaches to unsuspecting parents and teachers. This allows drugs claimed to improve attention and performance to be regularly handed out to children, and unreflectively endorsed by school leaders, yet the impacts of long-term usage have been shown to be profoundly damaging. This allows psychotherapy, executive coaching, and professional development programs of various shapes and sizes to proliferate at the very limits of what the market will bear in terms of quality and ethics. This allows the hopes of educators to be pinned on the latest technology or website that claims to be revolutionizing education. As I argue at length in Chapter 1, it is wrong to assume that educational benefits follow easily from emerging computer technologies, be it a search engine, Wiki, blog, or e-learning module with live streaming video. Informational technologies are *not*, by definition, educational technologies. The design of educational technologies must be a deeply deliberate practice, informed by philosophical meta-theory, human development, and the new sciences of learning (or so I argue in what follows). Today it is mostly market dynamics that determine what educational technologies are available, and there is no oversight or quality control in the educational technologies industries, which are rapidly growing nonetheless.

This is the context in which those who seek to shape the future of educational systems find themselves. Cultural trends and market dynamics work to counteract alternative forms of value and validly within educational configurations. Powerful political and economic forces have shaped mainstream education toward technocratic solutions combining standardized testing with biomedical technologies. For positive futures in education to gain traction we must find ways to innovate and respond to the dynamics of a globalized and crisis-ridden educational marketplace. This emerging educational frontier is what I am writing about here because it is uniquely potentiated to facilitate a transformation of the planetary world-system.

An Integral Meta-Theory of Education: Beyond Human Capital Theory

All the problems of philosophy are
encapsulated in the problem of education.

—John Dewey

I have been arguing that all current global crises might best be understood as crises of education. Wilber suggests this in several places, arguing that the crises of the biosphere are, in fact, crises of education and decision-making. Until enough of humanity ascends to higher levels of consciousness, capacity, and responsibility, even transformations of the legal system will not be enough to stave off ecological disaster. Citizens must not only know and follow the letter of the law, they must also understand why it should be considered reasonable. The world we live in now is hyper complex and crisis-ridden; this calls for new self-understandings and new forms of human capability. These require new forms of education.

The recent economic crisis has involved the best graduates from our most prestigious schools. The key players were our greatest test takers, our academic overachievers, and those who leveraged Ivy League success to land (unconscionably) high paying jobs in the financial sector. Their greed, incompetence, and narcissistic irreverence speak eloquently to the failure of our educational systems. The economic crisis is a crisis of capacity and decision-making, as the sheer complexity of the global economy has long outstripped the analytical tools used to understand it.[12] No business school in the world can prepare anyone to understand the unimaginable speed and complexity of today's capitalist world-economy.

Our political crises are multifold and entrenched, and they are also all educational at their root. The emergence of a "post-truth" democracy in which words have lost their power of persuasion (to be used mainly as weapons of slander) coincides directly with the dominance of reductive human capital theory-based educational reforms. Technology has opened spaces of possibility for truly deliberative forms of democracy, but they are being occupied by a generation of minds warped by inadequate and oppressive schooling, who are unable to reflectively participate in democratic discourse. Terror and fundamentalism are the result of educational initiatives, as is political apathy, which results from a crisis of identity that occurs when individuals gain their political subjectivity through entertainment and commercialized social media.

This brings me, finally, to our collective spiritual and personality crises, which are also educational at root. They appear in the everyday person's adoption of an abstract individualism and possessive materialism, as well as the run-of-the-mill nihilism that allows for passive conformity to social customs that perpetuate structural injustices. Unreasonable and joyless worldviews have emerged from the very fabric of our schooling and socialization patterns. For some time now, public schools have been designed explicitly so as *not* to be places that provide us with meaningful worldviews. Following from the separation of church and state, public schools long ago relinquished the task of addressing the *good* and *beautiful*, focusing instead on the transmission of "official knowledge" and marketable skills. But with the breakdown of family and community structures that traditionally provided for this kind of broader meaning-making, there is often nowhere for individuals to find the materials from which to build an understanding of self and cosmos—that is, except for schools and media unfit for this purpose.

These are the various ways education is implicated in the broader planetary *problématique*: survival (ecology), emancipation (economics), security (terror and fundamentalism), democracy (politics), and sanity (spirituality and personality). This provides a sense of just how broad our considerations must be as educators and why education is an inherently meta-theoretical endeavor. Each of the essays in this book presents an application of integral meta-theory in or around the field of education and attempts to demonstrate that it can be applied in the redesign of educational systems, including schools and technologies. I now turn directly to the task of providing an overview of integral theory. Readers less interested in meta-theoretical matters can skim these sections or skip ahead directly to Chapter 1.

Integral Meta-Theory: Getting Clear on the Big Picture

There is nothing so practical as a good theory.

—Kurt Lewin

At first pass the term "meta-theory" can simply be understood as referring to a type of super theory that organizes and subsumes more local, discipline-specific theories and concepts.[13] Roughly, whereas a theory within a discipline typically takes a particular part of the world as data, a meta-theory typically takes other theories as data. Things get even more complex when philosophy is rightly seen as wedded to meta-theory. One can also throw the whole discourse about "interdisciplinarity" and "transdisciplinarity" into the mix, which have themselves become highly fashionable buzzwords in the academy. When the net is cast broadly, meta-theories can be understood as a wide-ranging set of new approaches to understanding the nature of knowledge, reality, and human inquiry.

Meta-theory is a unique extension of more traditional modes of philosophy. First emerging in the latter half of the nineteenth century, meta-theory grew up as a response to advances in psychology that were transforming accepted beliefs about the nature of human knowledge, turning our most cherished God-given truths into evolved and fallible constructs. Meta-theory was also a response to socio-economic transformations affecting the institutionalization of knowledge production, specifically the birth of the complex departmentalized research university. Meta-theory emerged to serve an integrative and ethical function, positioning itself as responsible for bringing coherence and direction to academic discourses and reflective cultural practices. Of course, today meta-theorists claim to be doing all kinds of things, such as serving descriptive, deconstructive, or even decorative functions. I am aware of the various ways different meta-theorists understand themselves, but I choose to offer a vision that emphasizes the distinctly ethical and reconstructive core of meta-theoretical endeavoring. Others are welcome to tell stories that construe meta-theory differently, perhaps as a more recent and polyfocal form of academic activity. I personally prefer to see meta-theory as the continuation by new means of classic philosophical efforts, wherein conceptual innovations are made that bring coherence to the state of knowledge for the sake of shaping human history.[14]

Since its emergence in the wake of Darwin, meta-theory has always been about finding a place for humanity in an evolving universe, seeking to articulate a way of preserving human reason and morality in a thoroughgoing evolutionary context—including both natural and cultural evolution. Meta-theories have thus often focused on the distinctly normative nature of humanity, showing that we are the makers and followers of rules, values, and ideals, not just passive nodes in causal systems; we reflectively strive to create what *ought* to be from what *is*. This focus on the unique status of humanity in nature appears as one of the ways that meta-theories have kept alive more traditional philosophical and religious themes, including such problems as free will, post-conventional morality, and the possibility of creating radically new and more humane cultural and social conditions. The tie between meta-theory and religious or spiritual visions of humanity seems to be intrinsic. Because these theories are so broad, their content will tend toward areas traditionally the subject of philosophical or religious discourse. Even while meta-theories may not directly address these deep existential issues, many such issues are intrinsically relevant and are often raised despite the intention of authors to keep them off the table.[15]

As abstract and complex as these theories are, they are not disembodied "views from nowhere." Meta-theoretical constructs serve a discourse regulative function emerging from a kind of discursive mastery, which gives way to an ability to reflect on the norms of discourses and to pursue new ways of shaping those discourses. Meta-theoretical constructs help us adjudicate claims within and between disciplines, bringing both criticism and coherence. They also mediate between particular sciences and the everyday consciousness of the lifeworld, integrating the often fragmented state of academic knowledge, and creating new languages for understanding nature and humanity. Meta-theoretical languages articulate visions of reality beyond those prevalent within existing social conditions, including current scientific understandings of nature and the meaning of the evolutionary emergence of humanity. Meta-theorists traffic in constructs that lead beyond both nature and humanity. They provide languages designed to recreate humanity's self-understanding. Meta-theory has inherited from philosophy the function of providing for humanity's languages of self-transformation, which is the task of leading humanity beyond itself by rearticulating a shared vision of human nature and the nature of the universe.

I have written elsewhere about the nature of *integral* meta-theory in particular, looking at its relations to philosophy, interdisciplinarity, the sciences, developmental psychology, and education.[16] I draw much of my inspiration from Wilber, and have often adapted his "AQAL" (All Quadrants All Levels) approach to social reality (explained further below). But unlike Wilber I argue for a specific form of meta-theorizing that is predominantly normative, problem-focused, and methodologically pluralistic, and which serves as a basis for discourse-specific critique and dialectical comment—a role I have described as *the discourse regulative function of meta-theoretical endeavors.*[17] In general, meta-theories are theories that set the terms from which sub-theories are built, or that "norm the norms" by which sub-theories are validated and put into practice. Therefore, meta-theories are an important part of discourse within and beyond the academy. They function in complex ways, especially when they are inchoate or suppressed, which is often the case in postmodern culture.

An educational meta-theory in particular offers principles and models that apply across multiple sub-theories in education, from pedagogy and curriculum to policy and psychometrics. Meta-theories can bring coherence and quality to endeavors like education that are intrinsically transdisciplinary, complex, and amenable to research in several of the special sciences (i.e., psychology, sociology, and economics are all valid empirical perspectives on education). John Dewey offered perhaps the best and most well-known meta-theory of education, bringing psychology, sociology, politics, ethics, and epistemology together in his philosophy of pragmatism.[18] Since Dewey, however, there have been few others to consider education in comparable depth or breadth.

This lack of explicit meta-theorizing is not unique to the field of education. Following Jürgen Habermas and echoing Wilber, I have argued that one of the defining aspects of our postmodern culture is its lack of meta-theory and meta-narrative, and the related inability of individuals to build universalized and historicized self-understandings. According to this line of thought, it is no longer the singular ideological meta-narrative of modernity that inhibits the moral evolution of the species (such as Capitalism, Communists, and the Church, etc.). It is now the *absence* of any explicitly shared meta-narrative or meta-theory that inhibits enlightenment. Behind the polyvocal pastiche of our postmodern geo-historical moment, meta-theories and meta-narratives exist in abundance; they have simply been forced underground. As Bhaskar demonstrated in his ideology critique of positivism, one of the most powerful things a meta-theory can do is to convince the world it does not exist, or more typically, that there is simply no alternative.[19]

So when I propose that reductive human capital theory is the predominant educational meta-theory shaping education systems worldwide, I am not suggesting that it functions this way explicitly or by design. Rather, reductive human capital theory is an assumed and largely unspoken consensus, which is one of the reasons it is so insidious and pervasive. The idea at the core of reductive human capital theory as an educational meta-theory is that the main function of educational systems is to supply the economy with the next generation of workers. This idea has been active in political life for some time,[20] and can be seen as a successor to the idea that educational systems function to create pliable citizens and patriots.[21]

The idea that educational systems feed human capital into the economy organizes a related constellation of concepts and theoretical commitments (e.g., simple destratified economic models of human behavior, the abstract universalization of value, cost, and benefit, and the homogenization of system supported identities, among others). Human capital theory, in a variety of more or less explicit forms, has become the assumed consensus meta-theory for a wide variety of educational configurations—from large-scale educational policy and research to the ideals parents have for their children's education.

Because the discourse around human capital theory is very large with many complex and nuanced positions, I will be making reference to a particular species of *reductive human capital theory*. This is not so much a straw man as an ideal type. The term "reductive" is necessary because, as will become clear below, it is possible to conceive of integrally informed alternatives to human capital theory. These alternatives situate the moment of truth in human capital theory in terms of more complex and differentiated social theories, dislodging the primacy of instrumental reason, and deepening theorizing about individual agency, freedom, and choice. Reductive human capital is by definition incapable of dealing with complexity, agency, or dialectal and communicative reason. Using Bhaskar's terminology, this is because reductive human capital theory is *ontologically monovalent*—a form of thought committed to reducing the complexity of education as much as possible, concerned only with the control and prediction of closed systems.

As examples, I explore in Chapter 2 how the reductive-instrumental rationality of human capital theory can be seen in traditional approaches to standardized testing that make simplistic and untenable assumptions about teaching, learning, and school culture.[22] Yet despite the theoretical and empirical inadequacies of these approaches to testing, the dominant narrative in educational policy circles is that there is no alternative to these approaches for fostering accountability and efficiency in large-scale educational organizations.

Likewise, psychopharmacological approaches to educational underperformance are based on the idea of treating ADHD and related disorders as discrete disease entities, which involves untenable assumptions about the nature of learning, behavior, and human development. Conceiving academic underperformance as a medical condition exemplifies the distortions and simplifications of reductive human capital theory. Academic underperformance has a multitude of causes, from an individual student's troubles at home to the broader structures of an unjust standardized testing infrastructure. Yet the rhetoric surrounding ADHD locates the student's brain as the main problem, reframing underperformance and misbehavior as biological dysfunctions (which is effectively a depoliticization of deviance), thus cutting off any critical inquires into socio-cultural conditions in and around schools. Psychopharmacological approaches do prove useful for raising academic achievement as measured by performances on standardized tests—an outcome of such unquestioned value that it is viewed as an acceptable risk to have the brains (not to mention the self-understandings) of millions of children fundamentally alerted by the forced administration of psychotropic drugs.[23]

In contrast to reductive human capital theory, I argue for an integral meta-theory of education that embraces the complexity of education as a social phenomenon. As in my previous work with integral meta-theory of education, I am adopting a minimalist approach and only building the minimally complex meta-theory needed to make my argument: namely, that we need to fundamentally rethink schools and schooling in the context of current global transformations. I am working with a meta-theory composed of a four-fold (bio-psycho-socio-cultural) rendering of social reality (e.g., the four quadrants of Wilber's integral meta-theory), as well as an approach to learning and human development that emphasizes the importance of qualitatively distinct *levels of development* in the growth of human capacities, which unfold as a result of dynamic and embodied forms of learning.

The Four Quadrants: Or Why Education Is More Than Job Training

The most basic element of a non-reductive theory of education is a bio-psycho-socio-cultural model of social reality. Or more simply, following Wilber, a "four-quadrant" model of educational processes.[24] The *quadrants* represent the most general categories or divisions evident in human knowledge. They represent the most basic aspects of reality as we know it and must thus be included in any integral theory of education.

To understand the quadrants as *basic categories* is, technically speaking, to frame them in terms of a perennial philosophical ambition. From Aristotle, through Kant and Hegel, and down to C. S. Peirce and Wilfrid Sellars, there has been a project aimed at searching out the most *primordial distinctions* in terms of which to classify objects and forms of knowledge. Peirce marked a turn in this tradition by looking for these categories in the implicit structures of language and communication itself. He hit upon the idea that the categories should be aligned with the system of basic pronouns: I, We, and It. This insight, as followed up more recently by Habermas, points to the heart of our everyday language use and suggests a set of distinct "worlds," each with unique and irreducible properties: the subjective world, the intersubjective world, and the objective world. Refined in terms of linguistic analysis, this three-fold distinction ends up retrofitting a variety of perennial notions about certain great divisions in human knowledge: the Beautiful, the Good, the True; Art, Morals, Science; Self, Culture, Nature. This set of three "worlds" can also be understood as a system of basic perspectives or stances that can be taken up: first-person, second-person, and third-person.

The four-quadrant model, as articulated by Wilber, brings these philosophical strands together by graphically representing *the interiors and exteriors of individuals and collectives* (see Figure 2). Any and all events can be looked at in terms of all four quadrants, which provide the most basic insights necessary for taking an integral or comprehensive view of what is happening.

For example, take the course of an individual's educational biography as they move from preschool through higher education. This can be viewed predominantly in terms of the Upper-Right quadrant, or the exterior of the individual. Here the focus is on the behaviors and body of the individual, including where and when they were in schools, which classes they took, the organic effects of psychopharmacological agents, disciplinary actions, test scores, and a host of other objective facts about their education. But of course, every student is positioned in a network of institutional systems and processes that impact their education, including administrative bureaucracies, economic factors and funding, the built environments of schools, the use of computers and chalkboards to aid instruction, as well as the legal codes and policies of school systems and nations. These are all systems of *exteriors*, all disclosed through the Lower-Right quadrant, and they all play an important role in understanding anyone's educational biography.

So far so good, but there is more to education than these exterior factors; there are also the interiors of collectives, the Lower-Left quadrant. Here we are concerned with the transmission of knowledge, processes of hermeneutics and literacy, as well as the norms and practices of schools and the subcultures within them. And finally, there is the learning that takes place as it is felt and experienced by the student: the interior of the individual, the Upper-Left quadrant. Here we see the ideas they hold, the development of their capacities, the emotions and states they experience during their education, and the sense of self that develops as a result.

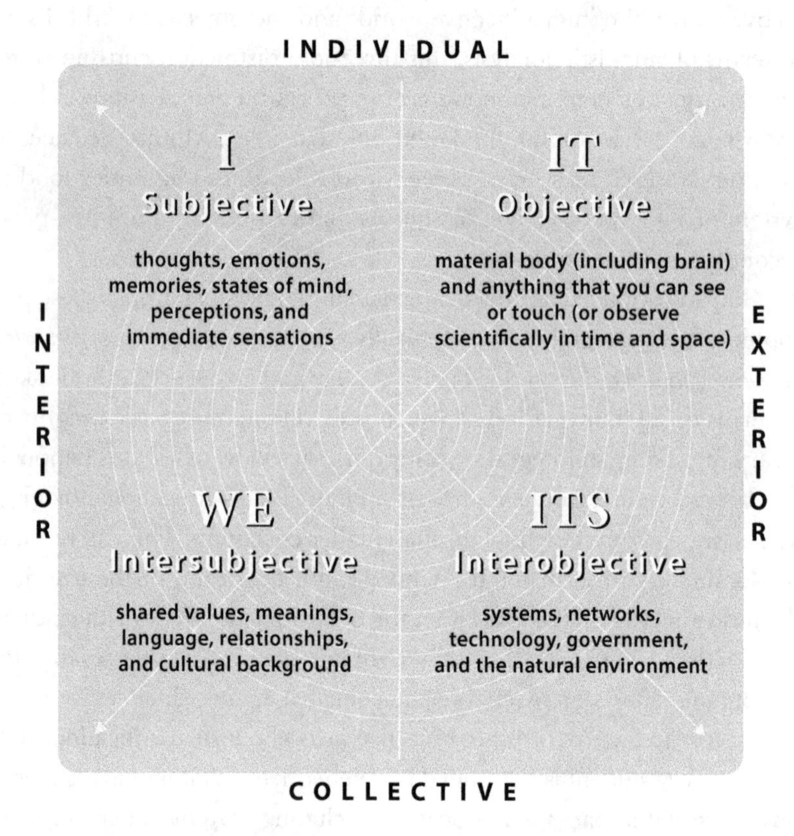

Figure 2: The Four Quadrants, adapted from: Wilber, K. (1995). *Sex, Ecology, Spirituality: The Spirit of Evolution.*

The point of the quadrants is to suggest that any view that leaves out any of these realities is partial and lacking some essential insight. The quadrants are a kind of quality-control mechanism for thought, built to ensure that we check off all the bases and keep an eye on all the relevant realities. Continuing with the example above, the point is certainly not to suggest that we are wrongheaded in adopting approaches that focus on education in terms of the Upper-Right quadrant (i.e., as a matter of test results and observed behavior). Echoing Wilber, the point is instead to suggest that such single-quadrant approaches are *true but partial.* It is essential to understand and work with the exterior physical realities of education, but it is also essential to understand and work with the interior realities of education. An approach that focuses on all these dimensions will be more humane and ethical as well as more truthful and useful. The quadrants are the basic scaffolding of an integral meta-theory of education, aiming to ensure comprehensiveness right off the bat.

The realities disclosed in each of the quadrants are inextricably intertwined and interanimated. They all evolve together in a complexly orchestrated "tetra-evolutionary" process. The quadrants do not frame static realities that are isolated from each other, but rather co-evolving realities that are mutually conditioning and mutually causational. In Wilber's terms, they tetra-arise, tetra-evolve, and are tetra-extensive. According to this model, social reality consists *at least* of individuals enmeshed in cultural and social systems that are reproduced in relation to natural realities. Said differently, the quadrant model is an attempt to represent the full complexity of the social realities addressed by the human sciences that can be applied in the study of education, which must account at least for the interplay of: individual agency and psychology; cultural/hermeneutic reproduction, communion and transmission; social systems and institutional structures; and the natural realities of the body and biosphere.

An integral meta-theory of education contrasts with reductive human capital theory. Education is conceived as not only or primarily about the limited technical challenge of arranging for the "functional fit" of individuals into the economy and social system. Education is also and primarily an ethical and cultural challenge concerning the meaning-making of individuals and groups. Whereas human capital theory would articulate the goals of an educational system in terms of what it accomplishes for social systems and economies, an integral meta-theory of education would articulate the goals of education in much broader terms, transcending but including a focus on the Lower-Right within the purview of an "all-quadrant" framework of educational values.

This does not mean that the Lower-Right is not a powerful factor when considering the shape of educational systems. Exactly the opposite is the case. The four-quadrant model implies a complex co-evolution of social systems, ecosystems, cultures, and personalities. I am arguing in this book that Lower-Right factors are going to soon be forcing humanity away from what we have known as schooling. Lower-Right structures—the world-system and its relation to the biosphere—are currently approaching the culmination of long-term trends and patterns.

These long-term trends and patterns represent the dynamics of the *longue durée* of historically-oriented sociologists. These are patterns that unfold over multiple decades as if they were natural processes, even though they are the emergent result of human actions.[25] I do not want to slide into a quadrant absolutism or Lower-Right determinism, which is the classic fallacy of Vulgar Marxism, for example. But I nevertheless maintain that these epochal shifts—of the world-system and biosphere—are the predominant drivers of change at this time, especially with regards to educational configurations. What this means is *not* that Lower-Right structures are *determining* what occurs in other quadrants, but rather that they set the environment, climate, and context in which the Upper and Lower-Left must adapt. At certain times in history Lower-Right contexts exert disproportionate influence; that is, specifically during times when these contexts are shifting rapidly and seemingly outside the intentional control of humanity.

The best example of this is, of course, the role of the climate as the context in which biological evolution has unfolded. From meteors (which are part of the "weather of the solar system") to Ice Ages, the climate has been an ever-present factor in evolution, catalyzing both extinctions and emergence. In human social systems, war and economic crises often have the same kind of impact as climatological catastrophe.[26] Coming seemingly out of nowhere, an economic crisis can destroy whole ways of life, just as wars can destroy whole populations. These "great storms of history" also give way to new emergent forms of social life, as massive energy is expended in adapting the cultural and personal realities to the new unprecedented contexts. Soon actual weather and climate change will impact human social systems profoundly, and will propel major changes in culture and personality. These trends are already being witnessed as the incidence of super-storms and drought increases. There are times when changes in the Lower-Right have a disproportionate impact on the other quadrants. We happen to live in one of those times.

An integral meta-theory of education states that the *goals* of education should not be predominantly concerned with Lower-Right outcomes; education is more than job training and socialization. Nevertheless, it is true that Lower-Right structures are currently massively impacting education, from the technologies that are touching countless minds and lives, to the rapidly escalating economic inequality that is a major determining factor of who has access to what forms of education. Major changes in the Lower-Right are soon to be upon us, and educational systems will be transformed. This means that education today cannot be primarily about achieving a functional fit between new generations and the existing social system, because the existing system is in a state of flux. Education today must prepare us for the future, even though the future is a moving target. This is another of the contradictions that beset our educational systems in this time of crisis, when it is unclear just what kind of world we are going to be living in tomorrow.

To foreshadow the discussions in Chapter 4, imagine, by way of illustration, a world only slightly different from our own in which a major industry has been newly automated. Perhaps all fast food service people no longer have jobs.[27] Yum! Brands, Inc. is one of the largest employers in the US, owning several fast food restaurant chains. Imagine they are now entirely "manned" by robots. Massive structural unemployment generated through the automation of service industries puts new political pressure behind the idea of a basic income guarantee and universal educational opportunity.[28] Societies lacking jobs in the past have often attempted to find an educational resolution to what is seen as a human capital crisis. This is what the Montgomery GI bill did after World War II, when our boys came home and too few jobs were waiting. The idea was: "send them to school and they will get tomorrow's jobs, with new and better skills." But what if tomorrow's jobs are now occupied by robots? Imagine if large populations no longer had the prospect of a job in any traditional sense of the term.

Deepen the thought experiment to consider our capitalist world-system transitioning into a new economic order in which the realities of job automation result in levels of structural unemployment that are profound. Imagine this labor market crisis is responded to not with greater repression and unnecessary exploitative white-collar labor, but with a new taxation system that redistributes wealth and provides a safety net of basic income. This frees individuals from the pressure to work any possible job available just to put food on the table. Imagine an economic system that does not revolve around the ceaseless accumulation of profit through exploited labor, nor on simple metrics of endless growth as an aspect of economic health.[29] Imagine instead a steady-state economics or a regenerative economics, which does not require simplistic linear and endless growth.[30] These are not social worlds that are right next door, but they are possible worlds that humanity could realistically create.

What would be possible in a post-capitalist world-system where job prospects did not dominate the agendas of educational systems? Different macroeconomic and technological conditions allow for different educational systems and possibilities. So when considering what is "the best educational system possible," we must ask whether this means the best possible *now*, or the best possible in *all possible social worlds*. This is exactly the question addressed in Chapter 4. A meta-theory of education must take into account the ideal social world that is implied by its visions for schooling, teaching, and learning. The ideal educational system implies an ideal society into which it fits. The four quadrants help in clarifying the true complexity of educational systems, which involve all aspects of reality. More implications of the four quadrants for education will be unfolded through the rest of the book. The goal here is to give an overview of the key meta-theoretical ideas that will be elaborated throughout. These also include ideas about the dynamics of learning and *levels of development* involved in the growth of human capability.

Levels of Development: Teacherly Authority and the Dynamics of Learning

I have argued that massive shifts in world-system dynamics are currently underway such that the cultural and personal learning curves for the next 50 years are precipitously steep. This brings meta-theoretical discussions directly to the question of how human capacities develop and the levels of development and types of competencies that we must cultivate in order to transform the current crises into opportunities. We must develop the capacities that will enable us to recreate the world-system for the betterment of humanity and the Earth. Needed are world-centric ethical capacities and profoundly embodied situational awareness. Needed are collaborative and loving mindsets, able to deal with loss and tragedy, able to rebuild with resilience, able to innovate ceaselessly and with alacrity. Education must promote growth into new levels of maturity. We need a new kind of grown-up. A minimalist integral meta-theory of education suggests some answers to these questions about human development and learning, which are the guiding principles in the design of a technological platform for integral education—but that is ahead of the story. Before that is discussed we must consider the addition of *levels of development* to the integral meta-theory of education being built here.

Along with quadrants, Wilber gives a special emphasis to levels of development (in all four quadrants). Part of the "meta" of his meta-theory is, for example, his presentation of charts comparing over 100 different developmental models, followed by a distillation of what most of these models have in common. Wilber's basic position is that you can choose whichever of these developmental models you wish—just make sure that you include at least one account of the vertical dimension of developmental or evolutionary depth. He often presents what he calls "an integral psychograph," which includes a dozen or so of the more popular and widely accepted models of development (including those I present in Figure 4), with an emphasis on the general similarity of their overall stages—while also pointing out their important differences. Developmental levels in general are a significant aspect of any comprehensive meta-theory, and Wilber has been an outspoken advocate of this from his first book. Here I begin to unpack the educational implications.

Born Built to Learn, but Needing Help

A common misconception in so-called progressive and alternative educational theory (i.e., alternative to human capital theory) is that students will learn better if they are more or less left alone in an environment rich with resources. That is, deschooling and constructivist pedagogies often take too far the (true and good) idea that real learning requires some degree of autonomy on the part of the student. They err in giving all educational impetus over to the student and radically ceding their own teacherly authority. In justifying this approach, they often say something like, "each of us already has within us everything we need to learn and acquire the capacities we desire." This is also a true and good idea, but it must be stated with a great deal more care and preciseness. Elsewhere, I have referred to simplistic renderings of this idea as the *cognitive maturity fallacy*.[31]

The cognitive maturity fallacy occurs when one takes as a given capabilities that are actually hard-won developmental achievements. Self-directed learning is exactly the kind of capability that should not be taken for granted in this way, as are many other forms of reasoning, including all higher level forms of moral judgment and self-understanding. An integral meta-theory of education rejects the cognitive maturity fallacy, and thus affirms a developmental view of human learning and education. This is perhaps best summarized by saying that humans grow and learn according to qualitatively distinct and sequentially-unfolding developmental levels of capacity, which are ethically, epistemologically, and politically important.

In rejecting the cognitive maturity fallacy and adopting a developmental view of human learning and education, we immediately face questions having to do with the problem of *teacherly authority*. The crux of the problem is that *not everyone knows what is good for them* (usually because what is good for them is absent, has been occluded, or is misunderstood). The implication of this fact is that at times we have a *responsibility* to exercise teacherly authority; those with greater knowledge and capacity often *ought* to act so as to raise others into the fullness of their capacities.

However, many progressive and alternative educators argue that teacherly authority is a stance taken up by oppressors in the context of unequal power relations. They see it as intrinsically tied to the use of force and as a part of education conceived as analogous to coercive human engineering. Indeed, this has been the case historically and in our present era, when politically conservative forces have embraced cynical and paternalistic forms of educational policy and practice.

Nevertheless, an integral meta-theory of education argues that *the constraint of freedom is necessary for enabling greater future freedoms*. If we take as a given capacitates such as self-directed learning and critical thinking, we end up abnegating our teacherly responsibilities and allowing more freedom too early than is healthy and appropriate. To be clear: freedom is unhealthy and inappropriate to the extent that exercising it disallows greater future freedom. A century ago, Dewey clearly understood this exact point and was at pains to make it clear to those in the progressive educational movement who at times acted in his name.[32] He documented and criticized educational environments that were so "free" they damaged students' future prospects for living a fully autonomous life (e.g., students not "naturally drawn" to reading and mathematics were allowed to remain illiterate and unable to multiply).

The fact that an individual's freedom is usually in some way overridden through education is a very important issue. It is relevant to education at all levels because it is part of all student-teacher dynamics. As already stated, children (and many adults) do not know what is good for them and often cannot be recruited to their own cause. The point here is that there are more and less acceptable ways to impinge upon someone's burgeoning autonomy. The difference between negative and positive forms of paternalism becomes extremely important when we adopt a developmental view of human learning and education. Such a view leads us to squarely confront the fact that individuals need to be educated *into* autonomy. Lack of education or exposure to the wrong kinds of education can imprison the mind, while access to the right kinds of education can liberate the mind. The question here is how to characterize the difference between educational relationships that are oppressive and those that are emancipatory. I argue that this difference can be directly intuited by engaging phenomenological methods to analyze the structures of moral consciousness that characterize educational relationships.[33]

Simply put, there is a difference between doing something *to* someone, doing something *for* someone, and doing something *with* someone. Ideally, education is undertaken *with* someone. Beyond a certain level of maturity, individuals can often be reasoned with about what is in their own interest, in which case teacher and student collaborate in a mutually educative undertaking. All good teaching requires that the teacher learn from their student, even if only to understand where they are coming from. Of course, this best-case scenario is not always going to be the case.

When it is clear that an individual is not willing or able to take responsibility for his or her own development, we are obligated to override this individual's autonomy to some degree. This is done unjustly when they are treated in ways they would not consent to under conditions of full knowledge. In coercive and unjust educational interventions, a person becomes someone they would not have chosen to be had they known what was possible and been empowered to choose. This is education done *to* them, not *for* them.

Alternatively, justice is served when we act in ways we believe an individual could not reasonably object to if they knew enough to make a decision that would be in their own interest. That is, it is possible to limit the freedom of another without this being merely a result of coercive power relations. The difference between coercive education and emancipatory education is the difference between doing something *to* someone and doing something *for* someone. Education that is *for* someone (despite their inability to consent) is close to the classic parental statement, "you'll thank me some day," which involves a kind of thought experiment in which considerations about the probability of future consent are informed by a recognition of the concrete singular individual in question, whose unique life trajectory is the foremost value being weighed. This counterfactual consent must be accompanied by an abiding and explicit desire to establish a cooperative relation with this individual *as soon as possible.*[34]

There is more to say on this, but the point here is that clarifying the differences between liberating and oppressive forms of teacherly authority has the potential to relieve the current postmodern squeamishness concerning the exercise of teacherly authority. It allows for a discussion of the fact that individuals often have a lot of learning to do before they have the capacity to make certain kinds of essential judgments. This discussion leads us to consider theories of human development as important to educational meta-theory. Theories of human development and learning specify the levels of capacity individuals move through as they learn, the dynamics of learning processes, and the forms of higher level capacity and judgment that are required to thrive in today's crisis-ridden world.

Scientific Theories of Human Development and Learning

During the first years of the new twentieth century, James Mark Baldwin would become the first psychologist to offer a complex view of human development in which a variety of different *learning sequences* unfold across qualitatively distinct developmental levels.[35] This set an important agenda for development science, wherein a *learning sequence* is defined as an empirically-grounded reconstruction of the levels or phases undergone during the acquisition of a specific capability, concept, or understanding. Decades after Baldwin, Heinz Werner and Jean Piaget would also offer theories of human development in which learning sequences figured prominently. Eventually, the moral psychologists Lawrence Kohlberg, Carol Gilligan, and Theo Linda Dawson would build learning sequences in the domain of moral judgment. Patricia King and Karen Kitchener built sequences for the domain of reflective judgment or critical thinking. Robbie Case did foundational work in the development of numeracy and interpersonal reasoning, while Kurt Fischer worked in socialization and about a dozen other skill areas.[36] For over a century researchers have been creating new methods and building empirically grounded models of specific learning sequences in a wide variety of domains. This general approach to researching development and learning continues to produce knowledge, with an increasing focus on individual differences and educational implications.

As a part of this tradition, Kurt Fischer's *Dynamic Skill Theory* has added a generative set of methods and concepts useful for researching and modeling learning sequences.[37] First outlined in the 1980s, the General Skill Scale (Figure 3) is the backbone of a comprehensive and dynamic approach to understanding development and learning. The Skill Scale is a model of the basic qualitative and structural transformations characteristic of the development of thought, emotion, and action across the lifespan. It has been empirically refined in light of decades of research.

In this context the term *skill* should be taken in a very general sense, as the most basic unit of psychological process. Unlike common connotations of the word, *skills* as Fischer defines them are richly multidimensional, involving emotion, cognition, context, and social support. Skills are built actively, dynamically, and by individuals in specific contexts, as I explain further below. Skills are also built hierarchically, with more complex ones transcending but including less complex ones. As individuals build unique skills in different domains, learning sequences unfold across the different tiers and levels: *actions* lay the groundwork for *representations*, which serve eventually as the basis for *abstractions*. Within each tier there is a series of levels, as the basic skill-type (action, representation, or abstraction) is coordinated into increasingly complex forms of organized behavior.

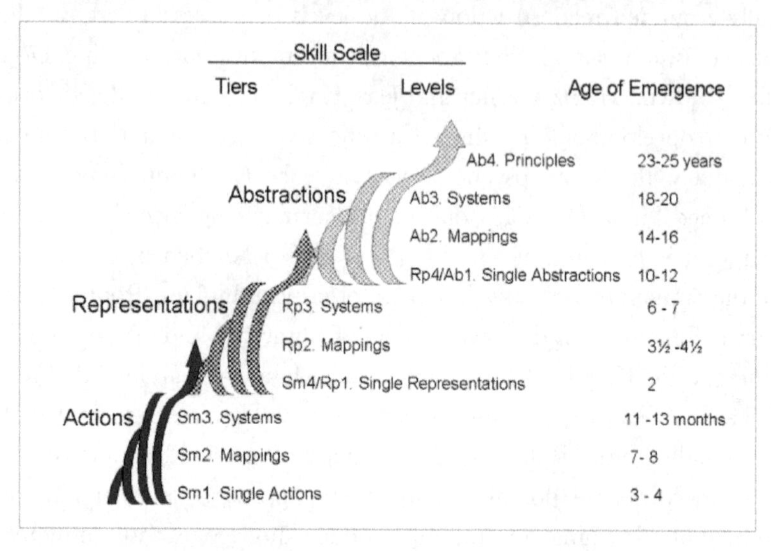

Figure 3: The Dynamic Skill Scale, based on: Fischer and Bidell (2006); with permission.

The Skill Scale is a model of the developmental processes that underlies learning in almost all domains. This model has been used to guide researchers in their analysis of patterns in human development, informing the investigation of how skill structures change and grow. Analyzing the diverse ways that learning unfolds over time in a given domain allows for the rational reconstruction of levels of development in that domain. This general technique has been used in a variety of domains, including mathematics, reflective judgment, and self-in-relationship, as already mentioned (see Figure 4). Ongoing research continues to reinforce the idea that the Skill Scale represents an important underlying dimension of human development and learning.[38]

<table>
<tr><th>Fischer (Skill Scale)</th><th>Kohlberg (moral)</th><th>Armon (good life)</th><th>Fowler (faith)</th><th>Kegan (self)</th></tr>
<tr><td>actions (1)</td><td rowspan="2">0: (magic/wish)</td><td rowspan="4">1: radical egocentrism</td><td rowspan="2">0: (undifferentiated)</td><td rowspan="2">0: incorporative</td></tr>
<tr><td>actions (2)</td></tr>
<tr><td>actions (3)</td><td rowspan="2">1: punish/ obey</td><td rowspan="2">1: magic/ projective</td><td rowspan="2">1: impulsive</td></tr>
<tr><td>representations (1)</td></tr>
<tr><td>representations (2)</td><td>2: naive hedonic</td><td>2: strategic egoic</td><td>2: mythic/literal</td><td>2: imperial</td></tr>
<tr><td>representations (3)</td><td rowspan="2">3: social approval</td><td rowspan="2">3: mutuality of affect</td><td rowspan="2">3: conventional</td><td rowspan="2">3: interpersonal</td></tr>
<tr><td>abstractions (1)</td></tr>
<tr><td>abstractions (2)</td><td>4: law and order</td><td>4: individuality</td><td>4: reflect individual</td><td>4: institutional</td></tr>
<tr><td>abstractions (3)</td><td>5: social contract</td><td>5: autonomy</td><td>5: integrative faith</td><td rowspan="3">5: interindividual</td></tr>
<tr><td>principles (1)</td><td>6: universal moral</td><td rowspan="2">6: universal ethic</td><td rowspan="2">6: universalizing faith</td></tr>
<tr><td>principles (2)</td><td>7: (universal spirt)</td></tr>
</table>

Figure 4: Levels of Development: a sample of systems with roughly approximate levels.[39] Fischer focuses on cognition; Kohlberg on moral judgment; Armon on judgments of the good life and value; Fowler on faith reasoning; Kegan on self-understanding.

Importantly, this tradition of research has focused in large part on the diversity and dynamism of human development. The emerging consensus regarding a common scale of development should not be seen as a reworking of the simple ladder-like, growth-to-goodness models of development that were popular in the 1960s and '70s. Instead, learning sequences are understood in terms of diverse pathways which individuals traverse in unique ways—even if they often work toward common goals. Researchers have tended to explain learning sequences in terms of a sequence of stages or ideal types, simplifying the messy dynamics of development into a single sequence of static levels. Simplifications like this are useful only insofar as they frame an understanding of how individual learners work, *in medias res*, to construct unique paths through this sequence of levels. Focusing on individual differences does not entail neglecting what is invariant and universal. The Skill Scale represents an important confluence of research concerning certain invariant processes underlying the diversity and variability of real human learning in context.

The models of Fischer, King and Kitchener, and others discussed above confirm what Piaget first showed nearly a century ago. Namely, that human judgment begins as fundamentally egocentric, lacking all of the qualities most associated with rationality.[40] Specifically, these early (but often quite persistent) forms of judgment are not based on establishing a relation of reciprocity between addresser and addressee relative to a shared understanding of the world. This is not because the individual is unwilling or deceptive, but because of *structural limits in their capacity for judgment*; they are unable to establish a third-person relation regarding their own validity claims. That is, they can't take their own ideas and beliefs as an object, let alone see them from your perspective.

Figure 4 displays a sampling of theories from the field of developmental psychology, each of which is presented as a sequence of levels in the growth of individual capacities across the domains of ethics, faith, and self-understanding. The idea of *levels of development* is most easily explained in the domain of morality. Here Kohlberg demonstrated that moral judgments develop through a series of levels, where each level brings about an increase in complexity, depth, and integration. Using broad brush strokes, in the moral domain we begin as egocentric, only concerned about ourselves. Then we come to identify with our family or tribe at ethnocentric levels. Our circle of compassion and care expands once again as we reach world-centric levels, where we come to embrace all humanity in our moral considerations. Finally, at the cosmo-centric level (Kohlberg's fabled 7th stage), we identify with all sentient beings that have ever been or will be. Development levels are levels of increasing embrace, increasing inclusiveness, and increasing capacity for action.

Scientific models of individual growth and learning make clear the complexity of personality and the accomplishment that is psychological maturity. In most cultures around the world, so-called "grown-ups" are usually quite immature relative to the full spectrum of human capacities and potentials that are latent inside them. Many grown-ups are actually emotionally young, having been infantilized by consumer culture and traditional religion or alienated from their own creative powers by dull and meaningless jobs. This is just to say that most grown-ups actually have a lot more growing up to do, which is part of the educational crisis characterizing our time. Overcoming neuroses, exploring latent potentials, and pursuing self-actualization are all part of what lies beyond merely conventional definitions of what it means to be a mature adult. A wide range of traditions in psychology provide guidance for the pursuit of complex and stable forms of human maturity. These traditions focus attention on the cultivation of wisdom, empathy, and emotional intelligence. Examples include popular therapeutic and group work focused on increasing the emotional resonance and authenticity of self-expression.[41]

While beyond the scope of this discussion, the models in Figure 4 provide detailed developmental stage sequences of personality and capacity growth. These models explain the different levels of complexity and capacity that individuals navigate as they grow up. We just looked at the example of moral development in which one's felt experience of love and care moves from egocentric, to ethnocentric, to world-centric, to cosmo-centric. Development unfolds for each of us as a series of unique learning sequences which make up the evolving aspects of our personality and capability. We all learn to walk and to speak, to ask questions, express our emotions, and argue our points, usually unaware of the developmental journeys that lead us to have those capacities. In fact, although we all learned to walk at different times and in different places, we all followed a similar learning sequence—a series of unfolding challenges, hurdles, setbacks, and successes. Likewise, with all the capacities that we have come to possess, each of us has grown up, developed, and emerged through a series of levels or stages similar to the ones in Figure 4. Understanding these various levels and learning sequences is essential for designing educational technologies, improving teaching and learning praxis, and promoting capacity development and personal transformation.

The Farther Reaches of Human Nature: Shifting, Unexplored, and Sometimes Dangerous Territory

The kinds of developmental processes described in the section above have been repeatedly made the subject of systematic study. Researchers observe and interview large numbers of people of diverse age and education and then rationally reconstruct levels and sequences based on observed behavior. Piaget pioneered these studies with a series of breathtakingly simple experiments. He showed that in the earliest and most rudimentary forms of human judgment, individuals are unable to even understand the need to justify their judgments, in part because "the child is incapable of differentiating clearly between relations of causality, of sequence, and of justification… which means that he is incapable of assigning a fixed function in speech to each of these relations."[42]

This quote can stand in for dozens of others that could be taken from Piaget's numerous studies on the development of reasoning and morality.[43] It also stands-in for the hundreds of quotes that could be taken from the theorists that followed him and confirmed and expanded on his findings.[44] These models imply that many forms of human judgment and action cannot be assumed as a given, and furthermore that the acquisition of many specific capacities requires a host of educational resources, which also cannot be assumed as a given. To be clear: this means that much of what we take as "common sense" and "rationality" is, in fact, a historically-emergent ecosystem of human capabilities which must be reconstructed by the individuals of each new generation and could, by implication, potentially cease to broadly characterize humanity if educational systems change significantly—for better and for worse.

This brings us back to the topic at hand, which concerns just what educational systems must be in place if humanity is to transform the unfolding planetary meta-crisis into an opportunity to rebuild the world-system in ways that benefit all. In particular, there are important questions as to what extent our current forms of "common sense" and "rationality" are enough to solve the problems facing us. Considering *levels of development* as an aspect of educational meta-theory often leads to questions about the so-called "farther reaches of human nature"—the post-formal, post-conventional, and trans-rational capacities that have been demonstrated by some small subsets of humanity (levels 5 and above in Figure 4). The evidence is clear that human potential includes capacities like world-centric morality, universal compassion, meta-paradigmatic thinking, and a whole slew of others. Evidence also suggests that these capacities are not now, nor have they ever been, connected to the purposes of schooling. At times these transnormal abilities have in fact been actively discouraged by the "ceiling effect" of nationalistic educational configurations.[45]

The Piaget quotes above center on the difference between, if you will, the prerational and rational. This marks the emergence of the understanding of simple forms of causality and entailment (logic) as well as the first grasp of hypothetic-deductive inquiry. This is a momentous leap and a critical moment in the course of human development. But Piaget always maintained that there were levels "beyond formal operations," even if he did not care to explore them.[46] A few contemporary researchers have pursued agendas focusing explicitly on the transnormal and post-conventional levels of development. They have demonstrated the profound differences between these levels and our so-called "common sense." While more research needs to be done—especially about the educational precursors and catalysts—the higher levels of human potential seem to provide access to new kinds of human capacities beyond what has been thus far commonly evolved. These higher (or later emerging) levels appear to be especially suited for handling complexity and are oriented around reflective ethical agency.

I have elsewhere criticized simple ideas about "growth-to-goodness."[47] However, my argument has never been that the higher levels are inappropriate goals to pursue through education. I have maintained that they ought not be the only goals and that their pursuit in place of other pursuits (such as emotional and shadow work) is potentially dangerous. That said (and with caveats in hand), there is no denying that the world today requires post-formal operational capacities and deep forms of critical discourse concerning the nature of knowledge and morality. These are the very forms of consciousness that must be *built into* any future technology platform for redesigning schools.

Wilber has claimed that according to some measures, the vast majority of humans on the planet are below the critical levels of capability that enable world-centric identity formation and reflective and democratic civic participation. To put it bluntly, in relation to some development models the majority of the world is deeply ethnocentric and irrational. Wilber raises the specter of Nazism, which was an unholy mixture of modern technology and pre-modern ethnocentrism.[48] He argues for social-system reforms and cultural innovations that would enable the transformation of human capabilities across a wide array of important lines, seeking to ensure that world-centric perspectives are available to all. These calls for the liberation of human capability and experience, transcending but including calls for economic welfare and equality, set Wilber in league with Amartya Sen, Martha Nussbaum, Jürgen Habermas, and Cornel West. These perspectives align with my broader arguments here about the need for radically new educational configurations capable of liberating human potential during this time of global transformation.

But notice that on one reading, Wilber's account presents a developmental spectrum in which Nazis are at the bottom and Global Peace Facilitators are at the top. The broad argument leans heavily, but not explicitly (or necessarily), on certain growth-to-goodness assumptions. It may be that on most scales many Nazis would score very low, but they would not score any lower than most of the "good guys" fighting against them in the 1940s. Moreover, and to the point, what about Hitler and the dozens of PhDs on his staff? Accounts of decision-making processes surrounding the genocidal "Final Solution" are convincing evidence that post-formal operational capabilities can be deployed for dreadful purposes.[49] Comparable evidence is ready at hand. Bernie Madoff and the rest of today's knowledge-economy robber-barons are clearly capable of meta-systemic reasoning and perspectival coordinations. Organized crime, multinational terrorist organizations, and modern totalitarian states all entail cognitive, emotional, and interpersonal tasks that make very complex demands on individuals. Success in these realms is a remarkable developmental accomplishment in many respects—although it is also deeply tragic and disturbing.

But personalities from history are not the best source of evidence about what the higher stages look like. Current research on adult development—covering up to and through the first of the post-conventional stages—presents more relevant data culled from carefully controlled observation and analysis. Of particular relevance are studies done on the *variability* of adults across contexts and domains and the *atypical developmental pathways* that result from atypical socialization contexts (e.g., abuse; neglect). Unless late-stage transformations are so radical that they reconfigure the basic structures of the body-mind (which there is little evidence for), we can reasonably assume that the dynamics of development evident in this data will remain in play all the way up.

In this regard Figure 5 is a picture worth more than 1,000 words.[50] It is a complex diachronic psychograph tracking a woman acting as a client in a psychotherapeutic dyad over the course of 118 conversational exchanges. The "beaded strings" near the top of the figure are indexes of variations in emotional valiance, while the jagged up-and-down lines track variations in level of development (upper line) and in the number of conceptual elements (lower line). The development levels are also called complexity levels or skill levels (Fischer, 1980), with levels 9, 10, 11, and 12 being Abstractions 1, Abstractions 2, Abstractions 3, and Principles 1, as outlined in Figures 3 and 4 above.[51]

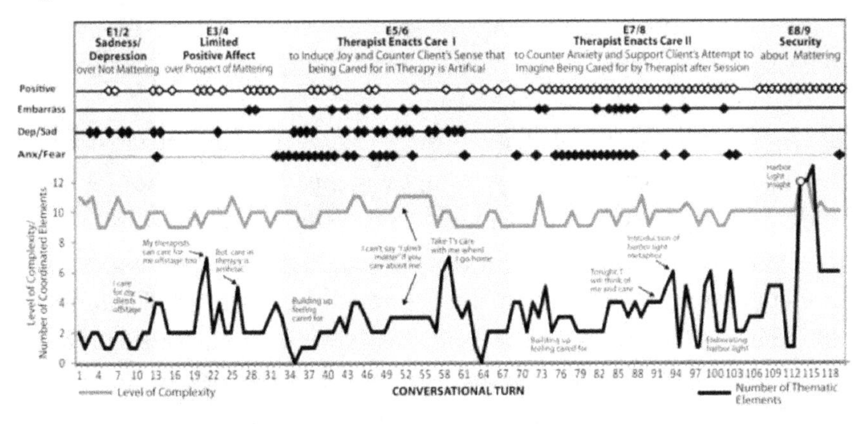

Figure 5: from Mascolo & Fischer (2010); with permission. A diachronic psychograph tracking a woman engaged as a client in a psychotherapeutic dyad over the course of 118 conversational exchanges.

The names of the levels—indeed the levels themselves—are not as important as the micro-developmental dynamics being tracked. This psychograph reveals complex patterns of covariation between developmental level, conceptual content, and emotion. Granted, this data only represents a sample of one, but that does not speak against it. In dynamic systems research, as well as in the use of case study methods, the examination of a single exemplary instance can be rigorously used as fodder for model building.[52] This is a kind of science that is more abductive than inductive, relying less on statistical inference and more on the detailed representation of particular instances; here "findings" frequently taking the shape of figures, graphs, and other iconic representational devices.[53]

I want to point out a single moment in the figure from the many possible moments of interest. The climax of the exchange, the Harbor Light Insight, comes at the end where the participant functions at level 12 for several exchanges and brings together almost twice as many conceptual elements all at once, all while experiencing unprecedented levels of positive affect. Note that there are fluctuations in developmental level throughout, which occur in a range between 9 and 11. As it all comes together toward the end of the exchange, however, a kind of phase shift occurs in the system, and post-formal operational capabilities are recruited during a moment of insight. These higher-stage capabilities are gone as quick as they set in, yet the insight proved to be an enduring therapeutic gain and a fulcrum for a change in the life trajectory of the patient.

These findings suggest that late-stage capabilities are fragile, domain specific, and context-sensitive accomplishments which can be stabilized over time, but are likely to remain transient optimal performances that are heavily dependent on social and environmental scaffolding. This is what we should expect if we think capabilities tetra-arise involving all four quadrants. The artifacts produced at the higher levels are *not* uniquely prone to be valuable. For example, transdisciplinary meta-theories are frequently cited as artifact-types clearly requiring the development of post-formal capabilities. But many of these kinds of sophisticated meta-theories are deeply flawed or radically partial. From Wolfram to Churchland to Wilson, highly complex theoretical edifices can be extremely reductionistic.[54] And as recent advances across a whole range of fields have demonstrated, even the most developed and complex theories can be seriously mistaken, or just plain *wrong*.[55] Everyone shows up differently beyond formal operations, even if it is true that certain universal deep-structural properties set the range of what is possible at these levels. In fact, in many domains there is a greater diversity of developmental pathways toward and through the higher stages than there are for the lower ones. Individuals suffering from clinical depression show unique configurations of emotion and cognition during late-stage growth, which dramatically affects their communication styles and self-understandings. Forms of highly reflective existential *ennui* require late-stage capabilities, as do the ironic and cynical forms of detachment that enable self-interested strategists to be successfully manipulative. People are not always admirable just because they are highly developed along certain important parameters. And just because someone has shown up in one context as highly developed does not mean they will show up in all contexts that same way. The farther reaches of human development are as messy and complex as the rest.

This point about the "messiness" or dynamic variability of development is an essential and often overlooked insight about learning and the nature of the mind. The science of human development shows that *your mind is not like a computer*. It is not linear, predictable, and programmable. Yet the metaphor of mind-as-computer dominates both academic cognitive science and common-sense thinking about human psychology, which in turn drives the design of educational technologies. They are now building computers as if to be used by computers. In the next section I argue that educators are not computer programmers and students are not passive machines. Instead of this way of thinking, I suggest that we ought to move toward a view in which educators are understood as environmental stewards tasked with nourishing the complex and evolving ecosystem that is the human mind—as Fischer's Dynamic Skill Theory suggests. Each person's mind is an ecosystem of evolving capacities, each and every mind is autonomous, creative, and unique, and each is worthy of respect. While the *mind-as-computer metaphor* contributes to the perpetuation of educational injustice and the deepening alienation of students, the *mind-as-ecosystem metaphor* suggests a more fair and creative future for education. The metaphors we use to talk and think about the nature of the mind have the power to change lives, for good or ill.

Your Mind Is NOT Like a Computer: Minding Our Metaphors About the Mind

Recent work in cognitive linguistics has demonstrated that metaphors play an essential role in science and in cognition more generally. The philosophers George Lakoff and Mark Johnson wrote a groundbreaking book, *Philosophy in the Flesh,* where they make this point very clearly. Metaphors form an inescapable and ubiquitous aspect of our meaning-making systems, especially when it comes to describing things we cannot see or do not quite understand, such as the human mind. We tend to speak about things we do not understand as if they worked like the things we do understand. This can be a powerful aid to understanding, but it can also lead to distortions, errors, and a comforting illusion of knowledge where there is really only confusion.

Historically, scientific models of the human mind have evolved through a series of metaphors. Freud used several metaphors to describe the mind, but the one with the most explanatory power was the metaphor of the steam engine. "Psychic energy" was understood as if it were steam compressed within a chamber; bottle up too much energy and tension, and it will explode elsewhere as a neurotic symptom that you cannot understand. Sex, of course, was the great pressure valve, a necessary way to release potentially dangerous buildups of energy. The dynamic workings of the mind, which Freud used to explain psychopathology, were all metaphorically related to the basic mechanisms that drove the machines that propelled the industrial revolution.

All this changed in the 1960s when cybernetics came on the scene, and soon computers replaced steam engines as the dominant metaphor for the mind. By the 1980s, the metaphor of the "mind-as-computer" was fully embraced by the emerging field of cognitive science, and this metaphor continues to dominate thinking today. By now it has even seeped into popular culture and become a part of our everyday school vernacular. According to this metaphor, the brain is hardware and the mind is software. The mind is fundamentally about "information processing," and our individual information processing units vary in terms of their speed and memory capacities. Smart students have a lot of RAM and fast download speeds. Students who are struggling just "don't have the bandwidth." If students follow the right programs and sub-routines they will encode the right information, which will be stored in memory and made available for retrieval later. Self-help websites today talk about "hacking your mind" to improve your performance, while countless tutors and even some widely-used curricula orient their pedagogy almost entirely around the idea that the mind can be treated like a computer.

This is, incidentally, a metaphor that many students and teachers instinctively reject after reflecting upon their own learning. In part they reject it simply for ethical reasons: *if the mind is a computer, then some of us must have some faulty hardware.* The idea that one is broken, defective, or somehow a lesser version is a conclusion many are unwilling to accept. And it is one that no caring teacher would ever foist upon his or her students.

It is remarkable just what a terrible metaphor the "mind-as-computer" actually is. For one, computers have no emotion. All computers work in the same way and process information in an identical manner. Give two computers the same input and you should expect to get the same output. Computers are not creative; they do what they are programed to do. They do not build knowledge, but merely process the knowledge put into them. Computers are not active, but passive. Computers are not internally complex. Even if they contain "parallel processors" they are still best characterized in terms of a single central processing unit. This assumption of unidimensionality is why the IQ and other reductive standardized tests fit so well with the mind-as-computer metaphor: IQ is just a measure of the size and strength of your central processing unit. And so it goes, as oversimplification is piled upon oversimplification, until a conception of the mind emerges that plays directly into one-size-fits-all ideas about education and pedagogy.[56]

A better metaphor can be found in the developmental tradition we have been discussing, beginning with the great Swiss psychologist and epistemologist, Jean Piaget. Piaget argued that the mind is best understood as an evolving organism—living, growing, and self-regulating in a metabolic relationship to its environment. More recent neo-Piagetians, headed by Fischer, have been talking about the mind as an *ecosystem.*

According to this view the mind is best understood as a complex and dynamic system—always in process, always changing, growing, and becoming more diverse and differentiated. At the same time that they grow in internal complexity, ecosystems also become more integrated and specialized, filling up their niches and fostering symbioses. Ecosystems are composed of a wide variety of independent and yet co-evolving species, so there is not one central "unit" that can serve as an overall measure of the ecosystem. Rather, to understand an ecosystem you must take multiple measurements in a variety of places across various time scales. Ecosystems are also sensitive and actively responsive to the larger environments in which they are nested. They can be easily disrupted and thrown off balance, but they are also generative and creative, self-regulating, and self-transcending. They are adaptable, open systems, and are constantly in a state of dynamic equilibrium. As ecosystems evolve they display non-linear growth, with jumps, dips, regressions, and daily and seasonal changes and rhythms. Their growth is not simple and linear, but messy and dynamic. And finally no two ecosystems are the same; every ecosystem is unique. Give two ecosystems the same input and you should not expect the same output.

Ideas about education based on the "mind-as-computer" metaphor	**Ideas about education based on the "mind-as-ecosystem" metaphor**
Student is passive and programmable. Emotion is a distraction from learning.	Student is active and autonomously growing. Emotion is the driving force of learning.
Variability between students is a problematic result of a glitch in their "hardware" (brain) or "software" (skills); it needs to be avoided and fixed.	Variability between students is expected as a natural result of dynamic self-organization and growth; it is fostered and leveraged.
The quality of the mind can be represented in terms of a single index of "computational power" (e.g., single high-stakes test: IQ; SAT, etc.).	The quality of the mind can be represented in terms of multiple measures of various skills and capacities, which co-evolve dynamically over time (e.g., multitudinous low-stakes embedded formative assessments).
Teaching practice is understood as being like computer programming: specific scripts are followed; information is "put into" students, who are then graded on outputs.	Teaching practice is understood as being like environmental stewardship: general principles are followed; educational environments are designed that nourish students, who then uniquely transform their environments.
Schools are run like computer factories or repair shops, where students are designed or repaired to specifications (standards) and evaluated on standardized performance tasks (testing).	Schools are run like conservation areas for the preservation of uniqueness and the fostering of self-actualization, where students are supported and nurtured, and then assessed in terms of their own organic progressions toward jointly constructed goals.

Table 1: Comparing the implications of two different metaphors about the mind.

To clarify, imagine that each different skill and idea you have is like a living organism: they all grow relative to the time and attention they are given, and as a result of being in some contexts rather than others. If all you do is put yourself in contexts where your attention goes into playing video games, then your skills and ideas related to video games will evolve. Some of these evolving video game skills might form symbiotic relations with other skills, such as eye-hand coordination or skills for collaboration and humor. All of your skills and ideas are co-evolving, sometimes joining together to create higher-order skills, and sometimes differentiating into sub-skills as they are refined relative to environmental niches. Your skills and ideas also compete for energy and exercise, as growing one set of skills (like playing violin) takes up the time and energy that would be needed to grow a different set of skills (such as doing algebra). You are an ecosystem of co-evolving skills and ideas, each developing at a different rate, with complex symbiotic and competitive relations emerging among them over time. You are not simply smart or dumb, having either a fast or slow information processing unit between your ears. Instead, you are an ever-changing, context sensitive, ecosystem in process, with no central tendency or summary statistic. You may have highly evolved skills in some contexts, and primitive ones in others. You may be on the verge of a major evolutionary leap forward (a great "A-HA!" is on the horizon), while at the moment you appear to be struggling. The only thing common is uniqueness, ceaseless change, and non-linear growth.

The mind-as-ecosystem metaphor allows educators to understand differences in how people learn, not as disabilities, but as alternative pathways of growth. Unlike the computer metaphor where variability between individuals is lamented as some kind of software glitch (amenable to a technical fix such as an ADHD drug or "drill and kill" test prep), the ecosystem metaphor suggests that variability is the norm. Variability should be expected and then leveraged. My dyslexia is a difference, not a disability.

The ecosystem metaphor also explains how and why performance and ability are radically *context sensitive*. In some contexts (such as class discussions), certain people feel smart and empowered, while in other contexts (such as when taking standardized tests), they feel incompetent and victimized. If the mind is both context sensitive and dynamically self-regulating, then this variability in performance makes sense. Change the context and you change what the mind can do. Relatedly, the idea that different skills and ideas evolve at different rates explains why so many individuals just seem so *lopsided*, with strong skills in some areas (such as mathematics), but weak skills in others areas (such as interpersonal relationships). But perhaps most importantly, the mind-as-ecosystem metaphor explains why traditional forms of schooling have appeared so counterproductive to so many reasonable and reflective critics: we are applying the wrong metaphor in the design of educational institutions.

One of the main reasons we stick with simplistic metaphors such as the "mind-as-computer" is because they do not challenge our status quo systems and processes. Fundamentally changing our dominant metaphor for the mind requires fundamentally changing our educational practices. It would make us change *everything*, from standardized testing to classroom activities. And this brings us to the heart of the issue: there are *injustices* done to students as a result of their being viewed and treated like something they are not. These metaphors about our minds matter because they impact how we understand and work with students. My first book, *Social Justice and Educational Measurement*, focuses on the social justice issues involved with contemporary standardized testing regimes in schools, and argues that part of securing a more just future for all students requires changing the way we think about the nature of the mind and how to measure it.

This book contains essays that address a wide range of issues about the future of schools, technology, and society. What holds the sprawling essays together is a new vision or metaphor of education based on integral meta-theory, which suggests that humanity is in transition from a world of educational scarcity to one of educational abundance. The meaning of education is changing along with the meaning of work, family, democracy, and nature. The essays here use meta-theory to embrace this change, to show why and how existing systems are failing, as well as why and how better systems are possible. There is no way into a better future without embracing at least some of the forms of educational abundance argued for here. We are—each unique individual is—the answer to the evolutionary crisis of our historical moment. However, the needed liberation of human potential on a massive scale cannot be done using the models of schooling we have inherited. Unprecedented forms and institutions are already emerging in which education happens for free—by the people for the people. My writing seeks to stoke these fires of educational innovation beyond schooling.

---

1. Thompson (2004, p. 49).

2. The "concrete utopian" ideal is not a religious vision of hope, but rather a political project and an important practice within ethics and philosophy. It consists of articulating preferable futures for society in a principled and realistic way, painting a picture of the practices and personalities that are attainable. It gives a glimpse of easily imaginable *utopian options* visible from the present. These then serve to guide praxis for individuals and groups, who act not in light of some ideal or abstract code but in light of an actual possible and preferable future. See: Rawls (1971); Bhaskar (1993); Benhabib (1986).

3. See: Clarence Karier's (1986) *The Individual, Society, and Education: A History of American Educational Ideas*. I weave various narratives concerning the history of education throughout this book, generally trying to pull from both critical and mainstream accounts. Karier is one of the pioneer critical historians of American education.

4. See: the education commodity proposition note on p. 245.

5. See: Ravich (2013) who documents the gold rush following the policy changes known as The Common Core Standards. High-end equity investors held conferences to discuss the expanded opportunities for profit making investments in the public education sector, including charter schools, education technologies, and consulting companies.

6. See: Wilber (1995). This point about the interior dimensions of the crisis of the biosphere is essential, and also includes other aspects such as depression due to alienation from nature and witnessing ecocide, as well as the guilt-ridden bad-consciousness of those overwhelmed by the moral complexity of our age.

7. This trend of being "in over our heads" has been noted by Wilber (1995); Kegan (1994); Habermas (1975); andJaques (1970; 1976), among others.

8. See: Stiglitz & Greenwald's (2014) *Creating a Learning Society: A New Approach to Growth, Development, and Social Progress*, where this argument is made from the perspective of human capital theory and evidence is given for the essential role of educa-

tion and learning in economic development and increases in standards of living. Along with Goldin and Katz's (2008) *The Race Between Education and Technology*, it represents the best of orthodox economic arguments for a wholesale refocusing on education as a macroeconomic priority. My arguments will transcend but include these arguments and point toward an even more radical valuing and re-visioning of education, one that leads us beyond the paradigms of economic growth and human capital theory, which I explicitly critique in Chapter 2.

9. See: Beck's (2001) *Individualization*, which traces the new forms of institutional life and postmodern work, and Arnett's (2006) *Emerging Adulthood*, which suggests a new phase of life after adolescence between the ages of 18 and 30, when individuals are confronted with fundamentally new social and economic realities. See also Graeber's (2015) *The Utopia of Rules*, on the life destroying qualities of bureaucracy and the institutional importance of reinforcing stupidity to maintain stability and predictability.

10. We feel we need education so desperately, in fact, that given its apparent scarcity we will pay almost anything to get it. Hence the student loan crisis, which is a direct result of the false scarcity created around education. I discuss student loan debt peonage in Chapter 4.

11. In stating it this way I am echoing Ramez Naam's (2013) *The Infinite Resource: The Power of Ideas on a Finite Planet*, giving primacy to the power of human thought and innovation, and putting education at the top of our priorities when considering world futures. But I do not agree with Naam's emphasis primarily on techno-scientific knowledge and physical instantiations thereof, such as technology and law. Naam explains his limited focus clearly: "the most valuable resource we have and that we have ever had is the sum of our human knowledge our comprehension of how the universe around us functions and how to manipulate it to our ends" (Naam, 2013, p. vii). Knowledge means scientific theory and technical control—period, end of story about human interiors. What about morality? What about the centuries of aesthetic discourse that has impacted our approaches to design? Naam's statement exemplifies what I mean when I say that human capital theory deals in simplistic renderings of the individual mind and learning. His statement *reduces discussions of human knowledge to discussions of techno-scientific control*. This is precisely the kind of profound and damaging truncation of human being and knowing that is explicitly counteracted by an integral meta-theory of education as discussed below. There is much more to human knowledge and interiority than techno-science, including the realms of ethics, art, and spirituality. An integral approach embraces the entirety of human being and knowing, and thus recognizes the possibility for educational innovation in more domains than just the scientific and technological.

12. I return to a discussion of econometrics and the epistemology of global markets in Chapter 3.

13. I have published elsewhere about the state of the discourse surrounding the term meta-theory, which has been so variously characterized. See: Stein (2015). For more on the field of meta-theory, see also: Edwards (2008); Fiske & Shweder (1986); Overton (2007); Ritzer (1991; 1992). On the related field interdisciplinary studies, see: Stein (2007), where I look at the works of Gibbons, Limoges, Nowotny, Schwartzman, Scott, & Trow (1994); and Klein (2005), among others.

14. It may be that I am only discussing a species of philosophical meta-theory, which can be set apart from scientific meta-theory (see: Ritzer, 1991). Or perhaps it should simply be called integral meta-theory. See: Edwards (2008); Esbjörn-Hargens & Zimmerman (2009); Hamilton (2008); Laszlo (2004); McIntosh (2007); Mascolo & Fischer (2010); Wilber (1995; 2000). I have no objections to the idea that what follows is merely a reconstruction of a certain type of integral meta theory. It may be that what I have in mind is not even meta-theory, but a kind of philosophy. Call it what you will in the long run; I call it meta-theory here for rhetorical purposes.

15. This is not a problem for my meta-theorizing (or Wilber's, as will become clear), but it is for some self-declared reductive meta-theoretical positions, such as eliminative materialism (the Churchlands), systems theory (Luhmann; Wolfram), and the various biocentric evolutionary syntheses (E.O. Wilson). The breadth of these meta-theories results in questions and visions of religious scope and significance, which the authors deal with either awkwardly or dismissively.

16. I discuss this in a series of papers, see: Stein (2009; 2010; 2010a; 2014; 2015).

17. Stein (2010).

18. Dewey (1916; 1929).

19. See: Bhaskar (1986). Recall "Adorno's famous adage that not just theory, but the *absence* of theory, becomes a material force 'when it seizes the masses'" (Bhaskar, 1993, p. 159). As I have already argued a few times, the *lack* of meta-theory can become a force that distorts and undermines our abilities to understand our true needs and the realities of the natural and social worlds. In the past, false consciousness was generated through the dissemination of totalizing worldviews that imposed on whole populations the meaning of everything. Today false consciousness results from fragmented and detotalized worldviews that impede us in making meaningful sense of anything. This

idea has echoed on the fringes of the academy and in a few leading minds since the great sociologist Daniel Bell first declared "the end of ideology." Many were not fooled by the decline of the Cold War rhetoric that followed in the wake of Bell's declaration. On the edges and in the wings were theorists who saw what was emerging and what has come to pass in the decades since: a "new normal" characterized not by repressive world order, but by de-repressive world disorder; not by the specter of total submission through integration, but of radical dissolution through fragmentation.

Each of the essays here is an exercise in politically emancipatory meta theory. This kind of meta-theory has an essential role to play as our species careens toward planetization. Humans are confronting the absolute limits of capitalism's domination of nature, both internal (our humanity) and external (the biosphere). In the midst of this crisis, the culture of late capitalism continues to churn out scientistic and irrational philosophies that "reify and naturalize knowledge, chiming with the logic of commodification, and cutting the ground from under critique [by] normaliz[ing] past and local changes, ideologies and freedoms [and denying change].... They detotalize, divide, and rule.... [Modern philosophies are] made for empire builders, manipulators, and the masters of $subjects_2$ who want to distract their eyes from the top of the $power_2$ relations on which they sit.... As they permeate down from the rarefied stratosphere of philosophy, irrealist ideologies act to disempower and fragment the agent" (Bhaskar, 1993, p. 159). We desperately need new meta-theories because the lack of a coherent worldview has become a source of repression and a cause of alienation.

20. Becker (1964).

21. This played out on a grand scale in the history of American education. See: Cremin (1970; 1980; 1988).

22. I discuss this at length in Stein (2016).

23. See: Chapter 2.

24. The four quadrants were originally articulated in Ken Wilber's (1995) *Sex, Ecology, Spirituality*.

25. For more on sociology and the *longue durée*, see: Wallerstein (2006).

26. Diamond (1999).

27. For a startling and provocative look into such a world of automation, with the example of service industries in particular, see: Marshall Brain's (2012) novel, *Mana:*

Two Visions of Humanity's Future. See also Jordan Greenhall's (2014) "The Coming Great Transition."

28. See: Chapter 4.

29. See: Chapter 3.

30. For an accessible overview of these important ideas, see: Eisenstein (2011).

31. Stein (forthcoming).

32. Dewey (1916; 1929).

33. See: Chapter 5.

34. Habermas (2003).

35. See: Baldwin (1906). James Mark Baldwin was a massive figure on the intellectual scene of his day. During the height of his influence he was mentioned in the same breath as William James, John Dewey, and Pierre Janet on both sides of the Atlantic. He was arguably the most significant American psychologist of the nineteenth century; while William James gave psychology a face, publishing the indelible *Principles of Psychology*, Baldwin gave it legs and institutionalized it, building labs and starting journals. His writings were widely cited and translated into many languages, and several of his books were considered standards in the field. And though his theories have had a lasting impact on a variety of areas—from developmental psychology (Kohlberg, 1981; Piaget, 1932) and psychoanalysis (Lacan, 1977) to evolutionary biology (Weber & Depew, 2007), evolutionary epistemology (Campbell, 1987), and integral theory (Wilber, 2000)—he is not the household name he once was. For more on Baldwin and his important meta-theoretical contribution, see: Stein (2015).

36. See: Werner (1957); Piaget (1932); Kohlberg (1984); King & Kitchener (1994); Case (1992); Watson & Fischer (1980); Siegler (1981). For an overview of recent approaches to learning sequences, see: Stein (2009a).

37. For overviews of Skill Theory, see: Fischer & Bidell (2006); Fischer (1980).

38. See: Fischer, Hand, & Russell (1984); Kitchener & Fischer (1990); Fischer & Kennedy (1997); Case (1992); Commons et al. (1998). In the wake of this confluence of research, Dawson & Stein (2008) confirmed the existence of a developmental dimen-

sion underlying a wide variety of learning sequences by applying a set of psychometric techniques. This resulted in a refinement of the basic principles of Skill Analysis—along with other comparable developmental assessment systems—and the construction of the most psychometrically validated and reliable developmental assessment system to date, the *Lectical Assessment System* (LAS). The LAS has been used to systemize the construction of learning sequences out of both longitudinal and cross-sectional data sets (Dawson-Tunik, 2004). This process for building learning sequences involves a three-step iterative method (described in detail elsewhere: Dawson-Tunik, 2004; Dawson & Stein, 2008). The LAS also makes possible a radically different form of standardized educational assessment, and in turn new forms of customizable educational technology, as I discuss at length later on.

39. Kegan (1982); Armon (1984); Kohlberg (1981); Fowler (1981).

40. It should be noted that this tradition of research and theory about levels of development has stood the test of time in terms of both scientific validity and cross-cultural universality. That these models have done well in cross-cultural studies is important, as this is a common criticism in postmodern contexts. As summarized by Gardiner & Kosmitzki (2004, p. 123) in their important *Lives Across Cultures: Cross-Cultural Human Development*, "These stages [levels of development] have been studied from a cross-cultural perspective, and research evidence suggests that some aspects may be universal (the sequence of levels) while others (the stage of formal operations) may not." That is, while many aspects of these stage models are universal, this does not mean that development unfolds identically in different cultures. As I will explain, development is a radically contextual and individual affair, even as universal patterns and processes are involved.

41. For a remarkable overview of contemporary approaches to therapy dealing in multiple dimensions of human development (maturity and emotion), see: Basseches & Mascolo's (2010) *Psychotherapy as a Developmental Process*. This is a book Harvard psychologist Robert Kegan described as "the closest thing we have to a 'unified field theory' for psychotherapy." For more on therapeutic practices that foster the multidimensionality of growing up, see: Forman (2010); Wilber, Engler, & Brown (1986); Sullivan (1984).

42. Piaget (1928, pp. 21-22). It is worth quoting Piaget at length on this point, as he so clearly explains just how different the egocentric, immature mind is from the mind that has been matured through socialization:

> It is because it is not detached from the ego that this sort of thinking does

> not know itself.... There is nothing in ego-centrism which tends to make thought conscious of itself.... The successive judgments which constitute the child's talk are not connected by explicit relations but are simply stuck together.... [This] absence of direction in the successive images and ideas... is itself the outcome of that lack of self-consciousness that characterizes all egocentric thought. Only by means of friction against other minds... does thought come to be conscious of its own aims and tendencies.... We have on many occasions stressed the point that the need for checking and demonstration is not a spontaneous growth in the life of the individual; it is on the contrary a social product. Demonstration [and justification] is the outcome of argument and the desire to convince. Thus the decline of ego-centrism and the growth of logical justification are part of the same process. (Piaget, 1928, pp. 11-15).

43. Piaget (1972).

44. Kohlberg (1981); Fischer & Bidell (2006). There has been some debate as to the degree that Piaget's work stands the test of time, or to what extent his work has been "disproven" or shown to be culturally biased. This is all quite blown out of proportion. I believe Piaget is one of the greatest minds of the twentieth century. I discuss Piaget at length in: Stein (2015). See also footnote 40.

45. For those researching the "higher levels of development," see: Commons, Richards, & Armon (1984); Pfaffenberger, Marko, & Combs (2011); Alexander & Langer (1990).

46. Piaget (1972).

47. The Growth-to-Goodness Assumptions

See: Stein (2014). The *growth-to-goodness assumptions* are a particularly problematic cluster of ideas having to do with the nature of human development and the trajectory of certain specific stage models. The idea is simply that when it comes to human development, "higher," late-emerging levels are by definition better than lower, earlier levels (i.e., in any learning sequences, level 5 is *always* better then level 2). Many developmentalists have unabashedly endorsed the notion that higher is better and that evolution is a process of growth-to goodness. According to this view which dates back to Baldwin, the *telos* of development ensures that later stages are characterized by increasingly adequate, increasingly integrative, and increasingly reconciliatory and redemptive cognitive and emotional processes.

The prehistory of Baldwin's *growth-to-goodness assumptions* goes back to Spinoza,

Schelling, and Kant, and especially the latter's third *Critique*—that dark and cryptic cipher that spawned Romanticism. Of course, Baldwin was not alone, as most psychologists and philosophers who endorsed evolution toward the end of the nineteenth century also endorsed a growth-to-goodness view (Farber, 1998). Baldwin would influence most of the major developmental psychologists over the next century. While the effect of his initial commitment to a growth-to-goodness view would fade, it would never entirely wear off. Kohlberg often slid into a kind of imminent teleology and neo-Aristotelianism (Habermas, 1993). Maslow (1971) and Loevinger (1976) would offer models where the characteristics of the highest levels were overtly more valuable. And all three posit that the highest levels are best described as integrative, liberating, wholesome, and healthy—fundamentally *worth* striving for.

More recently, Wilber and a host of others have used these models and their assumptions about the higher levels in the context of a broad discourse about human potential, transformation, and meaning-making. I say *assumptions* because all existing models that address "the farther reaches of human nature" are based on scant empirical evidence and lots of speculation, as nearly all of the above-mentioned theorists clearly say in print (see: Wilber, 2000). Current discussions in Wilber's wake deploy the term *integral* to signify the quality of the transformations that occur in late-stage development. The momentous leap to second tier values, the synthesizing power of vision-logic, and post-conventional morality are all considered indices of a deeper *integral consciousness*. This new emerging form of consciousness is tetra-located in individuals, cultural movements, and their respective biological, economic, and institutional configurations. This brings psychological models into contact with those from anthropology and cultural history that also view integral structures as the latest and most complex emerging evolutionary meta-trend (Gebser, 1985; Thompson, 2004; 2009). It is as if the *telos* of evolution ensures us an integral future. And so the story goes that higher is better because integral is higher.

The growth-to-goodness assumptions should not be confused with Wilber's psychological theory as a whole, which is polyvocal and rich with footnotes and caveats. The growth-to goodness assumptions are simply in the *zeitgeist*. They involve (but are not limited to) the following ideas: 1) the higher stages are intrinsically more valuable than lower ones; 2) the higher stages can be characterized as integral across the board; 3) the *whole person* transforms while attaining these levels; and 4) the emergence of this valuable integral consciousness has some degree of inevitably, being *the next big thing* on the evolutionary itinerary. Few of the theorists mentioned above admit being committed to these assumptions in any kind of unqualified or simple way. And yet it is hard to find in their works rich descriptions of the higher levels that don't unduly emphasize their positive attributes. They paint inspiring pictures of the higher levels, and in this respect their works serve an important ennobling function—a kind of provocative normative function urging us on by scientifically describing a realm of deeply admirable human potentials.

However, as will become clear, I argue that the higher levels don't always look so good. Many products of late-stage development are not worthy of being dubbed *integral* when we consider the term's normative uses. This means that the use of *integral* as a catch-all category for late-stage capabilities, dispositions, and related artifacts is both inaccurate and at variance with its normative use.

48. See: Wilber (2006) for these specific arguments, although the general idea that human capacity development is an essential component of the global situation is a refrain that runs throughout his work, as I have already pointed out.

49. See: Goldhagen's (1996) *Hitler's Willing Executioners* for disturbing evidence that the worst atrocities committed during WWII were not the result of simplistic and underdeveloped minds. It was, in fact, deeply educated and cultured people who were the most heinous perpetrators. Similarly, as I've already noted, the villains behind our current global economic injustices are the products of our so-called "best schools."

50. See: Mascolo & Fischer (2010) for more details, especially concerning methods.

51. In the parlance of Wilber's (2000) psychological model, spoken in the *lingua-Piagetian*, these are Late Concrete Operations, Early Formal Operations, Late Formal Operations, and Early Post-Formal (aka, Amber, Orange, Green, and Teal).

52. For dynamic system models in developmental psychology, see: Paul van Geert's (1994) *Dynamic Systems of Development*. For case study methods that make use of exemplary single instances, see: George & Bennett's (2005) *Case Studies and Theory Development in the Social Sciences*.

53. For more on representational devices and "topological psychology," see: Lewin (1936); Peirce (1933). Also see Catherine Elgin's wonderful *Considered Judgment* (1996).

54. Wolfram (2002); Kauffman (1993); Churchland (1996); Wilson (1975).

55. Kagan (2009).

56. A detailed discussion of educational measurement is reserved until Chapter 3. It should be said here that Dawson's *Lectical Assessment System* (LAS) is at the center of positive futures for testing. Forms of educational assessment are already available that allow for measuring student learning in terms of the ecosystem metaphor, i.e., dynamically tracking multiple variables across various timescales and looking at non-

linear patterning—all simultaneously providing diagnostic information. These tools have been built by Lectica, Inc., a non-profit built by Dawson, Fischer, and myself, dedicated to reforming standardized testing infrastructures in light of the new science of learning and the new and better metaphors for the mind that it implies. The vision is to supplant traditional forms of standardized testing and potentially usher in a new status quo in which each student can be viewed as a unique and evolving ecosystem of skills and ideas.

Chapter 1
Education in the Anthropocene: Futures Beyond Schooling

This was originally written by invitation for Ken Wilber's working group on integral geopolitics and the Ukraine. It is interesting to note that this working group was under surveillance and eventually contacted by U.S. intelligence agencies. It was never clear exactly why (or maybe I just can't tell you). Ultimately the group produced a website that collects work on integral politics and society written by scholar-practitioners from all over the world.

I argue in this essay that the current epoch of world-system transition requires that we replace outdated systems of schools with networks of decentralized education hubs that are technology intensive and staffed with citizen-teacher-scientists. Responding to an unprecedented crisis of human capability requires building an unprecedented educational infrastructure consisting of multitudinous public facilities. Each unique local facility combines a library, museum, computer center, community hub, childcare cooperative, and co-working space—all in one building.

This blueprint for a global network of educational hubs is the first of several concrete utopian visions I offer in this book—glimpses of the integral paideia. As the rest of the essays make clear, the creation of an education-centric society—a true "learning society"—will take more than getting everyone an Internet connection and an iPad. The integral paideia involves untold advances in educational technologies, only the beginnings of which are sketched in this essay. It will also involve radical changes in the authority dynamics and governance structures of educational organizations, which I discuss here under the idea of "deschooling," making new use of Ivan Illich's term. There are futures for education beyond schools. The longer we resist these possibilities beyond schooling—the longer we think "fixing" education means building bigger, better schools—the greater the probability we will leave future generations radically ill-equipped to deal with the planetary crises they will be facing.

Expanding our social imagination beyond familiar institutional realities is part of what integral theory can help us do, if it is used critically and creatively. This essay discusses themes raised throughout the book about the importance of theorizing education in complex ways, seeing existing institutions as in crisis, and articulating directions for preferable futures.

Living in a Time Between Worlds

Civilizations are mortal.

—Susan George

This essay offers arguments and speculations about the contemporary possibilities for large-scale adoptions of integral[1] educational practices at the level of a nation-state or global community. As a starting place I take the idea that the years between 2000 and 2050 represent a critical turning point in the history of humanity and the planet. This is a time of global transformation, and I am interested in how this period will impact the domains of schools, education, and learning. I argue that fundamental transformations of our social structures (economies and institutions), ecosystems (biosphere and agriculture), and consciousness (culture and identity) are upon us. These require a fundamentally new approach to education that entails the end of what we have known as schooling.

I base my belief that the next few decades will be a time of planetary transformation on results from the fields of world-systems analysis, futures studies, and heterodox macroeconomics, along with a growing body of scientific research suggesting that we have entered a new geological epoch known as the *Anthropocene*. This term was brought to prominence by Paul Crutzen, a Nobel Prize-winning atmospheric chemist, and has been reverberating through scientific, cultural, and political discourses ever since.[2] From the Greek roots *anthropo*, meaning "human," and *-cene*, meaning "new," this term is now being used to mark a formal unit of geologic time suggesting that humanity has so impacted the Earth's basic physical constituents (especially its atmospheric and chemical composition) that our age constitutes a new geological phase of planetary development.

This is only one of the latest scientific concepts to show the extent to which humanity's fate is now intertwined with the fate of the planet itself. Our decisions in the next decades will determine the future of the biosphere, the Earth's geological trajectory, and, of course, our survival as a species. This is not some controversial science—even climate change skeptics have to recognize the power of nuclear weapons to wipe the biosphere from the face of the planet's hard rock mantel. It is also impossible to overlook the sheer scope and impact of massive human infrastructures such as cities, dams, canals, and highway systems, which impact whole landscapes and ecosystems. An important fact here, just to get a sense of scale: between 2011 and 2013 the Chinese poured 50% more concrete than was poured in the United States during the whole of the twentieth century.[3] Imagine all the vast urban expanses of the US, and now expand them by half—and build it all in three years. The Chinese also have plans to dig another Panama Canal and to link the southern and northern tips of South America and Africa with transcontinental rail lines. The Earth is being impacted on a scale today that is almost impossible to comprehend.

Indeed, there is a great deal of objective evidence that Earth-system and socio-economic trends generative of the Anthropocene have been accelerating rapidly since 1950 (see Figures 1 and 2). It appears the Earth is being put in our hands and we are not prepared for the responsibility. Our species is reeling from the shock that comes from realizing that it is up to us to ensure the continuation of the Earth's life support systems. We are existentially intertwined in a common destiny, both as a species and as a biospheric community. A vast web of life now depends on our stewardship. This is a profound educational challenge and a historical opportunity.

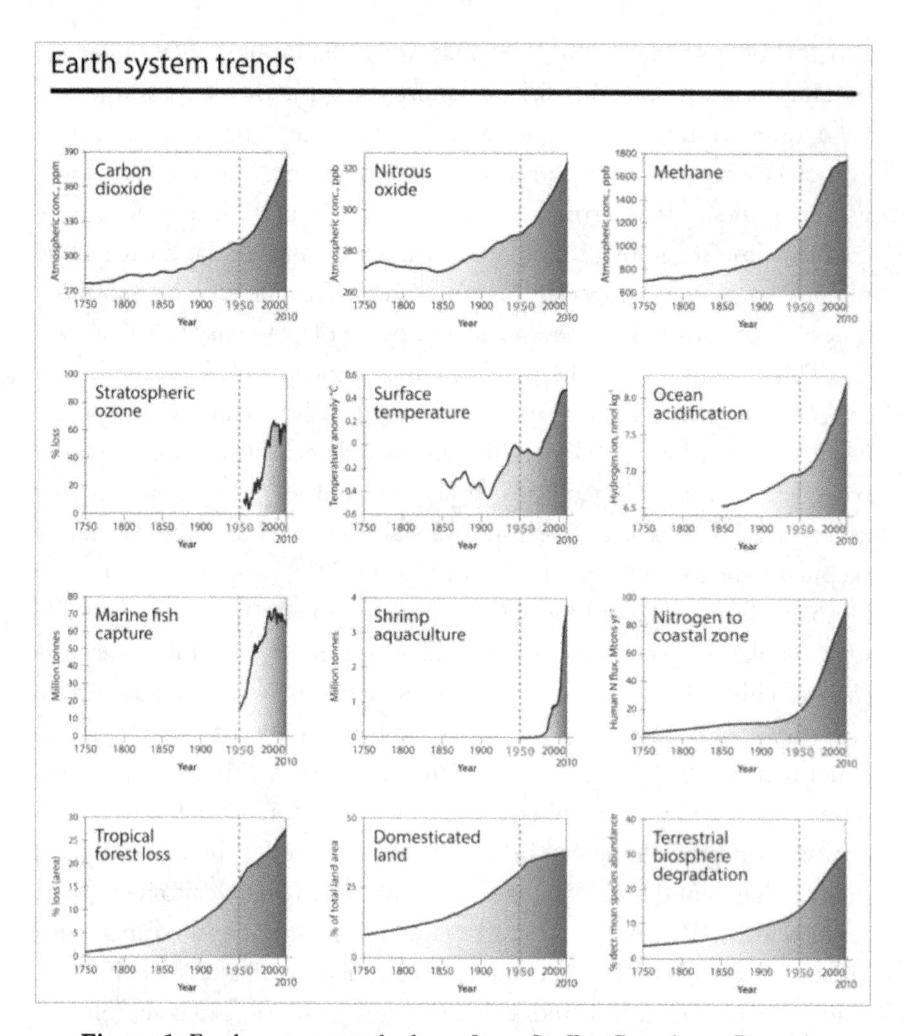

Figure 1: Earth-system trends charts from: Steffen, Broadgate, Deutsch, Gaffney, & Ludwig. (2015). "The Trajectory of the Anthropocene: The Great Acceleration." *The Anthropocene Review*, 2(1).

It is important to understand that the recent genesis of the Anthropocene is a direct result of the modern capitalist world-system, which began to emerge during the sixteenth century and which today represents the largest functionally integrated social unit the human species has ever created.[4] The ideas of "world-systems" and "world-ecologies" are essential for any serious thinking about evolutionary futures for the human

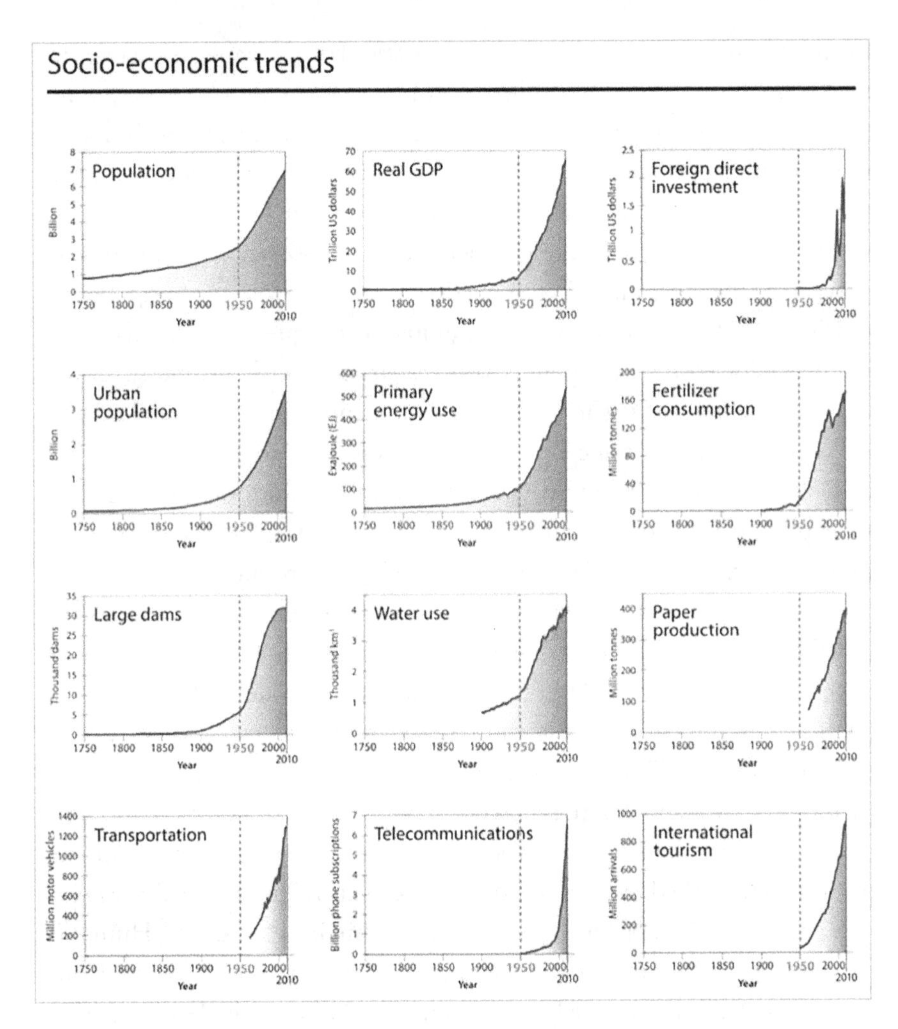

Figure 2: Socio-economic trends charts from: Steffen, Broadgate, Deutsch, Gaffney, & Ludwig. (2015). "The Trajectory of the Anthropocene: The Great Acceleration." *The Anthropocene Review*, 2(1).

---

species.[5] The fields of world-system analysis and world-ecology represent a growing transdisciplinary movement, encompassing economics, geography, politics, sociology, history, and ecology.

The modern world-system has been built around the availability of Cheap Nature. The discovery and exploitation of new frontiers of Cheap Nature (especially of energy, food, and labor) has long allowed for resolutions to capitalism's recurring *developmental crises*. For example, consider the pivotal switch in energy-commodity frontiers from wood to coal, which signaled the emergence of the so-called "second industrial revolution"—the revolution of steam engines and railroads that transformed whole continents. During the early eighteenth century in Western Europe and England, trees were becoming expensive as forests began competing for space with the agricultural land needed to feed growing city populations. Crisis was immanent until new mining techniques and labor-control regimes allowed for the opening of *underground* energy frontiers: massive veins of rich petro-fuels just there for the taking (taking as "free" millions of years of "work" done by natural processes). And best of all, it was available "outside" the existing conflicts and scarcities of the land. New Cheap Nature—problem solved. Of course, we all know the story of the petro-fuel era, the end of which we are seeing all around us.

It is likely that the dawning of the Anthropocene signals capitalism's *cumulative* or *epochal* crisis. The last frontiers of Cheap Nature are disappearing. The "taps" (resource flows, such as water, oil, and soil) are running out; the "sinks" (waste dumps, such as the atmosphere, oceans and human body) are filling up. There is nothing left "outside" the metabolism of the world-system. There is nowhere left to go to find new taps and sinks.

Human societies have always organized the use of nature. Nature has always then worked back upon society. Capitalism has unfolded *within* and as a part of the web of life, not outside it or somehow set apart.[6] Humanity is nature, even as we somehow manage to "destroy nature." How is that even possible? It is possible because humanity has already destroyed many *historical natures*. The capitalist world system in particular has run through multiple distinct world-ecologies, each with its own science, technics, and culture. The idea is in some ways simple: every historical era of the capitalist world-system has also involved a related *historical nature*—a way of mapping the biological world, including plants, animals, weather, oceans, continents and even "human nature." There have been many world-systems during the course of human history, and thus there have been many visions and versions of nature.

I leverage the language of crisis here and suggest that we have reached the ecological and geographical limits of capitalism.[7] Yet I mean only to point to the limits of nature as we know it now, the limits of our current historical nature in which nature is understood as providing energy that is scarce and food that is produced for profit. Nature, including human nature, is more than is dreamt of by human capital theory and neoclassical economics. This is a theme that plays out through the chapters to come in my discussion of metrics, social miracles, and the future of educational technologies.

A world-system is defined in terms of a geographical region that contains a singular division of labor, coherent political and bureaucratic apparatuses, and a distinct organization of the world-ecology. World-systems co-evolve with cultures, and there is (or has been at least since the 1970s) a truly planetary culture. Or better: a global ideology broadcast from a polycentric capitalist world-system touching every corner of the Earth. Previous world-systems were only planetary in ambition. Ultimately, they were circumscribed and competed with other world-systems on their fringes. So when trade and communication took place between ancient civilizations it was, in fact, an exchange between world-systems. This differs from what we know today, which is trade and communication between different societies within a single world-system. Previous world-systems such as those along the Nile and Indus river valleys were, to say the least, non-capitalist. They were based on economic systems, ideological formations, and personality structures vastly different from our own. The existence and continuation of the modern capitalist world-system has fundamentally changed the very frontiers of human possibility, while at the same time fundamentally altering the self-regulatory processes of the biosphere itself.

The modern capitalist world-system is now close to literally encompassing all of humanity while simultaneously exhausting the biosphere. This is something never before achieved by any existing historical world-system. Based on an analysis of long-term global trends in economics and political history, contemporary world-systems analysts argue that we have reached a crucial moment in geo-history. When any complex system reaches its structural limits, an evolutionary crisis ensues and a fundamentally new kind of system must be painfully and violently born.[8] It is no different with the complex dynamic systems that comprise humanity's planetary civilization. We are currently in just such an evolutionary crisis; we inhabit a transition between world-systems. This is another educational challenge and opportunity of our time.

Today we are witnessing simultaneous and interactive crises playing out amongst our social structures and their biospheric corollaries. The human-biosphere relationship is being fundamentally renegotiated. In the midst of all this *external* transformation there are related changes in human consciousness, culture, personality, and capability. Our global crises have an *interior* dimension as well.

Social media and popular culture suggest that we live in a time of *identity crises*, a time in which *the self-understanding of humanity is changing*. Throughout the world, basic institutions of government, finance, and education are suffering a crisis of legitimacy as the principles upon which public culture is founded deteriorate. In many places there is no shared sense of purpose or common ethical worldview upon which to base constitutional governance. The resources of the lifeworld for meaning-making and identity creation have become almost as depleted as the resources of the natural world.

Humanity's inability to understand itself is part of a cascading planetary phase shift. Our identity crisis is coinciding with the dawning of the Anthropocene; the educational challenges humanity faces in the coming decades are in large part about reconstructing our self-understanding as a species. Future educational configurations will require a response not only to the current global environmental and economic crises, but also to the current global identity crises. This is yet another educational challenge and opportunity of our time.

In what follows I trace these themes into the domains of schools, education, and learning. I argue that the *external crises* of world-system and biosphere and the *internal crises* of identity and legitimation all require a fundamentally new approach to education, entailing the end of what we have known as schooling. The external crises demand radically new infrastructures and a change in the basic platforms of educational technology—from blackboards and paper to screens and tablets—which are already making simplistic notions of schooling obsolete. Crises of culture, consciousness, and personality demand a reconstruction of academic knowledge and a release from the hidden curriculum of schools, which foster outdated modes of socialization and limiting forms of self-understanding.

The vision of education I offer is one in which dynamic forms of abundance and universal access replace static forms of scarcity and competition-based access. Education must no longer be something that is kept behind closed doors, requiring special privileges and capital to obtain. In a world pushed to the brink by complex challenges, education—like energy—must be made abundant and free if our species is to survive. Everyone everywhere must have access to educational resources that are good, true, and beautiful, even if only so that solutions can be found in time for the billions of community-level problems that are reverberating across our planet as it reels in crisis. Integral education looks beyond post-industrial schooling and current trends in global education reform and toward a radically different set of educational possibilities, which assume that the world of tomorrow will be very different from the world of today.

To be clear, I must deal with certain likely misunderstandings upfront, because the terms "schooling" and "educational technology" come fully loaded with preconceptions. While I am suggesting that we do away with schools, the vision of integral education I offer is not one of "home schooling" or "un-schooling" where parents shoulder the burden of education alone or with a small group of others who are "off the educational grid" in proper libertarian fashion.

The re-imagined educational system of networked "education hubs" I envision is no longer really about schools and schooling, that is true. But the institutions I am envisioning are nevertheless truly places in which the village raises the child. At times this does involve higher levels of parental engagement, and I take account of that by arguing for labor market reforms that would provide parents with space and time to create learning communities. I argue in general and throughout that the possibilities of education are directly tied into macroeconomic conditions and reforms, such as stipends for educationally active parents or basic income guarantees for all people.[9] These kinds of changes in social policy would make possible radically new forms of education in which lifelong learning and complex intergenerational relationships are central. The integral meta-theory of education outlined here allows us to fruitfully look into these kinds of concrete utopian possibilities. These are the possibilities that humanity could realize within alternative economic and institutional contexts. An integral meta-theory of education ought to hone our social imaginations and allow us to explore possible and preferable futures for educational systems both large and small.

As radical as this may sound, what I am arguing for here is also a position that embraces the accomplishments of the historically public schools built by nation states around the planet. These vast school systems of the modern world are not to be dismantled, shut down, or sold off to private enterprises, as is happening worldwide in what is now the largest privatization of educational institutions in history.[10] Our great school systems need to be repurposed and redesigned, transformed into unprecedented institutions that are a combination of public libraries, museums, co-working centers, computer labs, and cooperative child care centers. Funded to the hilt, staffed by citizen-teacher-scientists, these public and privately supported learning hubs would be the local centers of regionally decentralized pop-up classrooms, special interest groups, apprenticeship networks, and college and work preparation counseling. Giant schools built on the model of early twentieth century factories can be gutted, remodeled, and reborn, metaphorically and literally, to create the meta-industrial one-room schoolhouses of the future. In these places technologies will enable the formation of peer-to-peer networks of students and teachers of all ages, from all across the local region (or the world), without coercion or compromise. What enables these safe and efficient hubs of self-organizing educational configurations are fundamentally new kinds of educational technologies, which put almost unlimited knowledge in the palm of every person's hand.

A vision of truly game-changing educational technologies is already on the lips of many educational innovators. I argue here that a revolution in schooling based on new educational technologies will only occur after a radical critique of current trends in educational technology has swept away most of the products and artifacts we see today. Many of the existing self-declared "educational technologies" are built in light of reductive human capital theory, which simplifies the nature of learning and limits ideas about the purposes of education. As I explain below, not all informational environments are educational environments. Search engines and social networking sites are not epistemologically reflective, nor or they developmentally challenging, both of which are important aspects of healthy and powerful educational environments. Internet-facilitated informational environments often have no teacherly authority. Most open-source content platforms cede *all* authority to the user, which is the classic mistake of progressive and constructivist pedagogies, as discussed in the Introduction. An integral meta-theory of education allows us to consider the *levels of development* and *dynamics of learning* that unfold as an aspect of all learning processes, and to thus grasp the ethical importance of appropriately exercising teacherly authority.

The modern sciences of learning, which are ignored in the design of most educational technologies, tell us that learning is optimized when it involves sustained interpersonal relationships, emotional connection, embodiment, and dynamically interactive hands-on experiences. Based on the best of what we know about the dynamics of learning, educational technologies should be bringing people together *away* from screens–*not* isolating individuals alone in front of screens. Technologies ought to help us customize learning and provide universal access to information through useful, well organized, and curated content. They should not be the primary locus of attention or main source of interaction and instruction.

Internet and computer technologies have been thought of as the great equalizers and deliverers of world-class educational opportunities for all. But an edu-tech-utopia has not come to pass. The digital divide between those with technology and those without remains and grows wider with every advance in hardware and every new software update. Moreover, even those privileged few who have technology often find it pedagogically ineffective, as many educational technologies are simply bottling old wine in new casks—streaming talking-head lectures, multiple-choice quizzes, and readings via e-book. This is old-school didactic instruction packaged in twenty-first century garb.

Given this less than ideal state of educational technologies, I would like to suggest that there are some tentative minimal design principles that will move us toward more integral educational technologies. Integral educational technologies are those that facilitate real in-person relationships and peer-to-peer networks of collaborative interaction. Educational technologies should not be the focus of attention, but a scaffold for group participation. For example, technologies can help with content generation, give psychometrically sophisticated recommendations, and enable formative and non-invasive assessment. Integrally designed practices and activities direct users away from screens and into relationships. As I explain below, the computer is *not* the new teacher in the meta-industrial one-room schoolhouse. The computer is the new chalkboard and textbook, a technology that enables teaching and learning, and that works best when it is put to the side after sparking a conversation or activity.

With these key ideas foreshadowed and the general context set, I will now turn to considerations about the current educational landscape and begin to craft an argument that schools must be re-imagined if we are to survive this time of planetary transformation. Then, I turn to an exploration of educational technology trends, peer-to-peer networks, and the beginnings of an integral education platform. I allude here to what is discussed at length in other chapters, namely the macroeconomic and political structures that encircle educational institutions, leaving them caught up in the pressures and tribulations of broader world-system dynamics. I argue strongly that we should begin to design technologies that direct the resources of our communities toward a radically different set of educational futures, where the categories of schooling (such as GPA, class rank, standards and tests, aged-normed classes, subjects, majors, etc.) are the meaningless categories of a bygone bureaucracy.

Our task as educators today is to evolve the very form of schooling itself, looking beyond the institutional vestiges of a prior era and toward the emergence of educational configurations of almost unimaginable abundance, freedom, and efficiency. Educational systems must be created that can facilitate the emergence and stabilization of those capacities and mindsets that are necessary in this historical moment. These are, almost by definition, unattainable through conventional schooling. This is where integral education will thrive in the decades to come: where communities find new ways to work together to solve the problems facing their children and themselves; where new stories about our humanity are emerging; where new social possibilities are arising in the space between world-systems; and where the future of the biosphere and civilization are understood as intertwined.

Schools Are Dead. Long Live Schools.

... school is a dangerous place.

—John Taylor Gatto

If the world-system is in crisis—and there is every reason to think it is—this means the next 30 to 40 years will be a very interesting time. The global society that we live in has been pushed to the very brink of what its current regimes can handle, from energy to politics to economics. Historical records suggest that educational institutions play a unique role during cataclysmic transitions between world-systems and during the rise and fall of civilizations.[11] Educational institutions and their practices play an essential role in the deepest dynamics of cultural evolution. Educators today need to be able to step back and see their work in the context of current geopolitical tensions, climate change, multiple ongoing wars, an atmosphere of terror and surveillance, and unprecedented forms of economic inequality, all resulting from the trajectories of global capitalism. It has been argued that the dawning of humanity's capacity to build reflective educational practices represents the dawning of culture itself, so deep is the function of education in the propagation of the species.[12] This shows the importance of getting clear on current and near-future educational configurations and doing what we can to ensure that integral education comes to be widely practiced during this time of planetary transition.

My argument here is that in the not-so-distant future, integral education will likely come to have a great deal less to do with *schooling*. Of course, schools have had their place and have fulfilled important functions. But large public schools as we have known them are in the process of receding from the center of social life and will soon no longer be synonymous with education.

As I discuss in the Introduction, *integral education* is simply education that is *good, true,* and *beautiful.* Furthermore, it is education that is world-centric (at least) and designed according to an integral meta-theoretical framework of knowledge, human development, and social reality. I have published elsewhere about integral education. Here I will draw upon the minimalist integral meta-theory of education that I have previously contrasted with mainstream reductive human capital theories of education.[13] Reductive human capital theories of education dominate reform efforts worldwide and represent a trend toward the commodification of educational relationships, which in the long run will spell the end of large-scale state-run educational bureaucracies, as I explain below.

What we are witnessing today are the successes and failures of the educational systems built by nation states in the wake of the World Wars. In the decades since 1940, modern mass-schooling has done amazing things, especially in America and the post-industrial West. The post-war educational boom raised unprecedented numbers into higher education and lifted countless others out of mere functional literacy and menial employment. Public educational institutions were a main locus of civil rights reforms during the 1960s American cultural revolution. Schools were thus repositories of hope for a positive future in a time of great turmoil. During the course of the twentieth century, schools transformed from limited one-room institutions supplementing the family into huge factory-like bureaucracies. This profoundly impacted the life prospects of all children. In many ways schools came to supplant the family in the shaping of individual development.

The idea of schools as large-scale national institutions is perhaps best exemplified by the comprehensive American high school first designed in the late 1950s. This was the brainchild of James B. Conant, co-director of the Manhattan Project, co-founder of the Educational Testing Service, and key architect of the Cold War-inspired educational reconfigurations in the United States between 1947 and 1972.[14] The comprehensive high school—with thousands of students routed into tracks via testing—was the central vision of a public school system that would outpace the Soviet Union. It would be better ideologically because of its inclusiveness and openness. It would be a more efficient school system as well, accelerating the production of scientists and engineers who could ensure American hegemony. In achieving these goals Conant's post-war educational meritocracy was a largely successful social experiment.

Of course, there have been unintended side effects. I do not have the space here to unfold the ethical and economic aspects of stratified meritocratic educational systems that privilege social efficiency over social justice (this is something I discuss at length in my book, *Social Justice and Educational Measurement*). Suffice it to say that today what were once unprecedented (and in some ways inspiring) schools have long since reached the zenith of their effectiveness and appropriateness. School systems as we have known them have exhausted themselves and are becoming a dysfunctional part of the social system. It has now reached the point where schools have started to have the opposite of their intended effect. Even by the reductive standards of human capital theory, most school systems are failing insofar as they are not equipping upcoming generations with the skills and dispositions needed to maintain key functions in economic and governmental institutions.[15]

Since the 1980s, the American mass-schooling model has expanded. It has been dumbing-down culture, burdening students with billions of dollars of personal debt, and limiting our collective sense of what is possible economically, ethically, and personally. This is a strong claim substantiated by over a decade of educational theory and history. The recent writings of Michael Apple and Diane Ravitch alone demonstrate the extent to which recent trends in so-called "educational reform" have been misguided and have in fact been undermining student achievements, increasing inequality, and deprofessionalizing teachers.[16]

As this decades-old system lumbers into the twenty-first century, it grows increasingly inefficient and expensive. Eventually it will reach a crisis of legitimacy because of its own dysfunction, if it has not already. When this happens schools will no longer be seen as providers of opportunities and repositories of hope as they have been for so long. Instead, they will come to be seen as burdensome, arbitrary, and unjust, as encoding upon the self the norms and differences of a stratified society, and as providing opportunities for some at the expense of opportunities for others. Such a switch in perspective toward schooling signifies a loss of trust and faith in schools as public institutions. A legitimation crisis within the educational system is profoundly troubling and can fundamentally disrupt the reproduction and continuation of a society's way of life.

Deschooling: Integral Redux

Early on some educators foretold of an impending crisis as they saw the American mass-educational model spread around the globe. One of these early provocateurs, Ivan Illich, wrote the now classic book, *Deschooling Society*, published in 1971. It remains one of the most radical pieces of educational theory ever written. Just as the title suggests, Illich argues for getting rid of schools altogether and, in effect, taking education away from the nation-state and handing it back over to the local community, family, and individual. According to Illich, this is preferable because modern mass-schooling creates a culture in which individuals are dependent upon experts to tell them what to think, and are thus disempowered with regards to their own knowledge and learning. Moreover, schools as they have existed have too often been the ideological arm of nation-states or the philanthropic hobby-horses of the wealthiest citizens and commercial interests. The politicization and commodification of education deeply disturbed Illich, who believed education to be near the core of humanity's sacred duties of conviviality, care for the weak, and love of others.

Illich suggests that instead of going to schools all members of society should receive what is essentially an educational credit card. This card is filled with education-credits through governmental decree, which can be cashed in for learning time with elders and other experts throughout the community, and especially at certain public centers such as libraries and museums. The child and family are freed to engage in educational activities through decentralized pop-up classrooms, apprenticeships, and neighborhood or city-level educational organizations, such as skill exchanges, interest-based peer-matching systems, and student-teacher finding networks. Illich's deschooled society functions with a kind of alternative currency based on educational value, which facilitates exchange, cooperation, and accountability. With schools a thing of the past, communities and families make use of a new set of tools and resources to self-organize educational configurations, which will guide the young toward adulthood as well as provide lifelong education for adults.

Illich wrote all this before the Internet, at the very beginning of the Information Age. Yet he was imagining the kind of opportunities networked computers would soon make possible. Internet pioneers have mostly never read Illich, yet they are seeing to the reincarnation of his vision. New online education movements are drawing thousands away from public schools and colleges and into home schooling and self-education. Through the spread of artificial intelligence and the rise of massive free online courses (called MOOCs), there emerges a near-future prospect of having all the world's knowledge, along with an intelligent tutoring system, right in the palm of your hand. When this inevitability occurs, schools will appear openly as what they have been covertly for some time: relatively useless holding pens for youth left over from a previous era of capitalism.[17]

There was a time when public school systems raised the cultural center of gravity (and in some places they still do), but on the whole this time has passed. At this point, schools from kindergarten through university are structured such that students end up less developed than they would be if they spent the equivalent amount of time doing something else. This decline in teaching and learning has a great deal to do with the dominance of *reductive human capital theory* as an orienting theory of education in late capitalist societies. Reductive human capital theory has made educational systems into feeders of the economy. This has turned learning into something that can be simplistically measured, and teaching into something that can be done according to a script and under surveillance.

Beginning in the 1980s and leading up through the first decades of the twenty-first century, global educational systems became subject to a form of authoritarian modernization, wherein neoliberal reductive human-capital theorists aligned with conservative (and in the US, religious fundamentalist) political actors to create a hegemonic block.[18] During these decades, educational systems became increasingly characterized by career-oriented technical knowledge, conservative social values, standardized forms of curriculum and testing, authoritarian social relations, privatization, and marketization.

One of the essential pillars of this *Global Education Reform Movement* (aka: GERM[19]) has been sophisticated and self-conscious political organization and activism by political and economic conservatives. These trends are compounded by the efforts of the so-called "billionaire boys club,"[20] who have leveraged their positions as captains of industry to wield unrivaled influence over the shape of educational reform. They have so drastically shaped the funding landscape that many self-ascribed liberals have embraced policies that would previously have only appealed to conservatives (e.g., charter schools, school choice, marketization, accountability-oriented testing). The bottom line is this: a few wealthy organizations are drastically and unilaterally impacting the shape of schooling, displaying without disguise the interests and power of capital in shaping human development. All this supports the ideas of those who fear a return to the patterns of the Gilded Age just preceding the World Wars, which was the only other time in history in which the power of capital to shape education was so extreme.[21]

All of this makes clear the essentially *contradictory* role of education, which can be either a liberating factor or a force of oppression. While the drive to freedom cannot be totally vanquished, and always remains latent even in the most oppressed and "wretched of the earth" (Frantz Fanon's phrase, circa 1961), it is also true that oppressive forms of education can radically *disable* individuals, undercutting the development of capacities that are a precondition for participation in society. Of course, some will develop these capacities *despite* the system; counter-hegemonic practices are always present, even in the most repressive educational regimes.[22]

We live in a time in which there is great *urgency* concerning the cultural transmission of certain essential capacities, which are not guaranteed to re-emerge with each new generation. Many of the capacities that we take for granted (even ones as fundamental as "reasonable" judgment) are, in fact, historically emergent. They were at one time unprecedented and remain reliant upon the continuation of complex processes of cultural transmission and education. Just because these capacities have become taken-for-granted aspects of social life does not rule out their widespread disappearance due to socio-cultural regression or organized repression through oppressive education. Educationally induced cultural regression is a very real possibility in a time of profound crisis.

Consider the recent US Presidential Election of 2016, which involved the hijacking of teacherly authority in the public sphere by small groups interested in large-scale cultural and political disruption. In the case of the "Trump Insurgency"[23] this was accomplished through a combination of innovations in the use of social media, the intentional adoption of a simple and divisive political strategy, and the shameless use of the rhetorical power of media spectacle and scandal, which regress whole discourses below reasonable judgment forms. Facts and truths, let alone deeper structures, patterns, and realities, have no impact in the maelstrom of a 24-hour news cycle dominated by a contrived scandal and crisis. Repeated cycles like this led to a decline in trust and coherence between spectacle and spectator, and thus to a diffusion and undermining of teacherly authority ("who knows what/who to believe anymore?"). This happened in part because the postmodern Left has been unable to locate or justify its own teacherly authority, especially in the context of social media and the new decentralized content production platforms. These forms of communication technology are importantly different from those historically used in the interest of modern and postmodern teacherly authority. They have unique educational affordances that make obsolete many conventional ways of thinking about teacherly authority and its appropriate use.

Take for example, the Internet communications and political strategy company Cambridge Anayltica, which had a hand in both the election of Trump and in the Brexit campaign. Founded by an expert in psychometrics, this company leverages Big Data from social media to facilitate customized ad and content delivery that is targeted to an individual's psychological dispositions and vulnerabilities, as mined from their personal Internet usage.[24] Into the postmodern vacuum of teacherly authority (the space of "who knows what/who to believe anymore?") can be inserted any number of beliefs, and the longer the state of unknowing lasts, the greater the emotional desire to get clear answers. The technique of Cambridge Anayltica and those like them is to insert into this space not reasons and resources, but politically charged advertisements and ideological "edutainment" videos, with an emotional and cognitive combination that has been customized to known aspects of an individual's psychological makeup.[25] The result is that many individuals resolve the crisis of teacherly authority by relinquishing the demands of reasonable judgment and accepting the so-called "alternative facts." The recent eclipse of reason in the public sphere has sprung from the misuse of new and powerful educational technologies.

The implications could not be more serious given all that has been said here about the development of human capacity and the centrality of education in the project of emancipation. The capitalist world-system is undergoing a catastrophic bifurcation and will soon give way to radically new forms of social life. At the same time the biosphere is reeling and re-regulating as it is pushed beyond key thresholds by industrialized civilization. How will future generations be educated in this time of planetary transition? How will the predicted one billion climate refugees be educated as they are displaced by superstorms, rising waters, and drought? For that matter, how are the current millions of refugees from the Middle East being educated, as among them are children and young adults who are not only being physically (and violently) marginalized, but also becoming profoundly educationally impoverished? It should be clear that centralized school systems and large-scale bureaucracies for schooling are not the answer. So what will become of human capability, ideology, and freedom in the decades to come, as crises deepen and tensions escalate?

Social systems in crisis often overcompensate with moves toward heightening control, which can result in fear-based reifications of the very institutions most in need of change. Educational institutions are particularly prone to being co-opted by political forces during geopolitical tensions (just consider the massive science and math reforms that followed as a direct result of the launch of Sputnik).[26] As we continue down a path of escalating planetary crises the future of education hangs in the balance, and the educational configurations that emerge during this time of transition will shape the face of the world-system(s) to come. Will education, along with energy, be liberated from existing regimes and made free and abundant, bringing forth a fundamentally more equitable and just world-system? Or will it remain centralized, politicized, and oppressive, unresponsive to the needs of real individuals weathering multitudinous local crises?

The epoch that follows our own is not guaranteed to be safer, more equitable, or more just. Ecological sustainability and the mere preservation of the species are goals that can be met through radically unjust means.[27] This is why it is so important to remember that schools have not predominantly been built to educate individuals toward freedom and reflectively chosen pursuits of the good (although this has been the motive of their construction for some). Schools have been built largely to control and channel populations, disseminate what counts as "official knowledge," and socialize new generations into particular economic and social structures.[28] Broadly speaking, national school systems are not and never have been predominantly "for the people"; schools are and have been predominantly for the existing national economy and social system. Thus, when social systems are in periods of rapid transformation the role of schools becomes contradictory. They teach knowledge that is *no longer relevant*, socialize individuals into roles that *no longer exist*, and provide the mindsets needed to continue ways of life that are *rapidly disappearing*.

Educational configurations uncoupled from centralized control, however, serve a different role during times of civilizational transition. During the last Dark Age in Europe, it was a decentralized network of self-supporting monasteries that preserved certain key elements of knowledge and culture.[29] Relatively free from the armies, the plagues, and the cycles of economic turmoil, it was monasteries in the wilderness where some of the great cultural treasures of humanity were passed down from generation to generation, preserved despite the darkness. We are in search of equivalent forms of crisis-surviving educational configurations: the *meta-industrial temples of learning*; the one-room schoolhouses of tomorrow's global village; the institutions of learning that will see humanity through the coming planetary transformations.

Integral Educational Technologies and the End of Schools

> We don't need no education; we don't need no thought control.
>
> —Roger Waters (Pink Floyd)

Fundamental issues in the philosophy of education are obscured by the narrow concerns of contemporary educational scholars, focusing on the challenges of post-industrial schooling, global job markets, and "twenty-first century skills." Many critics and reformers seem blind to the remarkable changes impacting education worldwide. In the United States, large government-run "factory schools" are being closed and replaced by diverse and privately run "educational vendors," from brick-and-mortar charter schools to massive new platforms for online learning. Many issues that have long been at the center of educational debates are becoming irrelevant. Post-industrial schools are changing rapidly and are being profoundly impacted by a wide variety of technology-intensive educational options, from expensive iPad apps to Ivy League courses offered online for free. There are fundamentally new possibilities—and unprecedented problems—facing the hyper-educational communications ecosystem that has emerged now that the Information Age has reached a critical threshold.

Due to the crises of the world-system and accelerating trends in informational technologies, in the coming decades public schools around the globe will fragment into educational marketplaces. This will result in incredible diversity and stratification. I believe this will eventually give way to a radical rethinking of schooling almost by default, as direct-to-consumer offerings and innovations in artificial intelligence-based tutoring systems and social network coordinated pop-up classrooms begin to reshape the educational landscape. Given this opening and fragmentation, there are sweeping, almost science fiction-like vistas for educational futures—futures where state schools have disintegrated into thousands of for-profit "edushops" that sell software and face time, or where massive online public schools teach millions of students exactly the same ideas in exactly the same ways, as kids sit at home in front of state-distributed screens for hours on end. These are some of the futures we must fight.

Those preoccupied with "fixing" the existing system of schools do not stop to ask questions about what schools are for, who they serve, and what kind of civilization they perpetuate. As I have been discussing, our civilization is in transition. Across the planet major transformations are underway—in world-system and biosphere—that will decenter the core, reallocate resources, and recalibrate values, the economy, and nature itself. This is the task of education today: to confront the almost unimaginable design challenge of building an educational system that provides for the re-creation of civilization during a world-system transition. This challenge brings us face to face with the importance of education for humanity and the basic questions that structure education as a human endeavor.

This way of framing questions when thinking about contemporary educational systems transcends but includes contemporary debates about the shape of schools (which will be in flux for decades), and instead focuses on the fundamentals of educational philosophy and design. I seek here to clarify the need for educational technologies to be informed by a comprehensive philosophy or integral meta-theory of education, including findings from the new sciences of learning, developmental psychology, cognitive science, and affective neuroscience (i.e., *levels of development* and *the dynamics of learning,* as discussed in the Introduction). I argue for a fundamentally new approach to education, built around basic questions that I believe will shape major transformations in education during the coming century. Thought leadership in an era of educational innovation requires a focus on perennial design questions about the value and purpose of education, the mechanisms of learning and human development, and the technologies that structure the emergence of new capabilities.

Educational Technology Futures: More, Better, Faster, Now

Some researchers have argued that irrespective of the politics of education, *fundamental changes in educational technologies have rendered all prior educational systems obsolete.*[30] Focusing on the future of educational technology, a report from the National Science Foundation (NSF) task force on cyberlearning describes burgeoning markets for educational technologies that rely on high-speed Internet and powerful computing.[31] Post-industrial schooling will be built upon whatever new technologies come to play a dominant role in education. The NSF suggests that educational technologies will evolve in leaps and bounds, a fact perhaps best evidenced in the US by the transition of all standardized testing from pencil and bubble sheet to mouse and computer screen, following the Common Core educational assessment strategy. Needless to say, markets for educational technologies are booming.

There is a great deal of speculation concerning tomorrow's educational technologies—the emerging "edu-tech" industries. In particular, there are some important characteristics and trends in emerging educational technologies that are catalyzing a move away from schooling as we have known it, and toward more local, self-organizing, and integral forms. It is impossible to know what education will look like in the coming decades, but we can think through possible futures based on the trajectories of major trends characterizing emerging educational technologies:[32]

- **Technology saturation:** Computers and other networked devices will reach an increasingly large proportion of the population, especially students. Smartphones and other portable devices are already ubiquitous in many places.
- **Just in time learning:** Learners will use technologies that organize databases of resources that allow for instant access to whatever needs to be learned.
- **Customization:** Learners will use technologies that are responsive to individual differences as educational opportunities are guided by user preference and performance.
- **Scaffolding:** Learners will use technologies that structure the delivery of tasks and learning opportunities based on close to real-time assessments of performance.
- **Reflection:** Learners will use technologies that document the history of user performances and then present comparisons among users' histories. Technology will enable detailed portfolio management systems, templates, scoring interfaces, and databasing.
- **Distance learning and online education:** More education will take place at a distance through online learning environments, with improved efficacy due to advances in video conferencing and content-delivery systems.
- **Databases and electronic learning records:** With embedded assessments, and automated progress and behavior monitoring technologies, educational record keeping will

become as detailed and complex as medical record keeping.[33]

This list of trends and characteristics is not exhaustive, but it is nevertheless suggestive of what tomorrow's educational institutions will have to work with. The history of education teaches that advances in technology can alter practices and in turn alter the structure of the educational system. These trends are not benign or neutral, and they have the shape they do mainly as a result of market mechanisms driving trends in the tech industry. As a result of market-driven tech innovations, school systems are inundated with a seemingly endless stream of new technologies and software, which deeply impact the shape of teaching and learning.

New approaches to schooling inspired by human capital theory are aiming to leverage many of the technological trends listed above, including customization, scaffolding, and large-scale databasing. But they are mostly looking to carry out old forms of schooling using new technological instruments. A great deal of content will soon be administered via the Internet and at computer terminals or laptops. Many schools do not have the computers needed or will have to make upgrades to their existing systems to make this happen. The cost of ongoing tech-infrastructure upgrades alone—which are primarily being saddled by local districts—are already a large part of education budgets moving forward, and most of it will ultimately go into the hands of a few large technology corporations that sell specific hardware and software to schools.

These new educational environments make use of keyboard and mouse skills, as well as some limited web browsing. More subjects will eventually be brought into computer administered forms. It is not clear what the impact of the new technologies has been or will be. For example, we do not yet know how computer skills differ by social and economic stratum. As education expands to laptops and tablets, will there be differences in performance between students across different hardware and software interfaces? It also remains to be seen how more numerous and extended forms of screen time will affect students, as well as how using computers across more subjects will affect pedagogy and curricula.

Poor use of educational technology also contributes to making the experience of education into one where individuals feel alienated and powerless. As if taking B.F. Skinner's idea of "teaching machines" literally, computerized educational experiences make students feel like they are being taught by a machine. This is an uncanny experience of having critical life opportunities provided by seemingly mechanical means. It also obscures the fact that educational relationships always involve interpersonal and political realities. The computer is enabling a covert or hidden "conversation" (albeit one way) between the student and a wide range of interested parties, from the teacher and local school administrators, to the state and national Departments of Education, as well as research agencies, think tanks, and philanthropic investors.[34] Because of the perceived value and promise of technologies, there are initiatives to design new schools to use them. This has propelled the evolution of an "educational-technology industrial complex," which drives many of the tech-trends listed above.

It should be noted that surveillance, most of it benign but extensive, would be expanded as technology continues to evolve its role in schools. Video games and social networking sites capture thousands of data points per session about their users, all housed in a central data storage system that can be analyzed and searched.[35] Educational assessment technologies are still catching up when it comes to the use of real-time, computer-enabled behavior tracking. As teaching and learning move from pen, book, and paper to glowing screens and operating systems, educators can now make use of large-scale "learning-analytic" backends built into their e-learning platforms. This allows for cataloging student scores on practice and official tests, as well as what was Googled, read, or viewed, for how long, and where. Many schools that own the computers used by students withhold students' rights to privacy and allow administrators to remotely view student computer use, including webcams.[36] Embedded assessment takes on a whole new meaning when testing technology is literally embedded in students' lives twenty-four hours a day. School-networked tablets, computers, and smartphones are used by students inside and outside of school for academic and non-academic purposes.

Surveillance and privacy are only two of the ethical concerns regarding tomorrow's educational technologies. Advances in educational technology have always forced educators to reconsider the very nature of their task. If this list captures the characteristics of the technologies that will become essential to future educational configurations, then the goal here is to begin inquiring into the preferable directions for integral education. I believe we are looking at a possible system of education beyond schooling, one that is decentralized, locally customized, and self-organizing.

Failures of Educational Imagination: There Are Alternatives!

Let me be very clear about what I mean when I say educational configurations are going to need to become decentralized, locally customized, and self-organizing. Call it deschooling, rethinking schools, or just good old-fashioned educational radicalism, my argument is that schools as we are currently running them are incapable of changing rapidly enough to accommodate the planetary crises and transitions we face. It is as simple as that. Today's schools are unable to provide for the capacities future generations are going to need to survive. Something new must emerge from within the school systems of today, which are too quickly being dismantled, privatized, and inundated by new forms of disruptive technology. Allow me to contrast today's straining, hierarchical, and centralized school systems with tomorrow's decentralized education hub network, as a way of bringing home the vision I am arguing for here.

Imagine a young girl (let's call her Althea), from a family living just on the poverty line in a city recently beset by unemployment and ecological devastation due to climate change (e.g., she lives in a city like Detroit, but where there has been a drought for years). With water supply issues and generations of structural unemployment due to factory flight, local governments are overwhelmed. The few funds made available to schools have been used to shut down buildings and restructure districts, as the government seeks to save money by pushing more and more students into fewer and fewer buildings. Today Althea needs to get on a school bus and travel as much as two hours to get to one of the few large schools that have not been closed. The handful of charter schools that have emerged will not admit her because she has a learning disability; yet these same charter schools, which attract the wealthiest in the city, will take funds from the public coffers (and thus take funds away from those non-chartered public schools that must take all who apply).[37]

Once at school, Althea will sit in a desk and more often than not be instructed in a manner that could have been witnessed in any public school during the past 150 years. Just as Illich lamented 40 years ago (and Dewey 60 years before that), schooling still largely consists of teachers filling passive students with information and then asking them to recite it back. When computers are used it is typically to watch video lectures from outlets like Khan Academy or to engage in "research" through Google, Bing, or other corporate-backed search engines.[38] Computers thus aid in the delivery of didactic instruction, which is often further reduced to mere test prep. This makes the curriculum dense with facts, light on reflection, and mostly irrelevant to the students' interests and wishes. Just because there are a lot of computers in a school does not mean that the school is doing anything with them that truly improves teaching and learning.

Importantly, the majority of students will use their smartphones or other devices to access the Internet in a wide variety of ways outside of school (or in school, despite the rules). Althea will likely look at her smartphone screen while on the bus, sending text messages to a friend on a different bus while also looking at videos continually populating her social media feed. Modern myths about the benefits of youth computer-symbioses aside, research shows that adolescents and young adults largely use the Internet to engage advertisement-laden streaming content and social media. Students' spontaneous uses of (potentially) educational technologies largely mirror the ways their schools put these same technologies to use. Young people are made into passive consumers of spectacles and ideologically saturated "facts," delivered by talking heads and simplified to 140 characters or sound bytes. Where there is participation and engagement, young people are put in contexts where language and reason itself are restructured and disembodied by their medium of choice, be it Facebook, Twitter, or Instagram. The Internet does not facilitate the kind of transparent freedom of expression that is suitable for healthy socialization and learning. Rather social media-based forms of communication involve a basic funneling and distorting of expression and discourse, which become wrapped in surveillance by advertisers and government agencies and then packaged to induce narcissism and addiction.[39]

If this sounds unrealistically harsh, one needs only to read more about conditions in today's large urban public schools and the growing literature on computer-mediated forms of adolescent socialization.[40] Althea is unlikely to graduate. But she is more likely to graduate than her male peers, who are more likely to end up in jail in many US locales. She is likely to be only functionally literate and thus unlikely to pursue lifelong learning through reading, community and political engagement, or higher education. Having been stunted by inadequate education, she is also more likely to engage in unhealthy lifestyle choices such as forms of malnutrition that lead to chronic illness, or forms of media consumption and ideology formation that lead to a degradation of reflexive capacities and ultimately to political apathy and emotional instability.

Of course, there are some pockets of resistance and resilience in even the worst of today's educational configurations. However, these are largely the exception in today's financially squeezed and ideologically fragmented educational landscape. Under pressure from global forces (e.g., world-system induced structural unemployment; climate change induced local eco-disaster), the school system Althea attends has retreated to its minimum viable product: running buses longer, using fewer buildings, and selling off districts to private for-profit charter-school operators. School leaders are trying to make a system work that has been pushed to the point of failure. As pressures on the school system mount, surveillance, testing, and cost-cutting increase. The center cannot hold.

Now imagine a different reaction on the part of this same school system in the face of urban blight, structural unemployment, and climate change. In response to grassroots political pressure, neighborhood schools are repurposed as minimally staffed public spaces and hubs for parental and community engagement. These community centers are focused around a technology-enabled peer-to-peer networking and time-sharing platform, in which each parent and student has an account. This service provides opportunities for all children to be a part of regional educational configurations, leveraging computer technologies for logistics, communications, and curricular content delivery.[41] Some of what is available is self-organized by students, but much is organized by citizen-teacher-scientists and parent groups who are employed by the state or local school. All activities are logged and tracked in a common learning management system, which produces monthly reports to students, parents, and a skeletal crew of community administrators.

Investment capital that would be in charter schools is pooled with public funds and distributed across the system. Computers, tablets, and highly resourced community hubs (which are likely to be refurbished schools) are installed and maintained like public infrastructures. Hubs servicing Pre-K and the early years receive the most funding and are the most well staffed, needing to function in part as daycares and play spaces. Hubs for adolescents and young adults become more like co-working spaces and incubators for ideas and projects spearheaded by students, parents, and citizen-teacher-scientists. Some hubs would likely focus on the ecological crisis facing the city itself, and perhaps work to restore a local waterway. Involving the regional state university provides high-level access to scholar-practitioners who might work with students in navigating a transition to college. Ideally a locally unique education-to-job-or-college pipeline would be created through community forums, job fairs, and regional entrepreneurial innovation.

Depending on other macroeconomic and labor-market policy shifts, a considerable amount of parent time could be made available, and widespread community work and lifelong learning among adults might be fostered. For example, as I discuss in Chapter 4, irreversible structural unemployment lends weight to ideas about a basic income guarantee, beyond which educational possibilities open still further.[42] There are profound possibilities for educational configurations in post-capitalist economic contexts, where the need to have marketable skills recedes, and in its place emerges new needs for lifelong learning, self-education, and community. A truly ideal and just educational system would be freed from all subservience to economic considerations and entirely dedicated to the furtherance of human potential.[43]

In any case, back to the near-future thought experiment where Althea is now no longer riding two hours on a bus to get to an overcrowded school. Instead, she is waking up and working on her publicly provided tablet computer, confirming a meet-up with six girls who all live in her neighborhood. They all have an interest in writing and are meeting in the park under the supervision of two parents, both of whom have registered their availability and skills in the time-share network at the education hub.[44] The girls will spend two hours writing into a computer-generated prompt and then discussing what they wrote with each other and the adults.

After lunch at the local education hub (which is a refurbished elementary school and thus includes a cafeteria), the girls will go their separate ways to different activities. One girl takes public transport to an internship across town. Another goes with her mother to a music rehearsal, which was organized through the hub platform and brings students together from all over the city to create an orchestra. Althea is staying at the hub to join a class that will help her design a website where she can post her writing. She is joined by students of a variety of ages who all have an interest in website design. They are led by a local college student who is volunteering at the hub and teaches this course regularly. Each assignment he gives Althea is logged in the regional education platform, which consists of a learning management system and social network. At the end of the day, she sees that in two years she will have logged enough certified activities to be allowed to submit a college admissions portfolio to the numerous state and private universities interested in students from her innovative district.

This thought experiment may seem utopian, and it certainly raises more questions than it answers (some of which, however, I attempt to address in later chapters). The picture I just painted contains some features of current attempts to catalyze spontaneous and decentralized educational organizations, which are sprouting up in the spaces not filled by the current systems.[45] These spaces seek to allow for the creation and teaching of new forms of knowledge. They imply new visions of social, economic, and political life. These are educational spaces that engender a new vision of learning in a complex and emergent world.

Such an approach to education is alluring and potentially a more efficient and economical use of educational resources than traditional schools. And while it seems unwieldy and complex to "unleash" the youth from the confines of schools and then "trust" them to self-organize, it is nevertheless a seemingly far less damaging option for many young people given the state of their existing schools. While a network of education hubs would have its downsides and challenges, these downsides would be different from the downsides of the current system, which we know all too well (e.g., school-to-prison pipeline, low levels of functional literacy and critical thinking, and apathy and drudgery even among those who succeed). Radically transforming schooling is also preferable because it allows for a system that adapts to current realities, offering multiple options and pathways toward diverse capacities and opportunities, some of which involve a local school-to-job ecosystem and apprenticeship network.

However, before we can strongly endorse any alternative to schooling, we must get clear on just what a good, true, and beautiful education is. When there is a major cultural fork in the road it is good to break things down at an axiomatic level. Getting back to basics is essential in times when a wholesale redesign of educational configurations is in order. I now turn to foundational questions in educational technology design.

Integral Educational Technologies: Platforms Beyond Schooling

Some educational technologies can be used to subvert large-scale educational bureaucracy and innovate with local, decentralized solutions. As the technologies of education change and larger Lower-Right quadrant contexts shift demands on educational systems, the possibilities for rethinking schools increase. Things like pop-up classrooms using open-source academic courseware and freely available streaming lectures start to make a lot of sense. Trends in online education are already spurring changes in assessment technology and alternative forms of credentialing, which seek to change the very idea of what counts as education.

Over a longer time scale, these trends in educational technologies have the potential to transform education from a limited resource that is scare, expensive, and inequitably distributed, into an abundant resource: a universally accessible and non-rivalrous good. Modern school systems are predicated on the idea of meritocratic access to limited educational goods. This structures education in terms of zero-sum games of competition, which distorts what education should be about—namely cooperation toward a common future. Competition-based educational systems are the result of seeing education through the lens of reductive human capital theory, where the idea that one buys and owns a degree (and thus gains access to a job) dominates thinking about the purpose of schooling.

Radical new approaches to educational philosophy and design are desperately needed. If reforms continue to run according to human capital theory there will be increasing segregation of educational opportunities along economic lines, as well as outcome differentiations along the technological and pedagogical quality-vectors set by the new free market of educational enterprises. That is, there will be winners and losers in a climate of educational scarcity. Generational discontinuities and alienation are immanent, as millions of students are soon to be schooled through teacherless computer-based learning, without classrooms, playgrounds, bands, art, or sports teams. Some will come to occupy an educational underclass, systematically disempowered as political actors by the very institutions created to raise them as citizens.

A privileged few will be empowered by educational configurations the likes of which no humans have experienced before. Students can already put their hands on near limitless knowledge. Soon they will be using collaborative tools to put what they know to use in addressing the problems of their communities. Tomorrow's educational environments will ask students to learn for a lifetime from almost anywhere. This emerging educational frontier will create a new kind of humanity. In these days, we are once again *recreating* ourselves through the power of our own educational technologies. Doing so requires us to create and justify design principles for educational technologies of profound scope and impact. These ideas dovetail with realities emerging in the Internet and high-tech sectors, where ambitions to upload entire libraries are decades old. In this climate of intense possibility, let us dwell on pure potential. Let us stop and ask, in a structured way:

- What and whose knowledge should be passed on to future generations and why?
- How should this knowledge be organized, archived, made available, and taught?

Because of the breadth of these questions, a book would be needed to address these topics.[46] I only briefly run down the issues here in three broad areas: curriculum and meta-theory; learning science and technology; and self-organization through pro-social technology design.

Curriculum and Meta-Theory: What Is Knowledge?

The sheer quantity and diversity of human knowledge available for access through educational technologies is enormous. It is not far from the truth to say that one of history's greatest libraries is in the palm of your hand when you hold a smartphone. The recent proliferation of academic disciplines and subdisciplines and the booming publishing and web-content industries, all call for a new kind of curriculum that is built around a comprehensive philosophical meta-theory. In no other time during the history of educational systems has there been such a need for an orienting "theory of everything" as there is today. There is simply too much information to use. We are drowning in it. Educators are particularly pressed, as they must not only decide what and whose knowledge to learn themselves but also what and whose knowledge to teach future generations.

An integral meta-theory provides a coherent and ethically appropriate answer to the question posed above: *what* and *whose* knowledge ought to be preserved in the educational systems of tomorrow? Briefly, the answer is: *all of it and everyone's.*[47] Grappling with the full responsibility and complexity of passing on our knowledge ought to put us in a state of epistemic humility. Who are we to shape the minds of those who come after us? How can we even know what will be useful and meaningful to them? This deep line of educational questioning leads to a desire to get *all* knowledge into the educational technologies that are becoming so wildly distributed, somehow making sure that it is *all* there for generations to come. Epistemological comprehensiveness is a guiding design principle for future educational configurations, which are no longer driven by narrow goals of ideology and economics. Integral meta-theory in particular can provide a framework for prioritizing and organizing the totality of knowledge—a method for mapping the whole of what could be taught.

To give only the simplest of examples, imagine a website that structures ways for young people to form groups that work in local communities around environmental issues such as drought or pollution. The "issues" can be seen in terms of carbon emissions and the reaching of some specific quantitative threshold, reducing the number of cars and the gallons of fuel, or climate change and rising temperatures (all Right-Hand quadrant realities; all essential). However, equally as important are the cultural factors and the role of personality, emotion, and decision-making. So if this website is to function as a piece of integral educational technology—and not merely as an aspect of commerce or a branch of educational bureaucracy—it must have an all-quadrant view *built into the very architecture of the website*. Every young person who uses the website will be scaffolded to see their local issues in terms of all four quadrants. A non-reductive framing of the issue will be built into the informational environment itself.

Educational technologies capable of providing a platform for radically rethinking schools will need an orienting curricular philosophy that is epistemologically comprehensive but not indiscriminate, involving a complex matrix of evaluative weightings and prioritization. It may sound odd to even speak of a curriculum while at the same time talking about the end of schooling and the beginning of large-scale decentralized edu-tech driven learning. Curriculum is a blind spot in most accounts of the dawning educational technologies revolution and related computer-based school reform initiatives. We appear to have been so amazed by our unprecedented levels of *access* to information that we have forgotten how to ask questions about the *quality* of information. This absence is a symptom of reductive human capital theory, which seeks to depoliticize questions of curriculum and content, and instead shift the focus to efficiency, accountability, and the functional fit between the skill set "delivered" and the economy.

Education and the knowledge conveyed therein should be valuable and appropriate to the learner in their context. But this context is not *merely* economic. Basic questions concerning what humans ought to know and be able to do are complex ethically, politically, and epistemologically. The organization of knowledge and its presentation in a curriculum is a question that ties into some of the most ancient philosophical discussions on the purposes of education. According to the minimal integral meta-theory of education built here, one broad goal of education ought to be to develop those forms of post-conventional capabilities and personalities that are able to transform local culture and community. Another goal is the balancing of interiors and exteriors as the focus of learning, beyond human capital theory's orientation toward education as job training and functional fit in the economy. Ways need to be found to build these goals into the structure of an otherwise open-sourced platform for learning and collaboration. This depends in part, of course, on the technologies available and the ways they can be shaped in light of our knowledge about human development and learning.

Learning Science and Technology: Machines Don't Teach, They Help Teachers

Preserving the greatest possible amount of valuable knowledge is pointless if it is inaccessible because it is impossible to learn. Questions about the values and knowledge we want to instill are related to questions of pedagogy and teaching and learning practice. Here we must draw on scientific models, specifically those in developmental psychology, learning theory, and education, as well as technological concerns including strategies for storage and access. Assuming only that our integral educational technology must be useful to unknown humans from all walks of life and in all cultures, it must provide a *universally accessible content delivery system*. The ideal educational technology would contain an intelligent tutoring system that operationalizes the sciences of learning.[48]

Not all informational environments are educational environments—search engines are not teachers—so we must curate content and orchestrate its delivery according to the best of what we know about how learning occurs. Moreover, because we cannot know what future generations will need to learn, we must create educational technologies that are radically open, allowing for explorations in any direction while remaining carefully structured to ensure fidelity to the dynamics of learning. This means organizing all relevant knowledge in terms of both its *complexity and value*, similar to Wilber's proposal for a dizzyingly complex Giga Glossary.[49] As large as this task sounds—cataloging all that is worth knowing across all quadrants and the full spectrum of developmental levels—researchers are beginning to build knowledge networks, conceptual learning sequences, and developmental dictionaries that can serve as epistemologically sophisticated backends for intelligent tutoring systems.[50] Educational technology must make knowledge learnable, not just available.

A big part of learning is being with other people and cooperating across generations and skill levels. Technologies should be designed to facilitate collaborative in-person meet-ups, skill exchange, and interest group-based teach-ins; all forms of self-organizing educational community are essential for real learning. Screens should run applications that get users to go away from their screen and be with other people, interesting objects, and nature. Pro-social technologies that spawn peer-to-peer (P2P) networks will form the universally accessible platform for integral educational initiatives of the future.

The P2P movement is a perfect example of how emergent technological and organizational forms can enable the spontaneous emergence of integral educational initiatives. This movement is largely characterized by technology platforms that facilitate the spontaneous sharing of gifts and skills, self-organized problem solving, and non-hierarchical collaborations based on "bottom-up" rather than "top-down" solutions. The idea is to explicitly utilize collective intelligence in the design and implementation of solutions to some of the world's greatest problems. The P2P movement comes in many forms and holds tremendous promise. I am especially interested in *open platform cooperativism*, which seeks to put the most basic elements of platforms for online social networks and economic transactions back into the hands of users, and thus counteract trends toward surveillance and exploitative commercialization.[51] These kinds of emergent networks are the conditions required to enable the kind of educational futures I am envisioning here.

However, as these technologies currently exist, they facilitate less than optimal educational self-organization. Too many ostensibly P2P platforms are predicated on the "standardized differentiation" of personality types and the homogenization of expressive modalities. Too many ostensibly P2P platforms are predicated on the "standardized differentiation" of personality types and the homogenization of expressive modalities (see the important work of Michel Bauwens and the recent book by Steven Johnson, *Future Perfect*). I share Wilber's concerns about the principled lack of hierarchical structures in some P2P networks, which often (although not always) question traditional ranking by skill level or expertise.[52] This is problematic, as hierarchal relations are a ubiquitous property of the *specializations* that occur in natural networks, which makes their active suppression unnatural and ultimately self-defeating and contradictory (i.e., it takes a hierarchical assertion of power to suppress the emergence of hierarchies). Moreover, hierarchies are an essential aspect of human self-organization and problem solving (e.g., if you are the only medical doctor in the room, you are "in charge" if a medical emergency occurs; that would be your unique obligation).

Peer-to-peer networks are often still based on simplistic ideas about the nature of human *interiors*. What we already identified in the Introduction as the *cognitive maturity fallacy* is only one part. Outdated ideas about the nature of the self dominate the technologies of the so-called "Web 2.0." This is because the movement is mainly one of techno-economic optimists focused primarily on external structures. Thus we get platforms that claim universal representativeness, but are truly playgrounds for a privileged few. Wikipedia, for example, is a website where the vast majority of the content is produced by a relatively small number of well-educated white males, where paid consultants and content-creators curate high-profile pages; it is almost always ranked near the top of Google searches for particular topics. Or consider websites like Facebook, which is not technically a P2P phenomenon, although it is often cited as part of the new collaborative web. What is actually happening on Facebook, structurally, is that users both produce and consume their own content, which is then classified and leveraged as a medium for targeted advertisement and surveillance. The technologies of intimacy we use to communicate ourselves to the world literally force us to sell ourselves in the process, which leaves us feeling exploited. The co-optation of our personal communication as a means for selling advertisements reinforces the messages from our broader culture that the self is only a means to the end of profit making.[53]

These tools also contribute to deepening the sense many people have of disembodiment and displacement: the uncanny feeling that one is in a generic or non-unique place, *a placeless place*. As much as we are all participating together in cyberspace, we are often physically and emotionally isolated in physical space. This radical dislocation of identity is another lamentable postmodern moment in our culture (we feel totally ungrounded: post-biological, post-historical, post-geographical), and the new tools provided by the P2P movement often simply serve to hasten our descent into an existential nomadism of the abstract individual.

The now pervasive "pedagogies of the new media" and "identity-constituting screen cultures" are manifest in a barrage of images and spectacles. The user of a social networking website can be exposed to anything from almost anywhere in the world. This is a kind of pseudo-omniscience that cuts both ways. Screen cultures draw us out into the world in unprecedented detail (in high-def, as it were), while they also send us further into inwardness and isolation, sometimes fracturing our sense of self and personhood. The staged spectacles of late capitalism were used to orchestrate unity through nationalism and consumerism. Today predictable and profitable spectacles like the Super Bowl or Olympics are giving way to unplanned spectacles of disaster and terror that give fear-based public cultures an endless barrage of violent and confusing imagery. Adolescents (all of us really) are now socialized around the clock via screen viewing, which is usually of user-curated content, sometimes live-streaming from around the planet.

Much can be and has been accomplished through the coordination of *separate selves*, each understanding themself as independent and largely self-interested. But this is very different from a self-organizing cooperative in which each member understands their interdependence with all others and shares in a mutual understanding that there are no externalities. If we set the technological tools in the right cultural and individual contexts (that is, if we frame their use integrally), conditions can be made right for educational communities to spontaneously come together. Technology can allow larger and larger networks of collective intelligence and wisdom to emerge. Currently there are no technologies that are up to this task, although some are being developed.

Perhaps the best example of a technological platform that enables the self-organized emergence of educational communities is *Hylo*, developed by Edward West and team. Hylo.com is built to facilitate collaboration and resource exchange among large groups of purpose-aligned individuals. It is a social synergy engine, connecting real people in real communities so they can combine their unique gifts, skills and interests. It works by essentially making visible the opportunities to connect, collaborate, and share resources within and between individuals and communities. This can unlock collaboration, creativity, and resource flow, even in communities that have very little access to traditional financial resources. Were this platform to be generally adopted as an educational infrastructure within local well-resourced hubs, we would witness the spontaneous emergence and self-organization of educational cooperatives of various sizes across the planet, as democratically-minded world-centric individuals are brought together into diverse problem-focused, resource-sharing endeavors. This is a concrete utopian possibility in a very real sense, which means it is a possible future, not a dream. But it is a future we must create and not one inevitable for humanity.

Conclusion: Integral Education, Prospects and Probabilities

I have argued that there are major changes underway impacting humanity's social structures and their biospheric corollaries such that the next 50 years is by all accounts going to be a time of major global transformation. During this time educational systems as we have known them will be reworked in light of new technologies, shifting values, economic and climatological chaos, and new forms of human self-understanding and capability. Schooling in particular will be changing drastically in the coming decades. I believe integral education is likely to thrive in those places where schooling is least recognizable or nonexistent, where instead there are decentralized and self-organizing educational communities in which technologies have provided equal access to unprecedented levels of educational achievement. At the core of these new possibilities are educational technologies that are designed with an integral meta-theory of education in mind. Here, I have only touched on a vision of what certain radically new educational configurations might look like. My goal has been to spark the social imagination and set an agenda for future work in the field of integral education.

Can integral educational technologies impact humanity enough to facilitate a healthy world system transition? This is an issue that has immediate and direct implications for schooling in the coming years. An integral meta-theory of education contrasts with the fragmentation and biases of so much school curricula, as well as the randomness and blindspots of search engine generated Internet content, which has quickly become one of the most pervasive educational forces of our time.

The design requirements stemming from an integral meta-theory of education show the unscientific nature of so much "evidence-based" educational reform, especially in the areas of testing, pedagogy and online learning. Today the possibility of a science of education has yet to be realized, while the pretense of science nevertheless dominates the discourse of reformers. These lessons combine to suggest integral design requirements for educational technologies in general, which show (among other things) the limits and fallacies of current approaches to technology intensive education, which are increasingly centralizing and privatizing the administration of mass-schooling.[54]

---

1. Generally, I follow Wilber in adopting the term *integral* and discuss it at length in this book and elsewhere, see: Stein (2014).

2. The term "Anthropocene" entered the Oxford English Dictionary remarkably late, in June 2014. That is 15 years after it is agreed to have been first coined. See: Ian Angus' (2015) "When Did the Anthropocene Begin… and Why Does It Matter?"

3. Between 1900 and 1999, the US consumed 4,500 million tons of cement; between 2011 and 2013, the Chinese consumed 6,500 million tons of cement. In three years, the Chinese consumed 50% more concrete than the US did in the entire preceding century. See: David Harvey (2016a) and his "Senior Loeb Scholar Lecture" at the Harvard Graduate School of Design. Harvey points out that the real issue is not that they did it or *how much*, but rather: "*why* did the Chinese pour so much concrete?" The answer is that it was a classic macroeconomic crisis of overproduction and unemployment. The Chinese massively debt-financed internal investments in infrastructure and urban construction, mainly as a way to buy their own concrete and employ their own labor after losing 70 million jobs and whole markets for building materials during the 2007 US monetary crisis. Harvey's (2016) work in geography and in revitalizing Marxist theories of the production of space through uneven geographical development are essential in understanding the dynamics of present and future human-biosphere relationships, as I discuss further in Chapters 3 and 4.

4. For this very reason Jason Moore asks whether a better name for our current geological epoch would be the *Capitalocene*. See: Jason Moore's (2015) *Capitalism in the Web of Life*.

5. Wallerstein (2007); Moore (2015).

6. Moore is at pains to drive home this essential point about the co-constitution of society and nature. His notion of *double internality*—nature-in-society and society-in-nature—addresses this. As we will see with Wilber's quadrants, the differentiation of society from nature, or mind from brain, has its analytical usefulness. But heuristic *differentiations*, such as the quadrants, must not be reified into hard and fast *dissociations*. We differentiate only so we can better reintegrate at a higher level of synthesis and insight. Society and nature are not two and yet they are not one; we need concepts that capture their interanimation and co-evolution.

7. See: David Harvey's (2006) *Limits to Capital*. Capitalism tends to solve its problems by spreading out or putting things someplace else in space, the so-called "spatial fix." This worked when there were frontiers. We are probably nearing the end of spatial fixes.

8. Also see: Capra and Luisi's (2014) *The Systems View of Life*, for an up-to-date review of the literature on complex dynamical systems, autopoiesis, and other aspects of the sciences that study non-linear biological growth and evolution. Wallerstein's world-system analysis is directly influenced by Capra's theoretical forbearer, Ilya Prigogine, whose foundational work studied the patterns in dissipative structures far from equilibrium, which show emergence and spontaneous structuration. Prigogine foresaw a time when the social sciences could make use of the complex dynamical models being used in physics and systems biology. Importantly, we also encounter ideas from dynamical systems and the sciences of emergence when we look at human development and the nature of learning.

9. The idea of a basic income guarantee is one of the "Thirteen Social Miracles" discussed in Chapter 4.

10. This has been documented on global scale (see: Sahlberg, 2012). But it starts with policy changes in the US (see: Ravitch, 2013). Note also that the size and impact of public school systems have varied greatly between nation-states in the capitalist world-system. Although the story here focuses on American schools, the account offered is not addressed to any particular region or nation. Many of my suggestions may in fact work better in places without long-standing legacy institutions and entrenched

educational systems. In nations traditionally outside the "core states" of the world-system there may be greater openings for radically new forms of education to emerge.

11. See: the great historian of education, Lawrence Cremin's (1970) *American Education: The Colonial Experience*. Medieval and pre-colonial educational systems show how teaching and learning during the birth of new social orders require the invention of new forms of social cooperation and intergenerational transmission, including new kinds of assessment, new literacies, new languages, and new architectures.

12. Tomasello (1999); Dewey (1922).

13. Stein (2013). Also see: Chapter 2.

14. For some of the history surrounding Conant's educational vision, including the founding of the Educational Testing Service, see: Lemann (1999); Stein (2016).

15. When schools and other educational institutions are unable to reproduce society at the simple level of skills and dispositions, then key roles in the social fabric are not filled and whole systems can come undone. Habermas has called this a *capability crisis*, which often brings with it a *legitimation crisis* and a society-wide *identity crisis* (Habermas, 1975). If you doubt the modern world-system is in this situation, consider the US economic crisis (which involved our so-called "best minds") as well as the current state of presidential politics (the level of discourse is a major sign of declining educational systems).

16. This is a rich and important area of scholarship. See: Apple (2004; 2013); Ravitch (2010). Also see the work of the radical educational historian, Joel Spring's (1989) *The Sorting Machine Revisited*.

17. This may be taking it too far, but see the landmark text in critical theory of education, Bowles and Gintis' (1976/2011) *Schooling in Capitalist America: Educational Reform and the Contradictions of Economic Life*. This book lays out an essential theoretical tool in the critical theory of education known as the *correspondence principle*, which states that the social relationships within educational systems in a capitalist society will mirror or correspond to the social relationships that characterize commercial production and employment. One can trace several eras: an agrarian mode of production has an educational system built around one-room schoolhouses that are flexible, minimally resourced and relatively self-sufficient, but ultimately beholden to the rhythms of the farm. Factory production in industrial societies spawn large-scale mass-schooling run by bells and clocks and based on standardization. Post-industrial, late capitalist "cubi-

cal work" that involves screens and self-directed "white-collar" labor gives us schools modeled on tech startups that provide every student an individualized computer and workstation. The implications of the correspondence principle are many, but one is that schools exert a form of social control and conditioning that fosters the habits and self-understandings needed for participation in the economy and current division of labor. Macroeconomic changes are reflected in schools, which take on the shape needed by the economy.

18. Apple (2004; 2013).

19. Sahlberg (2012).

20. The term comes from a former G.W. Bush education cabinet member: Ravitch (2010).

21. The radically disproportionate power of capital resulting from wealth inequality is increasing daily—almost geometrically—and with mathematical certainty. See: Piketty (2014).

22. For more on counter-hegemonic educational practices, see: Apple (2013).

23. For a big picture on the election of Trump and the related "culture war" being fought over the right to shape the meta narrative of the future, see Jordan Greenhall's "Situational Assessment 2017: Trump Edition."

24. Cambridge Analytica is the most public face of a "global election management agency" that serves as a Big Data psychometric backend used by elites to manipulate the social and news media feeds of everyday people. This dangerous and almost invisible hijacking of teacherly authority is reshaping the culture and worldviews of millions worldwide (see: Grassegger & Krogerus' "The Data That Turned the World Upside Down"). Whereas prior modes of media were centralized and focused on creating a single story or narrative for everyone to buy into (e.g., National Public Radio; The New York Times), the new decentralized modes are focused on multiplying narratives and the disintegration of mutual understanding (e.g., Facebook; Twittter). With a kind of epistemic centrifugal force culture is pushed outward and apart, as identity politics splinter the public sphere into a solipsistic hall of mirrors. Once divided the people are then easily conquered; the vulnerabilities of subgroups allow them to be manipulated into consolidation and alignment along polarized party lines during the ideological (and advertising) push of an election season.

25. The psychometrics used at Cambridge Analytica are built around the OCEAN model of personality traits. Content is ultimately delivered based on the OCEAN diagnostic of emotional personality type in five dimensions: openness to experience, conscientiousness, extraversion, agreeableness, and neuroticism. It is important not to underestimate the way that the truncation of communication leads to a regression below reasonable judgment forms in public culture. Short duration streaming video, sentence length or image and word-based "memes," and the Tweet—for some these have usurped reasoned argumentation as a validation for teacherly authority.

26. Again, the Cold War reshaped American educational policy profoundly, largely laying the groundwork for the domination of reductive human capital theory as educational meta-theory. See: Cremin (1988); Lagemann (2000).

27. Activist and scholar of social revolutions, Micah White, sees exactly this possibility in his book *The End of Protest* (pp. 179-180): "I am haunted by an eco-fascist nightmare.... The ecological catastrophe will deepen and political leaders across the political spectrum will no longer deny climate change. They will see the political advantages of proclaiming themselves ecological saviours and of speaking in global terms. They will know the benefits of maintaining an emergency, or disaster capitalism.... I am concerned about the potential for scientific-oriented environmentalism to flip into a dark force in our world. I foresee that great tragedies could be carried out under the technocratic ecological flag. To join politics with catastrophic environmentalism is dangerous. It will attract the most power hungry... and the most calculative. Their lifeboat mentality will be the pretext for genocide and enslavement. And yet, some kind of universal ecological politics is absolutely necessary for the survival of humanity."

28. Again see: Bowles & Gintis (1976/2011).

29. Wallerstein (1974); Cremin (1970).

30. Collins & Halverson (2009).

31. Ibid.

32. These same trends are discussed in Stein (2016).

33. Based on: Collins & Halverson (2009); National Science Foundation (2008); Dawson & Stein (2011).

34. Stein (2016).

35. Pariser (2011).

36. Spring (2010).

37. Ravitch (2010); Kozol (2012).

38. Khan Academy is a great example of how new casks can be filled with old wine. Video lectures, even excellent ones, are merely a kind of didactic instruction, schooling's classic (and weakest) pedagogical practice. Moreover, Khan and his colleagues have neglected the learning sciences and ignore the role of developmental level in the design of their educational resources, which now include standardized tests tied into the US Common Core Standards.

39. For a rich anthropological and psychological description of what life is like spending all day in front of a screen, see: Thomas de Zengotita's (2006) *Mediated: How the Media Shapes Your World and the Way You Live in It*, and Nicholas Carr's (2011) *The Shallows: What the Internet Is Doing to Our Brains*.

40. Carr (2011); Kozol (2012).

41. Clearly the nature of these hubs and the technology they are built around is complex. This will occupy us later on. For now, assume it works and is built on integral design principles. There are, of course, other common concerns that this kind of system of hubs would favor students with intelligent and engaged parents. Students from these kinds of families will be advantaged no matter what educational configurations society provides for them. The purpose of public education has long been to level the playing field for those who are not so lucky. In the system I am envisioning here, even those children with so-called "bad" parents can simply be dropped off at an education hub, where they will have guidance and supervision from the citizen-teacher-scientists on staff. Ideally, however, this is a problem that can be largely solved in a single generation; as macroeconomic reforms and lifelong learning opportunities proliferate, we may begin to see fewer "bad" parents, who are themselves often the result of failed economic and educational systems.

42. See: "Thirteen Social Miracles," Chapter 4.

43. Again see: "Thirteen Social Miracles," or consider a vision like Buckminster Fuller's (1971) work on education, *Education Automation: Comprehensive Learning for Emergent Humanity*.
44. Parents are rightfully always worried about safety. But the system will get all parents to register, list skills, and then have performances continuously reviewed by peers,

as is done on Uber or other skill-sharing sites. Sounds complicated, but is it any more scheduled than many of today's lifestyles?

45. See: the numerous startup incubators, social labs, and pop-up classroom networks in cities like San Francisco, Boston, and New York. Also see: the Impact Hub, a co-working and education space out of LA, Oakland, and other cities worldwide.

46. Stein (manuscript in preparation).

47. This statement (that *everyone's* knowledge is worthy of preservation) is frequently met with critical responses about the need to distinguish between valuable and non-valuable or even dangerous ideas (i.e., what do we do with the neo-Nazi propaganda and censored textbooks?) This need for quality control is exactly the point. An integral approach to educational technologies contextualizes without censoring. The darkest ideologies of our past must never be forgotten; they must be taken as lessons, with future generations scaffolded into deeper reflections on the significance of human mistakes.

48. See: David Rose's work on *universal design for learning* in Gordon, Meyer & Rose's (2016) *Universal Design for Learning: Theory and Practice.*

49. Wilber (2006).

50. For a place where this kind of research is being done to improve education, see: Lectica, Inc. (www.Lectica.org).

51. Scholz & Schneider (2017).

52. Of course, we are not talking about pathological "dominator hierarchies," but rather about holarchies. See: Ken Wilber's (1995) *Sex, Ecology, Spirituality*, where the terms are used with reference to their originator, Riane Eisler.

53. It is hard to overestimate the impact that advertising has had on the direction of the Internet and the quality of website content. Micha White (2016, pp. 169-172) contextualizes the place of internet advertising in the history of the advertising industry's co-optation of communications media:

> For decades, corporations have consciously and strategically pursued the commercialization of culture. Their winning strategy has been to integrate advertising into public culture. By snatching the role of funding culture away from the people and their governments, corporations have

made us dependent on "free" information, entertainment, services and software that are subsidized by advertising and come at a grave cost to our psyches and our world. It would take a historian years to enumerate the many tactics that modern corporations have developed to ensure that public television, radio, transportation, newspapers and schools are inundated with commercial logos and ads. But when it comes to the Internet, the stages of the takeover are clear.... The advertising industry founded the Coalition for Advertising Supported Information and Entertainment (CASIE) in 1994, a task force whose core mission was to guarantee that into the future "advertising revenue must be a key funding source for information and entertainment in the evolving world of media...." CASIE was also instrumental in thwarting legislation to tax advertising on the Internet.... Within a decade, advertisers owned the Internet.... Google introduced advertising in 2001... [and then bought] DoubleClick, a leading online adverting company, for $3.1 billion, making the Internet search engine one of the world's largest advertising agencies. By 2014 advertising accounted for nearly 90 percent of Google's revenue.... Social networks such as Facebook, Instagram, Snapchat and Twitter have largely followed Google's strategy of offering free services.... [funded by] commercials on the sides of our screens and in our newsfeeds.

54. Stein (2016).

Chapter 2
Ethics and the New Education: Testing, Medication, and the Future of Human Capital

Most of this essay was presented at the 2013 Integral Theory Conference and later published in the Journal of Integral Theory and Practice. It brings together my work as a graduate student at Harvard on the ethics of educational psychopharmacology (ADHD medication) and on social justice and educational measurement (high-stakes testing). The discussion on ADHD meds is about an ethical distinction between designing children and raising them. The discussion on standardized testing involves a distinction between efficiency-oriented testing and justice-oriented testing. The unethical branch of each distinction is that which objectifies and instrumentalizes the student, whereas the ethical branch establishes a cooperative relationship. The unethical branch sees only the Right-Hand quadrants of the child and school (only bodies, brains, systems, and structures) with no sense of justice beyond efficiency, and no accounting for the student's self-understanding, emotions, or the school's culture and its meaning.

Every time I give a talk on these topics at schools or colleges, I am confronted by a school psychologist, teacher, or parent, upset that I have called into question the drugging of a large percentage of the student body (among boys, as much as 15%). The medicalization of academic underperformance is part of the ideology of contemporary schooling, wherein problems with the social structure are misunderstood as problems with the biology or psychology of the individuals within them. The argument goes something like this: "It's not the school's culture of high-stakes, low resources, and frequent teacher turnover that is the problem. It's the brains of all these children that are the problem—they all have some kind of organic dysfunction that makes it so they don't fit in. We must fix them by working upon their bodies and brains."

The integral paideia functions through non-coercive and creatively cooperative intergenerational exchange in the context of educational abundance. Children should be raised into their own. That means they are allowed to grow. Children should not be designed or worked upon as objects manufactured to our ideals. The argument here is not "anti-medication," nor is it "anti-testing" in any simple sense. I seek to put attention on the relationships and dynamics of power and educational authority rather than on the pill or test used, which is merely an instrument of deeper structural injustice. This essay touches on a theme raised by all the essays in this book: the need to liberate educational configurations from their colonization by the tentacles of power extruded by other social systems, be they pharmaceutical industries, standardized testing industrial complexes, or federal polices penned by distant lawmakers.

Introduction: Tomorrow's Child

During the first decade of the twenty-first century the global economy was set into crisis. National political discourse and policy became based on the idea of continued US technological and scientific superiority, more specifically the need for comprehensive educational reform to prepare American children for the techno-scientific economy of tomorrow. This climate saw federal testing policies set so that accountability metrics dominated school cultures. Prescription drugs for academic underperformance skyrocketed. Already large financial inequalities between school districts continued to increase and technological progress in the broader culture began outstripping school infrastructures by decades (with kids feeling like they're going back in time when they enter school buildings). This has led to the deterioration of teaching and learning in schools—failures that have been well documented.[1]

I argue here that there are issues deeper than the US educational system's *failures*; failures to provide adequate buildings, for example, or failures to foster a love of learning (its sins of omission, if you will). Recent decades have shown the system capable of committing sins of *commission*, where educational processes become unacceptable because of what is being *done to* students, not just because of what is *withheld*, lacking, or inequitably distributed. Two trends occupy my attention here: standardized testing and educational psychopharmacology. Tests and meds. These are the technocratic solutions to the educational crises of the twenty-first century. In this essay I show how they reveal the logic of reductive human capital theory and the structure of its coercive, de-agentifying, and instrumentalizing educational practices.

In order to better diagnose these pathologies of reductive human capital theory, I begin by laying out a set of normative meta-theoretical distinctions. I work from the minimalist integral meta-theory of education offered in the Introduction, and use this to look at some ethical issues involved with standardized testing infrastructures, briefly touching on the history of their use in the US as a function of human capital theory. My proposed integral meta-theory of education is employed to reveal ethically significant differences between *efficiency-oriented* testing practices and *justice-oriented* ones. I argue further that the recent epidemic of psychotropic drug prescriptions for school aged children is symbiotically (or dialectically) related to the dominance of efficiency-oriented testing infrastructures, both through their common roots in reductive human capital theory and through their practical in-the-classroom compatibilities (e.g., kids on meds do better on tests).

Then looking at the rhetoric and science surrounding the growth of educationally-oriented psychopharmacology, I deploy the same meta-theoretical approach to characterize the ethical difference between *designing* children and *raising* them. I conclude with a series of provocations and reflections directed at kindling the social imagination and reviving our sense that there are alternatives to dystopian educational futures. Tomorrow's child will inhabit the most pervasive, invasive, and complex educational configurations in history, but there are possibilities for integral education still—ways by which to bend geo-historical forces toward the creation and perpetuation of more humane, just, and liberating educational systems.[2]

Human Capital Metrics: Between Efficiency and Justice

> The more any quantitative social indicator (or even some qualitative indicator) is used for social decision-making, the more subject it will be to corruption pressures and the more apt it will be to distort and corrupt the social processes it is intended to monitor.... Achievement tests may well be valuable indicators of general school achievement under conditions of normal teaching aimed at general competence. But when test scores become the goal of the teaching process, they both lose their value as indicators of educational status and distort the educational process in undesirable ways.
>
> —*Campbell's law*, Donald T. Campbell (1975)

There are several broad socio-political motives for institutionalizing standardized educational measurement. As already discussed in the Introduction, human capital theory offers simplistic representations of complex educational processes, using terminology and measures amenable to certain kinds of legal, economic, and political decision-making. Decisions about the educational systems involve taxpayer money, conflicting values, and political disagreement, so appeals often need to be made to ostensibly unbiased and objective facts about schools, which many argue tests can provide. Modern educational systems face complexities of bureaucratization and legislation comparable to those faced by modern health care systems, where the need to measure both the cost and treatment effectiveness has transformed the nature of medicine.[3] Today, trends toward high-stakes accountability and efficiency monitoring practices (in which testing figures prominently) aim at transforming the delivery of educational goods into an instrumental market-driven activity. The result has been cultures dominated by *efficiency-oriented testing practices*, where measures built to yield system-level data for school leaders and political decision-makers shape the intimate educational experience of students.[4] These practices are focused on system-level monitoring and bureaucratic functions, such as allotting opportunities to students, determining program effectiveness, and fostering accountability in the system, among other things. *Justice-oriented testing practices*, on the other hand, transcend but include efficiency-oriented practices. Guided by a more comprehensive understanding of teaching, learning, and culture, they are focused on monitoring and enabling the fair distribution of basic educational goods and promoting the autonomous growth of individual students. Lessons from the history of testing will help illuminate this important distinction.

Educational Testing: A Brief History

The roots of modern educational testing can be found in the work of the earliest psychologists. Precisely engineered electrical equipment and newly invented psychometric techniques allowed for the kinds of precise measurements that brought early prestige to psychophysics and later to behaviorism. As psychology grew beyond the laboratory, the importance and prestige of measurement remained and the practice of mental testing became central to the identity of the emerging discipline. IQ testing in particular captured the public imagination and quickly found its way into the plans of policy makers and educational reformers. By 1930, IQ-style multiple-choice standardized testing was ubiquitous in American public schools, typically being used to track students into different groups for instruction and management.[5] This growing testing infrastructure also allowed for the beginnings of the "scientific management" (aka: human capital theory) of school operations. Educational researchers began, for the first time, to systematically use test results to inform their thinking about school improvements. These initial large-scale testing efforts were carried out under the banner of organizational efficiency and educational research. These tests offered the kind of objectivity and simplicity of representation that fit with the human capital theory-based arguments that were beginning to dominate an increasingly complex and politicized educational system.

In 1931 a young high school science teacher from Michigan solved a technological problem that IBM had been working on unsuccessfully for years: *automated test scoring*. The implications and subsequent technical developments (such as the Scantron machine) would facilitate the construction of the first national standardized testing infrastructure.[6] The centerpiece of this newly automated testing infrastructure was the Educational Testing Service

(ETS), which emerged in part as a result of the federal government's interest in exercising quality control and determining how best to fund research and development. Several waves of sweeping federal legislation during the Cold War consolidated the shape of late industrial-era education, including: funding to create the National Science Foundation (NSF) and promote science, technology, engineering, and math (STEM) education in K-12, civil rights, desegregation, and the War on Poverty programs (such as Head Start).

Federal government agencies began recruiting the testing industry to aid in policy and program evaluation studies.[7] As the human capital theory-based "scientific management" of educational reform drew widening support, federally mandated educational testing expanded, eventually including the National Assessment of Education Progress (NAEP), the Iowa Tests, and a host of other national K-12 tests. The federal influx of support for testing also led to broad concerns that the educational system was being turned into a kind of "sorting machine" for human capital, rewarding a limited set of educational trajectories through the use of tests that focused on mostly STEM-related skills and competencies. This was a vision of a national meritocracy.[8] The negative effects of increased testing on classroom practice continued to mount, as the high-stakes multiple-choice exam came to symbolize American education itself.[9]

Despite some clearly expressed concerns, continued advances in the computerized administration and scoring of tests fueled policy makers' ambitions to build a national K-12 testing infrastructure for use in program evaluation and systems-level accountability at the national level.[10] The final push toward a comprehensive federal testing infrastructure began with President G.H.W. Bush's *America 2000*, in which he proposed a national testing apparatus that would be tied into a national curriculum and used to ensure the equitable distribution of educational opportunity, as well as American competiveness in the global marketplace. President Clinton later endorsed the plan but backed off the idea of a national test. In 2001, *No Child Left Behind* (NCLB) provided a federal mandate to build a K-12 testing infrastructure for accountability purposes, but not in the form of a single national test. Instead, a decentralized, competition-oriented, and high-stakes set of testing practices was rolled out, inspired by human capital theory.[11] This spawned a rapidly expanding for-profit computer-intensive testing industry, which has proven to be error prone, corrupt, and dominated by simplistic psychological and psychometric theorizing. The Obama administration dismantled NCLB, but sustained a broad commitment to efficiency-oriented testing, putting millions of dollars into a "next generation" tech-enabled testing infrastructure that promises to increase the number of tests and the impact on school cultures, teaching, and curriculum.[12]

On the Difference Between Efficiency and Justice

From the perspective of an integral meta-theory of education and its commitments to an all-quadrant model of social reality and human action, the history of testing is one in which there is a profound and conspicuous *road not taken*. The earliest psychometric pioneers were guided by the idea that the psychological and social sciences could be leveraged to aid in the construction of a profoundly enlightened and liberating educational system. Just as standardized measurement infrastructures had revolutionized the physical sciences and brought incalculable social benefit (e.g., civil engineering and medicine), so would educational measurement—continually informed by cutting edge research—allow for the radical redesign of educational systems.

Psychologists, sociologists, and educators would soon dismantle the simplistic theories and models in psychology which had misguided the earliest approaches to testing. By the late 1960s, advances in the human sciences would yield complex, four-fold, bio-psycho-socio-cultural models of learning and culture. These advances opened the possibility for *justice-oriented testing practices* that would facilitate the mass-customization of individualized education and ensure the equitable distribution of resources and the fair treatment of individuals.

However, the urgency with which testing was institutionalized as a part of the war effort of previous decades (and in the context of rapid urbanization and public school expansion) led to a premature reification of the function and meaning of testing. Overwhelmed by the unprecedented complexity of administering modern school systems, and under increasing public pressure to prepare children to enter a rapidly industrializing economy, school leaders and administrators had little sympathy for those who were out to make testing more than a tool for bureaucratic efficiency.

The result has been that modern educational systems are dominated by testing infrastructures that neglect the all-quadrant complexity of social reality, levels of human development, and dynamics of human learning. History reveals that the growing prevalence of an efficiency-oriented view of how educational organizations should be managed propelled increases in the size and scope of testing infrastructures. Testing companies then funded and pursued the adoption of technological innovations enabling economies of scale (e.g., multiple-choice test item; the Scranton machine) in order to service a measurement-intensive system of educational institutions that were increasingly fetishizing efficiency. This way of viewing the nature of schools was imported as "scientific management" from industry. It characterizes school systems as if they are factories processing raw materials, with objectively measurable inputs and outputs, and where the dominant institutional virtue is efficiency.[13]

Efficiency-oriented testing practices are designed to simplify the complexity of educational configurations in order to facilitate certain kinds of data-driven managerial decision-making. They are tools for surveillance and system monitoring akin to the measurement infrastructures used in industry for quality control and cost-benefit analysis. Theodore Porter, an authority on the socio-political history of quantitative objectivity, explains this simple truth about decision-making in bureaucracies, especially public ones, where "mere experience or know-how is not sufficient to ground public expertise.... [because the public insists] that administrative decisions be depoliticized.... The ideal is a withdrawal of human agency.... Subjectivity creates responsibility. Impersonal rules can be almost as innocent as nature itself." Continuing from Porter's important book, *Trust in Numbers*:

> Cost-benefit analysis was intended from the beginning as a strategy for limiting the play of politics in public investment decision.... such regulations [would require the standardization of measurement procedures] throughout the government and [be] applied to almost every category of public action. The transformation of cost-benefit analysis into a universal standard of

> rationality... cannot be attributed to the megalomania of experts, but rather to bureaucratic conflict in a context of overwhelming public distrust. Though tools like this one can scarcely provide more than a guide to analysis and a language of debate, there has been strong pressure to make them into something more.

When turning to cite contemporary examples of the expansion of these decision procedures, Porter looks to educational bureaucracies, quoting from a prescient 1994 front page article in the *Los Angeles Times* about the plans of American college accreditation agencies to measure *how much* education students are receiving. "There is a very significant body of opinion in higher education," stated the accreditation agencies' representative, "that says to the public, 'Trust us. And don't require us to produce any evidence [of results].' What we're saying is that those days are over." Porter reflects on this drive toward accountability as a form of mechanical objectivity enabling the quantification of value for bureaucratic purposes. "Like every institution, the university must be refashioned as a panopticon to open it to surveillance by law courts and regulatory bureaucracies.... [subsuming its] activities within a 'culture of evidence.'"[14]

A culture of evidence is almost without exception a culture of measurement. Again, it is hard to reasonably deny the importance of this way of considering education. Why wouldn't we want objective evidence that public money and private tuitions create colleges that get results? It is precisely the simplicity and importance of these basic questions that make simplistic (usually quantitative) representations of educational processes so prone to misuse and overuse.

In some cases, cost-benefit analysis via high-stakes testing makes sense in schools. But it must always be remembered that what is measured are not objects, but people, and the traits of interest are not length, weight, or other manufacturing specifications, but qualities of mind, skill, and personality. This has led to a situation in which a system of categories built for purposes of instrumental rationality and control has become the dominant system of categories used in schools to guide the construction of students' self-understandings. There is perhaps no greater insight into the detrimental effects human capital theory has had on education during the past century than this: efficiency-oriented testing practices have come to provide the categories in terms of which students (and teachers and school communities) understand themselves. This state of affairs has become progressively worse during the past decade. Federal policies have increasingly promoted testing practices in which communities are shamed by school closings, where teachers' "value-added scores" are published in newspapers, and students' life prospects (and academic self-concepts) are shaped by forms of testing that are demonstrably inappropriate for these purposes.

The claim that contemporary testing infrastructures have led to systematically distorted forms of self-understanding is supported by the fact that the history of testing has been estranged from the rest of psychology and educational theory. During the century that gave us Dewey, Montessori, Steiner, and Piaget (among many others), the testing infrastructure changed primarily in response to advances in technology and the needs of bureaucrats—*not* in response to advances from the learning sciences that were progressively revealing the nature of how educational processes *ought* to be structured. That is, as advances in educational theory and developmental psychology opened possibilities for approaches to assessments based on meaningful, student-centered, and psychologically rigorous systems of categories and constructs, the dominant approach to testing remained focused on measuring under-theorized constructs (e.g., scholastic aptitude) using simplistic means (e.g., multiple-choice). Evidence continues to mount concerning the detrimental effects of these psychologically naive testing practices, especially their stigmatizing and disempowering impact on students, and their tendency to radically truncate the pedagogical and curricular options available to teachers.[15]

Importantly, this same reductive approach to understanding learning and teaching has led to a broad cultural movement in support of psychopharmacological solutions for educational underperformance. If testing facilitates the mischaracterization of students as objects amenable to instrumental manipulation, it is only a small step to re-imagine education in terms of actual physical interventions into the biology of the child. Moreover, because these interventions improve scores on the very tests that mischaracterized the child in the first place, the approaches are reciprocally reinforcing and create an ostensibly coherent approach to educational reform in the twenty-first century. This dialectically related ensemble of efficiency-oriented testing, psychopharmacology, and human capital theory is shaping the future of education as if there was no alternative.

> The radical rise in ADHD diagnoses by two thirds over the first decade of the millennium coincided with the implementation of the federal No Child Left Behind law that centered on high stakes standardized testing. The "high stakes" part of the high stakes testing puts economic sanctions on low test scores and rewards high test scores. As Maggie Koerth-Baker has observed, "...when a state passed laws punishing or rewarding schools for their standardized-test scores, ADHD diagnoses in that state would increase not long afterward. Nationwide, the rates of ADHD diagnosis increased by 22 percent in the first four years after No Child Left Behind was implemented." Studies that break down ADHD diagnosis by state confirm that the states with the greatest financial penalties under No Child Left Behind are also the states with the greatest rates of diagnosis, especially for youth below the poverty line.[16]

But there are alternatives. An integral meta-theory of education offers a complex multi-dimensional model of the mind, characterizing it as an evolving ecosystem. Measuring the mind is thus understood as being intrinsically ethically fraught. I have elsewhere argued for justice-oriented testing infrastructures, as well as for a kind of integral pluralism in the realm of psychological measurement.[17] These are a condition for the possibility of the educational futures I argue for in this book. Unless we think about testing in radically new ways we will continue to recreate the same injustices and inefficiencies that have plagued our educational systems for decades.[18]

Educational Psychopharmacology: Between Designing Children and Raising Them

> The neoliberal imperatives for testing, scripted lessons, and direct instruction for "higher outputs" have created institutional conditions and financial rewards and punishments so that ADHD symptoms of restlessness, inattentiveness, and hyperactivity have become more prevalent, numerous, and more likely to be identified. That is, the new culture of control in schools is inseparable from the trend for the radical rise in the medical pathologization of students. Reasonable individual responses (like restlessness) to repressive institutional conditions—like disassociation from the environment, extreme boredom, and inability to find relevance in the assignment—have become the basis for the identification of disease and the prescription of drugs. Moreover, the medical pathologizing of students is interwoven with neoliberal ideology in education in which knowledge, learning, and intelligence are understood through the register of economic competition, social mobility, and opportunity.... High stakes testing and drugging of students facilitates the expansion of the multi-billion dollar test and textbook publishing industry, and creates profits for the medico-pharmaceutical industry.
>
> —Kenneth J. Saltman (2016)

Today in schools around the world there are millions of children whose lives have been shaped by educationally oriented psychopharmacology. Although the numbers vary as a function of socio-economic conditions, there is a clear and striking global trend toward increasing use of ADHD medications.[19] Parenting and schooling practices have been transforming as a result. The media disseminate direct-to-consumer advertisements for key products, while biotech companies make huge profits from "child-focused" campaigns.[20] We find ourselves in a historically unprecedented situation facing complex moral issues. Discussing treatments for ADHD in particular, this section highlights the increasingly prominent role that psychotropic drugs play in contemporary educational configurations. These trends in educationally oriented psychopharmacology (like those discussed above regarding testing) reveal the pathologies and distortions of educational configurations dominated by reductive human capital theory.

Just as the large-scale institutionalization of efficiency-oriented testing infrastructures has been justified by the importation of management models from business and industry into education, so has the rapid increase in children's psychotropic drug prescriptions been justified by the importation of treatment models from medicine. In both cases, the ontological monovalence of reductive human capital theory has lent credibility to reductionist (flatland) models of education, which oversimplify the nature of learning processes, neglect the all-quadrant complexity of social reality, and characterize education as simply involving the prediction and control of closed systems. Scientific advances about the nature of learning and education are not motivating reform and large-scale implementation; rather these are motivated by an economically based desire to "optimize" a certain kind of educational system. Exploring the state of knowledge about ADHD, as well as the state of practices in schools, clarifies the dangers and injustices accompanying the medicalization of academic underachievement.

ADHD: Science, Controversy, and Ideology

ADHD is a disorder characterized by inattention, hyperactivity, and impulsiveness. It is a good predictor of negative academic and economic outcomes. Teachers are typically the first to suggest the possibility that a child might need an ADHD diagnosis, and roughly 75% of those diagnosed are male (three times as many as girls).[21] In 2011, 11% of all US children ages 4–17 were diagnosed with ADHD (6.4 million); 6.1% were taking ADHD drugs (4 million), with an estimated 8% to 35% of university students in the US using cognitive stimulants. In 2012, diagnoses of ADHD had risen 66% since the prior decade. Of those diagnosed, more than half are also diagnosed with conduct or oppositional defiant disorder. Family practice doctors—not child psychiatrists—handle most referrals and issue most diagnoses and treatments. The most common treatments involve the prescription of stimulant medications such as Ritalin and Adderall. The United States appears to be setting a global trend, as numbers reflecting the annual use of ADHD medications show major recent growth worldwide.[22]

This is where agreements about ADHD end. Facts about the causes of ADHD and the most effective treatments for it are complex, incomplete, and contested.[23] The long-standing "chemical imbalance" theory of ADHD suggests that executive function deficits involving the dopamine system are responsible for symptoms. However, it is questionable whether problems with executive function alone are necessary or sufficient for a manifestation of the disorder.[24] Moreover, genetic research guided by this hypothesis and looking for predictors of ADHD has been inconclusive, finding minimal evidence for the involvement of genes known to be involved with dopamine transporters and receptors.[25] And while neuroimaging work has revealed suggestive anatomical and functional differences in subjects with ADHD when compared to controls, most studies have been conducted using samples that are too small to yield conclusive results and that do not include children and adolescents. Some studies do suggest possible environmental causes, but most research focuses entirely on causal factors within the individual.[26] The most promising avenues for future research focus on multiple etiologies, diverse developmental pathways, and the effects of environmental factors. Researchers hope that these avenues might eventually shift diagnostic practices away from symptom identification and toward more complex and dynamic biomarkers of individual differences.[27]

The state of ADHD diagnosis and treatment is comparably complicated. As already mentioned, despite clear trends suggesting that certain practices of over-prescription are widespread, there are, in fact, very prominent regional differences in rates of diagnosis. These differences have led many to argue that ADHD is *under*-diagnosed in impoverished communities while it is *over*-diagnosed in wealthy and middle class ones.[28] Although the most common treatment for ADHD is stimulant prescription drugs, what studies there are about the efficacy of these treatments do not provide straightforward results. Studies originally suggesting that drugs worked better than behavioral therapy have been reanalyzed to reveal that, in reality, outcomes resulting from treatments involving drugs alone were less desirable than those that combined drugs with cognitive behavioral interventions, and these outcomes were only minimally superior to behavioral therapies alone.[29] Also, it is not at all clear that drug-induced symptom reductions (as measured using the American Psychological Association's *Diagnostic and Statistical Manual of Mental Disorders* [or DSM] criteria) necessarily lead to the desired improvements in academic achievement. Moreover, how stimulant drugs work to improve ADHD symptoms is not well understood, which is not surprising given the state of the aforementioned brain research.[30]

The realities "in the trenches" of school and family life look different and less ambivalent. The number of diagnoses and drug treatments continues to rise as if oblivious to the tentative and preliminary nature of the science. This has led some to stress that this is, simply and objectively, a dangerous and uncertain situation. Nuanced ethical arguments aside, very little is known about the impacts of long-term stimulant usage in childhood and adolescence. Research conducted on adults and animals has demonstrated that these drugs do have a set of undesirable physiological effects when used in large quantities over long periods, effects such as addiction and the stunting of growth.[31] It has also been demonstrated that symptoms return almost immediately when those who have found success with drug treatment discontinue the use of medication. This means that as the first generation of "Ritalin kids" find their way into college and the workforce they will continue treatment for symptoms, some having been on the drug for the vast majority of their lives—over 20 years. Ritalin and Adderall now rival alcohol and marijuana as the most widely used recreational drugs on college campuses, where they are typically taken in higher doses for off-label purposes. Billions of pills containing Schedule II substances are in circulation among an age group known for high-risk behavior. The possibility of an iatrogenic crisis affecting a whole generation of young adults worries many observers.[32]

Nevertheless, despite these uncertainties and risks, millions of children are diagnosed with ADHD and treated with medications, and the prevalence of these practices continues to increase. This suggests that trends in diagnoses and treatments for ADHD are more than the result of advances in the science and art of educational psychopharmacology—*the ideology of reductive human capital theory is involved.* There is evidence of close and questionable relations between drug companies and the disability advocacy groups (such as Children and Adults with Attention-Deficit Disorder, or CHADD) that have tirelessly worked at legitimizing ADHD as a widespread disorder amenable to drug treatment.[33] The rapid increase of ADHD prescriptions has been driven by the profit-seeking educational initiatives of pharmaceutical companies. What is a largely US-based industry targets teachers, parents, and family doctors with drug advertisements and educational materials that encourage diagnosis and prescription. These companies have created a gold mine. In 2010, the United States spent $7 billion on ADHD drugs. By 2015 that number had risen to $12.9 billion.[34]

There are also broad shifts in culture toward "blaming the brain" for what used to be considered moral failures or individual differences. There is a general acceptance of a "biomedical self" in both popular culture and the human sciences. These considerations are consistent with views that explain practices surrounding ADHD in terms of more general trends in the medicalization of the human condition. These theorists raise concerns about what it means to reframe underperformance and misbehavior as biological dysfunctions, suggesting it amounts to the individuation of social problems and the depoliticization of deviance.[35]

On the Difference Between Designing Children and Raising Children

In light of an integral meta-theory of education, it is easy to see the *partialness* of most current attempts at helping children with the symptoms typically associated with ADHD. The vast majority of approaches shift attention away from the quality of the educational configurations and toward the biology of the child. Instead of considering that social and cultural factors may be a part of the problem, the problem is located in the child's biological substrate. Thus, the child's brain is to be fixed to fit into available educational configurations, as opposed to fixing these configurations so they are responsive to the individual differences of the child.[36]

This approach to treatment is an artifact of reductive human capital theory, which guides the development of educationally oriented psychopharmacology, where medical means are used to affect educational ends. As opposed to adopting a polyfocal approach concerned with the interaction of numerous bio-psycho-social factors, a specific biological dysfunction is blamed and targeted with a specific biomedical intervention.

Just over a century ago some scientists began to suggest that education could be made akin to building or engineering, first suggesting the prospect of *designing children*. This approach entails that the internal dynamics and growth processes of individuals be taken as objects of manipulation—*working on* the life being shaped, as opposed to *working with* it.[37] Designing a child is a process in which a third-person perspective is adopted and an instrumental intervention is used to change behaviors, dispositions, and capabilities. In principle, there is no need to make use of relationships built on communication, compromise, or mutual expectation, no need to embrace the all-quadrant complexity of social reality. Instead, this approach amounts to a unilateral *construction* of who the child will become. Designing a child is a relationship with a monological structure of non-reciprocal imposition, established in light of the designer's goals for the child without input from the child or consideration of the child's goals. The child does *not* participate in shaping their life, but is acted on from the outside. The child experiences behavioral and dispositional changes resulting from processes beyond their control with results the child does not consider themselves responsible for producing.

This distinction between *designing* and *raising* concerns the structure of the educational relationship in question, not the risks of medication or the unsavory practices of the pharmaceutical industry (these are important, but not the heart of the issue). The line is drawn between relationships that respect the child's limited and burgeoning autonomy and those that override the child's nascent autonomy in the interest of goals to be imposed upon them. The distinction focuses on the way people intervene in children's lives, and establishing a continuum applicable in the analysis of any educational relationship. Biologically focused interventions tend toward design. They make it possible to get results (to change behavior as desired) without establishing the kinds of relationships typically associated with the raising of children. According to an integral meta-theory of education, children establish their identities in specific socio-cultural contexts and relationships that embody specific preferences and values. Development is a dynamic process of individuation through socialization; an individual *negotiates* their identity in relation to the desires of significant elders, peers, and broad cultural patterns. However, when educationally oriented psychopharmacology are used to affect the outcome of identity formation, a child's ability to negotiate their own identity can be lost, as the preferences of parents or prevalent cultural norms are literally *built* into their biology. As noted during the discussion of ADHD, most treatments do not involve questioning the socio-cultural contexts in which the child manifests symptoms. Instead, attention is focused on the biology of the child only, and it is not considered whether some of the norms and rules the child is being asked to conform to might be unreasonable. Importantly, educational configurations that work this way effectively instantiate a system of norms that is insensitive to dissent and that relies on an ability to design children who will conform. This is a violation of the child's autonomy (and anatomy)—literally disallowing the child's "self-legislative" ability, overriding their bodily sovereignty. Parents, cultures, or schools that severely constrain the choices available to children during identity formation are rightfully seen as repressive. All children have "the right to an open future" in which they can act autonomously and responsibly. All children have a right to participate in their own development. This brings us to the heart of the ethical violations that result from the dominance of reductive human capital theory as the meta-theory of education.[38]

Conclusion: Ethics and the New Education

I have woven a complex story about the impact of reductive human capital theory on contemporary educational configurations and the bad symbiosis between high-stakes testing and ADHD medication. Extrapolating the trends discussed suggests the emergence of a new kind of educational system in the coming decades. During the twilight of American dominance and in the context of unprecedented global interconnectedness and complexity, school systems are being redesigned to fit the strategic and instrumental needs of largely economic geo-historical interests and entities. Since the end of WWII, reductive human capital theory has set the terms by which educational possibilities are understood and pursued, resulting in a public education system of vast size and scope, conceived by policy makers as a "sorting machine" for human capital.[39] Now in the early years of the twenty-first century, this homogeneous public education system is being dismantled and replaced by a heterogeneous mixture of (for-profit) charter schools, online education providers, and what remains of traditional schools (increasingly underfunded and undervalued). What are emerging are the most complex, pervasive, and overtly economically driven educational configurations in history.

This new education is one in which the goal of the system is no longer to create citizens who share a common fund of knowledge and culture as a result of shared educational experiences. This Deweyian ideal (which while never achieved, did serve to counteract the total co-optation of public schools by economic interests) has been almost entirely dissolved by the relentless push of reductive human capital theory-inspired approaches. As discussed above, testing infrastructures have become the criterion by which educational institutions are evaluated and according to which students, teachers, and school leaders understand the goals of education. The resulting simplification of educational processes has short-circuited reflective discourse about the goals of education, creating the illusion that competing educational configurations can be compared as simply as comparing the bottom line of competing companies.

Add to this mix the trends discussed above concerning educational psychopharmacology, and a picture emerges in which students' nervous systems become part of the "system environment" that must be controlled in the interest of pursuing narrowly defined parameters of system success.[40] Just as manufacturing efficiencies are often achieved through the use of measurement practices that make invisible the collateral damage being done to the environment, the test-driven efficiencies of the new education involve collateral damage that is hidden in the brains and minds of students, beyond the realm of what is measured when considering the success of a school. That is, reductive human capital theory leads us to test-driven competitions between educational approaches that are intended to find solutions that work (i.e., raise test scores), without regard for how this success is achieved. We seek test-based notions of success even if it involves normalizing the large-scale administration of psychotropic drugs to children.

This goes against everything that has been shown to be effective in the realm of pedagogy, both in the learning sciences and in the politics, theory, and practice of critical and transformative educators.

> [ADHD] drugs used in conjunction with repressive pedagogies like scripted lessons, grit and other forms of resurgent behaviorism, have a political implication that is diametrically opposed to that of critical pedagogy. Critical pedagogy addresses experiences which are meaningful to students and helps them to comprehend those meaningful experiences in terms of the broader forces and struggles that produce those experiences. [ADHD] drugs are being overprescribed in order to work on the body to allow the mind to endure or even enjoy the focus on that which is meaningless so that students can study for standardized tests and their decontextualized content. This corporate dream of replacing thought with stimulation is the same dream of ending contemplative thought that animates the positivist school reforms of standardized testing, scripted lessons and the rest. Contemplative thought, the work of interpretation, cedes to the memorization and accumulation of decontextualized facts. In contemporary positivist school reforms such as standardized testing, the meanings behind the facts, the selection and value of truth claims are determined elsewhere by the ones who know, the experts, the test makers who sit in the offices of large corporations such as Educational Testing Services and Pearson NCS. Thought resides there, with them. The practice of drugging children for test preparation undermines intelligence, the work of interpretation and judgment of the meanings of texts and claims to truth.[41]

As argued above, the increasing prevalence of psychopharmacological approaches in education is due in large part to the way testing has distorted communication about the goals of education. Counteracting these trends requires changing the terms of the debate. Educators will be unable to demonstrate the effectiveness of non-psychiatric approaches for as long as the means used to measure effectiveness remain simplistic and reductive. Arguments about the irrationality and immorality of instrumental interventions into the brains of children will remain powerless for as long as there appear to be no alternative ways to succeed in the current system. This is a path toward an economically driven auto-transformation of the human nervous system, in which educational configurations are altering children's brains to fit the needs of an increasingly complex and exploitative economy. The continued unilateral *design* of the next generation by those currently in power is an unjust situation in which individuals are rendered incapable of taking responsibility for their own lives, denied the autonomous pursuit of a self-chosen conception of the good, and thus denied the freedom and self-respect typically given to responsible humans.[42]

Tomorrow's Child: Redesigning Education to Recreate the Economy

There are alternatives to these dystopian educational futures! The minimalist integral meta-theory of education I have used throughout suggests a way forward that would lead to a fundamentally redesigned educational system. The all-quadrant complexity of social reality suggests a "multiple bottom lines" approach to considering educational success. Beginning with the individual, it must be recognized that the reproduction of social realities is always accomplished through their transformation, specifically through the creative and autonomous actions of agents who are held responsible for what they say and do. Reductive human capital theory envisions a future that is simply a continuation of the present, whereas an integral meta-theory of education envisions a radically open future, dependent upon the creative actions of future generations. This leads to a focus on the conditions that foster the development of autonomous, reflective, and ethical individuals. This means building the educational system around the realities of human psychology and social relations, as opposed to building it around the needs of the economy.

Accomplishing such a profound shift in the priorities guiding educational design entails a new kind of testing infrastructure. It requires an approach to testing that can make meaningful learning visible, provide insights into the diverse needs of students, and thus monitor the true distribution of educational goods in society. Such justice-oriented testing practices must be based on insights from the learning sciences that enable the measurement of multi-dimensional learning processes, beyond the simplified, psychologically naive reductive human capital theory that is only interested in tests of "basic skills." This means designing a testing infrastructure that is intended to *directly* benefit teachers and students by providing them with scientific insights into their own teaching and learning processes. As opposed to tests built to simplify the complexity of educational configurations in order to aid administrators in decision-making, this would be a testing infrastructure that reveals the true complexity of learning processes to those undergoing them, empowering students and teachers to take control over their lives in the classroom. Current approaches are so far from this ideal of testing as a liberating technology that the possibility seems almost unimaginable, which has led many educators to spurn testing altogether. But a small group of learning scientists and philosophers has already begun radically redesigning tests, pioneering powerful new directions in large-scale standardized testing.[43]

The innovative redesign of large-scale testing makes it possible to imagine a system built in light of the true complexity and diversity of human development and learning, with an expansive and compassionate vocabulary of educational evaluation and assessment, and a multitude of acceptable educational outcomes. Instead of designing students to fit the imagined needs of tomorrow's economy, tomorrow's economy would be conceived as open, contingent, and malleable—an economy capable of evolving to reflect the creative freedom of individuals raised into the fullness of their autonomy, responsibility, and imagination.

Contemporary policy and ideology consider the function of the educational system as merely to supply our vast global economy with human capital, educating entrepreneurial global citizens or building skills for the global work force. But what if we turned this on its head? What if we understood the economy as merely an infrastructure enabling a vast educational system, with all of our entrepreneurial efforts channeled toward the betterment of human understanding and experience? Reductive human capital theory values only a limited subset of what is possible as human potential. The greatest benefit of reversing the relation between the educational system and the structure of the broader economy would be the resulting liberation of human potential. Humanity stands misshapen by radically partial valuations of its own possibilities. The educational frontier opens with new ideas about the values and possibilities of human life. These are more necessary now than ever, because the future is less predictable than it has ever been.

There have been cultures in which the young were educated into a form of life known by their parents and grandparents. And there have been cultures in which adults prepared children for new forms of life, which they did not know but could envision and understand. We live today in a culture in which we must prepare children for forms of life we cannot anticipate.[44] Elders can no longer claim to fully understand the experiences their children are having and will have. Education must not be what it has been. Our children are tomorrow's already. We must educate them openly, in the world, without pretension of profession. Their world will not be the one we have known; we must teach the teachers not to instill yesterday's knowledge, but to create spaces in which tomorrow's problems become visible.

---

1. Hursh (2008); Stecher, Vernez, & Steinberg (2010).

2. Dewey (1916; 1929).

3. Liebenau (1987).

4. Spring (1989); Habermas (1987).

5. Brown (1992); Gould (1996); Chapman (1988); Callahan (1964); Lagemann (2000).

6. Lemann (1999).

7. Campbell (1975).

8. Social Justice and Meritocracy

See: Spring (1989); Stein (2016). In one of the most influential educational works from his era (or any era), Jerome Bruner (1969) in *The Process of Education* ambivalently endorses the then-emerging meritocracy during the Cold War. He gives voice to concerns about its impact on individuals while also arguing for its necessity, inevitability, and value, given the overall goals deemed critical to national defense during the Cold War:

> The present National Defense Education Act is only a beginning.... The peril of success under the conditions [it promotes] is the growth of what has been called "meritocracy." Partly out of the inertia of present practice and partly [an inevitable consequence of the national security crisis], there will be a strong tendency to move the able student ahead faster and particularly to move him ahead if he shows early promise in technical or scientific fields. Planned carefully, such acceleration can be good for the student and for the nation. A meritocracy, however, implies a system of competition in which students are moved ahead and given further opportunities on the basis of their achievement, with position in later life increasingly and irreversibly determined by earlier school records. Not only later educational opportunities but subsequent job opportunities become increasingly fixed by earlier school performance. The late bloomer, the early rebel, the child from an educationally indifferent home—all of them, in a full-scale meritocracy, become victims of an often senseless irreversibility of decision. A meritocracy is likely to have several undesirable effects on the climate in which education occurs, though with advance planning we may be able to control them. One consequence may be an overemphasis upon examination performance.... If, further, the principal scholarships and prizes come increasingly to be awarded for merit in the sciences and mathematics, then we may also expect... that there will be a devaluation of other forms of scholarly enterprise.... (Bruner, 1969, pp. 76-80).

Bruner notes several important issues that were merely on the horizon at the time of his writing, and these issues would become increasingly central in the following decades. His ambivalence toward the emerging meritocracy reflects his sense that it was both inevitable and valuable as an aspect of national security, yet it was also potentially damaging to the educational system and the lives of individuals. He shared the belief (also held by those within the educational establishment) that insofar as scientists and engineers are needed to ensure the continued security of the country, then meritocratic mechanisms must be implemented to facilitate a steady supply of them.

Bruner focuses on the potential damage done to individuals, pointing out that meritocracy would unfairly impact the life prospects of individuals who do not fit the mold. Bruner studiously avoids explicitly arguing that rewards would be distributed along socio-economic lines, but his reference to "the early rebel [and] the child from an educationally indifferent home" points in this direction.

Bruner continues, warning that the narrow focus of the emerging test-based meritocracy is also likely to lead to the devaluation of humanistic scholarship. There is a tendency for testing-intensive policies to define the scope of what is educationally valuable; testing infrastructures *set the range of categories from which all may choose* through a kind of anonymous power (Busch, 2011). Bruner saw these significant dangers, but believed they could be avoided through proper planning (e.g., by ensuring a lack of bias and broadening the range of tested subjects). But these are not the core social justice issues raised by the institutionalization of a national test-based educational meritocracy. There are more fundamental issues that concern the relationship between testing and the very idea of meritocracy, which Bruner does not raise in the quote above.

First consider the very idea of a meritocracy. Merit is, by definition, a set of skills and traits deemed valuable in a specific socio-cultural context. Awarding merit is thus part of a broader incentivizing strategy toward pursuing the goods valued in a sociocultural context. This is a point clarified by Amartya Sen (2000, p. 5), who following Rawls argues that "the concept of 'merit' is deeply contingent on our views of a good society. Indeed, the notion of merit is fundamentally derivative.... [it is dependent] on the concept of 'the good' in the relevant society." There is no "'natural order' of 'merit' that is independent of our value system" (ibid., p. 10). Theories of merit must therefore draw upon other normative theories. "The rewarding of merit is, to adapt a Kantian distinction, a 'hypothetical imperative' that is dependent on the way we judge the success of a society; it does not involve a 'categorical imperative' on what should in any case be done" (ibid., p. 14).

Sen also argues that meritocracies do not typically take into account the scope of inequalities resulting from the reward of merit. They therefore tend to create unacceptable inequalities of wealth and opportunity. As discussed below, in this way even a meritocracy based on a truly disinterested and objective mechanism for rewarding merit can still be profoundly unreasonable and unfair. However, injustice does not necessarily follow from the reward of merit. It is possible to imagine a meritocracy where merit is defined such that social justice is pursued through its reward. Sen suggests that if such principles of justice were included in the overarching values of a society, then merit itself would be recast in "an inequality sensitive way.... [It is the] the ad hoc exclusion of *distributional* concerns from the objective function in terms of which merit is characterized.... [that] makes meritocracies more prone to generate economic inequality" (ibid., p. 15).

That is, if merit is defined in terms of a social ideal that *includes* considerations of distributive justice, then rewarding merit would mean rewarding those traits that lead individuals to advance a fair allocation of goods in society (e.g., perhaps traits such as generosity, moral sensitivity, etc.). But when merit is defined in ways that *exclude* such considerations, the traits deemed valuable are likely to be ones that generate greater inequalities when they are differentially rewarded (e.g., analytical intelligence, extrinsic motivation, etc.). This creates a situation wherein those already advantaged receive additional advantages and the position of the least well-off is made worse. Unfortunately, all known large-scale educational meritocracies define merit in terms of a narrow social ideal that does not include social justice as the goal pursued through its reward (Arrow, Bowles, & Durlauf, 2000).

Moreover, Sen (2000) argues that meritocracies can negatively impact the self-understandings of those involved, potentially undermining their ability to understand themselves as free and equal citizens. There is a tendency for rewards based on merit to be understood as if they are somehow *owed* to the recipient, a tendency for those with certain traits to feel they *deserve* the special advantages they have been given through meritocratic mechanisms. Likewise, those not rewarded come to understand themselves as *not deserving* rewards, as somehow less worthy of social support and acclaim than others. Sen notes that this results from definitions of merit that exclude broader considerations of social justice, and which define merit in terms of what individuals can contribute to overall social efficiency (e.g., economic productivity; technical knowledge). This leads individuals to see their own self-worth in terms of their position in a hierarchy, ranging from those at the top (who are capable of contributing to society) to those at the bottom (who are less productive and in many ways dependent upon the contributions of "their betters"). Moreover, because of the seeming objectivity of the mechanisms used to detect merit, an inequality-insensitive meritocracy can create the appearance that great discrepancies in wealth and opportunity are *legitimate and just*, systematically distorting everyone's sense of who is entitled to what and why.

9. Samelson (1990); Sacks (1999).

10. Phillips (2003).

11. Hess & Petrilli (2006); Toch (2006).

12. **No Child Left Behind: A Recipe for Injustice**

Trends in recent US testing policy and practice are something I discuss at length in my book, *Social Justice and Educational Measurement: John Rawls, the History of Testing, and the Future of Education*, but I will briefly discuss NCLB here.

Even a cursory review of the structures put in place by NCLB reveals that they were far from a neutral or beneficent force in schools, especially struggling ones. NCLB was complex and contained a wide variety of programs and sub-programs, but its main impetus was to put in place a form of efficiency-oriented testing that included the following features (based on Hess & Petrilli, 2006):

- States were expected to choose their own tests and the performance levels on them that would define "proficiency."
- All schools were required to test all students in reading and mathematics at regular intervals from third grade through high school.
- All states were required to establish timelines showing how *one hundred percent* of their students would reach proficiency by 2013-2014.
- All schools were required to make adequate yearly progress (AYP) toward the goal of *one hundred percent proficiency*.
- Any schools not making adequate progress would be labeled as "schools in need of improvement" (SINI), and would face increasingly onerous sanctions, including being shut down and "restructured."
- Schools that were required to restructure had a limited set of options, including: converting to a charter school; replacing the principal and staff; relinquishing control to private management; or turning over control of the school to the state.

It should be clear that there would be significant problems with a testing infrastructure built and institutionalized according to these policies. First, the system lacks objectivity as a result of each state being given the freedom to not only determine what tests are used but also what counts as proficient. The new Common Core Standards and Assessments seek to remedy exactly this problem by providing a single testing infrastructure for all schools. Increasing objectivity is a positive move in terms of justice and institutionalized measurement (see: Chapter 3). But lacking objectivity is only one of NCLB's ethical failings. Any testing infrastructure can do damage when it is coupled to a set of punitive and unreasonable high-stakes polices, no matter how well built and objective it is.

As the policies reviewed above indicate, NCLB was based on the idea that *one hundred percent* of students could be made proficient by 2014 (13 years from the date it was signed into law). Critics (Hess & Finn, 2007) have lampooned this as unreasonable sociologically, akin to proposing that cities be one hundred percent crime-free. NCLB also involves mathematical impossibilities that ignore the basic laws of statistics, such as the ubiquity of normal distributions and regressions to the mean. These are logical errors like the so-called "Lake Wobegon effect," which is a community where "all the children are above average."

Moreover, every school was expected to make consistent linear annual progress toward the goal of one hundred percent proficiency *or be punished*. The rhetoric was not that failing schools would be helped. They would, in fact, be shamed and shut down and new schools would be put in their place. Teachers and principals would lose their jobs and a new (often privately run) school would replace a public school that had (with its name, sports teams, and traditions) been a part of a community for decades.

This is the second basic ethical failure of NCLB: systems that further disadvantage those who are already disadvantaged are unjust. These are echoes of the problems with test-based meritocracies discussed above. This was an injustice built into the basic design of NCLB as a law, which was combined with a lack of objectivity and the setting of unreasonable goals (one hundred percent proficiency). It was a recipe for injustice.

> Because NCLB required states to promise that they would reach an impossible goal, the states adopted timetables agreeing to do what they could not do, no matter how hard teachers and principals tried.... With every passing year... more and more public schools failed to make AYP and were labeled as "failing." Even though some states lowered the cut scores (or passing marks) on their tests to make it easier for schools to meet their target, many still failed to make AYP toward 100 percent proficiency for every subgroup.... In the school year 2006-2007, 25,000 schools did not make AYP. In 2007-2008, the number grew to nearly 30,000, or 35.6 percent of all public schools.... The consequence of mandating an unattainable goal... was to undermine states that had been doing a reasonably good job... and to produce "a compliance-driven regimen that recreates the very pathologies it was intended to solve." (Ravitch, 2010, pp. 103-104).

13. Callahan (1964).

14. Porter (1996, p. 189; pp. 195-196; p. 198).

15. Stecher, Vernez, & Steinberg (2010).

16. Saltman (2016, p. 20). Saltman takes it deeper: "Proper self-discipline in the name of producing 'college and career readiness' increasingly brings together the imperative for students to use the tools of bodily control to be entrepreneurial 'subjects of capacity.' That is, proper attention is demanded of students to display test-based performance outcomes that allow the student to compete for shrinking access to the world of work, income, and commodity consumption." (Saltman, 2016, p. 19).

17. **Justice-Oriented Testing**

See: Stein & Heikkinen (2009); Stein (2016). In a just society, the educational system provides all students with basic educational goods as an essential entitlement, a basic right. The educational system also administers the fair differential allotment of a broader range of educational goods beyond those that are basic. That is, inequalities of access to all educational goods must be the result of fair process. Justice-oriented testing is characterized by both objectivity and fairness. This is an approach to testing practice wherein students' metrological rights are considered as a means for actualizing the broader commitments educational systems have to social justice. Justice-oriented testing infrastructures are built to ensure objectivity, but not at the expense of relevance or the possibility of directly benefiting students. This kind of testing infrastructure creates (and is created by) an educational system preoccupied with providing for the full range of educational primary goods, contributing to a system of background institutions that promote fair equality of opportunity, and facilitating the self-actualization of all students.

Needless to say, there has never been a pure instance of justice-oriented testing, just as there has never been a pure, ideal instance of efficiency-oriented testing. But this dynamic has been in evidence since the first testing infrastructures were built in the early decades of the twentieth century. Testing infrastructures have been built to shoulder the burden of accomplishing a variety of functions that are a necessary part of an educational system committed to social justice, including administering a kind of pure procedural justice in the allocation of opportunity, assuring the equitable distribution of educational primary goods, and identifying the unique learning needs of each student.

Justice-oriented testing is based on a fundamentally different way of thinking about educational reform than its efficiency-oriented counterpart. The goals to be met by justice-oriented testing are not given to the educational system and classroom, but emerge organically from within it. The requirement that tests be relevant and beneficial means bringing teachers and students directly into considerations about the design of new tests. This means new design principles. For example, consider the array of best practices and examples of "authentic assessment" compiled by the non-profit testing rights advocacy organization FairTest (see: www.FairTest.org). Nearly all of these examples are possible elements within a justice-oriented structure. Many involve collaborative projects run by and for teachers, with assessment practices such as complex low-stakes portfolio systems that combine qualitative and quantitative aspects, often clearly the result of a great deal of reflective objectivity and pedagogical rigor.

However, all of these approaches to testing and assessment can be subject to misuse or rendered useless as an educational aid. Even the best portfolio system is unable to serve justice in a school that is unable to provide students with skills and ideas worth showing off. Justice-oriented testing cannot exist so long as there are larger social forces inhibiting the educational system as a whole from providing the basic educational goods owed to all. Justice-oriented testing is a *part* of a just educational system, not a guarantee of it.

At its most extreme, the demands of justice-oriented testing reverse the typical dynamic between the educational system and the other institutions of the basic structure, positioning the goals of the educational system as superordinate to both economic and governmental goals. According to this view, the dynamics of education reform must expand outward from the schools to touch every sector of society, because many of the non-negotiable commitments of the educational system cannot be met through the reform of schools alone. This is an idea that will be discussed in Chapter 4, where the radically democratic implications of designing justice-oriented educational systems and testing infrastructures are elaborated as an aspect of the social miracles. The point to make here is that justice-oriented testing replaces the notion that "efficiency *is* justice" with the notion that "efficiency *serves* justice," thus positioning justice as the dominant institutional virtue and rearranging the commitments and relationships of the other institutions of society accordingly.

18. The Inefficiencies of Injustice

See: Stein (2016). Because of the injustices they create, efficiency-oriented testing infrastructures can counterintuitively result in higher levels of organizational *in*efficiency, typically as a result of escalating *surveillance and enforcement costs* (Bowles & Gintis, 1986). These costs are incurred by an organization when its members view the organization's structures as obstacles in opposition to their interests, or when any member is systematically disincentivized from performing their role. This is detailed in my discussion of efficiency-oriented testing infrastructures elsewhere (see: Stein, 2016), where I argue that in general quality-control measurement infrastructures tend to be expensive to build, maintain, and implement. This inevitably leads to concerns about the *cost of surveillance* needed to exercise certain kinds of quality control. In this case, NCLB can be understood to have created an educational environment in which teachers and students were the subject of quality-control surveillance on a massive scale.

The costs of surveillance are not only financial (ibid.). There are significant impacts on organizational cultures and individuals' self-understandings when surveillance (and related methods of enforcement) become necessary aspects of organizational functioning. This leads to organizations wherein individuals do their jobs a certain way *not* because they agree with the effectiveness of the technique and appropriateness of the task, but rather because the "quality" of their work is closely monitored and deviations from the mandated methods are punished. If they were not so strictly surveilled they would prefer to do things differently—*not* out of laziness or incompetence, but because they believe there really is a better way. The result is that less work gets done and quality suffers, accompanied by steadily increasing costs of surveillance, employee turnover, burnout, and discontent. Distractions and low morale impact enforcement practices, as do the increasing probabilities of active expressions of worker discontent, such as sabotage (e.g., cheating under NCLB could be understood as a kind of sabotage). Bowles and Gintis (1998, p. 6) speak to the literal price (in dollars) of injustice:

> Institutional structures supporting high levels of inequality [and injustice] are often costly to maintain.... [There is a cost] in enforcing inequality, in such forms as high levels of expenditure on work supervision and security.... [But there is a] positive relationship between efficiency and equality [in] that more equal societies may be capable of supporting [higher] levels of cooperation and trust.... Cooperation and trust are essential to economic performance [and efficiency].... Of course, trust and cooperation do not appear in conventional economic theory.

Costs of surveillance go up even more if the objectivity of the instruments used is hard to maintain. Poorly built equipment or the likelihood of human error (or deception) requires that testing be done under more strict and exacting conditions, which are more expensive both financially and psychologically. Costs also go up faster in industries where the "output" being measured is not a simple object like grain or a car, which can be tested and measured by means of uncontroversial physical instruments. In the so-called service industries (as some would have education become) where the product is more intangible, quality-control monitoring is not so easy and is often much more invasive, subjective, and expensive (ibid.). There is always a trade-off between the damage done to the product by testing it and the gains in quality that can be made through more testing (Busch, 2011). Apples must be tasted, fuel burned, and medicines used in order to determine and improve their quality. The more you test something, the better sense you will have of its quality and of how to improve it, but in doing so you will also have destroyed more of the product. The product begins to lose value due to increasing numbers of tests as the overall process becomes increasingly expensive. All of these lessons about the dynamics of institutionalized measurement apply in thinking about NCLB, where testing as quality-control surveillance was exercised in blanket fashion throughout the nation's educational system.

To bring this discussion home, it should be said that the latest testing infrastructures being built as part of the Common Core Standards continues what has been a more general trend of investing in surveillance technology. "Improved test security" is a major leg of the argument for investing in, at the federal and state levels, an entirely computerized testing infrastructure. The technology specifications are modeled on the platforms pioneered by ETS and its test security and computer center subsidiaries. It is not a coincidence that these new high-tech tests will make it impossible for teachers to get their hands on students' answer sheets at exactly the time when students' answers will begin to be used to officially determine each teacher's value. While there is a small countervailing discourse about the need to include teachers in building and evolving assessment practices (see the work complied by FairTest), the general trend is quite the contrary. The systemic disempowerment and de-professionalizing of teachers is understood as part of an effort to improve the quality of their practices. This is the kind of theory/practice inconsistency that marks an institutional configuration as unstable and crisis-prone (Bhaskar, 2012).

No doubt, it is important to monitor the quality of the educational processes that take place in schools and to ask questions such as: How good are the teachers in this school? How much has this child learned? This is essential. But the use of testing infrastructures as the dominant index of quality leads to a distortion of value. This is a distortion in the meaning of what counts as a good education, and it creates a new ideal of what teachers and students ought to be and do. Testing can distort the perception of value to such an extent that "quality control" becomes a counterproductive undertaking.

Attempts to "steer" a complex system (such as a school system) typically fail when they are undertaken by focusing narrowly on one aspect of that system. This is "steering" based on feedback that tracks only a few *true but partial* representations, and it is bound to fail (Buck & Villines, 2007). When the system being steered is one constituted by complex human relationships (like those between teachers and students), a narrow measure of quality control will distort these relationships, leading to an increasing sense of injustice. False measures engender false consciousness, disingenuousness, and systematically distorted communication (in the fully Habermasian sense of this term); or they occasion widespread discontent, disruption, push-back, subversion, and revolt, as witnessed in the Atlanta Public Schools cheating scandal (See: Stein, 2016).

In the long run, "steering" organizations like schools according to limited and misleading measures will create situations in which even the limited functions that are officially and objectively monitored start to decline. This decline in efficiency is in fact a result of systemic disruptions in the culture and social relations of the organization. These disruptions were initiated as part of an attempt to improve the very functions they are diminishing. This is the *inefficiency of injustice*: when the injustices that result from a policy undermine the goals for which that policy was initiated.

The *inefficiency of injustice* is a common and problematic pattern that besets many modernizing practices (Bowles & Gintis, 1998; Porter, 1996), especially authoritarian forms of modernization (Scott, 1998; Apple, 2001). NCLB was beset by inefficiencies stemming from injustice. Cheating, test-prep pedagogy, and rising costs of surveillance ultimately resulted in the "side-effect" of inefficiency due to injustice. Some of these problems can be resolved by improving testing practices: making better and more secure tests across a greater range of subjects. This is the direction in which testing is headed. Once again bolstered by technological advances and opportune political climates, testing infrastructures are expanding and increasing their size, scope, and significance.

19. Zito & Safer (2005); Scheffler et al. (2007).

20. Diller (2006); Rasmussen (2008).

21. Swanson et al. (1998); Sax & Kautz (2003); Schneider & Eisenberg (2006); Saltman (2016).

22. Jensen et al. (2001); Parens & Johnston (2009); Pastor & Reuben (2008); Scheffler et al. (2007).

23. Parens & Johnston (2009); Singh (2008).

24. Swanson et al. (2007); Sonuga-Barke (2005).

25. Li et al. (2006).

26. Seidman, Valera, & Makris (2005); Braun et al. (2006).

27. Nigg, Goldsmith, & Sachek (2004); Sonuga-Barke (2005); Chamberlain, Robbins, & Sahakian (2007); Singh & Rose (2009).

28. Diller (1999).

29. Carey (2000).

30. Loe & Feldman (2007); Singh (2008).

31. Hyman (2002); Rasmussen (2008).

32. Recall from the Preface that an iatrogenic condition is one that results *from* medical treatment. See: Ivan Illich's (1976) *Medical Nemesis* for a philosophical rundown of the multilevel iatrogenic impacts of industrialized for-profit medicine. For the iatrogenic impacts of ADHD meds in particular, see: Parens & Johnston (2009); Diller (2006); Rasmussen (2008); Healy (2002).

Perhaps most worrisome is the iatrogenic cascade that is leading tens of thousands of otherwise healthy children from ADHD diagnoses into manic depressive and bipolar conditions. The widely reported recent increase in childhood incidence of bipolar disorder directly corresponds to increases in ADHD medications. Robert Whitaker's

(2015) *Anatomy of an Epidemic* carefully details how the effects of common ADHD medications such as Adderall exactly mirror the mood swings and hyperarousal of depression and mania, essentially creating the bipolar child.

> [ADHD meds] cause children to cycle through arousal and dysphoric states on a *daily* basis.... Such arousal and dysphoric symptoms are the very symptoms that the National Institute of Mental Health identifies as characteristic of a bipolar child.... [Symptoms in children] include increased energy, intensified goal-directed activity, insomnia, irritability, agitation, and destructive outbursts. [And when the effects of the dose wear off each day there are] the symptoms of depression in children [including] loss of energy, social isolation, a loss of interest in activities (apathy) and a sad mood. In short, every child on a stimulant [ADHD med] turns a bit bipolar, and the risk that a child diagnosed with ADHD will move on to a bipolar diagnosis after being treated with a stimulant has been quantified.... Massachusetts General Hospital reported in 1996 that 15 of 140 children (11 percent) diagnosed with ADHD developed bipolar symptoms—which were not present at initial diagnosis—within four years. (Whitaker, 2015, pp. 237-238).

33. Conrad (2007); Rasmussen (2008); Fukuyama (2002); Saltman (2016).

34. Saltman (2016).

35. Elliot (2003); Kagan (2009); Healy (2002); Conrad (2007); Illich (1976).

36. Olfman (2006).

37. Pavlov (1927); Skinner (1938).

38. Nussbaum (2000); Feinberg (1992); United Nations (1989).

39. Spring (1989).

40. Habermas (1987).

41. Saltman (2016, p. 105).

42. Habermas (2003); Nussbaum (2006).

43. Stein, Dawson, & Fischer (2010).

44. Mead (1970).

Chapter 3
The Global Crisis of Measurement

The 2015 Integral Theory Conference was the first place I presented the material in this essay, which I had been compiling for some time as a part of my graduate studies. As I showed in the previous chapter on testing and show again in this essay, meta-theories are brought down to Earth (quite literally) in the form of measurement infrastructures. What a society chooses to measure is always tied into that society's shared narrative about the way the world works and what is valuable within it. Looking around at how things are measured and quantified can reveal a society's dominant and often implicit (or unarticulated) meta-theories. Think about the way gross domestic product (GDP) functions as a measure of economic health, and thus encodes an economic meta-theory that gives primacy to simple notions of endless growth. Or consider the ways that contemporary public education systems are continually under surveillance and being restructured, thanks to a certain kind of efficiency-oriented standardized testing, which encodes the meta-theory guiding schooling today—human capital theory.

These two examples clarify what I am calling a measurement crisis. A measurement crisis occurs when society loses touch with reality because it has institutionalized a systematically distorted measurement infrastructure. Below I discuss various aspects of what I characterize as a global crisis of measurement, including biometrics, econometrics, and measures of global climate change, among other things. Cultures intoxicated by a particular meta-theory will usually spawn a system of false measures. Measurement instruments and techniques will be built that appear to deal in realities but instead deal in demi-realities. Truncated representations of complex phenomena are taken as sufficient and revelatory when they are, in fact, insufficient and misleading. This is worse than flying blind, it is flying blind when you think you are seeing clearly.

As will become clear, the broader point of this chapter is that a wholesale revolution in measurement infrastructures is a necessary part of the world-system phase shift that is upon us. I take time in this chapter to cover both the history and contemporary diversity of measurement practices because it is important to see just how deep the issue of global measurement reform is. To give a sense of what is at stake, the only other measurement reforms of comparable significance and size involved the creation and global propagation of the metric system. Importantly, this was a movement intimately related to the French Revolution and the birth of the modern nation-state. Seen in this light, redesigning standardized testing infrastructures is only a small part of what needs to be done to open new educational frontiers and usher in the integral paideia.

Invisible Infrastructures Shape Our Lives and Social Justice Demands They Be Made Visible

No matter where you live on the planet, measurement infrastructures and related standards impact your daily life in countless ways. For example, the average American begins their day by waking up to an alarm clock. They flip on the light, put on some clothes, walk into their kitchen, open the fridge, and prepare breakfast.[1] They are not usually aware of the complex history of measurement practices and technologies that facilitate their simple morning routine. Nor do they suspect the massive global reach and ethical implications of the measures and standards that they take for granted every day.

The alarm clock involves the standardization of time measurement, which is a relatively recent occurrence, especially the mass-production of cheap and accurate clocks. Theorists such as Lewis Mumford have argued that the standardized measurement of time should be understood as the most important invention leading to the industrial revolution and the rapid advancement of capitalistic modes of production. Electricity that flows at the flip of a switch is the result of international standards for voltage, wiring, and safety, as well as recent advances in the ability to measure and regulate electrical currents. Take a look at your electric meter and you can see just how precisely and constantly your electricity use is measured. Measuring something is usually a necessary condition of being charged money for it. Monetization is an essential motive for measurement, a point to which I will return. Every light bulb, fixture, and appliance is standardized to ensure interchangeability and functionality. Clothes are all explicitly measured and standardized according to a variety of more or less reliable indices of size. This is a relatively recent way of standardizing mass-produced clothing, which has had a profound impact on the self-understanding and body image of millions. The size of the doorways of your bedroom and kitchen are likely to be standardized, as are the lengths of hallways, walls, and the dimensions of windows, all stemming from the coordination of massive national construction interests. Every item in the refrigerator is marked according to volume or weight. Certain nutritional qualities of food have been measured and the results are displayed on the container. One might see various other standards of quality on food packaging (itself usually a standardized box or carton), such as USDA Grade A, Organic, Free-Range, or Non-GMO, all involving the development of measurement and standardization procedures.[2]

Measures and standards impact nearly every aspect of our given lifeworld; they are a part of the daily feeling of taken-for-grantedness that underpins our psyches and relationships. The advantages and power of standardization and measurement are clear, and they are often rightly touted as codifications of scientific advance, public welfare, and economic progress. Without contemporary advances in measurement practices there would be no medical diagnostics, no auto safety regulations, no building codes, no indices of the quality or amount of food products. The list of ways that advances in measurement and standardization have increased human welfare is very long, and as the example discussed here shows, we unconsciously depend on the proper functioning of global measurement infrastructures a great deal in our everyday life.

Just by getting up and getting ready for the day, these global infrastructures for measurement and standardization also implicate each of us in a great deal of political and ethical complexity. Consider only the alarm clock. Put aside the history of time measurement (e.g., it was the Mesopotamians that gave us the 24-hour day and 7-day week, etc.), and focus only on the alarm clock's size, shape, and construction. The plastics that the clock is made from are the end result of global supply chains mediated by measures and standards at every step, from qualities and quantities of materials, to labor regulation, international trading standards, and complex accounting practices. Here is where it gets important to pay attention. Because of standards enforced by labor contracts in factories in China, as well as inaccuracies in measures of raw materials' toxicity levels, whole populations are being poisoned and exploited, and it is all being done by the book. That is, industry standards and scientific measurements are being used (often very carefully), yet their very use sanctions and legitimizes injustices. This is a civilized form of barbarism.[3]

Probe deeper into who designs, implements, and enforces these standards and measures and you find scientists, businessmen, and politicians who will likely never set foot in the factories most impacted by their decisions. Yet they will be able to monitor and surveil those factories from a distance through the abstract optics of their measures, which is one reason for their creation. It becomes clear just how many people are alienated from a sense of having any form of control over many essential aspects of their lives, such as safety and livelihood. The workers being poisoned and exploited are radically disempowered relative to the measurement regimes that subjugate them, especially the scientifically complex measure of toxicity, where the average workers are literally unable to understand the instrumentation and chemistry involved. The claim of scientific expertise (and the display of accompanying technologies) which back large-scale measurement practices often contributes to the anti-democratic ethos that surrounds the world of international standards and measurement.[4]

All this follows from a simple look at the measures and standards involved in producing the plastics in an alarm clock; I will not even get into the rest of the average American's daily morning routine. However, the point to remember is that when you touch your alarm clock in the morning to shut it off, it appears to you as simply ready at hand, a taken-for-granted part of the lifeworld; it is not seen as an outcome of a complex system involving injustices facilitated by official and scientific standards and measures. As long as everything works, fits, or otherwise adds up, we do not notice the multitude of measures that structure our lives. Their very taken-for-grantedness—their seeming invisibility—is at the core of their power and importance, as well as their danger and susceptibility for use as instruments of injustice.

Measures and standards are implicated in social justice because they quite literally *structure* our lives in profound ways, impacting the ways that we understand ourselves, the social world, and the nature of reality itself. They quite literally give shape to the physical environments we inhabit and the temporal durations that constitute the rhythms of our lives. They make some things possible and others impossible; they reveal certain aspects of reality while concealing others. Measures and standards facilitate cooperation and trust at a distance and across cultures, while also enabling complex institutional processes that are often exclusionary, exploitative, and oppressive. They constitute what the great moral theorist John Rawls would call *basic structures*.[5] Basic structures are social structures we enter into by virtue of entering into society at all. We are born into institutions and other social inventions and infrastructures that are not of our choosing, and they shape our life prospects from day one. Because measurement infrastructures are basic structures, they are intrinsically implicated in issues of social justice.

As I will explain, the history of measurement has been a history in which the privileged and empowered have been the creators and institutionalizers, while the oppressed and powerless have had no choice but to use their master's tools and definitions of reality.[6] This is a pattern that continues to this day, perhaps best exemplified by current trends in educational "reform," where in the United States billionaires who never set foot in a public school growing up (and who send their own children to private schools) swayed federal legislation toward the creation of a vast technologically intensive testing infrastructure that now dominates the entire public school system. New tests and measures are being forced upon teachers, and if they do not use them they can be fired. Educators are being disempowered, de-skilled, and rendered voiceless when it comes to some of the most *essential* aspect of their professional practice (i.e., assessment drives curriculum and pedagogy). Meanwhile, for-profit industries are poised to make billions off the privatization of one of the oldest and most inspiring public institutions in American history. There are important pockets of resistance to these hegemonic practices, but the trend is global. As Asian economies increasingly copy and exceed our test-obsessed approach to schooling, and efficiency-oriented, testing-intensive, and market-driven educational projects head the list of World Bank and Gates Foundation funded "reforms" throughout the developing world.[7]

But education is only one example; this is a ubiquitous pattern in the evolution of civilizations. The creation and institutionalization of measures and standards is a lopsided affair, where power is wielded by a few over the practices and definitions of reality that shape the lives of many. In recognizing this reality about the profound impact of measurement infrastructures and standards-based regulatory practices, new possibilities emerge for resistance and for re-visioning social realities. Bringing invisible infrastructures to light allows us to see if we are structuring our lifeworld so that social justice and human dignity reign.

In particular (and in keeping with the themes of this book), when thinking about how to orchestrate a global transition into a new world-system and new epoch of human-biosphere relationship, one focus should be on the redesign of standards and measurement infrastructures of global reach. At the very least this would involve the democratization of global standards-based regulatory practices, as well as absolute transparency and credibility in measurement science and practice. There is a future in which planetary justice exists, but to get there we must use the master's tools to dismantle the master's house—and measures and standards are some of the most powerful tools around.

This chapter is essentially a call for theorizing and activism around the pivotal role of our increasingly diverse and rapidly expanding measurement infrastructures and standards-based regulatory practices. Focusing on these basic structures and institutions is a unifying political strategy for those interested in progressive global action toward a more just world order (not the anti-globalization movement, but the movement for global justice). A narrative around the reform of measurement and standardization could serve to orchestrate a *decentered unity* of diverse political actors and organizations.

What do agricultural innovators, education reformers, climate change activists, anti-capitalist organizers, free-the-web techies, and holistic medical and psychology advocates all have in common? They all want to see *radical* changes in the basic measures, definitions of reality, and standards of practice that shape large-scale social projects. They are looking for a change in the *structural DNA* of society, a revolution in the source code. To redesign measures would be to rearrange the basic structures by which we live and work. It would not be the first time in history that a wholesale revolution in measurement fueled the fire of wholesale political revolution.[8]

Below I begin with a broad historical survey of how measures and standards have played a role in the evolution of civilizations. I deal with the philosophy of measurement in particular, and build a minimalist integral meta-theory of measurement. I explain how measurement infrastructures shape our perceptions of reality, our sense of what is true and false, real or illusion. They also impact how we view what is good and bad, just and unjust. Measures and standards are implicated in our group practices and cooperative endeavors as basic structures and tools, showing up across all the planes of social being and each of the four quadrants. I bring the story up-to-date and look at our current *global crises of measurement*, providing examples from domains as diverse as education, climatology, economics, and medicine. These are all domains where measures and standards are deeply politicized and thus subject to corruption, ideology, and often just plain bad science. I close with some speculations about preferable futures for global measurement infrastructures and standards-based regulatory practices, seeking to inform the creation of new approaches to the representation of complex global realities, especially transactions involving non-monetary value, measurements of psychological interiority, and the probabilistic modeling of non-linear dynamical systems.

Origins: The Mysticism, Mythology, and Politics of Ancient Measurement Practices

The relationship between social justice and measurement goes back to the origins of human civilization. Humans have almost always been engaged in measurement practices of various types, even prior to the creation of cities, agriculture, and complex divisions of labor. The very earliest human artifacts showing evidence of tool making and complex cooperation all demonstrate that even prehistoric humanity practiced basic forms of measurement. Constructing a spear, arrowhead, or shelter, or creating a musical instrument or article of clothing—all require engaging in measurement practices. These earliest forms of measurement were often informal, intuitive, and conducted by simply referencing the dimensions of one's own body (e.g., palm span, arm length, foot, etc.). In fact, all ancient cultures had measurement practices that were modeled on the dimensions and proportions of the human body. That the common root of all measurement can be found in the relationship between the human body and the natural world accounts for the intriguing similarities and seemingly mystical unity between architectural sites of ancient cultures that are widely dispersed in time and space. The simple elegance and beauty of many ancient structures can be attributed to their conformity with certain idealized proportions of the human body, usually inspired by (also cross-culturally common) mythologies about the parallels between the dimensions of the human form and the sacred structure of the universe itself.[9]

Early in human history, these anthropocentric measures became institutionalized and made part of the dynamics of religious authority and political power, especially in the first great empires that emerged in the Nile, Tigris, and Indus river valleys.[10] It was trade, massive construction projects, and agricultural planning that fueled these first large-scale standardizations and enforcements of measurement practices. The basic units of measurement still made reference to the human body, but they were no longer allowed to vary according to each individual's unique body and context. Instead, a single measure came to be decreed as valid throughout the land. For example, this often involved making the length of one specific foot (typically understood to be that of the king) into *the official foot.*[11]

While it was sometimes literally true that these sanctioned units were actual representations of the physical dimensions of the king's body, more often it was symbolic and mythic. The institutionalization of measures referencing the king's body modified and reinforced the myth of the sacred political microcosm/macrocosm: the body of the king and the body politic form a mystical unity, so the kingdom is built and run according to his bodily specifications. "The union of mystery and authority in one body was essential to the survival of kingship, and measure was a physical manifestation of both."[12] From the construction of the Great Pyramids to the building of Roman roads (straight as an arrow, with perfect uniformity of width), empires were built on standardized measures and their enforcement, accompanied by ideologies suggesting that the official measures were of legitimate and unassailable (even divine) origin. The close connections between empire, measurement, and ideology continue to this day, a theme I explore further below.

Taxation and marketplace transactions are also dependent on measures.[13] This is another reason that measurement practices have been codified and enforced by centralized political and religious powers, beginning early in the ancient world. Bushels (of oats), bales (of hay), areas (of land), and dimensions (of houses), have long been essential factors in determining rates of taxation and equity of exchange in the marketplace.[14] In ancient urban centers known for their trade and commerce, there were usually officials (sanctioned by the powers ruling the city) to regulate measurement practices in the marketplace. Tax collectors were always equipped with official measurement tools in order to resolve disputes over the size of bushels or the area of a farm field. Certain cities and their administrators became known for fair and just measurement practices, others for unjust ones. The connections between measurement and justice were apparent to the ancients, so much so that many of the first written legal documents (e.g., the constitutions of the Greek city-states) included extensive references to the regulation and standardizing of measures.[15]

Given the primacy of measurement in early civilizations, it is clear why measurement tools and practices became seen as markers of justice and civility. Measurement instruments often embodied in their construction the most sophisticated technologies of their day (e.g., incredibly precise metallurgy is needed to make scales and standard weights, as well as rods and other measures of length). Measures also played an essential role in the construction of monuments that (still) stagger the imagination. They also enable the coordination of trade and fostering fairness and mutual understanding in the marketplace. The difference between civilization and barbarism came to be seen as the difference between those who had good measures and those who did not.

It is no surprise then that ancient religious texts (especially the Bible) abound with reflections on measurement and the ethical significance of good, true, and just measures. The Talmud is explicit: "a false balance is an abomination to the Lord, but a just weight is his delight." The New Testament also contains important reflections on measures and justice, such as when Jesus knocks over the scales and measurement tools of the corrupt moneylenders who had set up shop in the temple. Further examples of ancient sacred texts that address the connections between measurement and humanity's sacred responsibilities can be listed, including examples from Eastern traditions such as Hinduism and Confucianism. They all amount to the same message: the reign of justice and truth on Earth depends upon humanity establishing just and true measures.

This religious theme was often deepened through explorations of the esoteric connections between measurement, sacred geometry, numerology, and archetypal imagery. It has long been believed that certain lengths, dimensions, and ratios are of sacred or divine origin. It was a common belief in the ancient world that God(s) bestowed to humans the tools of measurement and the exact lengths and weights that facilitated the emergence and growth of civilization. The Egyptians traced the birth of measurement to Thoth and the Greeks to Hermes, while monotheists traced their measures to God, typically through a specific prophet. In this framework, the just and true measure was thought to be the first, primordial, and divinely sanctioned measure. Isaac Newton himself expended great effort to determine the true length of the original *sacred cubit* (or *Solomonic cubit*)—the basic unit of length used to build the Temple of Jerusalem according to God's blueprint, as provided to King Solomon.. Knowing its true dimensions would allow for accurate reconstructions of the Temple and of Noah's Ark, the measurements of which are both described in detail in the Talmud. It was thought that building these according to exact specifications would implicate humanity in the creation of divine structures of tremendous power, creating a mystical home for God on Earth, thus ushering in the reign of Heaven. The mysticism of measurement and the religious aura and power surrounding measurement practices are often overlooked in accounts of the history of civilization and human culture.[16]

Modernity and Metrology: From Sacred Measurement to Scientific Measurement

Modernity began with a series of revolutions—the American, French, Scientific and Industrial—all during roughly a half-century (1760–1810). This revolutionary political and scientific climate also produced a profound revolution in measurement practices. The metric system, today known as the International System of Units, or the *Système International d'Unités* (abbreviated SI), is an invention that embodies all the ideals of the Enlightenment. The metric system in many ways represents the best of "the dignity or modernity" as described from Charles Taylor and Habermas to Wilber. The motives for its creation were complex, including scientific, economic, and ethical concerns. The result was the first global measurement infrastructure, an overthrow of anthropocentric measures, and eventually the widespread disappearance of regional and cultural differences in measurement practices.

When the scientific revolution began, Europe was in a state of great confusion and conflict concerning measurement practices. The Middle Ages brought a decline in centralized political regimes with the power to set official measures, which led to a proliferation and fragmentation of local measures. This became a serious impediment to the expansion of trade, and also caused problems for the burgeoning international collaborations taking place in many rapidly advancing sciences. It was a social justice issue as well, as measures were often under the control of the local guilds and property-owning lords and thus subject to corruption, leaving peasants and commoners open to measurement-enabled exploitation.[17] In the decades leading up to the French Revolution, major efforts were being made to address these issues.

Measurement was one of the chief agenda items dealt with by the first scientific organizations ever created: the Royal Society in England and the French Academy of Sciences. The need for greater regulations in measurement practices, universally standardized measures, and international coordination was clear, even if just to ensure the progress of science. What was not clear was how to go about determining what the new measures should be and how they could be broadly institutionalized. It was decided that in the wake of Newtonian science, which marked the emerging dominance of a science based on abstract universals and non-anthropocentric ideas, the basic units of measurement should not be based on the dimensions of the human body. Instead it was agreed that measurement should be based on something abstract and universal. In the end, a decision was made by the French Academy to have the length of the meter be a fraction of the length of the Earth's circumference. There was to be a global basis for a global measure. This decision is a fascinating glimpse into some of the first manifestations of world-centric consciousness.

However, it turns out that precisely determining the true dimensions of the Earth is extremely difficult. At the time, long-standing debates about whether the Earth is a perfect sphere were still being engaged, therefore the French Academy sponsored one of the largest scientific expeditions in history with the goal of measuring the meridian between Paris and Barcelona using highly advanced surveying technologies and techniques. The project took seven years, but was eventually completed and hailed as one of the great scientific achievements of the era. On August 1, 1793, the length of the meter was legally designated as the length equal to the ten-millionth part of the arc of the terrestrial meridian contained between the North Pole and the Equator. Years later after the metric system had spread far and wide, it became clear that critical errors had been made and that the meter was not truly related to the dimensions of the Earth as it had been claimed. The intricacies of this crucial moment in the history of science and measurement are beyond the scope of this book. The point is that the meter is as arbitrary a length as any previously institutionalized foot, and perhaps even more so, given that it is not tied to the dimensions of the human body.[18]

Beyond these scientific difficulties, it was the political and cultural challenges posed by traditional measures that proved the greatest barrier to the success of the metric system. As discussed in the next section, measurement infrastructures are difficult structures to change once they have been in place for a time.[19] In fact, it would require a wholesale revolution in social and political life (the French Revolution) to create an opening for the wholesale reform of measures. A revolutionary chant echoed through the streets of Paris: "one measure, for all people, for all time!" The large-scale standardization and redesign of measurement was a part of the rallying call of the revolution. Old measures were associated with the *Ancien Régime*. Eventually, supporting them would be cause for beheading during the Reign of Terror. The metric system was institutionalized by bayonet and guillotine.

The spread of the metric system coincided with unprecedented processes of standardization across whole swaths of social and institutional life, especially in industry. This was fueled by global trade and shipping on a scale never before imagined, involving railroads, steam engines, ocean liners, skyscrapers, and eventually cars and highways. And they were all built according to levels of exactness in measurement never before achieved. This was the result of new standards-based regulatory regimes of global scale, the first of which began in 1856 with the meeting of the International Association for Obtaining a Uniform Decimal System of Measures, Weights, and Coins. This organization's first president, the international banker Baron Rothschild, saw the clear result of international standardization as an assurance of quality control, interoperability, and efficiency in production on a global scale.[20] A series of organizations eventually led to the formation of the International Bureau of Weights and Measures, as well as the International Organization for Standardization, which I will discuss more below.

Following from these efforts of *haute finance* came the emergence of complex global industries such as pharmaceuticals, weaponry, energy, and large-scale agriculture, which thrived on the new planetary infrastructures of measurement and standards-based practice. As a result of this seemingly miraculous mixture of industrialization, scientific progress, and cultural modernity, standardization and measurement became part of the moral worldview of an emerging global order. Part of what transpired during this cultural transformation was the disenchantment of measurement and its domestication; the scientization and bureaucratization of measurement functioned to remove its auratic connections with religion and ancient forms of non-scientific power. However, the connections between measurement, power, and mystery can never be broken; they are simply reproduced at a higher level. Over time, tremendous power and mystery came to surround the cult of science.[21]

Integral Meta-Theory and the Nature of Measurement

Humanity must find a way beyond measures of total abstraction. While universalistic and scientific approaches to measurement brought much of the dignity of modernity, they also brought disaster. The metric system set the tone and tenor for the developments we see before us today: the widespread use of measures that are indifferent to interiority and incapable of capturing the dynamic variability of the local, contingent, and unique. Universalistic and scientific measures dominate global and local life across nearly every sector of experience and society, from agriculture to education to health care. Practices are seen as if they need to be standardized and measured, even if they never were before, and even if they defy standardization or would be better understood as personal and unique. This is an age of hyper-measurement, as more and more is measured every day in greater and greater detail.

Make no mistake: many standards and measures are good and necessary. We must not throw out the baby of rigorous measurement with the bathwater of modernity's disasters. The integral meta-theory of measurement being developed here aims to transcend but include pre-modern, modern, and postmodern perspectives on measurement. Nevertheless, taking an integral approach to measurement does mean overcoming the simplistic (and usually mindlessly quantitative) measures used today, which *are* the legacy of modernity. So-called "modern measurement" has fractured and diversified during the maelstrom of postmodern planetization. Today's measures still suffer from the abstract universality of modernity. In addition, they also suffer from a new postmodern form of standardized differentiation.[22] The universal is displaced by postmodern fragmentation and a diversification of measures ensues. Yet this new set of measurement-enabled standardized differentiations is equally as abstract and artificial as the single universal that was displaced.[23] The postmodern landscape of measures is one in which a hyper-measured self is shaped by a network of mostly superficial or fictional measures. While there are some true and just measures that must be protected, the best and most needed measures have yet to be built.

Before going on to look at measurements and standards in postmodern societies at the shape of our contemporary global crises of measurement, I want to bring together some insights from history and do some meta-theoretical work. In the Introduction I discuss the components of a minimalist meta-theory of education. I adopt a pragmatist's view of meta-theory and engage in meta-theorizing that is problem-focused and action-oriented, erring on the side of conceptual simplicity. The problem that focuses my meta-theoretical explorations here is the impact of measurement infrastructures and standards-based regulatory practices on personality structures and culture, and specifically on education. I will hone in meta-theoretically on the centrality of interiority and consciousness, using a simple bio-psycho-socio-cultural portrayal of reality provided by Wilber's quadrants.

Measures and standards can be built to address realities in any of the quadrants. That is, we have measures for physical realities (the metric system), systems of things (econometrics), cultural patterns (political polling), and psychological realities (standardized tests). These parentheticals are only examples; each quadrant can serve as the focus of any number of measures and standards. The vast majority of existing measures and standards address realities in the Right-Hand quadrants (i.e., physical realities and properties of physical systems). But more and more new standards and measures are being used that target interiors and cultural patterns, especially advertising and social network metrics, standardized testing, and political opinion research and polling.

Importantly, a measure or standard built to address a reality in any one quadrant will have impacts on all other quadrants. This is to say that no matter what quadrant a measure *focuses on*, the measure itself is an all-quadrant affair. Just because a measure focuses on some physical reality does not mean it has no psychological impact. And vice versa: measures of mental and cultural phenomena often result in very real physical impacts. For example, standardized tests (which are measures of interiority) result in whole schools being closed and a wide array of other physical results (such as being granted the right to walk into one college as opposed to another). Going the other way: measures of global temperature rise (complex physical measures) have profound impacts on personalities and culture.

Because of this ontological complexity, all measures can and should be evaluated beyond their objectivity and reliability, and beyond their usefulness for efficiency, quantification, and monetization (all Right-Hand quadrant qualities overvalued in contemporary measurement). Instead, all measures and standards should also be viewed in terms of their alignments with justice and beauty. It is never enough to only know how accurate a measure is, although accuracy is important. We must also know the degree to which it serves justice and beauty to use the measure. This is an ancient idea about measurement which we should try to remember today.

Modern and postmodern measures are predominantly instrumentalities of reductive thinking, focused on exteriors and objectivity, and neglecting rich representations of interiority (while nevertheless impacting interiority). Measurement infrastructures are tied into the very fabric of the lifeworld, a basic part of the background consensuses and agreed-upon definitions of reality that allow us to get along and cooperate. Picture a transaction at a gas station or grocery store, and now imagine it without agreed-upon measures; a situation wherein every exchange is contestable all the way down to the level of disagreements as to what the units of measure are. You can run this same thought experiment in a scientific laboratory or construction site. Without measures and standards of practice, nothing will get built and there will be no mutual understanding. Measures are basic structures in all quadrants. Instituting a measurement infrastructure or standards-based regime creates structures and habits across all quadrants.

Four additional principles are needed to round out this initial sketch of a minimalist integral meta-theory of measurement. Firstly, *measurement practices enact realities*. They serve as lenses and function to represent aspects of the world in ways that garner consensus, thus profoundly shaping individual and cultural perceptions of reality. They also function as technologies and tools that enable the construction and regulation of new realities, be they physical or social. Measures and standards are part of the reason we think and act the way we do. They are part of the reason why the modern world of houses, cities, cars, and institutions has the physical shape it does. From the size of doorways and alarm clocks to the pitch and angle of highway off-ramps, the organization of large-scale agriculture to the safety inspection of your car—the world looks and moves the way it does because we use certain measures and standards, and not others.

Secondly, *measurement is intrinsically related to power.* Those who have the power to create and institutionalize measures and standards control society. This is in part because standards and measures are unavoidably normative. They say how things *ought* to be, how practices and products *should* look. Therefore, instituting them is an act of power, because doing so means exercising control over people and things. People in particular are controlled through measures and standards. They are controlled not only in terms of their perceptions of reality, but also in terms of how cooperative endeavors are structured and trust is enabled. "In our [post] modern world [measures and] standards are arguably the most important manifestation of power relations.... Of concern here: *the ability to set the rules that others must follow, or to set the range of categories from which they may choose*" (emphasis in original).[24] This is a kind of anonymous power that is quite unlike the power of a tyrant or dictator. It is a subtle, hardly noted power, often only seen when basic social expectations are violated or technologies break.

Thirdly, *measurement induces reflection.* We see ourselves through our measures and standards. Measures have always been one of the ways we keep records, from tax collecting to the census. They allow us to systematize and quantify the things we care about by measuring the things that concern us intimately. Medical diagnostics, standardized tests, and tax forms are only a few of the measures that have us reflecting on who we are and what we are doing. There is a historical correlation between the availability of bathroom scales and incidents of anorexia, beginning with their widespread introduction into homes in the 1950s. There are also correlations between the rising number of diagnostic categories in the DSM and the rising number of individuals diagnosed as mentally ill. Climate change crusaders seek to change our whole conception of culture and self based on some very complex and breathtaking numbers. An increase in the GDP is enough to spark national celebrations of pride. All measures provide us with information; some do so about things that are deeply implicated in our personality and the ways that we regulate self-esteem. To measure something is to show it exists, and to think you see it clearly. This can be empowering or dangerously misleading.[25] The hyper-measured postmodern self is engaged in kaleidoscopic self-reflection, mediated by dozens of self-related measures (I discuss this new hyper-measured self further below).

Fourthly, *measures determine what counts as research and science*. Measures create the most basic systems of categories in terms of which scientific research is conducted. There are important standards that regulate scientific practice, including peer-review practices and rules of statistical inference, which are all implicated in crucial standards-based regulatory regimes such as FDA drug trials and environmental policy research. You cannot ask the right question if you do not have the right measures at your disposal. Frequently, you also cannot use existing data critically because presuppositions are built into the ontology of the existing measures. Measures are at the crux of paradigm shifts and cross-paradigmatic disagreements, another theme discussed further below. New measures bring with them new sciences, and new sciences often require the invention of new measures.[26] Thus part of redesigning measures is epistemological, as innovations in measurement lead to adventures in truth. To make a new measure is to catalyze an expansion of what can be known, as well as what "counts" as known from a social systems perspective.

There is much more that needs to be said about this minimalist integral meta-theory of measurement, especially concerning the prescriptive and political implications of the theory. However, I must go on for the sake of space, and for the meta-theory to make sense additional context is needed. Below I will explore contemporary post-modem measurement infrastructures and the future of measurement as a way of further elaborating the meta-theory of measurement outlined here.

Measurement Proliferates During Postmodern Planetization

Sociologists have recently converged on the fact that today's standards-based regulatory regimes and measurement infrastructures are the only rules and regulations that are implemented on a global scale. "Most standardizers [and metric makers] are private sector organizations or private persons. They are particularly common and important on the global stage, where they meet less competition from other rule setters; there is no world state with legislative power.... Rather than being controlled by states, many standardizers want to influence and control state policies.... Many of these standardizers are also highly successful."[27] The list of the non-governmental international organizations that function as standards-based administrators of measures is long: World Wide Fund for Nature (WWF); UNESCO; International Women's Rights Action Watch; International Organization for Standardization (ISO); OECD; International Labor Organization (ILO); and so on. This is a cursory overview leaving out whole realms such as finance, education, and ecology, each of which I discuss further below.[28]

All this standardization and measurement is an unprecedented state of affairs. This movement toward a hyper-measured humanity began right after WWII, but started picking up steam around 1970, when standards-based regulatory regimes and measurement infrastructures became part and parcel of neoliberal global policies toward increasing efficiencies in planetary trade and communications.[29] Today the postmodern world is overrun with measures and standards. And although we may not realize it, much of the anomie and injustice of the postmodern lifeworld is a result of the proliferation of the wrong kind of measures and standards. We do not face the pathology of the one-dimensional modern human, the distortion of individuals when they are all aligned against one abstract standard (although in some places and institutions we still face that). The postmodern condition involves the fragmentation of humanity, a multi-perspectival personality refracted through a prism of standardized differentiations and mass-customizations.[30]

The hyper-measured self is a result of many things, especially the recent increased emphasis on measurement in educational systems and so-called "human capital management systems." For example, ISO 9000, the human resource and management standards issued by the ISO, impacts the lives of millions of workers as the largest quality-control initiative for human capital management in the world. Not surprisingly, those most impacted by these standards (the millions of workers) have no say in their creation. They are created by a group of experts with ties to most major international corporations. ISO 9000 exemplifies trends in measurement-intensive accountability and efficiency-oriented practices for postmodern organizations. Now global, these trends began with Frederick Winslow

Taylor in the nineteenth century, whose simple use of a stopwatch (a crucial innovation in measurement technology) would allow him to optimize workflows and rebuild entire industries around the principles of measurement-intensive scientific management.[31] Today more sophisticated versions of the system sciences are applied to organizational governance and development, and they are always measurement-intensive. Most people involved in institutionalized life are thus subject to a whole array of measures over which they have little or no control.

It is worth discussing the International Organization for Standardization (ISO) at length because it brings to light some of the most important and hidden infrastructures behind our emerging planetary civilization.[32] Founded in 1947, the ISO is an international meta-organization, or organization of organizations.[33] It convenes United Nations-style conferences composed of member nations, private entities, and nearly the full set of organizations in the current transnational constellation (e.g., NATO, WTO, ILO, and OECD). All have a stake in standards and related measurement infrastructures that transcend borders, currencies, and cultures. The ISO is regarded by some as no less than the beginnings of a "world state." This is because the standards and related measures produced by the ISO regulate and format innumerable components of infrastructures, artifacts, spaces, and practices across multiple scales around the globe.

> Credit cards, all 0.76mm thin, slide into slots and readers all around the world. Screw threads conform to a given pitch. Every make of car shares the same dashboard pictograms. Batteries with consistent durations are sized to fit any device. Books, magazines, music, and audiovisual works are indexed with ISBN numbers. Paper sizes and the machines that handle them are standardized. RFID tags, transshipment containers, trucks, car seats, film speeds, protective clothing, book bindings, units of measure, personal identification numbers (PINs), and fasteners of all kinds conform to global standards. All of these shared standards emanate from the International Organization for Standardization, or ISO.... ISO presides over a multitude of technical standards that establish criteria for everything from

> roller bearings and refrigerants to lubricants and footwear. There are technical standards for the parameters of a JPEG (ISO/IEC:15444) or an MPEG (ISO/IEC:21000), for cooking pasta (ISO 7394-2:2008), and even a standard glass for wine tastings (ISO 3591:1977).[34]

As already mentioned, of particular interest is ISO 9000, which is about "quality" in management practices. That is, it is about the way people act on the job, especially when supervising other people, interacting with customers, or performing essential tasks. When you call a service provider and they tell you the call is monitored for "quality," they are talking in terms set by ISO 9000. Compliance with ISO 9000 is essential for any organization pursuing a global project or market. Compliance is a condition of trade policies within the European Union, for example. ISO 9000 is an outcome of a long history of theories, some already mentioned above and in Chapter 2, which praise and propagate efficiency-oriented forms of quantitative decision-making. These theories address the *process* of production or service delivery. They specify standards for the procedures and practices of a company, clarifying norms for their social patterns, service provisions, and corporate governance structures. Importantly, this is a drive to shape *dispositions*, "to habituate without specific content."[35] Quality has to do with standardization and measurement of *process*, not content. Quality is content-neutral, without history, face, or uniqueness. ISO 9000 thus spawns cultures built around obsessive data gathering and metrics, which are used to objectively measure "quality" and ensure it is being delivered.

The ISO 9000 standards are themselves (like all ISO standards) proprietary to the ISO, strictly protected and copyrighted, and available only at a price. This means that although the ISO often appears to serve as a public information source or intergovernmental body, it is actually a non-governmental organization, a business that sells access to its standards to a group of private voluntary clients, who the ISO protects and does not disclose. The ISO keeps no public records and is not required to share its dealings or the scope of its business and impact. It is maintained and staffed by the very corporations and organizations that it certifies. This leads to the creation of "self-certifying codes of conduct" where compliance to a new standard and related measure is displayed as a public "seal of approval," which has actually been self-constructed by a corporation as a smoke-screen against potential bad press or litigation.[36]

This kind of metric-based deception has been documented in the case of the ISO 14000 and its various programs for corporate social responsibility. These are used by multinational companies to cloak themselves "in a veneer of environmental excellence and social responsibility.... 'International standards' [and related measures] can be used to undermine the development of national environmental law and capacity by arbitrarily 'legitimizing norms that have been defined by special interests, and reassuring government officials and other stakeholders that practices are improving, based on enigmatic standards [and measures] that lie beyond the reach—or responsibility—of national authorities.'"[37]

The ISO exemplifies many of the contradictions and problems that beset our hyper-measured postmodern world. It is a private non-governmental organization that advises and impacts governments. It deals with consumers, not citizens. The ISO rolls out extensive platforms that impact the general public from the micro to the macro, but these platforms do not originate from open public discourse, or even political dialogue. The standards and measures created, sold, and disseminated by the ISO have encircled the planet in a kind of late capitalist "consensus reality" of homogenized processes and measurement-intensive regimes. These perpetuate layers of bureaucracy, procedure, and regulation, which are mostly content-neutral, demonstrating the almost invisible political power of measures in achieving global hegemony over dispositions, processes, and procedures.

Now let us return to our example of the morning routine. Our average Joe or Jane will now go to school, work, shopping, or a doctor's appointment, and in so doing be tied up in innumerable ISO standards. Consider the further implications of postmodern standards-based regulatory regimes on the formation of human personalities and cultural patterns. The move from modernity's homogeneity to postmodernity's standardized diversity is a move from less to more measurement, in terms of both sheer numbers of measures and magnitude of impacts. Postmodernism is about difference, and marking out more differences requires more measurement.

Our late capitalist commodity-intensive lifestyles are caught in a web of standardized differentiation. We are not being unified and homogenized as we were during modernity; we are being divided and isolated into a pastiche of mass-customized personalities via measurement-intensive standardization practices, from marketing to service industries, therapy, medicine, education, and fashion.

Global Crises of Measurement: Whose Measures, Whose Future?

To help gain an overview of the situation with regards to postmodern planetary measurement infrastructures, I'll follow the definition of measurement crisis I offered at the start of this chapter. A measurement crisis occurs when society loses touch with reality because it has institutionalized a systematically distorted measurement infrastructure. I call them *crises* because they are systemic and endemic, and because they signal a need for deep structural *transformation*.[38] All of these crises are interconnected, ricocheting between the system, the lifeworld, and the four quadrants of social reality. I cannot detail each of the following six crises here, due to limitations of space and the focus of this book. I offer only a brief rundown of the global crisis of measurement.[39]

Economic Crisis: Poverty, Inequality, and Econometrics

It has been known for some time that GDP (gross domestic product) is a simplistic misrepresentation of the health of any national economy. It is also a poor index of cultural modernity, human rights violations, and democracy.[40] Yet GDP continues to be discussed in a serious manner and continues to drive national economic agendas. Similarly, most representations of *profit* (the so-called bottom line) are also gross simplifications of what makes a company valuable. In both cases a simplistic quantitative index is used in summary and in place of a richer qualitative analysis, or even in place of a more complex quantitative analysis with multiple parameters.

One important thing missed by summary indices of economic systems (like GDP, or simple calculations of profit) is intra-systemic inequalities; the differences between the most well-off and the least well-off are disguised. Highly profitable companies and nations with rapidly rising GDP often house staggering inequalities of wealth. In fact, in many organizations the rate of profit and the rate of exploitation (and thus increasing inequality) are correlated.[41] The less you pay workers, the more you skim off the top, and the more profits go up. GDP is similar in that it is the perpetual expansion of the economy that drives numbers up; GDP increases as the things that used to be free are brought into the market and given a price. For example, this means that we would be *lowering* GDP by teaching people to grow their own food, or treat simple aliments with herbs they grow themselves, or start a free neighborhood parent group that shares childcare. On the other hand, opening a childcare center, herbal company, or commercial farm expands the economy and makes GDP go up. Take something that people can do or get for free and sell it back to them—that is what makes for economic value according to simplistic growth-oriented measures like GDP.[42]

I want to quote at length the work of economic historian Dirk Philipsen, whose research into the creation and history of GDP sheds critical light on the overwhelming impact of this simplistic measure. The list below describes some of the negative characteristics of GDP and its institutionalized use. Note that these characteristics could be used to describe many of the metrics that dominate discourse and practice in today's world.

1. **Quality-blind:** As a pure measure of quantity, GDP is entirely oblivious to questions of good or bad: toys, weapons, pornography, organic food, car wrecks—it matters not. Volume (of commercial transactions) is what matters; quality does not.
2. **People-blind:** As a simple measure of monetized output, everything about people and their lives outside of the cash nexus is ignored, and thus culturally devalued. What counts and what doesn't seems grotesque: lumber but not trees; energy but not vital resources; therapy but not health; Facebook but not community; the nanny, but not the mother.

3. **Justice-blind:** As a measure of pure volume, GDP says nothing about justice or equality. A community with extreme poverty amidst excessive wealth, ridden with crime and social strife, can have the same GDP as one we recognize as providing fair opportunities in a stable environment. In America today, one person, Bill Gates, owns as much wealth as the bottom 10 percent (or roughly twenty-five million) of Americans combined. GDP has nothing to say about that....
4. **Ecosystem-blind:** The planet and all its vital resources and ecosystem functions are not counted in GDP at all—it's like measuring personal well-being without including health of the body. Damage and depletion are not subtracted from the total, treating the earth like a "business in liquidation." Such neglect robs the poor and future generations of the essentials for a good life....
5. **Complexity-blind:** GDP reduces human and social complexity to a market transaction, and thus is incapable of necessary long-term and large-scale thinking. Short-term financial benefit is rewarded at the expense of investments in crucial developments and benefits such as environmental health, education, infrastructure, or basic equality.
6. **Accountability-blind:** GDP is accounting without accountability—a small group of experts and their product, GDP—yield immense power over the operation of our economy, yet neither one is responsible to society nor democratically accountable. In the grips of a spell, the underlying logic remains both hidden and immensely powerful.
7. **Purpose-blind:** In the end, as a simple measure of volume, GDP is entirely blind to the most important question of all: what should be the objective and direction of our economy? GDP counts guns, but not security; medical equipment, but not health; computers, but not education. One cannot measure what one does not ask about. As a result, what

> gets measured is essentially the speed and volume by which we turn "resources into garbage." Some argue this includes human beings, increasingly driven into "an engulfing sense of purposelessness."[43]

Clearly there is vast and contested terrain beyond the debate over GDP and the distortion of human cooperation due to the hypertrophying of the profit motive. Metric-based distortions of value seep into the economy at all levels. Consider, for example, the role of credit and financial rating agencies and the dozens of other standards-based measurement-intensive activities involved in high finance, where the ISO's influence can also be found. The recent economic crisis was largely the result of inadequate and deceptive ratings applied to collateralized debt obligations (or CDOs); indeed, most predatory high-finance runs on deceptive "metrics."[44] The pretense of having reliable and "true" measurements of risk and return was used to distort perceptions of reality and to create whole realms of fictitious capital.[45] Of course, all measurement-enabled fictions (or measurement-induced demi-realities) eventually come crashing down, especially when they run up against the actual limits of the biosphere.

Ecological Crisis: The Politics of Measurement and Complex Systems

The ontology and epistemology of the climate change debate have been explored in depth from the perspective of integral meta-theories.[46] Less explored are the ways that measurement and quantification impact climate epistemologies and contribute to the increasingly pluralized ontologies of the climate debate. Knowledge is rendered in the terms provided by metrics, especially quantitative and scientific knowledge. The climate change debate has become so deeply politicized that trustworthy measures are hard to find. At the heart of every climatological debate is the interpretation, use, or placement of a measurement instrument (or thousands of them in the case of global temperature readings, where thermometers are tracked over decades, dotted across the entire surface of the Earth). The nightly news abounds with results and percentages gleaned from measures we know very little about. Sometimes the numbers put us at ease, but more often they cause us distress. The mass media is engaged in uncertainty management through manipulations in measurement and the representation of quantitative data.[47] There is, of course, a lot to say on the science and politics of climate change indicators, which is an important subplot in the recent social and political history of quantitative objectivity.[48]

More important, I believe, is the fact that as the climate crisis deepens there will be a proliferation of standards and measures related to sustainability, ecological accounting, and environmental law. This brings to mind the specter of an eco-fascist dystopia of hyper-measured and standardized humans, radically curtailed in their freedoms due to the precarious ecological limbo in which they find themselves. The need to *strictly* enforce future environmental regulations due to extreme climate disruption and delicate ecosystem balances will create conflicts around measures as simple as ounces of water and particles of CO_2. In the context of a future where humanity is engaged in a reflective and delicate balancing act with the biosphere, environmental standards-based regulations and related measures will be some of the most important and politically contentious issues on the world stage.

As the ecological crisis deepens we must remember that there are *unjust* ways toward achieving sustainable futures. Sustainability does not entail justice; sustainability is a Lower-Right quadrant value (a systems-maintenance idea) and can be achieved by means of any number of socio-cultural forms. We must make a moral commitment to the idea that sustainability requires social justice. The future of ecological regulations, standards, and measures must be democratized and made integral, as I discuss further below. Of course, as already discussed, Wilber noted some time ago that the ecological crisis is better thought of as a crisis of consciousness—the noosphere is the problem, not the biosphere—what we see is truly a crisis of decision-making, resulting from erroneous and demi-real worldviews. So politics is near the heart of the solution to the ecological crisis.

Political Crisis: Voting, Polling, and the Representation of Interiors

The ancient world provides accounts of many different voting technologies used in the city states along the Mediterranean: the volume of clapping hands in an assembly; the weight of pebbles dropped in different buckets by a crowd; hands raised; and of course, casting paper ballots. Still other peoples decided to have arguments, to debate, and to have a jury of deliberators with rules of evidence and discourse.[49] These are different technologies for measuring the sentiments and beliefs of a group of people. Discourse, argumentation, and decisions by juries are good, because they are more participatory and qualitative. But the benefit of a simple vote is its straightforward and quantitative right/wrong determination. Whereas arguments can always be questioned, a vote seems cut and dried. Voting is also anonymous and can easily scale beyond the assembly to the city or country as a whole. Nevertheless, voting is a crude technology invented thousands of years ago, and does not do a good job of representing the complexity and stratified nature of human interiorities. It is not a good basis for the election of officials or for the creation of law.

Political polling currently supplements voting as a window into what *the people* are thinking. But these are also crude tools that oversimplify thoughts and feelings to numbers and statistics. Again, this is not wrong in principle (numbers are essential), it is just a very partial view of things, especially interiorities. Opinion polls and large-scale survey-based profiles of populations can often be manipulative and misleading precisely because of their quantitative clarity.[50] These polls are composed of what survey builders call selected response items (or multiple choice questions); they literarily put words in your mouth. The instrument itself is rigid and forces a wide diversity of thought and feeling into a very constrained set of possible responses. Moreover, the sample size and demographics of the populations claimed to be representative are usually not. For example, most political polling is restricted to landline phones, and is rarely done on cell phones; a random sample of landlines is very different from a random sample of cell phone holders, both generationally and socio-economically. Details of survey design and sample construction aside, voting and polling provide a form of democracy where the people only get to say yes or no, or rate it on a scale from 1 to 5.

This is very different from what is often called *deliberative democracy*,[51] where instead of spectatorship and voting, citizens are engaged in discussions and cooperative decision-making. This is essentially a transition from a quantitative to a qualitative representation of interiorities (from voting to discussing), and is a very important deepening of the truest aspects of our great democratic traditions. For over a century we have known that this works wonders at the level of the local cooperative.[52] Bringing deliberative democracy to scale for a city, nation-state, or global community requires leveraging new web technologies that deal with qualitative argumentation in quantitative ways (e.g., gathering text-analytics meta-data on deliberative forums as a means of emergent policy creation). We must use technology as a way to lift and make audible *all* of the voices. This means finding ways to deal with "big data" about human interiority. The future of deliberative democracy is web-based, localized, and predicated on the aforementioned educational prerequisites, freedom of information, and basic guarantees for health care.[53]

Health Care Crisis: Biometrics, Diagnostic Categories, and the Future of Medicine

Similar to education, medical diagnostics can be used to improve science and treatment, but they can also be used to bureaucratize organizational processes toward the delivery of care under the headings of profit and accountability. Ideally medical measures and standards would be driven by science and used to expand understanding and provide increasingly accurate and specialized care. However, the shadow of medical diagnostics is long.[54] Today official standards (such as the DSM and Merck Manual) are built by profit-oriented organizations, and public oversight commissions (such as the FDA) have been shown to be infiltrated by the very companies most in need of oversight (recall the "self-certifying codes of conduct" we saw in the case of the ISO). Moreover, as the health care system continues to expand the politicization of medical measurements, standards of practice and record keeping will continue to increase.

The measurement of the human body for medical purposes is a very old practice. So is the use of medical measures to stigmatize, institutionalize, and oppress alternative populations and deviance in lifestyle.[55] Diagnostic categories define who is sick and who is not. They define what is a disease (and thus what is covered by insurance) and what is not. Diagnostic measures always reveal some things while hiding others. They typically characterize aliments as discrete disease entities, amenable to a specific localized and targeted fix. Compare this to diagnostics in Eastern medicine, where an aliment is put in the context of a whole body energy system. Medical diagnostics often standardize the human body and life course too formally, and can result in misunderstandings about the nature of disease and individual differences.[56] Without a major reform in measures and standards in medicine, future health care systems will continue to become increasingly counterproductive, resource-intensive, and a source of iatrogenic disease. Of course, the mind and body are connected, so it would make sense that crises in health care systems would correlate with crises in personality systems.

Personality Crisis: The Hyper-Reality and Hyper-Reflectivity of the Over-Measured Lifestyle

As discussed above (and I have theorized about elsewhere), there is a species-wide identity crisis in which humanity is currently embroiled.[57] We have been fractured into a thousand images of humanity, each with competing worldviews and competing definitions of human origins, the self, soul, and mind. Our species is playing out an identity crisis on the world stage, and for the first time we are collectively facing the fact we do not know what it means to be human.[58]

In the postmodern West where lifestyle and worldview pluralism reign, you can pick any self-related measure (intelligence, money, credentials, fitness, etc.) and find a group that hypertrophies it. There are a wide variety of new technology-enabled self-related measures, from Facebook "likes" to smartphone apps that track your steps and calories. The measures impacting our personal lives also include the meta-data gathered and tagged as a routine part of government surveillance, as well as the advertisement-generating backends built into social media and online marketplaces; these measure us, categorize us, and then shape our experiences in ways that are hard to perceive and beyond our control. We are over-measured, super-standardized, and caught in a web of complex self-shaping infrastructures—all this right at the moment when we are least sure of what the shape of our humanity ought to be. The old stories about human identity—the old ideals and standards of human character, health, and livelihood—have dissolved. In their place is a pastiche of ideals, lifestyles, and standardized differentiations, without an overarching form or narrative. Standardized testing in schools has been at the heart of this confusion about who we are and what we are capable of learning and creating.

Educational Crisis: Testing, Standards, and Marketization

My first book, which was based on my dissertation research, is focused on the history of standardized testing and the social justice issues implicated in testing.[59] Much of what I say here is elaborated upon at greater length in that book. In it I note that the great critical theorist of education, Michael Apple, pointed out (well before Bush's No Child Left Behind and Obama's Common Core Standards) that American schools could much more easily be turned into a marketplace if there were national standards and national tests. This is because there would then be a single clear matrix of competition and comparison between schools. Apple's words were prophetic. The US educational system is undergoing a transformation into a largely market-driven and privately run collection of enterprises. Things have changed so rapidly and radically that even mainstream one-time conservative policy makers are beginning to take note.[60] And standardized testing is at the center of this sweeping revolution in mass education.

The entire movement toward marketization is based on the presumption that testing can be used to quantify and thus monetize educational value. This involves an oversimplification of educational value and an overvaluation of tests as measures of educational processes. It is a thoroughgoing non-integral, flatland policy, that is only focused on the Lower-Right quadrant. Nevertheless, during the coming decades there will be a testing-based overhaul of US public schools. State-run schools will largely be replaced by a diverse and socio-economically stratified educational marketplace, with tests and standards playing a major role toward ensuring that vouchers are spent on schools that meet state testing benchmarks.

Large-scale standardized testing has perpetrated a form of injustice with long and complex roots in the control and categorization of urban populations, especially laborers and the poor. Testing has forever been part of the scientization of education, as well as the commercialization of psychology.[61] Today testing is being used to surveil and discipline whole schools and districts that are threatened yearly with being shut down and replaced by privately run charter-school chains. The people most impacted by the tests (teachers and students) are the farthest away from influence over the nature and content of the tests.[62]

Preferable futures for educational assessment involve the democratization of authority structures in schools and the elimination of all high-stakes practices and policies in favor of formative, developmental, and transformative approaches—a move toward truly authentic assessment. There are real possibilities for justice-oriented approaches to assessment and student evaluation, as well as the use of learning sciences and diagnostic technologies to improve student learning.[63]

Tomorrow's Metrics: Toward a Global Cooperative Forum on Integral Metrology

I have briefly reviewed five of the global crises of measurement that are currently unfolding in the context of postmodern planetization. All of these crises have been set in the context of integral meta-theory, which drew our focus to the impact of measurement infrastructures on interiorities (i.e., the four-quadrant impact of measurement infrastructures). Pre-modern and modern forms of measurement were discussed, which helped to clarify several meta-theoretical principles concerning the nature of measurement. Measures are intrinsically related to power. Measures create realities by structuring thought and decision-making. Measures make science by dictating what counts as official knowledge.

The goal of these explorations has been to shed light on some of the hidden (and not so hidden) *basic structures* that shape our late-capitalist global society.[64] I believe that if we continue looking beneath the surface at these kinds of basic structures, we might begin to hack the source code of socio-cultural evolution—especially if we begin to tinker with the structures impacting educational configurations. As a way of preparing for the radical social miracles suggested in the next chapter, I want to conclude this chapter with some reflections on global futures for measurement, especially what will be needed to create an educational system capable of navigating the transition to a new world-system.

From a scientific perspective, the heart of the issue is the long-awaited paradigm shift toward the new sciences of chaos, complexity, and emergence.[65] Measurement is fundamentally different in these sciences, which assume non-linearity in growth and behavior. When trying to understand truly complex or chaotic phenomena, one or two measurements taken of one or two variables will never be enough. Complex dynamical systems can only be studied by use of multitudinous measures across multiple time-scales, tracking non-linear dynamics in the growth and behavior of the system. The old paradigm[66] thinks in terms of linear growth, averages, and summary statistics; this is the heroic modernity that brought us the metric system, IQ testing, and one-size-fits-all medical care. The new paradigm thinks in terms of non-linear dynamic growth, uniqueness, and stratified ontologies (intra-systemic complexity requiring multiple measures); we have yet to see what a society built on these kinds of metrics would bring.

Another way to think about this is as the difference between a science of averages and statistics and a science of the individual and of dynamic modeling—the so-called "new science of the individual" or the sciences of uniqueness.[67] The basic idea is that *simplistic summary statistics are totally inadequate for the task of understanding dynamic systems*. Note that all the systems that are in crisis are dynamic, complex, and non-linear: economies, ecologies, human minds, and human bodies. None of these can be understood based on assumptions of linearity or measures that track only a single variable but claim to capture the majority of important variance. The future of measurement must go from the linear and simple to the non-linear and complex. This would mean that if we only have tools for tracking linear growth and behavior we should not talk and act like we have a handle on non-linear dynamics. Consider again the figure representing the therapeutic dyad that concluded the Introduction (see: p. 47); that is the messy reality of teaching, learning, and human transformation. This is what needs to be understood if we want to really have "evidence-based" practices in education and health care.

Along with the indeterminacy and complexity of these new measures, there would be an opening toward a more detailed and nuanced tracking of interiorities, worldviews, emotions, and consciousness. New abilities for accurately measuring interiorities should bolster democracy and education, allowing our institutions (schools, governments, companies, etc.) to begin listening and responding to people instead of classifying, categorizing, and monetizing them. We live in a world where there are enormous numbers of people whose lives are shaped by institutions of enormous scope (health care, education, transportation, food systems, etc.). These organizations are usually governed by standards-based regimes that are not accountable to those most impacted by their policies. Most large organizations are far from democratic and limit discussions of interiority to human resource retreats. Myers-Briggs tests and leadership profiles are used as an afterthought, and little is made of the internal states of the vast majority of employees. Their internal lives, thoughts, and emotions have no impact on the future of the policies that impact their work and daily responsibilities (e.g., ISO 9000). Innovations in the measurement and representation of interiority are necessary for the future of the democratic regulation of large-scale organizations.

Along with these new representations of interiors, we also need new representations of value to facilitate the emergence of a post-capitalist socio-sphere. As discussed in the next chapter, structural unemployment is an inevitable outcome of technological advance.[68] This means that large movements will emerge toward the pursuit of *unpaid* labor in economies of care, environmental stewardship, volunteer service, and other opportunities for human innovation and initiative, beyond the limits set when we measure value in terms of money. These opportunities will remain closed so long as money is the only representation of value that enables exchange and reward for service. Alternative currencies and time and skill sharing cooperatives are only the first wave of an emerging post-capitalist, post-money economy.[69] Without money as the dominant metric governing society, what alternative hierarchies of value might emerge? Again, by redesigning the basic measures a whole new realm of social possibilities comes into view. This idea ties directly into the discussion of a basic income guarantee in the next chapter.

Part of this measurement-enabled redesign of the economy would also involve the inclusion of justice-oriented economic indices such as the "Gini coefficient," which many economists prefer to GDP as a measure of national economies.[70] This could be deepened in terms of an even more explicit inequality index: a dynamic integral measure of the alethic truth of inequality, including indices of interiority, health, education, and human rights. The work of Nussbaum and Sen in these directions is promising, as are proposals for a global graduated income tax to redistribute ever-widening inequalities in wealth.[71]

Beyond these specifics, the meta-theory suggests that all measures and standards should be evaluated in terms of their impacts across all quadrants. All measures should be judged on their truth, goodness, and beauty. This means that discourse about metrics needs to be expanded beyond ISO experts behind closed doors. Only by seeing into the lived experiences of those most impacted by a measure can we get a sense of the degree to which its use engenders justice and beauty. This is another strand in the arguments unfolded throughout this discussion in favor of democratizing the creation of measurement infrastructures and standards. Democracy and expertise appear as almost necessarily in conflict. This has been a long-standing misconception: that the dominion of experts over society somehow precludes democratic participation.[72] In fact, this is a narrow and educationally simplistic way to think about decision-making in our complex techno-scientific society. Emerging research around civic data and participatory and deliberative forms of democracy suggest another way forward, where experts handle some aspects of measurement and standardization while deliberative democratic decision-making determines the parameters of use, as well as the ethical and policy implications.

Another clear outcome of the integral meta-theory of measurement is the centrality of *uniqueness* as an aspect of measurement practice. We must learn to respect the irreducibility of subjectivity and the irreducibility of the sacred and unique in every object and person. Measurement is about what things have in common: weight, price, length, and so on. All mark out dimensions of *sameness*. But measurement also provides parameters in terms of which an object can be located as unique. To stick with physical measurement (although the same truth applies in other realms): every object in the forest beyond my window has a weight and length, and in this way they are all the same. But every object would yield a unique combination of length and weight; there are no two trees or rocks or flowers that are the same (you can take the "every snowflake is unique" principle and generalize it to basically all of nature, especially living systems). The point is that measures reveal sameness, and can be used to standardize or homogenize perception. Or, measures can be used as a way to literally reveal and see uniqueness, to display individual differences, and (ideally) to valorize the immeasurable. To use measures as a matrix to reveal uniqueness you need enough of them to mark out a state-space with complex dimensionality. Integral metrological pluralism can yield a *constellational* unity in diversity—a representation of uniqueness.

Even from these initial insights it is clear that integral meta-theories could be used for mobilizing a social justice movement around measurement and standards-based regimes. Few other issues are as encompassing of as many global issues, or as amenable to meta-theoretical interventions; measurement infrastructures are a deep-structural lever, especially at the international level. Moreover, nearly every major progressive activist camp is calling for the redesign of measures, from education to health care, the environment, and Occupy Wall Street. What would be the impact of an international movement to organize for *a new global standards-based regime*? There have been some so-called "global constitutions" put forward by those seeking to lift planetary consciousness, but they have no teeth and no details. What we need is a clear call for international law at the level of standards and measures, and a call for the democratization of decision-making about these crucial infrastructures.

---

1. See: Busch (2011); Stein (2016). There are, of course, many other morning routines that could be discussed which might represent a more diverse slice of human life on the planet. For example, waking up in a slum in Calcutta to the sun, climbing out of a self-made structure of shipping packages and sheet metal, etc. I chose the average American in part because it is so familiar, but also because the postmodern West is by far the most measured and standardized socio-cultural epoch in history, so it serves as a very good example.

2. See: Mumford (1934) for more on the role of the clock in the genesis of the capitalist world-system. Throughout this book I will be talking about measures and standards, and on a larger scale, about measurement infrastructures and standards-based regulatory practices and regimes. These are distinct but related aspects of our contemporary techno-scientific society. Measures are instruments of various types that reliably differentially respond to specific qualities of interests and thus establish systems of categories and other classificatory schemes. Classic examples are thermometers, clocks, and tape measures. Other measures include standardized tests used in schools, medical diagnostics used in hospitals, tax forms used by the IRS, and quality-control checklists used in factories. Standards are different yet inseparable from measurement. They function to put measures in context by giving meaning to the results produced by them. A standard is a codified ideal—an explicit account of how certain processes, objects, and people *ought* to be. Classic examples include standards for food quality, educational standards, or standards for car fuel-efficiency and emissions. Once a standard is determined, measures are used to determine the degree to which the standard is being met. So while a measure can exist without a standard, a standard without a measure has no teeth and cannot be enforced in any rigorous way. Standards and measures work together to create realities and shape experience. As will be explained, measures and standards usually have long and complex histories. In postmodern societies measures and standards are proliferating at a breathtaking rate, addressing everything from psychological disease to the biochemistry of endangered wetlands. The implications of this increased standardization and measurement are reverberating throughout culture and personality structures. To foreshadow the arguments offered below, standards and measures can be made to address realities in any of the four quadrants, and a standard or measure institutionalized in any one quadrant has ramifications in all the rest. There is a small but growing literature on these topics. See: Busch (2011); Lampland & Star (2009); Brunsson & Jacobsson (2000); Tavernor (2007); Kula (1986); Duncan (1984).

3. Harvey (2005).

4. Busch (2011).

5. Rawls (1971); Stein (2016).

6. Kula (1986); Scott (1998).

7. As already discussed, this trend is sometimes referred to as the *Global Education Reform Movement* (aka: GERM). See: Sahlberg (2012).

8. I am referring here to the relation between the metric system and the French Revolution. Part of overthrowing the crown and aristocrats meant overthrowing their measures, which had long been used as instrument of injustice. I will discuss this further in the next section. See: Tavernor (2007); Kula (1986).

9. Michell (1972).

10. See: Mumford (1967); Tavernor (2007). It has been argued that the ancient Egyptians first invented standardized measures in tandem with geometry in order to redistribute land and levy taxes each year after the Nile's annual flood destroyed the previous year's plots. While the true origins of geometry may lie elsewhere, it is undoubtedly true that the first standardized measurement practices were invented in response to pressing social needs (Duncan, 1984). Measurement practices (involving measurement instruments and norms for their use) are as old as civilization itself and were some of the first social institutions ever established. Scales and measuring rods have been found among pre-civilized humans, and all ancient civilizations had complex systems of weights and measures. Historical accounts tell of an astonishing diversity of pre-modern measurement practices, all of them built out of necessity and evolving in response to the needs of their creators. Peoples in regions where land was scarce had precise measures of area, whereas peoples in regions with abundant land had more approximate measures. Those who dealt in gold had complex systems of precise scales for trading, while those dealing in oats or hay had systems of bushels and baskets, no less complex, but certainly less precise.

11. **Measures as Basic Structures and Subjects of Justice**

Measurement systems emerged and were institutionalized to address recurring social situations in which coordinated action depends upon the creation of a shared understanding of specific qualities and quantities in the objective world. Innovations in measurement stem from situations in our social life where it is necessary to achieve mutual understanding about a state of affairs that is repeatedly problematic, yet also consistently objectively determinable. These types of situations have a similar epistemological structure. They require multiple parties to be able to verify the amount or quality of some thing or things that concern them. Measurement systems are part of those social practices that require the reliable differential determination of objective traits in objects of concern. Considering even the most basic instance of measurement bears out this way of thinking.

If I measure a wooden board by myself as I build a table (say by laying down the length of my arm from elbow to finger tips and marking it as one *ell*), then through the act of measurement I have positioned the board in a space of meaning to which I ascribe universal intersubjective validity. That is to say, in the practice of measuring the board I am, in effect, saying that anybody and everybody who measured this board this way would find the same thing. Of course, my forearm may be longer or shorter than yours. As soon as one friend shows up to help me build, we are thrown into a negotiation about how precise an *ell* we need and whose arm it will be if a judgment must be made. This begins a process of refinement that, over the long run, results in a tape measure, marked in both metric and United States customary units, which any modern table builder would use off the shelf without a second thought. Usually, commonly used measures slip into the background and become part of our taken-for-granted measurement infrastructures. They become an unquestioned condition for the possibility of a vast amount of highly coordinated social actions.

Measurement infrastructures form a part of society's basic structure because they shape social life in fundamental ways, specifically by providing a means for coordinating social action in relation to objective realities. Consider the measurement practices involved in scientific research, engineering, and economic exchange, or in the administration of basic governmental tasks such as taxation. Measurement practices can facilitate these complex social activities because they provide a reliable index of reality that has been codified to consistently generate a broad consensus, which is ideally universal. Thus measurement infrastructures—like legal infrastructures—are both systems of knowledge and systems for guiding action and administering conduct (Habermas, 1996). They require knowledge about the invariant properties of objects and occurrences, which in turn entail the creation of instruments and practices that reliably differentially respond to those properties. Reflectively (sometimes scientifically) codified measurement practices then come to structure broad swaths of social life, often to the point of being woven into systems of law. Collections of measurement practices often congeal into an infrastructure and come to function as a taken-for-granted aspect of social life, so much so that unjust systems of measurement have been perpetuated for centuries due to sheer force of habit. This was the case with some systems used to administer taxation under feudalism in medieval Europe, a process of social inertia often aided by the rule of law (Kula, 1986; Wallerstein, 1974).

12. See: Tavernor (2007, p. 34); Kula (1986). History shows that measurement infrastructures have been (and continue to be) invented and institutionalized for social uses and wedded to systems of law. Aristotle's research for his *Politics* included a comprehensive survey of the existing city-states' constitutions. While the full fruits of his research were lost, what remains suggests that measurement practices, especially in the market and the field, were a major concern for those seeking to administer justice in the ancient world. It is no coincidence that the first ancient systems of measurement were accompanied by the first legal codes, or that legal systems and measurement systems have co-evolved since the dawn of civilization (Duncan, 1984). In fact, measurement practices were some of the first institutions to qualify as what Rawls would

call "basic structures of society."

It is no surprise then that many of the largest social and scientific undertakings in early modern history were focused on creating measurement infrastructures for science, industry, and government. The standardization of measures for temperature, distance, and weight dominated scientific discourse from the seventeenth through the nineteenth centuries, eventually resulting in the establishment of international standards for measurement, which were understood as a precondition for scientific collaboration (Tavernor, 2007). The rapid invention of agricultural technologies, mills, and eventually the steam engine necessitated the large-scale institutionalization of the standardized measures being created by scientists, many of whom were on the payroll of industrial benefactors (Porter, 1996). In the socio-political arena, the building of nation-states entailed monumental undertakings in the design and construction of measurement infrastructures; taxation, military technology and inscription, economic exchange, and many other measurement-intensive activities were necessitated by modern governments (Scott, 1998).

Because of their unique and irreplaceable social functions (e.g., their role as basic structures), measurement infrastructures have been the focus of some of the most intense and prolonged political and scientific efforts in history (Alder, 2003). This has resulted in a world-historical process during which multitudinous local measurement practices that evolved naturally in all societies have been systematically replaced by measures that are centralized, scientific, government-sanctioned, and internationally calibrated. The most famous instance of this process was, of course, the institutionalization of the metric system in the wake of the French Revolution. In this case, Enlightenment ideology posited that objective, standardized measurement was a primary means for facilitating both social justice and scientific progress. As one rallying call during the revolution put it, "one law, one weight, one measure.... For all people, for all time!" (Kula, 1986, Ch. 22 and 24). These ideals led to the international proliferation of the metric system and its eventual near-universal adoption by all the nations on Earth. Of course, as I discuss later on, the complex history of this process is nothing like a linear story of progress in which the new "true" measures were welcomed by all people.

13. In Aristotle's political anthropology, he recounts the societal need for Metronomi (commissioners of weights and measures) to be appointed by lot and tasked with seeing "that sellers [in the market] use fair weights and measures" (*Constitution of Athens*, Ch. 51. See: Ross, 1921). "There were also *Sitophylaces* (corn commissioners)... who watched over prices and the weight of loaves [of bread sold at market], which they had the power to standardize" (Duncan, 1984, p. 13). The earliest legal systems functioned to establish, among other things, measurement infrastructures as basic structures by using the force of law to ensure that specific measurement practices would be reliably regarded as the "true measure" (e.g., sometimes literally the king's foot). Like other

basic structures such as those for voting and jurisprudence (which are also the subject of ancient constitutions), the institutionalization of measurement practices serves to facilitate trust between strangers, mutual understanding at a distance, and fairness through the standardized treatment of cases. But this same constellation of law and measurement can be (and has been) used to exploit, systematically discriminate, and fallaciously justify inequity.

14. It should be noted that one of the functions of *money* is to reduce all other measures used in the marketplace to one universal measure of value. While it is easy to exchange like-for-like (2 bushels of my oats is equal in value to 2 bushels of your oats), it is hard to exchange dissimilar commodities, especially when they involve different basic units of measure (how many bushels of my oats is equal to 3 gallons of your wine?). Money serves as a kind of meta-metric that facilitates cross-metric value exchange (5 bushels of oats is equal to 20 dollars, which is equal to 3 gallons of wine). Suffice it to say that the power of money to reduce all measures to one is also the source of its greatest danger. Money homogenizes value and renders invisible many important differences between commodities. Also, the quantitative structure of money encourages the quantification of value, which promotes the proliferation of value measurement, even in areas where value is impossible to represent in simple quantitative terms (i.e., turning things into commodities that are not best understood as commodities, such as human lives and labor). Innovations in measurement that allow for non-monetary representations of value are discussed below. Money is also discussed below, where econometric indices are considered as an aspect of the current global crises of measurement. However, a full discussion of the connections between measurement and money, as well between alternative currencies and measurement, are beyond the scope of this book. For more on this important topic, see Chapter 4, as well as: Eisenstein (2011); Harvey (2014); Marx (1867/1977).

15. Consider the result of different laws governing the jurisdiction and powers of ancient and medieval commissioners of weights and measures, who roamed the marketplaces attempting to regulate the use of metrics (e.g., scales, rods, bushels, and loaves). Kula (1986) reports of wide variations between markets that were only miles apart, with ethnic and religious differences often resulting in different rights with respect to measurement. Wealthy merchant guilds found ways to change legal codes in order to allow them the power to regulate their own measures, which then inevitably changed in response to the needs of the guild. When yields are good, the bushel (or whatever is the standard unit of exchange) is big; when yields are poor, the bushel is small, yet the price of the bushel (its exchange value) remains unchanged (Kula, 1986, pp. 43-71).

This kind of metric manipulation was common practice and remained a ubiquitous part of economic life for centuries. It is important to understand how unit setting differs from price setting as a means for merchants to offset unexpected problems with supply or production. This is an issue we will return to when we discuss the manipulation of educational measurement systems, where units (e.g., cut-off scores) are set differently in different places, or change in the same place from year to year, often in order to offset problems with "production" (e.g., lowering the cut-off score for next year ensures the appearance that a school is producing students as good as or better than last year).

In modern economies, when yields are poor it is the price that goes up, but the unit (or measure) remains unchanged—a trend starkly exemplified by the worth of a gallon of gasoline, the size of which remains constant despite the highly variable and politicized nature of its cost. In ancient and medieval markets, it was more often the unit or measure that fluctuated in response to problems with supply or production. The loaf of bread, a staple of ancient and medieval life in almost all of Europe, was a basic unit of exchange, structuring the access most city dwellers had to one of their most basic sources of nourishment. But the loaf was a notoriously unstandardized unit, fluctuating largely in response to the supply of grains, sometimes imperceptibly, sometimes enough to incite a riot. For this reason many local political authorities regulated the size of the loaf to ensure fairness, but also for other governmental reasons such as to mitigate the risk of famine, build up supplies for war, or head off political upheavals (Kula, 1986, pp. 71-80). As discussed below, it was not until the metric system was spread via political revolution, colonialism, and scientism that many of our basic units of measure and exchange became "impersonal," ostensibly scientific, and generally perceived as fair; these measures and units thus became objective social facts that are now a part of the taken-for-granted infrastructures that facilitate coordinated social action.

Measurement was a political preoccupation in the ancient world and continued as such for centuries, with measurement infrastructures remaining a perennially contested subject in the expanding discourse about social justice leading up through the Enlightenment. The role of measurement infrastructures in contributing to the background justice of a society was understood early; the ideal of just measurement had been codified in a variety of ancient and medieval texts, from constitutions to religious scripture. Yet it would be centuries before many basic measurement infrastructures attained the universal and objective status they had always been counterfactually ascribed.

16. From such a perspective, in this book I am arguing that activism addressing the redesign of education, measurement infrastructures, and standards-based regulatory practices should be understood as a kind of *sacred activism*. It is an endeavor to make measurement practices sacred again by reclaiming ancient ideas about the role of measurement in the creation of basic structures that align with natural realities as well as human aspirations for justice, truth, and beauty.

17. A classic example of measurement-enabled injustice from this time involves the millers who owned the local mill, the only place local farmers could take their grains to be processed. Millers would collect grains to be milled in bushels of a size that they controlled and return processed flour in sacks also of a size that they controlled. It was not uncommon at certain times of the year for a miller to increase the size of the bushel while decreasing the size of the sack, thus leaving him with a larger surplus of flour which he could then use or sell. There was no way to prosecute these kinds of metrological injustices, because there was no centralized power regulating measurement practices. This was such a common problem that many medieval religious parables include stories of bizarre punishments in the afterlife for millers and merchants who engaged in underhanded measurement practices (see: Kula, 1986, for dozens of comparable examples, from bartenders with variably sized "pint" glasses, to pimps with watches that run fast). As I discuss, one of the great benefits of modern forms of standardized measurement is that they eliminate these kinds of simple measurement-enabled injustices. Of course, we now have measurement-enabled injustices of a much more complex and subtle nature. But at least we can trust that a pint is a pint no matter what bar you go to, and that a gallon is a gallon, regardless of the gas station.

18. See: Alder (2003); Tavernor (2007). I am focusing on *length* here as a matter of convenience and clarity. The metric system also standardizes units for volume and mass, but these are based ultimately on the length of the meter (the details of the conversion of length into weight and volume are too long to go into here). Interestingly, during the height of the metric reformers' ambitions, they proposed a metric standard of time which would have decimalized time measurement by creating a 10-month year, a 10-day week, and a 10-hour day. This was part of a broader revolutionary plan to de-Christianize the calendar and make it scientific. These efforts at reforming time and calendrical measurement failed in part because of the power of the clock and watchmaking guilds, but also due to the profound disruptions it required of deeply set traditional rhythms of life, work, and holiday.

19. This is a phenomenon known in sociological literature as *path dependence* (Busch, 2011; Luhmann, 1995). Once a complex system is far enough along a particular path it becomes cheaper and easier to just stay on that path (at least in the short-term). Once a measurement infrastructure is in place it creates conditions around itself (called layering or interoperability); as infrastructures become geared into one another they become very hard to change. This is one of the reasons that the United States does not use the metric system. The US had already gone too far down the road of standardizing its own measures and fostering industrialization; it was too late to retrofit all railroads and factories in the country. I will return to a discussion of path dependence below.

20. Porter (1996); Busch (2011); Scott (1998).

21. For more on the cult of science, see: Mumford (1967); Wilber (1995). Consider the esoteric rituals involved with today's metric system:

> [The meter] took on a new significance and it was accorded mythological, even sacred status. The installation of the definitive prototypes in the underground vault in the grounds of the International Bureau [of Weights and Measures] at Sèvres on 28 September 1889 took the form of a ceremony of deposition. This was to be re-enacted every six years, a procedure more familiar to a religious sect or secret society than a rational scientific organisation. It involved four keys of admission that were distributed among the foreign signatories of the International Committee. When they met sexennially at Sèvres, four designated delegates were required to bring the key they had retained, enter the underground vault, and inspect and confirm the safe condition of the prototype standards.... To ensure its longevity—for all people, for all times—its scientist-custodians [keep the "true" meter] out of reach of common humanity at large, [controlling] the metric system independently of nations.... On 14 October 1960 it was agreed to return to a truly "natural" and scientifically verifiable definition for the metre rod derived from the radiation of the orange-red light emitted by the radioactive kypton-86 atom, so that the metre would equal 1,650,763.73 wavelengths in vacuum.... Since 1983 it has been defined more simply (though it is no easier to comprehend) as the distance that light travels in a vacuum in the fraction of time of 1/299,792,458 of a second.... While a fundamental unit for all times had been settled on, it is one that can be comprehended only by scientists and verified in a laboratory under their control.... It [the meter] has no relation to human form, the shape or extent of the earth, or to any form at all.... It is a measure of everything and nothing. It is culturally removed from the mainstream experience of society. It is a measure of total abstraction. (Tavernor, 2007, pp. 149-151).

22. Busch (2011) explores the nature of standardized differentiation in detail as an aspect of neoliberal commercial and advertising innovations.

23. Consider the realm of psychological measurement as an example of how the move from modern to postmodern is a move from the standardization of a single abstract universal to the standardization of differences. In the early decades of the twentieth century there was one test that really mattered: the IQ test. It claimed to measure a

single index of your mental worth and was broadly institutionalized as such across a wide array of gatekeeping institutions. Today there are literally hundreds of distinct psychological measurement techniques (thousands depending on your definition of testing). Instead of taking one or two high-stakes IQ tests, children now take dozens of high-stakes standardized tests (hundreds depending on which state in the US you live in). Many of these new tests are just as illusory and ideological as early IQ tests, yet their sheer quantity and diversity impact and shape our lives and self-understandings. The hyper-measured self is a uniquely postmodern phenomenon I discuss more later on.

24. Busch (2011, p. 28).

25. Thinking and acting as if you are measuring something doesn't mean you *actually* are measuring that thing. Consider constructs like scholastic aptitude or GDP, which seem important, but are clearly just oversimplifications. They serve more or less as useful fictions we've agreed to tell ourselves about complex realities. These are measurement induced *demi-realities*, to draw on a term from Bhaskar. "*Demi*" means to make smaller, to half or diminish. Demi-realities are not wrong or mere illusion, but they are truncated, smaller, partial experiences of reality, often the result of ideological distortion due to oppressive social systems.

Commodity fetishism is the classic example of a demi-reality. When you buy something off the shelf in a store thousands of miles away from where it is built or grown, you come to have a very narrow and partial view of what it is you are actually buying. Interestingly enough, in a store you mostly just see the price, which is taken as a simple unidimensional measure of the value of the commodity. Everything that occurred thousands of miles away (all the people and sweat) is reduced down to a simple number. This is one of the lessons of Bhaskar's neo-Marxist views: that money creates demi-realities and distorts our sense of what is real and of what is actually valuable.

In any case, psychology as a science is particularly prone to measurement induced demi-realities. This has been especially true when psychology has served those moneyed powers interested in the reform of schools. The IQ-testing movement during the early decades of the last century is a perfect case in point. A very simplistic form of thinking about the genetic heritability of IQ created a school system largely built around this fiction. Even though there is no such thing as IQ as they defined it and claimed to measure it, IQ existed nonetheless. Your IQ was certainly very real when it kept you from entering the country at Ellis Island, or led to your sterilization in the Jim Crow South (see: Stein, 2016).

26. Kuhn (1962); Peirce (1866).

27. Brunsson & Jacobsson (2000, pp. 2-3). Also see: Busch (2011).

28. And, of course, there have always been public sector and state-run standards-based regimes and measurement infrastructures. These peaked with modernity, and have since been supplanted by non-governmental international organizations as the dominant players in large-scale standardization and measurement (Brunsson & Jacobsson, 2000).

29. See: Harvey (2005); Busch (2011). This is why London is simply not as far away from New York as it used to be. Where it once took a person, commodity, or news headline weeks to get from London to New York, it now happens in hours. Perishable foods are trucked across continents and are easier to obtain than foods grown locally; gadgets for my house are shipped across oceans and are easier and cheaper to buy than gadgets produced in my state. Wars on the other side of the globe are streamed into my living room in high-definition, but I have hundreds of channels and could just as easily watch a live soccer match in Dubai. Distant friends and family are closer than ever, as are strangers and celebrities, who are never more than a click away from being with me almost anywhere. The list goes on of the ways in which we are living in a smaller, faster, and more interconnected world than at any time in history. For more on the important idea of "time-space compression," see: Harvey (1990). Elsewhere I discuss the psychological and emotional impacts of the pseudo-omniscience that results from extreme time-space compression, especially from the instantaneous and relentless coverage of the profit-driven news media.

30. Harvey (1990).

31. Scientifically promoting efficiency in industrial production was a massive international movement led by Frederick Taylor, which involved the extensive use of measurement practices and the reorganization of the lives of workers around new objective measures. The efficiency movement was often referred to as a kind of revolution, and Taylor was often compared to Marx, even by Stalin himself. Importantly, the movement involved an ethical argument about the *justice of efficiency*. This is the idea that a "perfectly efficient system" is by definition just, because it wastes nothing and allows all to contribute to the whole. When this idea is held as the dominant institutional imperative, efficiency overrides individual autonomy in the name of administering justice for the sake of the whole and in the long run. This complex relation between efficiency and justice, and the intensive role of measurement therein, is the central theme of my (2016) book, *Social Justice and Educational Measurement: John Rawls, the History of Testing, and the Future of Education*.

32. My account is based on Easterling (2014), who positions the ISO in the context of her theory of *extrastatecraft*, or the design of transnational spaces and infrastructures

by mostly private entities and other non-state powers such as the ISO, which is a private non-governmental organization (NGO) of global reach.

33. Ahrne & Brunsson (2008).

34. Easterling (2014, pp. 171-172).

35. Easterling (2014, p. 187).

36. The OECD has reported on these "self-certifying codes of conduct," which played out in the labor and human rights violations at Apple and Nike. See: Gereffi, Garcia-Johnson, & Sasser's (2001) "The NGO-Industrial Complex."

37. See: Judith Kimerling's (2001) "International Standards in Ecuador's Amazon Oil Fields: The Privatization of Environmental Law." Quoted in Easterling (2014, p. 200).

38. I am speaking here in the strictly Wilberian (1995; 2000; 2006) sense of the term *transformation*, as a need for vertical structural transcendence and reorganization.

39. There are lots of other areas where potentially bad measures are proliferating. For example, judges are now using "predictive algorithmic sentencing," which claims to measure the likelihood of reincarceration. Using a system known as Correctional Offender Management Profiling for Alternative Sanctions, or COMPAS, a single "likelihood of reincarceration" number is given to the judge, who considers it as an aspect of sentencing (Angwin, Larson, Mattu, & Kirchner, 2016). Less scary (but still a bad sign) are the new measures of academic productivity and status (e.g., publication ranking systems) that are factored into contracts and hiring and firing. There are also metrics that determine statuses as diverse as university accreditation, hospital quality, and human rights violations. The growing global network of measurement infrastructures is vast and fascinating. See: Busch (2011); Easterling (2014).

40. Sen (1982); Philipsen (2015).

41. Bowles & Gintis (1998); Harvey (2006).

42. Eisenstein (2011).

43. This list of seven is quoted from Philipsen (2015, pp. 156-157).

44. George (2010).

45. For more on the dynamics of "fictitious capital" (or value in the form of debt, credit, and speculation) which plays a pivotal role in the boom-bust cycles of the capitalist world-economy, as well as more specifically in the most recent economic crisis of 2007, see David Harvey's (2006) *Limits to Capital*, as well as his (2011) *The Enigma of Capital*. The classic formulation of this idea can be found in Chapter 29 of Volume 3 of Marx's *Capital*. Fictitious capital is very real and is legally enforced, as are the profits made from it. However, the capital involved *is* fictitious. It is "money that is thrown into circulation as capital without any material basis in commodities or productive activity" (Harvey, 2006, p. 95). This is a kind of tradable and redeemable claim to wealth that is used despite the fact that the tangible assets represented are themselves vastly inflated in price or entirely non-existent. According to mainstream financial economics, fictitious capital is "the net present value of future cash flows." We sometimes simply talk about these kinds of economic phenomena as "speculative bubbles."

46. Esbjörn-Hargens (2010).

47. Chomsky (2004).

48. Porter (1996).

49. Duncan (1984).

50. Scott (1998).

51. Habermas (1996).

52. Buck & Villines (2007).

53. I talk more about democracy and its relation to other basic social goods in the next chapter.

54. Illich (1976); Nelkin & Tancredi (1989).

55. Foucault (1973).

56. Capra & Luisi (2014).

57. Stein (2015).

58. To avoid any misunderstanding, it should be said that humanity has *never* known

its true identity and purpose. This is not something we once knew and have forgotten, or something we lost and must now find. No doubt, certain cultures have previously been *convinced* of a particular identity and purpose for all humans, and there have been visionaries who've offered their stunning guesses at the riddle of our being. The difference now is not ignorance—we've always been ignorant—the difference is that there is now widespread knowledge of our ignorance and an unprecedented groping toward truly new answers; answers that are post-dogmatic, post-disciplinary/academic, post-conventional, and transnational/ethnic. Don't misread the recent upwelling of fundamentalist religion as a sign to the contrary. This reactive—and often violent—grasping and entrenchment of tradition is driven precisely by the now inescapable and hegemonic force of *alternative stories* about the meaning of humanity. The biggest sacrilege—and what looks to fundamentalist cultures like godlessness—is really the "storylessness" of postmodern culture, which stems in part from its (pseudo)-scientific basis; a non-foundationalist, open-ended, "choose your own adventure" worldview that glibly dismisses ancient traditions by citing the latest scientific headline, and then dismisses that headline when a newer study is released.

59. Stein (2016).

60. Ravitch (2013).

61. Gould (1996); Spring (1989).

62. Stein (2016); Hagopian (2014).

63. Stein (2016).

64. In complex societies social action is a highly coordinated affair, involving economic, legal, and political systems. This network of institutions congeals our shared *basic structures*, which set the terms of social cooperation and distribute the advantages that result from it. According to Rawls, the basic structure of a society establishes the "background justice" that conditions and shapes the lives of each member. Not every social structure is a part of the basic structure because not every institution has deep and pervasive effects on the shape of society. Basic structures are those that touch all members in some way, especially in determining their access to basic rights and goods. Rawls argues that these structures should be the primary focus of ethical frameworks concerning social justice because they set the conditions in terms of which the actions of *all* individuals, groups, and associations take place. No matter how free and fair a specific interaction between people appears to be, we cannot say it is just without understanding the broader social institutions in which it occurs. This was a lesson learned

clearly in the segregated American south, where ostensibly fair and uncoerced interactions at "separate but equal" businesses and schools were, in fact, reinforcing unjust legal structures that grossly distorted human relationships. "Thus we seem forced to start with an account of a just basic structure. It is as if the most important agreement is that which establishes the principles to govern this structure" (Rawls, 1999, p. 257). "We enter it only by birth and exit only by death.... The institutions of the basic structure have deep and long-term social effects and in fundamental ways shape citizens' character and aims, the kinds of persons they are and aspire to be" (Rawls, 1996, p. 68).

Rawls argues that fairness ought to govern the design of all basic structures. This is because basic structures are a non-negotiable precondition of life in a complex society. We do not opt into or join up with society; we are always already members of it, and will always live in terms of at least some of its basic structures. Of course, individuals can emigrate between societies, but they cannot return to a state of nature. We participate in basic structures of one type or another from the day we are born until the day we die. We participate in these structures and conduct our lives according to them, yet we did not choose them—we just happened to be born in a certain time and place. They shape our fate as if they are a part of nature, yet they are social constructions (Searle, 1995). Therefore, the arrangement of these basic structures is of special ethical concern, especially their bearing on the life prospects of individuals belonging to different groups, be those economic, generational, religious, or what have you. There are many acceptable ways to design institutions that one can freely *choose* to be a part of, such as a club (which charges for membership) or a scientific association (which excludes non-experts), but when an institution is a part of the basic structure that everyone *must* participate in, different organizational principles should be applied. According to Rawls, justice must be the dominant design principle for institutions such as legal systems, tax codes, and educational systems, which shape the very fabric of social life by structuring the terms of collaboration and the distribution of benefits.

Measurement practices were some of the first social institutions to function as basic structures and to become the subject of theories about social justice. Measurement practices exemplify what basic structures are and how they function to create the background justice of a society. Lessons from historical metrology will clarify the relation between measurement practices (as basic structures) and social justice. This sets the stage for an exploration of the ways in which educational measurement practices have many of the same social justice implications as physical ones, serving as basic structures and as a part of legal codes, as well as being implicated in the distribution of basic social goods.

65. Capra & Luisi (2014); Wilber (1995).

66. Importantly, the use of the term *paradigm* in this context is precise and appropriate,

not New Age or po-mo. As Wilber (1995) has pointed out, when Kuhn spoke of paradigms he was speaking of scientific injunctions, and often literally of measurement instruments and measurement practices. The term is widely used in a broader way to mean worldview or cultural outlook, but it is really more about the methods, equipment, and presuppositions that allow a certain form of everyday conventional science. The measures used in one paradigm are often literally non-transferable into others, which is why a reality that exists (i.e., can be detected and seen) in one does not exist in the other. Changing the very instrumentalities of scientific practice (changing the tools used to do measurement) is quite literally changing the paradigm.

67. Rose, Rouhani, & Fischer (2013).

68. Greenhall (2014).

69. Harvey (2014); Eisenstein (2011). Also see: the social miracles discussed in the next chapter. A basic income guarantee would also change the impact of money as a hegemonic measure of value.

70. Piketty (2014).

71. Nussbaum (2006); Sen (1982); Piketty (2014).

72. Beck (1992); Busch (2011).

Chapter 4
Thirteen Social Miracles: Creating Educational Abundance

I began to keep a running list of social miracles as a college student while reading Ken Wilber in conjunction with futures studies during an intense winter in western Massachusetts. The idea was simple: use the quadrants to organize the kind of scenario planning that was being done by futurists in governments and business. Scenario planning is about imagining near-future possible worlds following a principled method of grounded speculation. There are many methods one can use to paint a concrete utopian vision of alternatives to our current social realities. I was particularly interested in "black swan" scenarios, where some kind of extremely unlikely event occurs in one quadrant that sends shock waves through the rest. For example, a classic futures studies trope involves a series of medical breakthroughs that allow humans to routinely live over 200 years. This innovation in the Upper-Right quadrant has implications for the following: self-understanding in the Upper-Left ("What changes would occur in human psychology if life expectancy was 200 years?"); culture in the Lower-Left ("What meanings do family, nation, and species have, when life is centuries long?"); and social systems such as economies in the Lower-Right ("What happens to job markets when someone can hold a job for a century?").

As interesting as this is, radical life-extension technologies are not the kinds of miracles I have in mind here. I am interested instead in "social miracles," which are more cultural and political than scientific. While the majority of speculation about the future focuses on great leaps in science and technology, the futures scenarios I offer here focus instead on great leaps in human morality and political consciousness. This is an important departure from the dystopian techno-scientific futures that dominate public consciousness. From sci-fi movies to the nightly news, it is apocalyptic techno-science gone wrong, consumed by the youth in particular. Popular images of positive futures likewise hinge on new breakthroughs in techno-science. Sometimes it appears that our future is one in which humanity is either destroyed by techno-science or saved by it. In either case, as a culture we are starved for visions of the future that involve radically different political and moral innovations. We long for visions of breakthroughs in consciousness and culture.

It is important to understand that what stops humanity from living in a world of justice and abundance is not a lack of necessary technology and science. The culture of late-capitalism would have us believe that only scientific miracles will save humanity, and preferably those that will turn a profit and help maintain economic growth (so-called "disaster capitalism"). But the truth is that only social miracles will save us. What stops humanity from living in a world of justice and abundance are the stories we tell ourselves about ourselves, the rules we have made up that now govern our cooperation, and the legacies of illusion and dishonesty that continue to blind us to our actual situation as a species.

It is clear that the social miracles enumerated in this essay would catalyze the emergence of an integral paideia. They are a condition for the possibility of the next stage of human socio-cultural evolution. Less clear are the concrete next steps we need to take to make these miracles a reality. The beauty of this essay, in a way, is that it does not need to address how to bring them about—it is only tasked with dwelling in pure possibility.

Social Miracles: Human Nature and the Abundance of Learning

> …I like to call it *the more beautiful world our hearts know is possible.*
>
> —Charles Eisenstein

Because I am a philosopher of education I am often asked my ideas about what an "ideal school" is like. I used to answer these questions the best I could by sketching out plans for some impossibly amazing school system. I was usually met with the predictable: "Yes, but how do we pay for that?" Or the more interesting: "Who will employ students so unconventionally schooled?" And even the truly insightful: "Won't people educated in that way become unhappy in our society?" Indeed, my best philosophical ideas about what makes for a good education were beside the point given most people's current perceptions of what is possible. It turns out that when someone asks about the "best" or "ideal" school they are usually asking a different question, something more like: "What is the best of what is possible, given the current state of educational policy and economic realities?"

I no longer answer this question. Instead, when it is asked, I use it as an opportunity to discuss all the other social systems *surrounding* educational institutions. Other aspects of society often need to change in order for anything like an ideal educational system to exist. Instead of focusing on the design of an ideal form of schooling, I turn here to the question of *what else* needs to be in place for educational configurations to be truly ideal. Which is to say, what broader social conditions need to be in place to enable educational institutions to be at their best, impacting all students in radically positive ways, enabling self-actualization of the whole person from childhood through old age? Forget what is possible right now; what in our hearts do we want for our children and ourselves?[1]

Something fundamentally different from what we have now is usually the answer. While a privileged few have access to truly remarkable educational opportunities, the vast majority of the world languishes in a state of contrived educational scarcity. Information Age technologies were supposed to liberate all knowledge and bring education to the masses, but instead they have been hijacked by advertising firms and Big Brother. Paywalls block most academic content while intellectual property regimes are spreading to cover nearly everything, making something that is infinitely reproducible at next to no cost into something finite and expensive.[2] Educational institutions are run like gated communities, with complex passwords and customs necessary to gain entry. Only so many degrees get handed out each year at elite colleges, and statistics demonstrate that the college admissions process is one of the most intensely competitive situations in the whole of our society.[3] Putting adolescents in this position is a postmodern rite of passage, an initiation into a dog-eat-dog adulthood. We are used to a world in which education is treated as a scarce resource. It appears too often as a zero-sum game in which schooling is about job training for a job market that is increasingly unpredictable, competitive, and shrinking. Truncating educational horizons in this way destroys human potential to the point of becoming a structural injustice.[4]

Educational systems are inseparable from the cultural, social, and economic systems that surround them. This must be remembered when thinking about what an educational system ought to be like. When imagining preferable futures for educational systems we must also think through the surrounding structural constraints, the environment in which an educational system is seeking to thrive. For an educational system to thrive it must be in some balance with the other systems of society. A school system that produces manual laborers when the economy needs computer scientists is a blunt example of a failing system. But a school system that produces computer scientists when society needs computer scientists still fails in light of an integral meta-theory of education. What are the computers to be used for? What is their moral and aesthetic value? What are the cultures of the companies and households populated by computer scientists? Educational systems create cultures and personalities, even as they are the creations of cultures and personalities.

The classic question that has driven educational reform since the nineteenth century has been: "Can education change society?"[5] Evidence suggests that it can, but that change runs in both directions. Changes in society impact education, just as changes in education impact society. This is an important dynamic and involves a bi-directionality of causality which is common in the social sciences dealing in complexity.[6] What this dynamic implies is that educational reform can begin in many places, including changes in labor markets, family systems, military service requirements, and social welfare programs. It is interesting and important to think about public policy and law from the perspective of its educational impact.[7] Every policy, law, and measurement infrastructure is educative; this is clear. So it then becomes a question of how much and in what ways such seemingly non-educational structures are actually having an educational impact. Some measures and laws are directly educative, such as when a new measurement of food quality draws attention to the conditions under which the food is produced, making consumers think about their purchase. Other policies and laws are indirectly educative, such as when labor market policies that base hiring and firing on test scores create conditions that inhibit the development of cultural stability within schools; in these cases cheating undermines trust between students and teachers.[8]

A true "learning society" would not just find opportunities for learning within existing systems of law, culture, and labor markets, but create whole new systems guided by the idea of maximizing educational opportunities for lifelong learning. This is the vision I am offering here: educational abundance resulting from the repositioning of learning and human development as a dominant social value. To put it quite simply: most of our major social structures, such as labor markets and legal systems, are designed to promote economic growth—*period*.[9] What if they were designed to promote human development and learning instead? What if the goal of society—as encoded in its very legal structures—was not endless accumulation of wealth but the endless actualization of human potential?

Importantly, as I explore below, economic growth and the actualization of human potentials are related. We now depend on many forms of material abundance, made possible as a result of over four centuries of growth-oriented structures within the capitalist world-system. Capitalism, like all socio-economic systems, is also a system of human capacities. Basic structures and institutions shape the skills and dispositions of the people who work and live within them. Capitalism as a social system has shaped the face of the Earth more than any other, and has also remade the human mind and heart. It has made possible an abundance of human creativity, skill, and intelligence along certain lines, but it has also *constrained* human development along other lines. Economic factors have often dictated both what is passed on to the next generation and what resources are available for doing so. In some areas we have explored human potential magnificently, while in others we have literally suppressed exploration.[10]

I am interested in the social conditions that will enable a future of educational abundance in which the frontiers of human potential are opened wide. This chapter is an exercise in looking beyond schools toward broader opportunities for educational impact, such as macroeconomic reforms with educational provisions and entitlements, or reforms in social welfare programs that enable lifelong learning as a basic social good. The demands of social justice require the redesign of social structures in all sectors so that educational configurations can be transformed in ways that ensure all people get what they need.

I am looking beyond schools in order to re-imagine education, but I am also looking beyond the realm of what our culture tells us is possible. That is, I am looking out beyond the limits of our current stories (or meta-theories) about what human society is and can be. The set of ideas offered here are referred to as "miracles" because they appear "supernatural" to conventional consciousness. They seem impossible—almost against the laws of human nature—and it seems naive to suggest these as political ambitions. And to an extent this *is* merely an exercise or thought experiment in concrete utopian theorizing. I've discussed elsewhere the use of thought experiments in philosophy, which I believe can serve to structure and scaffold reflection.[11] I am choosing to systematically explore the implications of these social miracles as a way of peaking over into a "blue sky" vision of educational futures.[12]

In terms of integral meta-theory, every social miracle discussed is an "all-quadrant affair." Although some begin within a certain quadrant such as Lower-Right (e.g., legal structures), they initiate a cascade of changes as the ramifications play out across the other three quadrants. Most of these miracles are focused on Lower-Right structures simply because, as explained in the first two chapters, the time of global transition in which we live is a time when Lower-Right structures are exercising a disproportionate influence upon the shape of culture and personality.

Each miracle enables educational abundance and is enabled by educational abundance. These miracles are necessary if we want to see the widespread democratization of educational opportunity, and they would also be a natural consequence of this democratization. This is not a paradox; it is a dialectical tension and part of the dynamic praxis of politics and education.

Here is a list of all thirteen social miracles:

1. Debt jubilee for students (and nations)
2. Basic income guarantee
3. Integral decentralized social safety net
4. Actual democratic governments and workplaces
5. Public regulation of investment and finance sectors
6. Legal and economic systems that value the biosphere for its own sake
7. Renewable and inexhaustible energy
8. Reappropriation of the land: agriculture and geography
9. Total planetary demilitarization
10. Mutual respect between all major world religions
11. Absence of oppression based on race, gender, sexual orientation, etc.
12. Universal de-alienation and re-humanization
13. Science and technology in the interest of human flourishing and exploration

Clearly each social miracle deserves a book (or a shelf of books), yet I have put them into a single chapter. The accounts are thus brief and to the point. I can only scratch the surface here, so my goal is not to articulate a comprehensive political platform for an education-centric society, but rather to offer the first words toward such a platform. Investigating each of these miracles, as well as their cumulative and interactive effects, is intended to clarify the social conditions needed to enable the emergence of radically new educational configurations, free from the dictates of the capitalist world-system and its legacy institutions. These miracles are not going to happen tomorrow, but they nevertheless represent symbols of our shared social trajectory on this finite planet in the throes of evolutionary crisis.

1. Debt Jubilee for Students (and Nations)

In the ancient world, jubilees were known to occur once a generation or so, when leaders and priests would make a decree that abolished all debt, both economic and moral. This practice has been well-documented in archaeological and textual evidence, which suggest that it was a widespread and cross-cultural occurrence. The jubilee was a time of celebration and reconciliation, as the entire social system was basically rebooted.[13] The jubilee was a designated time in which the whole society transitioned into a radically new story about itself. Everything was turned on its head, especially the dynamic between those burdened by debt and those overseeing and profiting from its repayment.

Today we live in a world that is overrun by peonage and other forms of economic bondage.[14] Depression, anxiety, and destroyed families often result from predatory mortgages, credit cards, and educational loan practices. On a larger scale, consider the geopolitical tensions that circulate around the IMF and World Bank debt repayments; in all cases, the structures forced upon the indebted by virtue of their status are, to put it mildly, far from conducive to the realization of lifelong learning and the actualization of human potentials. When you owe a lot of money, you don't take the job you want that fits with your unique gifts; you take whatever job you can find that offers enough to pay your bills. Likewise, if you occupy a position in the government of a country that owes a lot of money to the IMF, you do not pursue economic policies coherent with what the region's people are seeking, nor do you allow for the emergence of social welfare programs that put human welfare above profit; instead you implement policies that maximize the revenues available for debt repayment.[15]

An honest view of the global economic situation suggests that we must "reboot" this whole system of economic inequality and injustice. We need changes at the personal scale (e.g., educational debt, medical debt, mortgages, credit cards, etc.) and also at the national and international scale, as North/South inequality has become almost irreversibly encoded in structures of debt relations.

Needless to say, such a global jubilee seems impossible. And it is impossible according to the current ways of understanding human nature and social reality. Nevertheless there are currently several projects that are aiming to initiate jubilees of debt forgiveness on multiple scales. One initiative known as "the rolling jubilee" has been working to buy debt, which is traded in the financial sector at pennies on the dollar, and then is simply expunged from the record, making it disappear. These efforts have so far focused on medical debts and student loans debts, the idea being that nobody should have to go into debt because they got sick or sought out higher education.[16]

Student loan debt in the United States alone constitutes one of the largest speculative bubbles in modern times. Currently, the total student loan debt is estimated to be approximately $1.4 trillion and growing daily (close to $3,000 per second by some estimates). The average individual owes over $37,000, but a growing percentage owe over $150,000. The average monthly payment is $393, but ranges up to over $1,000 for some private loans and/or combinations of loans across multiple financial service providers. Student loans are paid off over an average of 20 years, with many only finally being settled in old age, if ever. Approximately 5 million federal student loan debtors are in default, a number that is also growing daily. At any scale this is a lot of money. More disturbingly, at the rate things are going it appears that much of the educational debt currently owed will never be repaid. A loan is taken out to get certain skills, which then lead to a job providing reimbursements insufficient to repay that loan. This pattern is systemic. This is why I called the student debt situation a speculative bubble. All parties are banking on the diploma being worth a certain amount on the labor market, but often it is not.

Understand also that many schools and colleges are themselves in various forms of debt. The same financial institutions loaning to schools that want to build new classrooms are also loaning to students who want to fill those new classrooms. The schools take the student loan money and use it to pay off debt, essentially paying the bank back with the bank's own money. At the end of the day it is the students who are paying interest for decades after graduation, essentially footing the bill for the whole operation. This is similar in structure to the speculative real estate bubble that contributed to sinking the US economy in 2007–2008. In that case it was the same banks financing developers to build houses that also financed the mortgages of people who wanted to live in those houses. These schemes all work fine until one of the parties fails to come through, which is inevitable. It is usually the person taking out the mortgage or the student loan who pays the price when the spreadsheets need to balance out.[17]

The point here concerns the broad injustice and inefficiency of running a debt-based system of education, which requires that vast populations take on personal debt to gain access to basic educational goods. Thoughts of future debt payments influence how students choose their major and then their job, and prospects of taking on more debt limits access to graduate school.[18] Those who attend school do so knowing that the cost is perpetual indebtedness. This encodes a monetary logic into the educational experience, which I have called the logic of the *education commodity proposition.*[19]

The logic of the education commodity proposition is simple. If money is scarce, and education costs money, then I start to think about education in terms of money, which reduces education to a commodity. The classic example is: *how much education are we getting for our tax dollars?* This question has driven the implementation of vast standardized testing regimes intended to measure and monetize *how much.* Student loans force us to consider the relative economic and quantitative worth of diplomas from various schools in various fields. This is not the place to linger on the education commodity proposition (see endnote 19), except to say that it is exactly what Socrates warned about long ago in Athens. The Sophists sold education to the highest bidder, and then would tell the children of the ruling oligarchs exactly what they wanted to hear.

The role of student-as-consumer undermines the role of student-as-learner. When a consumer has taken out a loan to make their purchase, they tend to be quite concerned about their return on investment and will pull "the customer is always right" card.[20] Where the *consumer* is always right, the *learner* is actually interested in being proven wrong and in benefiting from that experience. Freeing students from a debt-based system of education would free them to be learners again, instead of consumers caught up in the calculating logic of self-interest. A future free from student loan debt would be a future in which there was a great deal less economic exploitation and a great deal more learning and self-actualization. Establishing a basic income guarantee would take this one step further and radically remove money from its perverse place at the center of our personal and collective lives.

2. Basic Income Guarantee

Every person has a basic right to live, regardless of the economic value they contribute to society. The idea here is of *a system of unconditional income to every person*. Each individual gets the same monthly payment that is adjusted to some democratically agreed upon standard of living. They can spend it how they will, and if they want more they are free to work for it. Ideas like this were important for national policy thinking in the United States and around the world as early as the 1970s. They disappeared for a few decades, but are now back on the agendas of many governments. However, to date there has never been a widespread implementation of a basic income guarantee, although there are visible and important political movements working toward it in some countries today.

For some of the best work in this area today, see the writings of Scott Santens, especially the book, *Basic Income Guarantee*, which reviews over 80 years of debates on the issue and clarifies a series of realistic proposals. Of course, the big question here is the same as with the proposed jubilee and the integral social safety net discussed next: how can we afford it? Despite the protestations of mainstream economic thinking, the problem is not affordability; the problem is a lack of imagination. As Santens explains it, a basic income guarantee is more than affordable; it makes good economic sense:

> Because inequality has reached such extreme degrees, and because we already spend so much money on existing government programs no longer necessary with a basic income for all, the required price tag is not an income tax increase of 60 percent. It's not even an income tax increase of 35 percent or 25 percent. It's a potential income tax increase of under 20 percent. And because a very small amount of people have an almost unimaginable amount of money at the very top, a basic income could actually decrease almost everyone else's income tax burdens except for theirs. Keeping in mind our present level of inequality and its negative effects on economic growth, this is actually even exactly what the richest should want, because although they would pay more in taxes for

> universal basic income, leaving them a slightly thinner although still very thick slice of the overall pie, the slice of the pie itself would grow, leaving even them better off as well. This is largely due to economic multiplier effects where $1 given to those with lower incomes has three times the growth effects on GDP as giving the same $1 to those who already have a great many dollars. Meanwhile, as if all of the above isn't enough to show how affordable a $1,000 per month universal basic income actually is, it's vital we understand just how much less we can spend as a society, simply by preventing all the costs of poverty that we'd never have to pay in the first place anymore. And if we also care about what we're going to do about all the jobs technology stands to eliminate in the years ahead, we should definitely care about figuring out how we can all be better off in an economy that actually works better with fewer jobs instead of worse off in an economy that's fundamentally broken. It's disappointing all of this economic complexity in regards to the affordability of basic income is nowhere to be found within [mainstream economics]. For this is a discussion we need to be having, and not one to be so easily dismissed as too expensive. Instead, we should consider the distinct possibility that continuing on without basic income is what potentially carries the highest price tag of all.[21]

Providing an income guarantee would have profound effects on the nature of the economy, the process of human development, and the structure of social relations. Imagine growing up and thinking about your future without worrying about the *need* to make a living. Imagine building a cooperative venture with a dynamic team of individuals without having to worry if the work you do will be able to turn enough of a profit to support you all. For most people today, the scarcity of money is a barrier to the actualization of their most important potentials (of course, too much money can also be a barrier). We distort our unique gifts into the shape of the job *we need* instead of being freed to find or create the job that *needs us*. Similarly, a scarcity of money is a barrier to the formation of truly cooperative enterprises and local decentralized forms of schooling. We distort intergenerational relationships in order to make time more profitable. We can't build the educational institutions we know we need because they have to be profitable in the traditional sense.

At the deepest level, such an income guarantee sends a message to every person that life is a gift and a right. Sustaining your own life is not something you should need to fight for or come into an oppressive and exploitative wage-labor relationship to accomplish. Think about the fact that we are the only species in the biosphere cut off from unmediated access to the food and shelter we need to survive. Yes, animals have to "work" for their food, but they don't have to participate in an exploitive wage labor system. Modern humans are the only animals that have to make and use money in order to get what they need to survive. And money does not grow on trees. Unless you are somehow otherwise cared for, if you do not join the wage labor system, you do not eat. This connection between money and basic survival gives money and paid work a remarkable existential power, and explains to some extent why money can come to be confused with life and value itself. A basic income guarantee would sever this existential connection between money and life by providing a basic kind of social abundance that says to everyone, "you have *a right* to exist; you don't have to earn it."

Think also about the ceaseless progress being made in the automation of so many jobs due to advancements in robotics; there will increasingly be systemic technological causes of unemployment and underemployment. Widespread automation is already putting machines in place of humans doing many of today's jobs, such as harvesting, food service, retail, and manufacturing. This frees humans from what is often dull and dehumanizing labor. But it also "frees" millions from their livelihoods. A basic income guarantee (in conjunction with the other miracles outlined here) could turn this process of advanced automation into a edu-tech-utopia, where instead of doing dull jobs that are not rewarding, individuals have the freedom to explore other aspect of their personalities, unique gifts, and interests. Education could then surpass employment as the dominant category of social life. Again, fundamentally "rebooting" our economy is an essential condition for liberating educational abundance.

3. Integral Decentralized Social Safety Net

Following the jubilee and a basic income guarantee naturally comes the idea of a general social safety net, especially free *quality* health care and free *quality* education through graduate school. This has been on many political agendas since the end of WWII, but its implementation has been geographically uneven. When and where there have been moves to implement these systems there have remained major concerns about the meaning of the term "quality." Of course, the word "free" is important, but it is easier to see what "free" means when you go to the doctor than to know what it means to have "quality" treatment.

Roughly speaking, an education guided by integral meta-theory would be *quality* education—one that is good, true, and beautiful. Beyond just providing universal education, there is a need to institute the right kind of education in the right kind of way. The same applies for all other institutions of the integral safety net. As Foucault, Habermas, and others demonstrated in their critiques of the welfare state, when governments build huge bureaucracies to handle education, health, and other social entitlements, they are too often alienating, inefficient, and infantilizing. Instead of the "one-size-fits-all" dependency-inducing welfare state, the integral social safety net must be engineered to emerge from a complex orchestration of decentralized cooperative hubs, such as the kinds I discuss in the first chapter. It cannot be a top-down system, out of touch with those being helped, and run by some centralized bureaucracy.

It cannot be stressed enough that an integral social safety net must *not* be modeled on the social welfare state of the Old Left, nor on the market-based service industries of the New Right. The idea here is to empower local communities in ways that increase freedom, choice, and innovation (the best of a market-based system), while also assuring that these are available to *everyone* through fair channels of distribution (the best of the state-based solutions). This means transforming things like education and health care into abundant and "non-rivalrous" goods, creating systems in which more education or health for me does not mean less education and health for you. Creating this kind of abundance of basic social goods will require a large-scale reorganization of the entire economic system (hence the basic income guarantee and the jubilee already discussed). The issue of providing this kind of community-based universal support for all people, regardless of gender, ability, or race, is one of the great social justice issues of the twenty-first century, especially in the Global South.[22]

The entitlements provided by an integral social safety net should be understood as a condition for the possibility of the widespread emergence of educational abundance. Said another way: lack of access to basic health care, sanitation, and safety can explain a great deal of the continued widespread under-actualization of human potential globally. We are squandering human potential because we simply have not built enough structures of mutual support and cooperative aid. In a world of almost unimaginable wealth and resources, only a privileged few are in a position to truly benefit. How can people even begin to reflect on the nature of their gifts, talents, and social visions—how can they even begin to self-consciously educate themselves and their communities—when they are suffering and dying from simple diseases and are unable to read or write?

Like the basic income guarantee, an integral social safety net institutionalizes the ethical principle that everyone has a right to live and develop free from oppression and deprivation. Social justice demands that the conditions of the least well-off in society be taken as the main index of social health and well-being.[23] The situations of the least well-off must be elevated above the inhuman, disposable, and untouchable, where so many now languish. Today the pain of these injustices can be felt reverberating throughout the lifeworld, poisoning even the once pristine opulence of the most privileged and empowered. Each and every human has a right to flourish and must be provided with the basic assurances and resources that make it possible for them to do so.

4. Democratic Governments, Workplaces, and Schools

Even with the aforementioned social miracles accomplished we would still need to find ways to come together in places of production, cooperation, and mutual endeavoring. We will always need to find ways to accomplish the functions performed by governments and corporations, including infrastructure maintenance, security and policing, distribution of goods and services, assurance of measures and standards, and countless other operations that require large-scale formalized systems of cooperation over time and space. Educational systems are tied into all other social systems, while each is also caught up in the dynamics of our broader planetary transformation. Today the most common forms of organization and governance are in crisis. Many democracies around the world (but especially in the United States) have largely devolved into dysfunctional oligarchies. Public participation has regressed into the viewing of carefully crafted political spectacles, which are followed by voting—a process akin to watching advertising and then going out to make a purchase. And, of course, there are still countless millions living in societies that are radically non-democratic and openly opposed to the principles of democratic governance. These regimes range from totalitarian dictatorships to fundamentalist theocracies, creating geopolitical pockets of unspeakable suffering and appalling ignorance.

Needless to say, non-democratic forms of governance are antithetical to the emergence of educational abundance. They squelch human potential. Indeed, from the perspective of an *educative democracy*,[24] most of what passes for democracy today (spectatorship and voting) is inadequate. The governance structure conducive to an education-centric society is what Habermas has called *deliberative democracy*,[25] which I have already discussed in the previous chapter. This is a form of governance in which each individual offers their voice, not just their vote. The goal is to institutionalize processes for consensus-making through structured and deliberative engagement and discourse. This is democracy beyond the forced choice of voting. There is obviously more to say about this than space allows, and of course, technological and cultural structures would need to be established to radicalize democracy in this way. The point here is that nothing short of this form of governance will allow for the possibility of educational abundance. Nothing short of true democracy can ensure the realization of human potential.

Deliberative and educative forms of democracy must be spread throughout all sectors of society. Today, while many governments declare themselves to be democracies (even if they are not quite living up to that ideal), almost all workplaces and corporations are run according to explicitly authoritarian governance structures (although they would never call them that, of course). Employees in most companies have no input in the formulation of polices that impact their lives, often in substantial ways. Employees can usually be fired and disciplined without due process.

Make no mistake: we are not talking about unionization. A labor union can be as undemocratic and self-interested as any corporation. In many cases, this is why unions call for higher wages in exchange for the rights of workers to control their work environment, as well as the structure of their tasks, rhythms, and specializations (i.e., taking money in exchange for autonomy and control over the conditions of one's own labor). Allowing educative democracy to flourish means creating ways for each individual to participate in the governance of the organization. Again, democratic participation should not be thought of in terms of spectating/voting, but in terms of a deliberative and participative co-creating of organizational structures and cultures.

John Dewey used to argue that true democracy is intrinsically educational because it is a process that seeks a continued opening into new experience and learning. Our current democracies are at their best when they spark reasonable and reflective discourse. Beyond spectatorship and sportsman-like jeering, people can come together in ways such that their words matter and they have the power to decide what is best for their lives and communities. In a true democracy the organization of collective life itself becomes a form of education, and educational abundance emerges from the very fabric of human self-government.

5. Public Regulation of Investment and Finance Sectors

Just as we will always need to perform many of the functions performed by governments today, so we will always need a credit system or some other way to create currencies and to fund educational organizations. Although many things would change with guaranteed income, we would still need to invest in ventures that take time and are capital intensive, such as building and maintaining a system of roads, or opening a store or school. Related to the need for a radical democratization of governance and workplaces is the need for transparent public oversight of investment and finance.

First and foremost would be a drastic reining-in of the speculative and destructive markets for "fictitious capital" that have become the main activities of Wall Street and other global financial centers. As recent history attests, recklessness and lawlessness in the world's financial centers can set the entire global economy into crisis. There is no true or unique social need being met by these endeavors to expand and complexify financial markets and transactions. These are activities undertaken simply to produce profits for a small number of individuals. Banks should serve the people and create value only insofar as they enable the expression of human potentials through the extension of credit and the facilitation of value transactions. Banks do not need to be (and have not always been) profit centers, and could instead be cooperative credit unions that are mainly centers of accounting and transaction.

Be it loans, venture capital, or philanthropy, where money is lent, invested, or donated there arises a new future and a new way of life. Today this idea is embodied in the heroic ideal of the entrepreneur who has a vision, finds investors that believe in his ability to accomplish it, and then changes the world (hopefully for the better), often while getting rich in the process. Our society has been transformed by such heroic entrepreneurs—from food to computers, cars to entertainment. Our lives are touched every day by commodities and services that began as a dream in someone's garage. One essential dimension of our response to global crises will be finding ways to ensure creative and timely eruptions of ingenuity and personal initiative. All of the economically-oriented social miracles being suggested here are aimed at the goal of unleashing creativity, uniqueness, and cooperative initiatives. Anyone who thinks that being liberated from debt and provided with an income guarantee would make people lazy and disincentivize work does not understand human nature. Freed from work as a necessity, we would all be in a position to take up work as a vocation and carve out a unique path for ourselves. Entrepreneurial energies would be everywhere.

Look beneath the surface of today's entrepreneurial energies, into who gets money to fund which projects. You will find that of the countless numbers of possible investments, the vast majority are limited to those that are deemed "profitable" along a very narrowly defined set of financial parameters. Try to get a bank or venture capitalist to finance an idea that is wonderful for the world but will never turn a profit and you'll see just how stark a reality this is. Unfortunately, educational organizations often fit this mold. The dominant motive guiding the investment of surplus money is the creation of more surplus money. Interest-earning loans and investments that require returns are the mechanisms by which capital grows simply by virtue of having been hoarded by some and needed by others. In this context, not using profits to create more profits is considered "throwing money away." Or it is considered philanthropy.

Giving away money is admirable and has done the world an enormous amount of good.[26] But philanthropy is only true to its name (*philo* = love, *antho* = human) when it is done in the spirit of the gift and in the service of educational abundance. This means that money is used in ways beholden to the values of those most impacted by the gift. Some admirable individuals have truly embraced these forms of "good-hearted" philanthropy. Yet even if we (generously) assume that the wealthiest among us are all engaged in good-hearted philanthropy, the fact remains that a very small number of people are deciding what to do with the overwhelming majority of the world's money. Good-hearted philanthropy or not, unilateral decisions are being made by an economic elite that impact our lives in innumerable ways. Individuals are wielding democratically unaccountable power on a vast scale and shaping the lives of countless millions whose voices are never heard. Indeed, those most often helped by philanthropic causes are the least empowered to take control of their lives (e.g., children, the poor, those at risk, and the disenfranchised of the developing world). While the services and goods provided are often essential and helpful in the short-term, the model is too often one based on separation and alienation —not cooperation, unity, and empowerment.

The philanthropic energies surrounding school reforms in the United States are a perfect case in point. Three major philanthropies stemming from *private* companies dominate the educational reform landscape of the *public* school system. Their power has had such an impact (e.g., shaping federal policy and the composition of university education faculty) that there has been vocal criticism of the "Billionaire Boys Club," even from formerly conservative education leaders.[27] Why do such a small number of very wealthy people get to shape the future of a *public* institution in a democracy? Put aside the fact that the foundations in question are all tied to huge corporations, and it could be argued that they are reforming schools so as to produce future generations of predictable employees and consumers. This would be in keeping with the history of educational reform in the US, where the philanthropic initiatives of the capitalist class have always remade education in their own interests.[28]

But let us assume that today's billionaires are not misusing their influence and are doing good-hearted philanthropy. Even then, they still have too much unaccountable power for a truly democratic society to accept. Thousands of teachers and millions of students have no voice in shaping the future of their own schools, while a few individuals with a lot of money (and often zero background in education) are able to change the face of the entire school system.

Imagine a social miracle wherein humanity has democratized decision-making about the reinvestment of all surplus social value. That is, imagine if all the surplus money went into a common, publicly controlled fund that was essentially used like a vast Kickstarter platform, where projects of all sizes would be funded through the democratically determined allocation of society's surplus resources. The realities surrounding the democratization of investment and radically cooperative banking raise complex technological and legal problems which are beyond the scope of this discussion. The idea here is simply to suggest that for money to go where it really needs to go—to create a world of educational abundance—there may be no better way than to open up investment decisions to "street level" voices. Let the teachers and students have an essential voice in determining the directions of school reform. Let local populations be involved in decisions about the relief work and infrastructure development that so greatly impact their day-to-day lives.

This is doubly necessary in the context of the planetary meta-crisis that is the focus of this book, where unprecedented and ethically complex situations are emerging in rapid succession all over the world. Each requires a unique response, usually involving new ways of liberating the creative energies of those on the ground. To face these kinds of dynamic challenges, we need a radically new way to think about investment and how we can create new worlds through the allocation of money and other forms of currency. Educational abundance can be enabled by freeing up the circulation of capital, which should be unleashed from its ties to the moneyed-elite and sent coursing through self-organizing educational configurations. Only by making use of a radically new means for redistribution of the total social surplus can we enable the spontaneous and sustainable formation of networks of educational hubs, as outlined in Chapter 1. Money is important, and changing the way we create, use, and conceive it is part of what we must do to make sure there will be a livable planet for future generations to be educated upon.

6. Legal and Economic Systems That Value the Biosphere for Its Own Sake

All of these economic and social miracles can occur even as the Earth and biosphere continue to be destroyed. Even if we address economic injustice at its root, all will be for nothing so long as we continue to relate to the natural world as if it were an inexhaustible resource for human consumption. In a sense this is *the* focus point of the planetary transformation underway: our dawning awareness of just how fragile and precarious our existence on Earth is. This precariousness is due in part to our misuse and exploitation of the biosphere.

For decades humanity was mostly ignorant of the widespread extinctions going on around us. However, as consciousness of these ecological tragedies has risen, we are now serving as real-time witnesses to increasingly tragic forms of ecological devastation. Environmental issues are on a lot of minds, which was not the case just 40 years ago. But even with ecological consciousness raised for some, nothing short of a radical society-wide reorientation in our relation to the biosphere will be enough to accomplish the profound changes necessary for humanity's survival in the coming decades. Changing our worldview vis-à-vis the biosphere—ideally in such a way as to problematize the duality of humanity/biosphere itself—is one of the central educational issues of our time. Ecological realities framed by complexity science will be a major focus in the curriculum and thematic content of tomorrow's educational systems, even if only because we will need to better understand the dynamics of the biosphere in order to survive.

We must become that evolutionarily unprecedented species that consciously seeks to preserve all other species. We must find ways to save what is left and to be stewards of the emergence and continuation of all future life. This requires *laws and infrastructures that value the natural world in a non-instrumental way*. We must all come to see (as many ancient and indigenous cultures did and do) that nature is more than what it can do for us. It is intrinsically valuable, complex and autonomous. It has its own non-human forms of consciousness and interiority, its own non-human purposes, values, and social processes. It is worthy of a deep respect and reverence beyond its instrumental value. We are one with nature—literally intertwined with and constituted by nature—and therefore what we do to nature we do to ourselves.

To put it bluntly: respecting the biosphere in this way will not be profitable in the traditional sense of the word.[29] Despite the continued "green-washing" of status quo business models, there is no way to make a profit in any traditional sense by capitalizing on what needs to be done to transform humanity's relation to the biosphere. For example, the preservation of large tracts of land and the dismantling of entire industries is not business as usual. Educating children into anti-consumerist lifestyles and ecological awareness is also not good for business as usual (imagine if a whole generation *really* did not buy things that were bad for the environment). As the discussion of finance above suggests, it is hard to raise money for ventures that will not turn a monetary profit, let alone ones that literally depend on *gifting* (as in the donation of land to conservation). The desire to create "green jobs" on the model of regular jobs too often requires that "green businesses" be run like status quo capitalist enterprises, thus creating their own externalities and narrowing their focus from delivering value and benefit to growing the market share and increasing revenues. To make the changes necessary to give the biosphere the respect and autonomy it deserves, we need to radically change the ways we think about, measure, and value the natural world. Instead of its utility, we must come to value the natural world for its beauty, uniqueness, and our sacred interconnectedness with it. But how does one "account" for these kinds of values in the context of community policy? How do we include the immeasurable and invaluable in legal and economic systems? Said another way: how does one structure a cooperative enterprise dedicated to ecological health so that it can be sustained in its mission despite its focus on *non-monetizable forms of value creation*? The answer involves the creation of legal and economic systems that place an intrinsic value on the natural world, granting it rights, and providing innovative accounting and measurement systems to track and monitor human impacts.

Note that the idea here is not to "save" the biosphere in order to save humanity, which is an understandable but problematic view of the situation. The idea that we must seek total instrumental control over the biosphere to ensure our own survival will soon emerge as a part of arguments for large-scale geo-engineering projects. As planetary crises deepen and spread, techno-optimists will increasingly argue that we should begin re-engineering the biosphere, finding ways to use technology and science to control things like weather, biodiversity, and atmospheric composition. These ideas stem from the species-wide identity crisis accompanying the planetary transition currently underway. The very real *uniqueness* of humanity in nature has long been mistaken as a sign that we are *separate* from the rest of nature.[30] As a result of this confusion we have acted as if the whole biosphere exists for our benefit. Moreover, we have recently come to believe that through technology we might somehow control the whole of nature, engineering it to ensure its continued support for us. Explaining it this way clarifies the illusions and confusions behind ecological strategies based on furthering the technological control of nature. How can humanity, which is utterly dependent on the *gifts* of nature, ever aspire to become responsible for the existence of those very gifts? How can a single strand in the web of life ever expect to be responsible for the whole? Granted we are a very complex and deeply conscious aspect of nature, but we are still *a part* of nature. Seeking total control over the natural world is an *insane* way to think about humanity's role as a member of the biospheric community. And yet we have long been educating children into this view of our relationship to the natural world.

Sanity requires that we recognize the reality of our interconnectedness with nature, as well as the intrinsic value of the biosphere itself. This means pursuing strategies of deepening connection and respect. We must learn to *cooperate* with nature, not control it. This means we must set out to build technologies and practices that mimic, participate in, and optimize ongoing natural processes, rather than seeking to change, undermine, or instrumentalize them. Doing this especially involves the creation of legal and economic systems that foster stewardship and preservation, not exploitation and control. Humanity's future is inextricably tied into the future of the biosphere. We must embrace our unique role, not as the master of nature, but as partner, descendant, kin, and lover. Without this as a given, educational abundance is impossible.[31]

7. Renewable and Inexhaustible Energy

Clearly related to the ecological issues discussed above are the issues involved with the so-called "energy crisis." We are so mired in political and economic conflict about the future of energy that the idea of a world run by clean, renewable, and inexhaustible energy seems like an impossible dream. In fact, it is just as possible as any of the other miracles listed here, if not more so. And like the other miracles, it depends less on technological innovations than on innovations in our culture and the ways we understand ourselves and our most important values and purposes. Many of the necessary inventions and alternatives already exist, a fact widely known and lamented by advocates of alternative energies for decades. The problem is not technological as much as it is political and economic; like the above discussion about debt and income, we are looking at the monopolization of essential resources by a small few. Energy is made scarce and expensive because production and access is controlled by huge corporations seeking large profits. Energy is not naturally scarce, as some things are (such as oil and diamonds).[32] Alternative technologies have been systematically sidelined and shelved in order to secure the continuation of status quo perceptions of scarcity.

Even if we were to put aside arguments about peak oil and the ecological damages that result from the consumption of fossil fuels, there are strong ethical and political arguments for the decentralization and technological disruption of our major global energy regimes. Centralized energy distribution involves the continued construction and maintenance of massive infrastructure projects (e.g., dams, power plants, power lines, and pipelines) which displace individuals and unevenly distribute the social impacts of energy infrastructure (e.g., the poor and disadvantaged are more likely to live next to power lines, downwind from coal burning power plants, etc.). Current energy regimes also create profoundly dangerous geopolitical tensions, which center around who has access to the precious few places on the globe where fossil fuel extraction is possible. As perceptions of crises surrounding conventional forms of energy deepen, these geopolitical tensions will become increasingly problematic and could threaten to undo the fragile peace that exists between the world's military powers.

Most profoundly, however, the centralized and profit-driven energy regimes of today radically disempower individuals and communities, often robbing them of any possibility for actualizing and sustaining educational abundance. We find ourselves at the mercy of vast and unaccountable systems in order to do such basic things as heat our schools, travel, cook, and communicate electronically—just to mention a few of the countless ways our lives and dreams require energy. Our access to energy shapes the ways in which we understand what is possible for ourselves and our communities. In some places, it has even been made illegal to "get off the grid." While energy independence and self-sufficiency are touted as goals for nation-states, the individual citizens within those states are made increasingly dependent on outdated and exploitative modes of energy distribution. Every day, people are forced to be on the receiving end of an energy system that is massively complex and resource intensive, and which is becoming more precarious by the day.

This would be an unfortunate but unavoidable situation if energy were truly scarce and difficult to produce, as it appears to be today. But the truth is that energy scarcity is a myth, just like the myth of educational scarcity. There is an overwhelming abundance of energy throughout the universe and here on Earth; from the sun, wind, and waves, to the as yet untapped energy thought to be stored in the very matrix of space-time itself (sometimes called zero-point energy). The problem is not a scarcity of energy; the problem is the politically generated scarcity of *access* to energy.

Because energy seems so scarce, many children and adults are educated into a worldview in which using *less* energy is a moral good. The idea that humanity's future will need to require less energy, and that we must seek to conserve and cut back on energy use, stems from our misunderstanding of energy as scarce. As the crises of planetization spread and new technologies for energy proliferate, we will come to see that the real question is not how we can ration out finite amounts of energy, but rather how we can best use and distribute *infinite* amounts of energy. Like the aforementioned reorientations of humanity's relationship to money and nature, when we change the way we think about energy a great deal else changes. First and foremost, the way that decisions are made would change from a mentality based on scarcity to one based on abundance. Social justice, educational abundance, and the liberation of human potentials would take precedence over efficiency and profit as the ideals governing the construction of energy infrastructures. This would result in a future where energy is localized and radically decentralized based on a wide variety of universally available technologies that generate renewable and clean electricity. There are possible futures in which energy is localized to the level of the household, where there is simply no need to encircle the world with electrical cables. Imagine providing every individual with the technologies they need to create enough free and clean energy to power their home, grow a business, and travel.[33] This is literally a condition that *empowers* the growth of decentralized educational organizations, and makes possible a kind of world-transforming educational revolution resulting from innovations in the geographical organization of human societies. An energy miracle allows for radically new ways of thinking about how we organize ourselves across the face of the planet, birthing new possibilities for de-urbanization and re-urbanization, new forms of regionalism, and new practices in agriculture and cooperative co-habitation and learning.

8. Reappropriation of the Land: Agriculture and Geography

While there may be an infinite amount of energy available to us, there is not an infinite amount of land. The Earth only has so much space, and more specifically, only so much habitable land and arable soil.[34] This fact is a very important aspect of the current planetary transformation, as we are reaching the limits of how we have managed and partitioned the land. To put it simply, we are running out of land to farm. This is due in large part to the way we are currently making use of what we have.

Agricultural practices cover almost half the surface of the Earth, and yet we still have food shortages and places where starvation is all too common. As discussed above with regard to energy, the sheer scale and centralization of large agribusiness has created a food system so complex and wasteful that it is straining to stay viable. As weather patterns continue to increasingly "disobey" our civilization's expectations, it will become clear that the current food system is rigid and not adaptable. Those looking to technological fixes in genetic engineering and supersized industrialized farms are pursuing a strategy of separation and control that will ultimately fail. As explored above, the strategies that respond with sanity to the planetary crises will not seek total control over nature, but rather seek to facilitate the emergence of a cooperative and complex symbiotic relationship between humanity and the natural world, which includes agriculture.

The arable land must be given back to the people and we must each know again what it is to grow, process, learn about, and live within our local food system. The once widespread practice of personal farming and intimacy with the sources of one's food seems almost impossible to imagine because of our current relationships to food. And yet there is abundant proof that permaculture practices and local food systems could replace the current centralized and commoditized food industry.[35] Moreover, schools that include gardens and experiences with farms have been shown to benefit students from all walks of life in profound ways.[36] We must reconnect the people with the means to obtain their own subsistence and break the ties between the availability of food and the wage labor and monetary system. This radical redesign of agricultural land use is part of a more universal reappropriation of the land.

Humanity does more with land than just grow food. There are nearly 200 countries on the globe, each marking off a distinct piece of land within its borders. The Earth is thus etched with a complex system of imaginary lines. These lines do not exist in nature; they are only as real as the political stories we tell about them. Importantly, distributions of arable agricultural land are not evenly spread across each region, nor are other crucial necessities of life such as water. In the coming years profoundly important events for humanity will unfold at the intersection of our future of food systems (including water) and these imaginary lines we call borders. As researchers have documented for decades, modern famines are political events, not natural disasters.[37]

Border formations have proliferated during the last century, as have disputes about what regions of land belong to which people. Virtually *all* of the borders and claims to land ownership that now exist can be traced back to some kind of theft, violence, or war. The actual use and ownership of the land has mainly been directed by private enterprises, as large corporations and their networks of suppliers have shaped whole cities and regions more than most governments ever dreamed possible. Urbanization is as important as any other major trend shaping the planet during the last hundred years and is deeply implicated in the dynamics of the planetary transition. Billions of human lives are profoundly shaped by the cities they live in, and yet who shapes these cities? Today a small number of real estate and industrial developers work with city governments to transform tomorrow's landscapes, skylines, and highways.[38] In China new cities are being designed and built within months, the way that suburban tract housing is built throughout the US. Just as cookie-cutter houses are no place to raise a unique child or build a unique community, cookie-cutter postmodern cityscapes are antithetical to educational abundance and the realization of diverse forms of human potential. Social justice would be served by democratizing the development of all future geographies, especially urban development and housing. And it starts with simply blowing clean the lines in the sand; along with the global debt jubilee would come a radical redrawing of our borders.

Borders are also deeply related to the history of modern schooling. School systems as we know them are an invention of the modern nation state and have been deeply etched by the legacies of nationalism and related forms of militarism and industrialism. Without the ideologies of modern nationalism it is unlikely we would have the kinds of large-scale public school systems we see today. As nation-states are now succumbing to crises of legitimacy, subsumed in global trade agreements and criss-crossed by corporations beholden to no state, the shape of a "post-national constellation" is coming into view.[39] What are the educational systems that are likely to thrive in the post-national era of planetary culture? This question hinges on the future of borders, which impact who can travel where, have access to which resources, and claim which rights and freedoms.

For what reasons should we have any borders? Why mark off regions for governance and separations between peoples? When Habermas writes about the emergence of a "post-national constellation," he does not imagine a world without differentiations or even a world without nations. Beyond our current borders are better and truer ones, arrangements of the land that facilitate improvements in regional governance as well as economic and cultural health. These new borders would not be the legacy of blood and exploitation, imperialism, and colonial oppression, but instantiations of functional differentiations and specializations between geographical regions, which emerge from the uniqueness of specific places and people.

Lewis Mumford and others involved in the post-war re-imagining of American urban centers saw the need for regional federations of cities, which grouped populations in ways that were often at odds with the political and arbitrary groupings of states. For example, the Connecticut River Valley supports a system of urban and agricultural centers that currently requires complex infrastructural and commercial integrations across four state borders (Vermont, New Hampshire, Massachusetts, and Connecticut). Mumford proposed that this geographically unique region would function better as a relatively autonomous political and economic unity, and that similar regional units should be formed in other regions and contiguous urban corridors. His idea was that the land itself yields unique culture and opportunities for cooperative ventures, but it must be optimally organized and justly administered and measured. How would the Earth be divided if social justice and the flourishing of educational abundance were the main goals for marking differentiation between regions?

With this kind of post-national regionalism comes the possibility for education systems with new purposes serving new populations. There are cultures, economies, and ecosystems that are alive and relevant to students, and they are often not those that have historically been the focus of nationalistic textbooks and curricula. Beyond nationalism is *cosmopolitan localism.*[40]

This is an educational approach capable of integrating the universal values of a global humanity with the particular histories and regional needs held by self-organizing communities of various scales. This would be an educational system grounded well enough in the local region to route students through local apprenticeships, while also being globally networked to educational opportunities in distant regions. The curriculum would be of planetary scope while also grounded in ongoing and detailed investigations of what is right around the corner at the local pond or park.

But first we must stop and roll back the new imperialism of late capitalism's post-colonial appropriation of the great wilderness areas of Africa and South America. Unknown to most, multinational corporations are currently buying massive tracts of land on these continents, amounting to many tens of thousands of square miles.[41] This social miracle would be realized when all governments cede all land back to the people, remortgage all property, and re-examine all ownership rights and land use contracts. In the great global commons to come it may be that the most important borders are those that mark the territories into which we do not roam, where nature has been left to regenerate and evolve beyond our watchful eye. With basic geographical justice and efficiency established, we could then—for the first time as a species self-aware of its evolutionary position—decide how to collectively manage the land we live on. The planetary transformation that is now occurring is like a flood that will wash away the fences and walls we have put up between us. As it was in ancient Egypt in the wake of the Nile's periodic flood, the land will be redrawn, just as it will be made fertile again.

9. Total Planetary Demilitarization

No borders will be redrawn so long as armies patrol them ceaselessly. Moreover, any and all of these social miracles would be for nothing if the wrong individual gained access to the right kind of weapons. In fact, many of these concrete utopian ideas seem unreasonable precisely because we think: "Great. Beautiful idea, but someone will control the guns and bombs. Then what?"

Carroll Quigley, the great theorist of civilizational evolution and historian of the modern world, has argued convincingly that there is an inverse relationship between robust forms of democracy and advances in weapons systems and technologies.[42] The greatest moments of democratic governance in history (when political power was truly in the hands of the people) occurred when the most advanced weapons technologies in existence were accessible and easily mastered by any common person. During these times the possibility of a spontaneously emergent people's army was very real. Consider the American Revolutionary War, where an army of amateurs defeated a great world power. The British Army had nothing more powerful than what could be built, purchased, and used by a ragtag group of farmers. But as Western civilization evolved and military tactics and scientifically designed weapons systems advanced, the means of violence became centralized. Military power became overwhelming and its deployment the province of highly trained experts. The possibility of anything like the American Revolution happening again became impossible, as the military-industrial complex took on a life of its own.[43] Democracy cannot last in socio-cultural conditions where the threat of violence is so great, or where the means of violence are so drastically centralized in the hands of so few. One of the main motives for setting humanity on a course toward radical planetary disarmament is that doing so is a condition for the possibility of true equality, freedom, and democracy.

It seems impossible for humans to live in a world without weapons of mass destruction and systems that administer structural violence. We are told by biologists, psychologists, and the media that humans are violent by nature—a warlike species. War is in our blood and history. Our educational systems have been deeply linked to the creation of war, and war is part of our civil religion and the way we worship and make a spectacle of the state. Some argue that our entire economy is based on war; others argue that without war there would be no moral progress. We create codes of honor and testify to the depth of the profound intimacy and brotherhood that emerges in the midst of war. Yet, simultaneously, each of us knows in our hearts that all war must end if humanity is to survive.

It almost goes without saying that we cannot simply throw down our weapons and disband our armies tomorrow. The world has become violent and some people and groups are heavily armed. Before war can end, widespread disarmament is necessary. Today weapons are everywhere, and in some places daily life is dominated by the presence of deadly force in the hands of a few. It is becoming increasingly easy to gain access to weapons of tremendous destructive power. Experts believe that within a decade we may see scenarios where a small rogue group can threaten to wipe an entire city off the map.[44] Until this situation changes we will need armies, but we will also need to fundamentally alter the meaning of violence and the nature of what it means to be a warrior.[45]

For millennia, all wars (even so-called "just wars") have been fought according to the logic of externalities, separation, and de-humanization. Wars are fought under the pretense of a humanity educated into believing that people are divisible into "good guys" and "bad guys." Military history shows us that humans can be trained to believe that unique individuals are ultimately expendable and replaceable. It is not a coincidence that the standardized uniform was first invented to outfit solders. Indeed, much of what we associate with standardized testing and school organizations based on ranking and sorting first originated in the army.[46] Dressing massive numbers of humans in identical uniforms symbolically extinguishes all traces of individuality and uniqueness within groups, while also signaling the divisibility of humanity as a whole into distinct and competing groups, each with its own outfit. The power of the uniform and flag resides in their symbolic capacity to fuse and meld individuals into a featureless group in which uniqueness is (often gleefully) denied in favor of strict conformity, homogeneity, and predictability. In the anonymity of a standardized military organization, individuals are empowered to behave in ways they otherwise would not. Expunging individuality expunges accountability, as everyone disappears into the faceless mass. More deeply, when the prospect of self-actualization is denied, the power of self-expression is perverted into a kind of compensatory self-assertion and self-aggrandizement. The anonymized self lashes out, desperate to be seen, in escalating extremes of violence.[47] So while the global situation requires that warfare cannot end tomorrow, all of these inhuman aspects of militarism must nevertheless be phased out as soon as possible.

But what would it mean to wage a war in which there were no true enemies? Moreover, is there *ever* such a thing as the justified use of lethal force? In a sense, the ethical use of violence is exactly what a community police force should represent. Self-governance entails the power to self-police, specifically through the democratic appointment of officials tasked with enforcing laws. This is the ideal of *a police force of and for the people.* It is the only acceptable way of conceiving the limited role armed conflict will have in a future following total planetary demilitarization. This sets up the possibility of educating individuals into a non-militarized world, a world in which the "legitimate use of violence" is understood as a limited and ultimately self-defeating social necessity.

In the worst-case scenario, humanity responds to the current planetary transition in ways that emphasize existing divisions and conflicts, and the result is total war on a scale never before seen—a war none of us is likely to survive. In the best-case scenario, the species-wide unity required by humanity's response to world-system transitions will bring about a strategic de-escalation of geopolitical conflicts, followed by massive celebratory public disarmaments based on mutual trust. Eventually there would remain only a decentralized global police force, one of the many democratically governed cooperatives guided by the steady and sustained deliberations of cosmopolitan localism. Importantly, this vision of a unified humanity has been one of the educational messages offered by the great world religions since their inception.

10. Mutual Respect Between Major Religions of the World

Beautiful visions of a world without war are a part of the esoteric and mystical core found in all of the great religious traditions. Of course, looking at the history of religion might lead one to believe otherwise. Religious conflict has dominated human history, and has re-emerged in postmodern society under the guise of religious extremism and ideologically motivated terrorism. Religion appears as a force of division and violence in today's world, so much so that some believe humanity's future depends on the dissolution of religion. This is a deeply tragic state of affairs. Of all the social miracles the emergence of mutual respect between all religions appears at times to be both the most unrealistic and the most imminently possible.

The deep tragedy of today's religions (or better, the tragic irony of their current state) stems from the fact that *all* religious traditions point toward an overarching unity of sacred beliefs, especially as they are understood by their most sophisticated practitioners. The wisest in every tradition have *always* spoken of the inherent unity of all religions.[48] The current state of religious conflict and fragmentation is really a perversion of the true message of every tradition—a perversion largely orchestrated through the systematic distortion of education about the true message of the great religious traditions. Since Aldous Huxley first wrote *The Perennial Philosophy*, the common mystical core of all religions has been explicit and understood. The unity of all religions is revealed in the highest wisdom of each. This has motivated some religious leaders to pursue a strategy for uniting all religions in a global alliance of world spirituality.[49]

Orchestrating a unity of all the world's religions does not mean annihilating the differences between them. Indeed, every religion has a unique voice and fosters unique personalities and cultures. A global alliance for world spirituality would be a place where each religion is honored for its unique lights and gifts, but also criticized, held, and healed in relation to its own unique shadow and history. Every tradition has beautiful texts full of wisdom that should be read the world over, and every tradition has texts that are an embarrassment, which reek of parochial times and places, and of patriarchy and bigotry. We must all lose face together before we can look each other in the eyes again; only then can we learn to recognize the unique and valuable wisdom that remains in the "other," as well as in ourselves.[50]

The problem today is not with the most advanced adepts and saints who already hold a vision of the world spirituality of tomorrow. Instead, the problem lies with the billions of believers who hold conventional or fundamentalist worldviews,[51] as well as the narrow-minded and dangerously charismatic leaders they often follow. Given these realities it is necessary to see how the social miracle of inter-religious cooperation would be impacted and facilitated by the other social miracles we have been discussing. What kind of lives would the mass of religious believers lead in the wake of a global jubilee, totalized demilitarization, and the institutionalization of an integral social safety net? Would we still have violent extremism if the differences between the global haves and have-nots were dissolved and every individual had access to a world-class education? How much "bad religion" is really just a pathological displacement of emotions resulting from the injustices and humiliations suffered at the hands of an exploitative global economy and social system full of racism and prejudice?

Religion is not the cause of violent extremism; religion has been perverted by a global society gone slightly mad, building educational systems that perpetrate illusions about our most valuable ideals. Re-imagining the future of religion is an essential part of retooling educational systems during this time of planetary transformation. Religious traditions are some of the most important and potent cultural resources we have that deal with matters of ultimate significance such as life and death, the meaning of existence, and the inviolable dignity of each and every human being. These themes are part of the core of an integral education, as I explain in the next chapter. They are also a condition for the possibility of the next social miracle, that of a truly just society.

11. Absence of Oppression Based on Race, Gender, Sexual Orientation, etc.

Historically, religious differences have been at the center of some of the most violent and oppressive social systems in history. Uniting and transforming the world's religions would therefore bring a great deal of peace and justice in its wake. But there are other long-standing forms of oppression and dehumanization that are not tied to religion. The list includes near universal subordination and oppression of women, insidious and recalcitrant forms of racial and ethnic prejudice; discrimination based on economic class, gender identity, and sexual orientation; ableism; ageism; and a sprawling array of other disgraceful realities that tear and fray at the social fabric of our civilization. These are oppressive social realities based on difference that create tremendous suffering and fundamentally undermine the possibility of educational abundance. Often, tragically, the very qualities that make one subject to these forms of oppression are the same qualities that make up one's most essential potentials and educational possibilities.

Oppression based on difference is perpetuated by social and cultural systems (Lower-Right and Lower-Left quadrants). The founder of world-systems analysis, Immanuel Wallerstein, has demonstrated with copious historical evidence and sociological analysis that the majority of the forms of oppression based on difference that we encounter today are unique and stem from the dynamics of the capitalist world-system. In Wallerstein's essay, "Intellectuals in an Age of Transition," he sets the history of racism and related injustices in the context of the total world-system transition taking place between 2000 and 2015:

> Ever since the French Revolution, every state has had "citizens" as opposed to "subjects." Citizens have rights. Citizens are equal participants in the political decision making of their state. Except that, ever since the concept was launched, virtually every state has tried hard to limit the applicability of the concept in reality. One of the ways this has been done is that the world-system has reified a whole series of binary distinctions and given them political importance to a degree unknown before: bourgeois/middle class/proletarian/working class; man/woman; White/Black (or person of color); breadwinner/housewife; productive worker/unproductive person; sexually mainstream/sexually aberrant; the educated/the masses; honest citizen/criminal; normal/mentally abnormal; of legal age/a minor; civilized/uncivilized. And of course there are more. What one has to note about these binary distinctions, all elaborated theoretically in great detail in the 19th century, is that they build on ancient distinctions but give to them a salience, an interconnectedness, and a rigidity that they seldom had before. What we have also to note is that the consequence of each binary distinction that is made salient is the restriction of effective citizenship. Citizenship as a concept theoretically includes everyone. The binary distinctions reduce this "everyone" to a relatively small minority of the population. This can be easily measured by looking at suffrage rights and even more at the degree of acceptability of real political participation.[52]

While there are individuals who have been shaped so completely by the delusions of their society that they go out of their way to perpetuate hateful acts, most oppression and prejudice is impersonal and based on subtle social mechanisms, often imperceptible to those involved.[53] It is important to understand that the systems of discrimination that plague our civilization are *social constructions*, and not the result of some inherent human evil or biologically ingrained disposition to be prejudiced. Just as the popular scientific press likes to tell us that evolution has made us selfish and individualistic, so they also like to argue that we are by nature afraid of those different from us, and that we somehow evolved to be racist and sexist. This is simply not true. Rather, the systems of discrimination and oppression that exist today are the result of a long and complex socio-cultural history, including economic and educational systems that *reproduce* it. Breaking these systems apart requires fundamentally disrupting business as usual. However, real change will not happen overnight, as breaking these systems apart also requires undoing centuries of injustice.

Importantly, integral meta-theory deals with issues of diversity, difference, and oppression in a sophisticated manner.[54] This is because the concept of the Unique Self straddles the line between the universal and the particular, and it is at this intersection that the unique person resides. Historically, modernity has emphasized sameness, universals, and a single acceptable identity (e.g., the white male head of an upper-middle class family with 2.5 kids and a dog in the yard behind a white picket fence). The heterogeneous and different were denied and repressed in favor of the universal. If you did not fit this universal ideal of the human, you were marginalized (or worse). Postmodernity, on the other hand, has emphasized the different, particular, and local over the universal. This has often resulted in the inflation of difference into specialness, spawning regressive and narcissistic forms of identity politics which have fragmented the political landscape into countless camps, each promoting its particular issue as *the* issue. New forms of education must transcend but include both of these views on identity, locating the individual at the intersection of the universal and particular. This holds open a space for recognizing both what we all have in common and the ways we are each different; embracing the universal without denying the particular, and embracing the particular without denying the universal. Only with such a framework for human identity in place can we begin to coherently and compassionately address the legacy of discrimination and oppression we have inherited. And only after addressing this legacy can we be freed from alienation and emerge into the fullness of our humanity.

12. Universal De-Alienation and Re-Humanization

All of these social miracles set the stage for the emergence of a new kind of human, one that is the outcome of true educational abundance, social justice, and freedom. This was Marx's vision as a young man (as expressed in his *Economic and Philosophic Manuscripts* of 1844), and it has since been the dream of countless utopians and political visionaries. This is a vision concerning the emergence of a human that is *truly human*, without blemish or distortion due to injustice and oppression. We live in a world in which so many people's lives are distorted by unjust social realities that we have no idea what humanity is truly capable of becoming. Each individual has massive reserves of untapped potential, often squandered and neglected during the struggle to make a living and conform to social roles that deny individual potency and uniqueness. We are alienated from our true nature, dehumanized by the forms of socialization that dominate our culture. As contemporary critical theorist David Harvey explains (working from the text of André Gorz's *Critique of Economic Reason*), alienation is a complex idea:

> The verb to alienate has a variety of meanings.... As a passive psychological term alienation means to become isolated and estranged from some valued connectivity. It is experienced and internalized as a feeling of sorrow and grief at some indefinable loss that cannot be recuperated. As an active psychological state it means to be angry and hostile at being or feeling oppressed, deprived, or dispossessed and to act out that anger and hostility, lashing out sometimes without any clear definitive reason or rational target, against the world in general. Alienated behaviors can arise, for example, because people feel frustrated

> at the lack of life chances or because their quest for freedom ended up in domination.... "The essential question" [from an economic perspective], Gorz writes, "is the extent to which.... involvement in one's work implies the enrichment or sacrificing of one's individual being.... Working," Gorz insists, "is not just the creation of economic wealth; it is also always a means of self-creation [ZS: a means of education]. Therefore we must also ask *a propos* the contents of our work whether the work produces the kind of men and women we wish humanity to be made of." We know that many if not most of those at work are not happy with what they do. A recent comprehensive Gallup survey in the USA showed, for example, that about 70 per cent of full-time workers either hated going to work or had mentally checked out and become, in effect, saboteurs spreading discontent everywhere and thereby costing their employer a great deal in the form of lost efficienc.[55]

This estrangement from our true nature is not a necessary aspect of human existence. Humanity can choose to begin a process of universal de-alienation and re-humanization through the prioritization of educational abundance as a social value. This is perhaps the greatest result that could be hoped for from the combination of all the social miracles we have been enumerating: the universal availability of opportunities for personal development, and the absolute priority of self-actualization and social participation for all individuals. No longer alienated from self, nature, and culture by forced entry into the wage labor system; no longer tied up in debt and dependent upon expensive, inefficient, and ineffective health and educational systems. Surrounded by an abundance of educational opportunities drawing on the diverse and practical wisdom of their communities, new generations will be educated into a new world that we cannot imagine, where future humans will be as different from us as we are from our archaic "cave men" ancestors. The future can produce a breathtaking proliferation of human potentials; innovators, polymaths, and artists may abound. Parents, teachers, and caregivers may emerge in the contexts of plenitude, the de-alienated heroes and creators of tomorrow. The sheer scale of the creativity unleashed would push us beyond the Earth and beyond anything that seems possible today.

13. Science and Technology in the Interest of Human Flourishing and Exploration

The realization of these social miracles would mark the beginning of a new era in human history. Imagine a future in which world peace and social justice are taken for granted as aspects of life on Earth. In this future each and every individual is free to grow and learn endlessly in the context of educational abundance. On such a planet, history will no longer be propelled by conflict, scarcity, and fear. What then will humanity do? More specifically, with our *interiors* liberated through the democratization of educational abundance, what would be the nature of our *exterior* endeavors?

It is likely we would be compelled by our very nature to expand our quest for knowledge and to discover new worlds. Historically, space travel has been undertaken for militaristic and nationalistic reasons, and is now quickly turning into a for-profit industry. Many hold the idea that outer space is simply another resource to be exploited for profit. It is speculated that the first trillionaires will be the CEOs of space mining operations that extract rare metals from asteroids. There is also a related vision of space travel that dominates science fiction and even popular science media, wherein humanity is driven to space by necessity, essentially forced to flee a dying Earth. In these dystopian narratives we are driven to the stars because of our failures here on Earth, and the discovery of new worlds takes place in the shadow of great tragedy and despair. Needless to say, scenarios such as these are far from ideal as motivations for expanding humanity's reach into outer space. They reflect a certain sense that there is no alternative to our current forms of social life and economic organization. Yet if our social systems were arranged differently, space exploration would be a natural outgrowth of the abundance and curiosity of humanity.[56] There will be no viable future for humanity in space if we simply try to bring today's status quo models beyond Earth's atmosphere.

Another task for humanity is to explore the possibilities of artificial life and intelligence, and to grapple with the ethical and theological implications of the coming technological singularity. There are many ideas offered about the fast-approaching future of hyper-technology: where computers become self-aware and autonomous (artificial intelligence), where biotechnology has gained the power to fundamentally intervene in the genetic code (artificial life), and where the human mind-brain has been merged, expanded, and controlled through carbon-silicon computer interface (human cyborgization). These are all dealing in the realms of the possible, but theorists who discuss these ideas spend too little time thinking through what is probable and preferable. Too many futurists are simplistic techno-optimists, "biologists and engineers intoxicated by science fiction."[57] They do not show any sensitivity or sophistication concerning the educational, socio-cultural, economic, and political realities that must be in place for a world with these kinds of technologies to be *humane* in any reasonable sense of the word. Without the social miracles elaborated here, science and technology will contribute more than anything else to the self-inflicted extinction of the species.

There is understandable fear, excitement, and confusion surrounding these ideas about accelerated futures for technology and science. These emotions mostly result from certain distortions in the way that humanity understands itself and its relationship to its own creations. Alienated from our labor and each other and surrounded by technological systems we do not understand, we have become immature and irresponsible. We either fear that we cannot control ourselves, or we assume that self-control is not a problem. We have actually come to misunderstand the work of our own hands. We imagine ourselves to be like the sorcerer's apprentice, in possession of great powers we cannot control and that may destroy us. Or we see ourselves as masters of the universe, able to wield immense power unproblematically. We must grow out of these inarticulate and depoliticized visions and begin to take more seriously the ways in which the science and technologies of tomorrow will impact our sense of being human and our ability to maintain a just society.

The future of technology and science is profoundly dependent upon the transformation of humanity's self-understanding and its forms of political and economic organization. When no longer compelled by war and profit, and when no longer convinced of our specialness and separateness from nature, what might our future technologies look like? The idea that we will create malevolent artificial intelligence bent on the destruction of humanity is a projection of our own fears and shame. Building advanced technologies that arise from a radically different sense of our own humanity could result in new forms of consciousness and life, beyond our current imagination and our sense of what is possible. Yet ultimately we must seek to ensure that these possibilities foster richer and deeper human flourishing, enabling the emergence and spread of educational abundance and lifting humanity up into new realms of love, care, and justice—the ideal seeds for the design of an educational system in the world-system of tomorrow.

---

1. Eisenstein's idea of *the more beautiful world our hearts know is possible* is some of the inspiration for the notion of social miracles I lay out here.

2. Greenhall (2017).

3. Something like less than 5 percent of those who apply to Harvard as undergraduates get in. There are few job markets anywhere like that. As for the limited spots and diplomas, while graduating classes have expanded, they are still capped. Compare this limited form of credentialing with an unlimited form, such as those offered on websites that teach you to be proficient in software, like Lynda.com. Here there is unlimited access and admission is not an issue. Of course, there are reasons why we are allowed to make certificates and credentials for some things and not others.

4. **Educational Basic Goods, Again**

In a well-ordered and just society the publicly supported school system is intended to supplement what is provided by the family in order to ensure the equitable distribution of *educational primary goods*: the basic opportunities for human development guaranteed to all. Importantly, one can argue for public funding and support for schools while not arguing explicitly for a public school system *per se* (e.g., a single state-run bureaucracy), remaining open to the idea of a publicly funded system of private schools (Freeman, 2007). But the lack of a clear commitment to a state-run public school system is not an argument in favor of the *privatization* of schooling. I would argue for a *system* of schools—not a marketplace of schools—coordinated and designed to ensure the just profusion of educational goods and opportunities.

Providing for educational primary goods is a social responsibility that cannot be met using market mechanisms as the sole determinant of transactions and allotments.

If it is a system of private schools that is to sustain a just society, it must be designed and regulated to ensure that its schools serve the public conception of justice, and thus cohere and contribute to the background justice of the broader basic structure. A system of private schools that remained economically stratified from generation to generation, for example, would segregate the education of social classes, and thus undermine the self-understandings and dispositions of free and equal citizenship. Such a school system would be unable to serve as part of the basic structure in a just society (Rawls, 1971).

In a just society, schools must provide for the development of individuals who have all the basic capabilities needed to participate in that society as free and equal citizens. Education is positioned alongside other basic rights and entitlements to primary goods, such as freedom of movement, freedom of conscience, right to due process, and entitlements to adequate food and shelter. There is an "amount" of education owed to everyone, which Rawls specifies as the amount prerequisite for social participation and for securing the equal value of political liberties. As Rawls explains, the constitution of a just society is "required to assure that the basic needs of all citizens can be met so that they can take part in political and social life.... Below a certain level of material and social well-being, and of training and education, people simply cannot take part in society as citizens, much less as equal citizens" (Rawls, 1996, p. 166).

The second responsibility of public schools in a just society (providing for the basic skills needed to pursue a self-chosen conception of the good life) is more subtle and complex than the first. Considerations about justice are different from considerations about what is valuable or good. Beyond the requirements set by justice (e.g., that one's pursuit of the good life cannot be predicated on limiting the good pursued by others), citizens are free to give meaning, direction, and value to their lives in whatever ways they see fit. Schools share a large part of the responsibility for making this freedom a reality. By some readings this suggests that schools should be designed as all-purpose opportunity providers, which is an impossible task. Schools cannot provide the means for everyone to pursue anything and everything; they only exist to provide the means to the further education required to advance a reasonable conception of the good life. Typically, other educational institutions are involved in an individual's self-chosen pursuit of a meaningful life, but public schools are responsible for providing a way into the exercise of this basic freedom to pursue further education. This entails that schools be designed accordingly. They must be fair to competing values and worldviews by not unduly privileging one over another, while also providing a wide enough range of skills and a wide enough exposure to cultural differences that students understand themselves as freely making reflective decisions about the value and direction of their own lives.

Generally stated, in a just society no conception of the good compatible with justice is to be made inaccessible through schooling, while no specific good compatible with justice is to be favored. That is, justice requires that a society's basic structures be fair to all reasonable values and ideals of the good life (Rawls, 1999). However, this does not mean that all possible worldviews and values are present in society or open to students. "The full range of values is too extensive to fit into any one social world" (Rawls, 2001, p. 155).

As Rawls (2001, pp. 154-155) explains, picking up a theme that is central to the work of Isaiah Berlin, "there is no social world without loss." There is no society that can accept and accommodate all ways of life. Of course, we often rightfully lament the limited space (as it were) of social worlds, and of our own society in particular. We regret how these excluded forms of life leave an effect on our culture and social structure through their absence. This is because nearly all forms of social life that are reasonable will make possible the flowering of certain unique and fundamental values. But Rawls suggests that the inevitable exclusion of some reasonable forms of life is not to be mistaken for arbitrary bias or for injustice. A just liberal society may have far more space than other social worlds but it cannot be without loss. That no social world can include all forms of life is a fact rooted in the nature of our fallible human values and the finitude of our world. A great deal of human tragedy reflects this.

Likewise, not all of the values and visions of the good life that are made accessible through schooling can be realized by an individual. Rawls considers this an unavoidable fact of social life, and argues that the basic structures of society must be designed to coordinate the interanimation of individuals who build their lives around diverse social enterprises and forms of life. In several places he offers the ideal of a harmonious "social union of social unions" as a way of characterizing the higher-order unity that is playing out through the coordination of diversity, all of which is enabled by basic structures that are just. This provides a way of thinking about the goal of an educational system that is not built to promote one vision of the good, but rather to enable the flourishing of individuals who pursue a diversity of goods within a framework of just institutions that privilege none.

Rawls (1971) argues that in a fully just society each individual will seek his or her version of the good in ways that are unique. In so doing they therefore depend on others to do things they could not have done, as well as things they might have done but did not. For educators in particular it is tempting to believe that each child might somehow realize all of their diverse powers—that some exemplary individuals might become complete exemplars of humanity. This is impossible, according to Rawls. He argues that the very nature of human sociability is such that we are by ourselves mere parts of what we might be. We must always look to others to attain the skills, capacities, and dispositions that we must leave aside or lack altogether. The good attained through collaboration in a common culture far exceeds the work that could be done by even the most remarkable individual. Through participation in fair systems of cooperation we cease to be mere fragments; the parts of ourselves that we have cultivated are combined into a wider arrangement. Rawls argues that overcoming alienating divisions of labor is not accomplished by each person becoming a complete embodiment of the full range of human capacities, but rather by each person's "willing and meaningful work within a just social union of social unions in which all can freely participate as they so incline" (Rawls, 1971, p. 464).

An educational system that can prepare individuals to reflectively navigate this kind of openness and plurality of goods requires the reconsideration of a wide variety of school practices, from tracking, grade, and ranking to curriculum design and pedagogy. We must know that these practices shape the life prospects and worldviews of students.

5. Apple (2013).

6. The causality implied here is not linear or unidirectional, but complex and dynamic. Both directions of analysis—that education shapes society and society shapes education—are needed in thinking through any given educational practice because both dynamics are always simultaneously in play. This kind of co-determination or reciprocal constitution is a common theoretical idea in the social sciences, especially when what is being explained is an evolving institutional formation (Bowles & Gintis, 1986; Habermas, 1987). The classic statement of this view is that "people create cultures and cultures create people" (i.e., people come to be who they are because of the culture they live in, while this culture itself is the result of the actions of the people who live in it). The idea in this case is that school systems create testing infrastructures and testing infrastructures create school systems. This is not a paradox, but a way of thinking about social realities that requires some degree of comfort with non-linear causality and normative facts.

Importantly, this way of thinking reveals that some socio-cultural dynamics are prone to self-reinforcing directionality; authoritarian cultures create authoritarian individuals who further contribute to the creation of a more authoritarian culture, which then creates even more staunchly authoritarian individuals, and so on in a kind of autocatalytic spiral (Bowles & Gintis, 1986). Analyzing the impacts of testing requires characterizing the complexity of this kind of self-reinforcing directionality as an important property in the dynamic between schooling and testing. Embracing the complexity of social system bi-directionality helps see what we are really dealing with as educators seeking to change society.

7. See: Rosenberg (2002), who refers to this approach as *educational democracy* or *educative democracy*.

8. Widespread cheating in schools is usually organized by teachers as a result of the combination of certain forms of testing and certain forms of perceived scarcity in educational goods. You cheat because you want the pay-off; for many teachers the pay-off

is simply keeping their job. Students don't cheat en masse because the whole point is to gain competitive advantage, which usually, when you reach the end of the line of rationalization, is about the possibility of a job in the future. See: Stein (2016) for more on the cultures of schools plagued by widespread cheating and its impact on students.

9. Harvey (2016).

10. Murphy (1992).

11. Some philosophical methods involve the use of complex representational devices, which can be thought of as structured models or thought experiments. More broadly, model-based reasoning in the sciences involves the deployment of a variety of "useful fictions" that simplify phenomena and exemplify the properties or processes of interest (Elgin, 1996). One of the most common kinds of models is the miniature, such as the scale models used in engineering and systems biology that represent large structures or long timelines in ways that "shrink" them down so they can be seen at a glance. Pulling the miracles into a constellational unity creates such a miniature; it aims to bring a larger complex whole into view by shrinking it down and distilling its most important properties. This means stepping back from the particular arguments to gain a view of the whole, which is facilitated by its being "chunked" into a set of related examples that can be scanned at a glance.

12. These social miracles are just as improbable as the emergence of life from matter, or human culture from animal instincts. Yet, those events happened. The genesis of the biosphere on Earth is nearly as amazing as the explosion of everything from nothing. As Stephen Jay Gould and many others have demonstrated, the sheer statistical improbability of such an occurrence is truly mind blowing. For good overviews of these issues, see Kauffman's (1993) *The Origins of Order*, and Capra & Luisi's (2014) *The Systems View of Life*. For a discussion of the compounding improbabilities involved in the emergence of "higher-order" life forms (i.e., beyond the already stupefying improbability of primordial ooze), see: Ward & Brownlee's (2000) *Rare Earth*. In non-scientific parlance, the term "impossible" comes to mind when considering these kinds of figures; and yet, here we are. The universe seems to be in the business of miraculous emergence. See: Gafni & Stein's (forthcoming) *The Universe: A Love Story*.

13. For more on the important and sacred ancient practice of the jubilee and a deepening of the themes raised here about it, see David Graeber's remarkable (2011) book, *Debt: The First 5,000 Years*. For more on these topics, see also: Eisenstein (2011); Piketty (2014).

14. The word *peon* is important to use in a historically informed way. The history of

debt peons is important to understand as continuous with today's situation, where vast numbers are perpetually indebted.

15. When governments scramble to repay debts or undergo economic restructuring at the hands of international agencies, it often results in the use of authoritarian politics to build extensive Lower-Right infrastructures that support a few specific industries (see: Harvey, 2011). This creates the worst kind of crony capitalism and has consistently generated unspeakable human rights violations, all just to repay a loan (and sometimes this loan was taken out by a now dead dictator, who simply made off with the money for himself).

16. www.rollingjubilee.org

17. See: Harvey (2016) and Despain (manuscript in preparation) for more on the financialization of higher education.

18. One-time graduate students are some of the most indebted people around—including this author.

19. **The Education Commodity Proposition**

See: Stein (2016). The education commodity proposition appears in institutional cultures as a simplification of decision procedures. It is comparable to the simplifications in decision-making that accompany what political economists call the "labor commodity proposition" (Bowles & Gintis, 1986). One of the foundations of the capitalist economy is the idea that individuals are free to sell their labor as a commodity that is fundamentally no different from other commodities, being part of a marketplace with price competitions governed by supply and demand. The labor commodity proposition (i.e., that labor is just like any other commodity) justifies, among other things, the persistence of efficiency-oriented decision procedures and data-driven management strategies in which labor is represented as if it were simply another purchasable component in the production process, to be sought for as cheaply as possible and utilized with maximal efficiency.

Of course, labor is actually unlike other commodities (such as a TV or car), because labor is *inalienable* from the person who "sells" it. You cannot separate the laborer from the labor. When I sell you my TV in exchange for a sum of money, you walk away with the TV and I walk away with the money. But when I sell you my labor, I must live through the work to be done. The valuation of my labor (assigning it a numerical, cash value) and my fulfillment of the employment contract (exchanging my labor for what it is deemed to be worth) implicate me both physically and psychologically in a way that the exchange of my TV for cash does not.

The analogy between labor and other commodities breaks down once the economy is understood not merely as a system of exchange, but also as a system of employment. It is not just *things* that are caught up in market dynamics; there are also *people* being exchanged, their capacities and time being purchased (ibid.). Framing economic issues in terms of the analogy "labor is a commodity" removes considerations about the human side of the labor-exchange relationship, simplifying its representation in terms of monetary units, and depoliticizing it by turning it into an impersonal relationship (like the selling of a TV) to be negotiated and determined in terms of what the market will bear, as opposed to what justice requires due to the involvement of *persons*. An oversimplification similar to the labor commodity proposition accompanies the use of large-scale standardized testing infrastructures. It is this oversimplification that is referred to as the *education commodity proposition*.

Testing can be used to put a number on a "unit" of education, giving it a quantitative value and making it amenable to certain kinds of decision-making calculations, such as cost-benefit analysis and the estimation of returns on investment. That is, testing allows educational processes to be conceived as if they are no different from other commodities, simplifying their representation to monetary transactions that can be considered in terms of economic efficiencies.

On the "logic" of the education commodity proposition

The discussion in this section is not intended as a presentation of facts about the existing educational system, nor as a sociological and economic analysis, but rather as a demonstration of the "logic" resulting from the terms of the education commodity proposition. While much of what is discussed does occur in schools today, the goal here is only to "run the model"—to explore the implications of thinking about education as merely a conversion of test scores into financial terms. The presentation is thus one-sided, focusing on only the most basic thought-forms spawned by the education commodity proposition. This does not imply that these ways of thinking and decision-making dominate all educational organizations, or that there are not important forms of resistance. Critical reflections and observations referencing the current state of education are offered along the way, but a detailed analysis of how the education commodity proposition has impacted schools is presented elsewhere (Stein, 2016).

There is a lot of reasoning that can be done based on the terms of the education commodity proposition. This way of thinking has created a powerful and seemingly irreplaceable function for testing in many educational configurations. The education commodity proposition influences a great deal of educational policy because it is a straightforward and seemingly necessary way to think about schools in economic terms. It appears necessary mainly because economic factors bear down strongly on so many school systems, and many educators have no choice but to foreground their financials. This trend is intensified by federal policies that force schools to compete for funds based on test scores, and by the fact that an increasing number of schools are simply being run like businesses (many are set up as for-profit ventures). This sense of financial necessity, which increases the prevalence and power of the education commodity proposition, constitutes part of the "logic" unfolded in what follows.

On the return of investments in education

The clearest examples of the education commodity proposition involve those who *invest* in educational processes, such as governments, philanthropies, and venture capital. Simply put, if the *amount* of education you are getting for your investment is represented (only or predominately) by the numbers generated on tests, then moving these numbers becomes the only way to "see" those changes in the value of the educational process, which is the intended result of the investment. If you do not measure it you cannot monetize it, and if you cannot monetize something then you cannot technically "see" if an economic investment has worked. This summarizes the main problem facing governments that invest tax dollars in public education and are then required to demonstrate that this public money was well spent. The watchword here is "accountability." In these situations test scores are used to translate (or re-represent) the value of educational processes in economic terms. The same kind of decision procedures are used by philanthropic donors and venture capitalists, both of whom must demonstrate due diligence when putting money toward the improvement of education. Improvements can only be monetized if they can be measured in ways amenable to quantitative demonstrations of return on investment.

Of course, the education commodity proposition also frames the decision-making of those who are responsible for organizing educational institutions. It impacts the thinking of school leaders who are concerned about their own budgets and the effectiveness and efficiency of their internal policies. For example, the value of a new math curriculum is easily turned into a question about the relationship between its cost and the test-score gains that result. If the math curriculum that produces the best scores is too expensive, then the next best affordable option will be chosen, often irrespective of other salient differences between the two curriculums. Curricular decision-making becomes guided by the calculus of cost-benefit analysis, which removes a wide variety of complex considerations from the table by distilling the problem down to its "essence": economic efficiency. More importantly, suppose this next best curriculum produces test-score gains but causes students to dislike math, creates misunderstandings not detected by the test, or results in teacher burnout. These are just a few examples of differences in educational value that easily and regularly escape measurement and therefore are not included in the official calculation of what a curriculum is "worth."

It is clear that the education commodity proposition shapes the decision procedures of those who *invest* in educational institutions (e.g., governments and philanthropies) as well as those who serve as administrators in them (e.g., school leaders). But its impact extends beyond those who are in these positions, affecting nearly every individual with a stake in the educational system. On the one hand, it shapes the thinking of those who provide educational services—those who "*sell*" education. This group includes teachers, who exchange their educational labor for a paycheck, as well as organizations such as colleges, independent schools, and tutoring/test-prep companies that provide educational goods in exchange for a fee. On the other hand, the education commodity proposition also shapes the thinking of educational *consumers*, namely students, who exchange their time and money for educational goods, sometimes voluntarily (e.g., higher education) and sometimes not (i.e., young children are mandated consumers of education). Importantly, students are also the *product* of educational processes, and thus embody the educational value provided to them by the institution they attend. This complex dual role of being both a consumer and a product puts students in an extremely vulnerable position, as testing-intensive determinations of educational value come to dominate not only their choices and actions, but also how they are treated by teachers and administrators, which fundamentally impacts their self-understandings.

On the "value-added" by teachers

Teachers occupy a unique position in school systems because, according to the terms of the education commodity proposition, they can be understood as selling a distinct type of *educational labor.* That is, they exchange their ability to teach for the means of their livelihood. This is important because above all other educational goods potentially conceived as commodities (from books to computers), it is *teaching* that has the most potential to add value to educational processes. It is also one of the most *expensive* aspects of schooling. Therefore, teaching is (and has been since the late nineteenth century) one of the central focuses of testing-intensive determinations of the value of educational processes. Yet like all forms of labor, teaching is *inalienable* from the teacher. Unlike improved school buildings, lunch programs, or technologies, determinations of the educational value-added by a teacher concerns the work done by an individual who can adapt the nature of that work to the methods used to determine its value. Teachers often come to understand their own work according to the measurement categories used to determine its value, which can distort educational processes in profound ways.

The problem of determining the educational value-added by individual teachers easily lends itself to simplification through cost-benefit analysis via testing. Two cheap inexperienced teachers whose students show moderate gains can be hired for the price of one veteran teacher whose students show gains that are only slightly larger, controlling costs while providing for twice the number of students. Of course, there are countless *undetected* forms of educational value provided by teachers that are not factored into such calculations, such as their ability to foster independent thinking, deal with interpersonal struggles, or bring hope and humor into the lives of their students. Likewise, bad teachers can raise test scores while off-loading the collateral damage done by their pedagogy onto *unmeasured* facets of students' lives by creating toxic levels of stress, promoting mind-numbing test prep approaches to learning, or by simply focusing attention only on those students whose improvements are key to raising the aggregate class score (e.g., ignoring the top of the class who will score well regardless, as well as the bottom who will score poorly even if they show gains).

This is how the education commodity proposition comes to structure the thinking and actions of teachers: *they adapt their teaching to the terms used to quantify it.* The full range of educational values made possible through a teacher's abilities cannot be represented in terms of test-score gains, so teachers put their energies toward those values that can be. While tenure and seniority can limit the impact of this approach to quantifying educational value, they do not eliminate it. This is because students (and their parents) and administrators often perceive a teacher's value according to the terms of the education commodity proposition, even if the teacher does not (Ravitch, 2013).

On students as consumers and products

Students themselves are subject to the terms of the education commodity proposition in more complex and ethically fraught ways than any other participants in the educational system. According to the terms of the education commodity proposition, students are cast as consumers of educational goods who are free to make complex judgments about the value of the institutions they choose to enter. Of course, younger students technically have no choice because their parents or guardians choose for them as proxies, but the idea remains that families have an interest in making informed decisions about the value of their educational options. Because school systems are routinely ranked according to test scores, test results often determine what neighborhood or suburb a family chooses to live in; the more affluent the family, the easier it is to make that educational criterion a top decisive priority.

Those families who are not free to choose where to live are told they are free to participate in appeals to improve the goods offered by their local schools. However, because any proposed programs require increases or reallocations of funding, debates about their value are likely to be reduced to questions about test-score gains. Suggested improvements that do not lend themselves to test-based quantifications of value are not likely to be carried out unless a program can somehow be characterized in those terms (e.g., the now classic: "music classes will improve scores on math tests"). Existing programs that cannot prove their value in those terms, regardless of the other values they bring, are likely to be the first programs cut when funds are tight. The terms of the education commodity proposition create an atmosphere in which the impact of local school governance is limited by the metrics available.

Of course, private school enrollments are not due merely to geographical proximity; you can go (or send your child) wherever you want. These schools are free to pursue a variety of direct-to-consumer advertisements. Educational marketing strategies regularly include test scores, or college-placement statistics mediated by test scores. Sports programs and extra-curricular activities can also be represented in ways that quantify their value, usually in terms of college placements and scholarships. College placement itself can be represented in terms of differentials in probable future earnings. Likewise, other privately-run educational providers, such as tutors, test-prep services, and educational consultants, aim to attract potential customers with statistics about test-score gains and resulting downstream financial benefits. Dissatisfied customers are free to go elsewhere, but their choices are still tied to whatever means are available to put a number on the value of the education being provided. The simplicity of these representations, the ease of integrating them into economic calculations, and the lack of trusted alternatives combine to create an environment in which it is difficult for students to understand their options in any other terms.

Of course, regardless of where students go to school and the range of options that are open to them, in the US they are forced by law to spend a large portion of their waking hours in school until the age of 16, or 18 in some states. Even at the college level, where students are finally free to choose for themselves where to go or whether to go at all, the economic drawbacks of not attending college are perceived to be so great that it has become a kind of forced choice. Those who do not attend typically describe themselves as unable to go (usually for financial reasons); they do *not* describe themselves as unwilling or as not wanting to go (Darling-Hammond, 2010). This means that the marketplace for education is unlike the marketplaces that exist for other goods. Markets for the vast majority of other goods are not predicated on legally mandated consumption or long-term negative drawbacks resulting from a failure to consume (notable exceptions are the health care and insurance industries).

The contemporary rhetoric concerning "school choice," which leans heavily in favor of a privatized school system that functions more like a "true marketplace," tends to ignore the fact that the vast majority of marketplaces are entered and exited voluntarily (Ravitch, 2010). This is a point that will be returned to throughout: educational primary goods are not commodities, they are entitlements (i.e., access to these goods is *a basic right*), and their just dissemination requires decision procedures that transcend but include those emphasized by the education commodity proposition.

As discussed throughout with reference to current trends in federal reforms, the idea of school choice and the related analogy of the student-as-consumer obscures the fact that students are also the *product* of the educational system. Children are not mere customers in the market for educational goods, they are also the product or "output" of the educational system. School systems want to measure the quality of their output, so test scores are used to objectively represent changes in students' abilities (i.e., "learning" is understood as test-score gains). The terms of the education commodity proposition allow us to literally represent students' psychological lives as objects with quantitative properties that can be monetized. When an educational process is evaluated in these terms, students are understood as an "output" or "product" of the educational system. Students are the depositories of the value-added by investments in a new curriculum or teaching staff. It is in students' skills and capabilities where the value-added measurement must be detected. If more money is put into a school then better students ought to come out. In order to know *how much* better the students are, their intellects and skills must be rendered quantifiable. This way of thinking characterizes students as a kind of "raw material" that is worked over as it makes its way through production processes. This is about the dominance of human capital theory as a framework for efficiency-oriented educational reform. Also see: Stein (2013).

20. This blurring of the distinction between student and consumer is the root of some difficulties on college campuses, where students are increasingly seeking to censor the ideas they disagree with. They are aware that each moment they are on campus is costing them future income and freedom. They are consumers going into debt to be in school. They are thus entitled to "have it their way," as they would when purchasing any other commodity.

21. Santens (2015).

22. Nussbaum (2006).

23. See: Stein (2016). It is not enough that everyone is ensured certain basic freedoms; everyone must also be ensured of the conditions that enable the exercise of those freedoms. Just because everyone has the freedom to run for political office does not mean that society is structured so that this freedom is worth the same to everyone. In the US, for example, only a select subset of very wealthy citizens can *in fact* run for office, because there are unconscionably minimal regulations on the financial backing of political campaigns. Beyond securing an equally adequate scheme of freedoms for all, a just basic structure must also secure the equal value of those freedoms. All must be in a position to *exercise* their freedoms, not merely to *have* them (Habermas, 1996). This requires designing social institutions that will ensure a fair distribution of the resources that are essential for exercising the liberties of equal citizenship.

It is important to understand that for Rawls, distributive justice is not about how to divide up a pot of money or some collection of material goods resulting from social cooperation. He offers instead the idea that there are certain *primary goods* that must be fairly distributed in order to ensure everyone the status of free and equal citizenship. A list of primary goods evolved during various iterations of Rawls' theory, including (among other things) money, education, health care, and the social bases of self-respect. However, enumerating such a list is not the best way to understand primary goods and their fair distribution.

Early on, Rawls (1971, p. 79) offered a broader definition of what he had in mind: primary goods are those things that any reasonable person would desire, regardless of whatever else they desire. That is, primary goods are the "all-purpose means" of equal citizenship—what *anyone* would need to pursue *any* reasonable conception of the good as a member of a just society. Primary goods are those resources needed by each to allow for the continued equality of all.

Primary goods are thus the most appropriate basis of social comparisons for determining the positions of the most and least well-off in society. Making social comparisons based on an index of Rawlsian primary goods takes into account more than just wealth, which is only one among many primary goods affecting the ability of individuals to exercise their freedoms. For example, consider a society in which the least financially well-off are given greater wealth in exchange for their right to vote and their freedom to choose an occupation, creating depoliticized but comfortable middle-class citizen-employee-slaves, who would otherwise be that society's poorest. Such an arrangement, while raising their "standard of living," would not change the status of this group as the least well-off according to an index of Rawlsian primary goods. Stripping a class of individuals of their political freedoms ensures their unequal status as citizens and undermines the social bases of their self-respect. This radically counteracts whatever freedoms might accrue from their improved financial situation, such as greater freedom as consumers.

None of this is to say that poverty is not devastating and disempowering. In fact, Rawls does more than almost any other contemporary political theorist to argue for the necessity of undertaking major redistributions of wealth, including the idea that a just society must establish a social minimum. The point is that, beyond money, we must be concerned with a broader set of primary goods (defined as the all-purpose means of equal citizenship) when considering questions of distributive justice.

This approach allows for more complex and meaningful questions about what constitutes a *fair* distribution of goods, transcending but including concerns about wealth. While the first principle of justice requires that a society's basic structure secures an equally adequate scheme of basic liberties for all, the second principle requires that this basic structure also give appropriate shape to those inequalities that inevitably result from the activities of individuals as they exercise their basic freedoms. The goal is not to create *perfect equality* where everyone has the same amount of everything (as in some utopian socialism), but rather to create *fair inequalities*, such that irrespective of where individuals are in the range between the best and least well-off, they understand themselves and their fellow citizens as participants in a fair system of cooperation—that they are each where they are as a result of institutions that all would agree to participate in.

Rawls is concerned with specifying permissible ranges and types of social inequality specifically focused on securing each person's status as a free and equal citizen. Therefore the second principle can be read as suggesting that *equality of opportunity* is necessary for creating a society in which inequalities are fair. Moreover, because even fairly earned advantages tend to create unfair situations in the long run (due to the cumulative accrual of benefits to those with greater advantage), inequalities must be structured so that they always benefit the least well-off in order to secure continued fairness.

24. Again see: Rosenberg (2002). Of course, the idea goes back to Dewey's (1916) *Democracy and Education.*

25. Habermas (1996; 1999).

26. See: Twist (2003). There are a remarkable number of truly good philanthropists in the world today, and one of our great hopes is that those who have money will invest it in ways that ultimately transform humanity's very need for money as we now know it. Integral philanthropy takes into account not only the four quadrants but also the degree to which philanthropists themselves are "grown-ups" (i.e., their structure-stage development, state awareness, and self-realization). See the promising work of Jennifer Jones' (2015) *Beyond Generosity: The Action Logics in Philanthropy*, presented at the 2015 Integral Theory Conference. This is "using money to destroy money" as Eisenstein (2011) puts it.

27. Ravitch (2013); Stein (2016).

28. For more on the impact of capitalist philanthropy on education, see the works of Bowles & Gintis; Apple; and Spring.

29. "Saving the biosphere" will be profitable in a more complex and holistic sense—a sense that emerges when value creation is not simply reduced to the creation of money. See: Eisenstein (2011); Hawken, Lovins, & Lovins (2010). There are already a wide variety of "ecological accounting" infrastructures that can measure a vast array of value parameters that are typically excluded from calculations of cost and profit. These are a good start, but mere Right-Hand quadrant measures are insufficient and will remain liable to distortion and "green washing" until human consciousness itself changes and the significance of these alternative forms of value are integrated into the ways we understand ourselves, value each other, and coordinate social behavior. For example, imagine a day when a company's performance on ecological impact measures will give its CEO greater reputation, admiration, and heroic fame than any CEO ever garnered in the nineteenth or twentieth centuries. If we survive it will be because a new culture emerges in which there are radically different hierarchies of social value from those now in place.

30. **Uniqueness, Separateness, and Specialness**

See: Stein & Gafni's (forthcoming) *Towards a New Politics of Evolutionary Love*. Problems arise when uniqueness is misunderstood in terms of separateness, and then when this sense of separateness is deepened into claims about *specialness*. Consider, for example, how humanity has understood itself in relation to the biosphere, and how this has contributed to the current multi-faceted ecological crises we now face. Humans are without a doubt unique in the natural world. Indeed, every creature is unique. But humans have a set of capacities that seem to single us out and make it almost impossible for us to ignore the importance of our own uniqueness. This valid insight into our own uniqueness has been the root of a great deal of anthropocentrism in which uniqueness is being mistaken for separateness. We have come to understand ourselves as separate from nature, as truly set apart and as not beholden to the same laws and processes. This sense of being separate has transformed into a sense of specialness, a kind of species-narcissism fostering the idea that we can endlessly burden and take from the biosphere without repercussion. We pollute, exploit, and otherwise destroy the biosphere because we understand it as separate from us, as some vast "other." We think in terms of "externalities" because we have mistaken our uniqueness for separateness. Yet in reality, everything we do to the Earth we do to ourselves. We are unique precisely because of the way we are interconnected with the rest of the biosphere; our uniqueness arises out of our inseparable connection to all living things on Earth. Each species is unique, and each plays a role in a vast symbiotic web of life; humanity's task is to understand its unique role. The future requires a strategy of deepening union and integration, not of further separation through technologies of control, prediction, and dominance. The new politics of evolutionary love is based on recognizing that all beings are irreducibly unique and thus worthy of respect, dignity, and preservation.

Of course, there is something odd about saying that everything is unique, because this makes being unique into something that everything has in common. It seems like a contradiction to say that everything is the same insofar as everything shares in the quality of being unique. This is an important and sometimes mind-bending paradox. But it is essential to see that the reality of uniqueness does not contradict the reality of sameness. Both sameness and uniqueness arise out of interconnection. Just as everything in the universe is unique in relation to everything else, so everything in the universe is the same as everything else. Take any two objects or events and you can list countless ways that they share in common properties and qualities. Even two things that seemingly have nothing in common, like the President of the United States and a grain of sand in the Sahara Desert, both have a nearly endless number of things that are the same about them, such as that they both occupy space and time, can be found on Earth, are composed of atoms, and so on.

Integral meta-theory can help make sense of this. The orienting generalizations of integral meta-theory (the four quadrants, levels, lines, etc.) can all be thought of as constituting a *matrix of sameness*. Everything manifests across all four quadrants. Everybody develops through levels of consciousness, involving different lines of development. Alternatively, however, the elements of integral meta-theory can be understood as constituting a *matrix of uniqueness*. Everything is positioned in a unique way according to the quadrants. No two people have an identical profile of levels and lines; we each have a unique psychograph. Integral meta-theory can thus clarify the ways that we are all the same, while at the same time showing us how we are each unique. This is an essential antidote to the problems of both modernity (emphasizing abstract universals, such as sameness) and postmodernity (emphasizing concrete particularities, such as specialness).

With its focus on *both* the universal and the particular, integral meta-theory makes clear the tragic flaw in what is sometimes referred to as "heroic modernism." This approach can be found in the design of one-size-fits-all architecture, medicine, and schooling. Just try taking a person who uses a wheelchair into any building of high-modernist architecture. Or try being a learning-disabled student in any of our modernized schools. The abstract universal is the bedrock of bureaucratic structure and the efficiency of modern industry and science. Commodities are strictly engineered and manufactured to be as identical as possible, as are experimental situations and chemical compounds standardized for drug research. The modern world has largely been a world of homogenizing influences and a general triumph of the abstract universal, the spreading of *sameness*.

Of course, there has been a rebellion against modernity's false universals and abstract categories. Postmodernism runs to the other extreme, as the universal is denied in favor of the particular, special, and separate. Postmodern culture has been largely about the intersections of the local, ephemeral, and non-generalizable, which are understood to be more real and valuable than the universal, either as statistical average or as static ideal. This has yielded a world rife with narrow identity politics, worldview fragmentation, and increasingly niche markets for increasingly customized goods. The postmodern world promises to be one in which our sense of what is common and shared in public life dwindles as the languages that express our differences and separateness proliferate.

As just discussed, separateness and specialness are distortions of uniqueness, not expressions of it. Someone truly convinced of their own uniqueness and intrinsic value would have no need to pathologically impress it upon others. They would also have a greater capacity to recognize the uniqueness of others and to see the reality of their interconnections and interdependencies. It is a paradox laced with no sense of irony that the cure for the narcissism that plagues our culture is, in fact, a deepening of considerations about uniqueness and a new culture of mutual recognition in which true uniqueness can flourish.

31. And educational abundance is a condition for the possibility of making this shift in our view of nature and in redesigning technology to create a symbiotic relationship between humanity and the biosphere. Again, this is a two-way causation where social systems can inter-participate and co-evolve with nature.

32. Of course, diamonds are not scarce in other parts of the universe. Some scientists speculate that there are likely to be asteroids or planets elsewhere in our galaxy that are composed largely of diamonds. Others believe there is evidence to suggest that diamonds might compose an entire stratum of the Earth's inner structure, deep within the mantel. In any case, it is philosophically interesting to question if there is anything like true scarcity in nature. Certainly there are local pockets of natural scarcity, but when viewing nature as a whole, *abundance* seems to be the overwhelming fact and the predominant plot line in the story.

33. For an account of just how radical ecologically responsible energy and technology futures could be, see Tony Seba's (2014) techno-optimist vision, *Clean Disruption of Energy and Transportation: How Silicon Valley Will Make Oil, Nuclear, Natural Gas, Coal, Electric Utilities and Conventional Cars Obsolete by 2030.*

34. Later on I will discuss the idea that humanity might one day leave Earth to find more land elsewhere in the solar system or galaxy. Note that some extreme techno-optimists would use this prospect as a justification for not fearing or grieving the current profound mismanaging of Earth, as if we have some back-up plan. As I explain, the exploration of new worlds must come from a motivation of abundance and exploration, not from the necessity of survival or the pursuit of profit.

35. See: Eisenstein (2011; 2012). There is not space to pursue a longer discussion of the reforms that are needed for our food systems (including water). Needless to say, there are deep connections between each of the other social miracles and the food system, which depends on energy, money, and everything else. I am not suggesting that everyone become a farmer; far from it. But I am arguing for a radical rethinking of where farming takes place and who does it. Just as I have suggested decentralizing other major infrastructures in ways that empower local regional cooperatives, I am also suggesting this as a way to think about the future of food systems. I also believe that we should think about food systems as educational opportunities and use them as a chance to teach the next generation about the most basic elemental forces that sustain their life and the life of the Earth.

36. See: Jane S. Hirschi's (2015) *Ripe for Change: Garden-Based Learning in Schools.*

37. See: Susan George's (1977) groundbreaking work, *How the Other Half Dies: The Real Reasons for World Hunger.*

38. See: Harvey (2009; 2013). Governments do a great deal to shape the land, but the ways they do this almost always involve collusion with and construction of large-scale private enterprises which are not accountable to the public, despite wielding vast powers to transform the land. The only exceptions to this rule were the actually existing communist regimes, which used state powers alone to organize urbanization and large-scale transformations of the land. Of course, this approach had its own disastrous consequences. What both approaches share is a lack of deliberative democratic input on the part of the people most impacted by land changes.

39. See: Habermas (2001). Here Habermas picks up the "concrete utopian" project of imagining (along with Kant) a cosmopolitan world community of all peoples and the related idea of the *world citizen* with a world-centric identity.

40. Cosmopolitan simply means citizen of the cosmos or world. See: Hill (2009), who offers a *cosmopolitan* ethic that is a universalist, post-postmodern, global, and integral moral orientation.

41. George (2010); Harvey (2011).

42. Quigley (1961; 1983).

43. See: Micah White's (2016) *The End of Protest* on how the recent militarization of police forces has squelched the possibility of organized civil disobedience. Protests as we have known them are over. The use of *excessive* force by militarized police units against US citizens is one of the untold stories of our historical moment. The US supports some forms of radical protest in other countries, such as those in the Middle East aided by US forces during the Arab Spring. However, the US government does not condone dissent at home. For example, the centralized intelligence and command and control apparatus of the Department of Defense was deployed to carry out the counter-revolutionary military tactics that systematically destroyed dozens of Occupy encampments across the country in a single day, ultimately breaking the back of the movement.

44. Robb (2008).

45. The board of the Center for Integral Wisdom includes Mark Divine, perhaps the greatest living Navy SEAL. He is part of a project focused on redefining the meaning of the warrior ethic. This project focuses on the emergence of the World Centric

Warrior: a person who is drawn to *fight* for humanity as an expression of their Unique Self. The ideal of a new kind of warrior is necessary for the creation of a global police union, actualized as a decentralized, self-organizing collective or cooperative dedicated to the use of righteous force. This goal of a people's police force assumes the kinds of disarmament and demilitarization discussed in the body of the text.

46. See: Lewis Mumford's (1934) classic, *Technics and Civilization*. Many of the large-scale industrial processes that have come to characterize (and homogenize) the modern world were first developed in the context of military operations, including precisely standardized commodity production, geospatially dispersed supply chain management, and complex computerized informational systems.

47. See: René Girard (1989) for more on *mimetic violence*.

48. Integral meta-theory provides some sophisticated ways to differentiate between various forms of religious belief. There is not space to go into this important topic here, except to say that there is a tremendous diversity of belief systems *within* any given religion. All faiths run a range from literalist and fundamentalist, to conventional "Sunday church-goers," and on to the post-conventional esoteric mystics. The great theologian and developmental psychologist, James W. Fowler, researched these stages as distinct levels of religious belief in his book *Stages of Faith*. Any view of religion that does not take into account this kind of intra-doctrinal developmental variability is missing some of the most important dynamics of our "post-secular age." See: Wilber (2005; 2006); DiPerna (2012).

49. This is a vision going back to the first great public religious figures of the modern age. Today, witness the Dalai Lama and the Pope, both of whom say things that would lead you to believe they do not hold theirs as the only path to truth.

50. See: Adi Da Samraj's (2006) *Not-Two Is Peace* for more on the idea that we must all lose face together before we can look each other in the eyes across our differences.

51. There are some theorists with knowledge of integral meta-theory who maintain that fundamentalist and conventional religious beliefs are a natural part of developing through the various levels of development. While it is true that lower level structure-stages tend toward literalism and simplicity in practice and belief, the extreme and often violent forms of religion we see today are best understood as *pathological distortions* of lower level capacities. The idea of a global alliance of world spirituality is *not* dependent upon everyone becoming a post-conventional saint. Rather, the idea is that post-conventional religious leaders would collaborate in the establishment of new

conventions, which when coupled with the socio-economic miracles already discussed could ensure healthy manifestations of all faiths at all levels.

52. Wallerstein (2003, pp. 21-22).

53. Johnson (2001).

54. For an excellent overview of how integral meta-theory in general deals with these issues, see: Forman (2010), especially Chapter 13.

55. Harvey (2014, p. 267; pp. 270-272).

56. It is interesting to note that one of the most popular science fiction franchises of all time, *Star Trek*, presents a future in which interstellar exploration is undertaken by humans in a radically non-capitalistic and overtly communist way. As David Graeber explains in his remarkable essay, "Of Flying Cars and the Declining Rate of Profit," in *The Utopia of Rules* (pp. 125-126): "*Star Trek* characters live under a regime of explicit communism. Social classes have been eliminated. So too have divisions based on race, gender, or ethnic origin. The very existence of money, in earlier periods, is considered a weird and somewhat amusing historical curiosity. Menial labor has been automated into nonexistence. Floors clean themselves. Food, clothing, tools and weapons can be whisked into existence at will with a mere expenditure of energy, and even energy does not seem to be rationed in any significant way. All this did raise some hackles.... conservatives and libertarians on the Internet also began to take notice, filling newsgroups and other electronic forums with condemnations of the show as leftist propaganda. But suddenly, we learned that money had not entirely disappeared. There was latinum. Those who traded in it, however, were an odious race who seemed to be almost exactly modeled on Medieval Christian stereotypes of Jews, expect with oversized ears instead of oversized noses. (Amusingly, they were given a name, Ferengi, that is actually the Arabic and Hindi term for 'annoying white person.') On the other hand, the suggestion that the Federation was promoting communism was undercut by the introduction of the Borg, a hostile civilization so utterly communistic that individuality had been effaced completely, sucking any sentient life form it assimilated into one terrifying beehive mind."

57. Habermas (2003, p. 15).

Chapter 5
On Spiritual Teachers and the Postmodern Marketplace for Religious Education

This was written as part of my work with the Center for Integral Wisdom (CIW). Large sections were published in the Journal of Integral Theory and Practice, as well as in Integral Review. The CIW is the brainchild of Marc Gafni, Ken Wilber, myself, Sally Kempton, Lori Galperin, Daniel Schmachtenberger, and about a dozen other thought leaders who are seeking to change the source code of public culture and raise the general level of consciousness and conversation, including the so-called "debate" between science and religion.

My work with the CIW has been controversial. Religion, spirituality, sacred experience, transformative ritual, the re-enchantment of nature—call God what you will—the topic is not for most polite conversation. As I explore in this essay, holding deeply religious sentiments is a source of personal embarrassment in modern scientific culture. Some of my academic colleagues have scratched their heads in wonder at my involvement with this organization, given its focus on questions and practices of a spiritual bent. My intention has always been to participate in an original religious culture capable of creating a new sense of the sacred, and to come to terms with our post-secular age in which religion has reasserted its world-historic role. Reframing religiosity is controversial in and of itself.

Then there is Marc Gafni, who is a lightning rod for controversy. I am one of the people who have seen inside the life of this "postmodern spiritual teacher," and I offer reports from behind the scenes and deep within the texts. There are no special powers or magical qualities of enlightenment to report—although Gafni is a post-conventional personality if there ever was one—nor are there any demons, sociopaths, or geniuses of deception and manipulation. There is only humanity in its most articulate forms, woven with tragedy, brilliance, and Eros.

There is no Buddha-Nature, Christ Consciousness, or Aurobindian Supermind that will be coming to save us. There will be no Great World Teacher, no Great Prophet. There is no Great Prophesy, only the everyday prophesies of caregiving, cooperation, goodwill, and decency that make us capable of civilization. It is just we humans, warts and all, who must save the world. Those out to "take down a false prophet" betray their simplistic beliefs and projections—as if there was a "true prophet" to whom we would owe as much allegiance as the false prophet merits scorn. We must become more mature in our conceptions of religious teacherly authority, as I discuss at some length in this essay.

One essential question that must be dealt with in the integral paideia is the question of the relationship of the human to the sacred. How should future generations be taught about that which is of ultimate concern, about what is holy, and about the histories and beliefs of the world's great religions? How does one exercise teacherly authority with regards to spirituality? If we can't answer these questions then we have little to say to the vast majority of humanity who are believers of one sort or another. As religiously motivated extremism and violence increase during the world-system transition, we must seek new ways to reclaim the higher truths of religion for the sake of civilization.

Religiosity Revisited

> Sociologically speaking I have not studied any of the new, de-institutionalized and de-differentiated forms of religiosity.... Maybe not everything on the market is Californian claptrap or neopaganism.
>
> —Jürgen Habermas[1]

There has been a resurgence of interest in religious phenomena in recent years. Scholars and intellectuals from diverse camps have been reflecting anew on the role of faith, reason, and religion in the public sphere, while mainstream media outlets focus countless hours on religious topics and events. Religious actions and policies have been a ubiquitous aspect of twenty-first century politics and culture, and yet for a significant period in intellectual history, sociologists, psychologists, and philosophers were predicting the decline of religion.[2] The "disenchantment of nature" and the modernization of culture and industry were predicted to disintegrate structures of religious authority. And indeed they did in many major respects, rendering the separation of church and state and the rise of scientific knowledge production processes. However, for most of the post-industrial West (but especially Americans), religion never stopped exercising a major influence, especially in the realm of moral education. For the majority of the rest of the world, local religious life continues to be of profound significance, even as local customs are transformed by a growing influx of global communications and commerce. The "decline of religion hypothesis" has not panned out, leading some to suggest that we have entered a "post-secular" era.[3] Religion is a key node in the emerging transnational constellations that will radically shape the future of global civilization.

This chapter explores contemporary structures of *religious authority* and how they are legitimated and justified. I am especially interested in the unique kind of *teacherly authority* that occurs in educational contexts where teachers and students are focused on religious topics. Moreover, it will be the non(or quasi)-institutionalized religious teacher (aka: *the spiritual teacher*) to whom I will give the most attention. The dynamics of religious authority in other parts of the world are complex and important—from terrorism to liberation theology—but I focus on the post-industrial West because it is where I live and because I think it is a site of new and complex emerging forms of religious authority.

Of course, the term *religion* and its cognates have been variously defined,[4] and these days other words have come to have comparable definitions. Religiosity has become *spirituality*, and the religious, *the spiritual.* I will tend toward a usage wherein religion has connotations of institutionalization, while spirituality is related with non-institutionalized and often eclectic beliefs and practices. Importantly, both terms refer to configurations of education, practice, and belief that are basically ways of addressing topics of ultimate concern. That religion (and thus spirituality) has to do with topics of ultimate concern is an idea expressed by the great theologian Paul Tillich,[5] who argues that religion and spirituality have to do with the human condition understood in its broadest possible context. Ultimate concerns include such themes as the meaning of life, death, love, God, and morality. More recent and unavoidably religious topics would include *the self-inflicted extinction of the human species*—the "end of days" as they appear today, if you will.

Eschatological "end of days" visions remain common in the broad public imagination, from movies to the nightly news. After Hiroshima and the Nuremberg trials, and now in the context of an ecological crisis of unknown proportions, the idea that every human could die as a result of human decisions is a consideration that is hard to ignore. Also in the culture and hard to ignore is the related idea of a universe in which humanity has come and gone, flourishing for a time only to be extinguished. Evoking religious themes is very difficult to avoid when discussing these topics, let alone when issuing action-orienting counsel as a parent or teacher. Thus some speak of the irreplaceable (and often untapped) semantic potentials that reside in religious language.[6]

However, at least since Kant (who wrote that a good child of the Enlightenment should be embarrassed to be caught praying) the use of religious language has come with a great deal of baggage. This is the result of shifting views about the justification of *religious validity claims* and related processes for legitimizing *religious authority*. New configurations of religious authority have emerged during the course of socio-cultural evolution. Today there is a set of co-existing religious authority structures and related worldviews wherein the dynamics of authority vary greatly. These different normative structures result in very different educational practices, and in particular very different kinds of teachers and teachings.

As I will explore below, the *spiritual teacher* is a fascinating and newly emergent role in postmodern and multicultural societies. This is an individual without an official position in a religious organization who nevertheless appeals to the public at large, while assuming (and often being granted) a certain type of moral and religious authority. This is a unique form of authority in that it is more or less non-institutionalized and typically built around market transactions and exchanges (books, lectures, retreats, etc.). The spiritual teacher—like the religious fundamentalist—is a uniquely modern figure and agent. Spiritual teachers are also unique because they can appeal to a much wider variety of sources to ostensibly justify their claims and legitimize their *teacherly authority*. The traditional religious teacher (e.g., a rabbi or priest) typically justifies their authority in terms of a specific lineage of teachers, teachings, and practices. The spiritual teacher, on the other hand, will justify their authority in ways often totally unaffiliated with any one religious tradition. While it is true that the dynamics of teacherly authority vary even within a single tradition, it is still the case that spiritual teachers are authorities with more ambiguous and complex modes for securing the legitimacy of their authority.

The goal here is not to describe the current spiritual marketplace, but to build a language that might allow us to discuss the value of the various wares on offer. In other words, the aim here is to offer an evaluative framework (or the first words in a "language of strong evaluation"[7]) that can be used to sort the good teachers from the bad ones.[8] I begin by positioning the spiritual teacher in the context of eclectic traditions in the history of American moral education. The world of spiritual teachers contains new forms of teacherly authority and new teachings and forms of teacherly practice. Later on, as an example I look at Marc Gafni's teachings of Unique Self, as expressed in his book *Radical Kabbalah*.

Postmodern spiritual teachings are important because they are yet another indicator of major recent reconfigurations of religious authority in America. We must take a socio-philosophical look at the predicament of authority faced by twenty-first century spiritual teachers. This means characterizing the dynamics of teacherly authority and the varieties of educational configurations that surround what Habermas has called "the new de-institutionalized forms of religiosity."[9] Ultimately, it should be possible to offer a set of normative distinctions intended to help clarify the value and validity of emerging spiritual teachings and forms of teacherly authority and teachearly practice. I want to clarify ideas about how to separate the "California claptrap" from the forms of religious language and practice that make a legitimate claim as "vehicles for possible truth contents."[10]

Many popular spiritual teachings, such as those offered by Eckhart

Tolle or Byron Katie, stand outside religious traditions. These are not teachings based on any lineage, and are without scholarly depth, reference, or precedence. While they are not engaged with any particular religious tradition, they may reference them and may have practiced with teachers from traditions. It has been clear to me for some time that this divorce from lineage and tradition leads both to a newfangled form of postmodern guru worshiping (where personal charisma makes up for the poor quality of the teaching) and to a retreat into *ad hominem* arguments against specific teachings (where personal attacks take the place of reasoned debate). So it is that these teachings draw much of their power from their non-denominational character (their "spiritual but not religious" flavor) and from the personal revelations and insights of their authors. These are the postmodern freelance shamans, the so-called "spiritual teachers."

On Spiritual Teachers: Religious and Moral Education During the End of Days

> Religious traditions have a special power to articulate moral intuitions, especially with regard to vulnerable forms of communal life.... This potential makes religious speech into a serious vehicle for possible truth contents.... We cannot exclude that they involve semantic potentials capable of exercising an inspirational force on society *as a whole* as soon as they divulge their profane truth contents.
>
> —Jürgen Habermas[11]

Nearly all of the world's most important educational institutions began as the result of religious organizations,[12] and without a doubt the most influential teachers have been religious ones. After all, what were Christ and Buddha if not teachers? Moreover, the ultimate purpose of education (a good life, if you will) has nearly always been understood as a religious question. Likewise, the world's religions are attempts to educate humanity, for better and for worse. In the United States, for example, the most successful educational initiatives of the eighteenth and nineteenth centuries were not the struggling public schools, but networks of religious organizations and revivals. The so-called "Great Awakenings" that swept across the country between 1730 and 1910 have been convincingly characterized as complex educational configurations, with organized economic and institutional arrangements, information dissemination strategies, teacher training, and youth outreach. The complex public school system that emerged in the twentieth century was imbued with a potent kind of American "civil religion," which is just now coming under scrutiny as trends toward multiculturalism have forced changes in American ideology.

Today the extramural markets for religious education have never been bigger or more diverse. Everyday people are increasingly lured toward fundamentalist revivals or New Age retreats, or else distracted by endless streams of religious books, television programs, and web content. So while the public schools have been famously and controversially separated from religion, the majority of the population nevertheless participates in religious educational configurations of some variety. Some of these configurations simply involve private schools or churches, while others involve publishing and media outlets, and still others involve spiritual teachers of one type or another.

It is interesting to look into what historical precedence there is for the role of the spiritual teacher in America. It should first be noted that a distinctly modern understanding of religious authority has allowed revival and evangelical movements to overwhelmingly characterize religious life in the United States. Historically this is a land in which any Protestant farm boy with a bible and a voice could conceivably establish a ministry and a flock. The democratization of authority that has characterized modernity cannot be separated from the antinomianism of the Reformation and the concomitant individualization of religious insight and attainment. The early American colonists and revolutionaries exemplified these emerging modern forms of religious practice and belief, which were anti-dogmatic, pluralistic, and highly individualized. Hundreds of different religious groups could be found in New York City when its population was still only several hundred thousand.[13]

At least since the literary awakening spawned by the American Transcendentalists, an influx of Eastern religious traditions has broadened the horizons of non-denominational spiritual seekers. Specifically, the important influence of Ralph Waldo Emerson as a religious educator has not gone unnoticed; he was perhaps the first best-selling author, lecture-circuit running, post-traditional American spiritual teacher.[14] The 1890s saw both the popular appeal and scholarly praise of William James' *The Varieties of Religious Experience* and Swami Vivekananda's influential appearance at the Parliament of the World's Religions in Chicago. These events signaled the end of a century in which multitudinous religious configurations diversified across the country—a trend that would continue throughout the next century and into our own.

After World War II, large swaths of the subculture (especially on the West Coast) firmly embraced the Eastern traditions they had been flirting with for decades. Multicultural, pop-cultural, and psychoactive spiritual marketplaces would evolve, breaking into mainstream consciousness with the emergence of celebrities who worshiped gurus from India and Harvard professors writing books while tripping on LSD. As if in reaction to the almost anarchistic eclecticisms of the spiritual counterculture, a new wave of evangelical Christianity began to flourish in the closing decades of the century. A large, wealthy, and politically powerful network of Christian religious organizations established massive and effective educational configurations that shaped the life of the country as a whole, and continue to do so today. By contrast, the spiritual counterculture expanded, diversified, and commercialized into a polycentric and dynamic marketplace, but with little political influence and only pockets of wealth and institutional organization.

Today Americans are paradoxically the most *religious* and the most *modern*; the most *spiritual* and the most *materialistic*.[15] There are a vast array of religious and spiritual teachers and teachings on display or for sale. Most individuals are not forced into one form of religious engagement, but are positioned to reflectively choose among many. This is an unprecedentedly complex educational environment that is no doubt greatly affecting the life trajectories of current generations. In particular, we must ask ourselves: where and how are processes of moral education being carried out and justified? To whom and for what kinds of reasons do we grant a teacher the *authority* to shape the religious and spiritual contours of our lives? When we choose to join a church, begin meditation instruction, change our behaviors in light of a "self-help" book, or participate in religious observances, we moderns must ask: why these teachings? Why this teacher and not some other? The indelible pluralism of the contemporary scene has engendered unique configurations of religious authority. The result has been educational dynamics that are ambiguous and obscure, with forms of authority ranging from the self-effacing total control of the classic guru to the relativistic self-indulgence of teachers manipulating the postmodern spiritual marketplace. These different forms of teacherly authority warrant more careful attention.

The Structure of Teacherly Authority

> The teacher has a peculiar form of authority.... It is viewed as nonproblematic, and necessary, because, (1) it is effecting development, and (2) it is *phase-temporary* or *phase-specific*. That is, the teacher's authority over the pupil is temporary; it effectively evaporates once the pupil's degree of understanding approaches that of the teacher.... Phase-specific authority seems inescapable in any process of education (development).... Either religious teachers are there to bring you up to their level of understanding—in which case their authority is phase-temporary—or they exist to keep you in your place, which by definition is somewhere below or under them.
>
> —Ken Wilber[16]

Today in most of the post-industrial West, the terms *religious authority* and *moral authority* have negative connotations, often used as terms of derision or cynicism. The terms *scientific authority* and *medical authority* have enjoyed non-ironic usage for the past half-century or so, but are also frequently and increasingly focuses of concern. *Political authority* is of course the type of authority most well known, and its contestation is what we typically call history. New global conditions (particularly transnational economic and ecological crises) are jeopardizing the authority of national governments, and there is growing concern about the shape of the global authorities to come, from the UN to Google. Closer to home, in our own lives we grant and are given authority over a wide variety of spheres, from the cook's dominion over the kitchen to the raising of children. The structure of authority is complex—from the micro to the macro—but it always involves relationships in which normative force is non-reciprocally distributed. Authority is therefore a dynamic property of relationships wherein one party is granted unique responsibilities and allowances with regards to the other. For example, the parent acts with authority over the child in setting rules, the scientist speaks with authority to the press about research findings, and the teacher lectures authoritatively to the student about a subject in which they share an interest. In each case, one role (parent, scientist, teacher) is positioned asymmetrically "above" the other, and there is an imbalance of knowledge and power (among other things). Importantly, for authority to work this asymmetry must be recognized and agreed to by all parties. If you speak as an authority but are not recognized as one by your audience, you will not affect your audience as an authority might. Authority must be granted or given—one must *arrange* to be seen as an authority.

Importantly, the ways in which authority is negotiated and arranged tell us if it is *justified* or *unjustified*. There has been a great deal of discussion about what "good" and "bad" forms of authority look like. The dynamics of authority have been discussed in the sociological literature[17] and tied into postmodern critical studies of the relationship between knowledge and power.[18] Likewise, there is research in developmental psychology about authority, where several taxonomies of authority-type are already in use.[19] It has also been a topic in post-positivist philosophy of science (epistemic authority)[20] and in political theory.[21]

The dynamics of *teacherly authority* have received less attention, and the unique forms of authority deployed by twenty-first century spiritual teachers have received almost none.[22] Institutionalized forms of teacherly authority have existed throughout history, from ancient apprenticeship systems to post-industrial public school systems. Informal non-institutionalized forms of teacherly authority have also been common throughout history. The basic structure of teacherly authority is such an important part of human interaction (and serves such an essential function in the transmission of cultures, skills, and knowledge) that some theorists have suggested it is a species-specific trait unique to *homo sapiens*.[23]

Teacherly authority is a property of relationships where *knowledge* is non-reciprocally distributed. Both parties recognize this, and both agree that the person with more knowledge is entitled to instruct, teach, inform, or otherwise assist the other. Contrast this with political authority or parental authority, where power and the legitimate use of force are the qualities that are non-reciprocally distributed. Of course, parents and politicians can be teachers, and different forms of authority can overlap and interact. For example, scientific authority is easily turned into teacherly authority, and a disgraced leader can maintain political authority even after losing their status as a moral authority. The point here is not to give a definitive classification of authority types, but rather to focus on the structure of teacherly authority itself, and on religious or spiritual teacherly authority in particular.

If I grant you teacherly authority, I give you the right to lead me in my thinking. I trust you to tell me what is good and bad in the way of belief, and I consent to do as you instruct so that my mind might be changed along the lines you suggest. While there are debates about the differences between implicit and explicit knowledge and the differences between skills, knowledge, dispositions, and capabilities, the basic structure of teacherly authority is simple: just use the psychological constructs that make the most sense for the interaction in question. Sometimes it's a skill (like tying a shoe). Sometimes it's knowledge (like American history). Regardless of *what* is being dealt with, teacherly authority concerns relationships established when you and I don't meet on equal epistemic ground, and I would like to be brought up to where you stand. We mutually recognize this and consent to the authority dynamics that allow you to be the teacher and me the student.

It is in the *legitimacy* and *justification* of teacherly authority where things get truly complex. Teacherly authority allows one person to influence the development of another, which entails a source of legitimacy and some form of related justification. Teacherly authority needs to be situated (usually institutionally) and to have some form of backing (such as reasons and principles). *Who* is seen as a legitimate authority and *why* are they seen that way? For example, in a contemporary American public school the classroom teacher is not the final source of authority. Instead, legitimate teacherly authority is radically distributed from textbook publishers to the heads of school. This polycentric form of legitimacy is backed by a variety of modern political, economic, and philosophical justificatory strategies. This is very different from the teacherly authority of a parent offering instructions to their child in personal responsibility, where there is only one source of legitimacy backed by the kinds of informal justificatory strategies that color family life ("because I said so" being a classic parental justificatory trump card). The structure of teacherly authority has to do with both *who* has authority and *why* they have it.

But of course, there is also the essential *how* and *what* of teacherly authority: *how* does the teacher exercise their authority and *what* is being taught? These aspects interact with the aspects just discussed to yield a complex picture of the different possible configurations of teacherly authority. To return to the example of American public education, the classroom teacher is one source of legitimate authority in a complex network of teachers who are justified by the state to teach a broad curriculum during a limited part of the day through the use of didactic instruction methods. Contrast this with ancient apprentice systems that often involved a single legitimate source of teacherly authority, one justified by both tradition and demonstrated mastery, exercising control over almost the entire day and life of the apprentice, and using hands-on techniques and threats of corporal punishment to instill a range of professional skills.

History teaches that when the *what* is religious subject matter and the *who* is a religious or spiritual teacher, the configurations of teacherly authority become powerful and potentially problematic. Moreover, as the sketch offered above suggests, configurations of teacherly authority have changed during the course of history such that today there are multitudinous educational endeavors characterized by a wide variety of authority dynamics.

Unique Self: Reclaiming the Personal and Democratizing Enlightenment

> In modern societies, religious doctrine has to accommodate itself to the unavoidable competition with other forms of faith, and other claims to truth.... Thus modern faith becomes reflexive. Only through self-criticism can it stabilize the inclusive attitude that it assumes within a universe of discourse *delimited* by secular knowledge and *shared* with other religions. This decentered background consciousness of the relativity of one's own standpoint... [is] characteristic of the modern form of religious faith.
>
> —Jürgen Habermas[24]

I now turn to an examination of Marc Gafni's Unique Self Theory as an example of contemporary spiritual teachings. Unique Self Theory stands out from the field in terms of the complexity and adequacy of what it offers. On the one hand, these teachings are post-traditional in that they speak to a broad swath of the public who are not exclusively located within or identified with any particular spiritual or religious tradition. On the other hand, they are based on fundamentally different arguments than other teachings in the genre—arguments that stem from a breadth and depth of scholarship. These teachings differentiate from the great traditions but they do not disassociate from them. Virtually all of the other teachings in this genre fail to make these kinds of arguments, and wind up disassociating from the great religious lineages without being able to generate any comparable source of breadth and depth. Gafni's teachings aspire to advance sophisticated scholarship and practice within a specific religious tradition (Judaism), while also moving beyond a merely academic impetus and impact toward an emancipatory intent. The key observation here is that Gafni is not only a significant third-person scholar of his native tradition of Kabbalah, he is also an advanced first and second-person adept within the tradition, possessed of realization received from the lineage.[25]

The core value of these teachings is that they reconfirm (in a compelling scholarly fashion) some of the most central ethical tenants of Western civilization. Moreover, they do so by reminding us that the Judeo-Christian tradition contains a radical enlightenment teaching, with a message about the collective awakening of *everyone everywhere*. Gafni calls this the "democratization of enlightenment." This is a theological metaphysics justifying the reign of an Absolute Democracy in which each must live so that all will have the ability and dignity to be heard, known, and counted. The mystical core of the great democratic political revolutions can be found in the cipher of ancient texts, reinterpreted in each age (and again today) in order to enliven the struggle to create a world conducive to human liberation. As Habermas has stressed, there is currently no replacement for the world-disclosing power of religious language, especially in its capacity to give voice to the profound vulnerabilities, interdependencies, and potentialities of human social life.

The core innovation enabling the democratization of enlightenment is what Gafni calls *the reclaiming of the personal*. This idea is presented most clearly where he offers a comparison between two models of Self, his own model of Unique Self and Andrew Cohen's Authentic Self or Evolutionary Self (a comparison undertaken in detail in Gafni's book *Self in Integral Evolutionary Mysticism: Two Models and Why They Matter*). He notes that in classic enlightenment teachings from the East, the key transformation is from the personal to the impersonal. For example, Cohen's community (now disbanded) was for many years called the Impersonal Enlightenment Fellowship. This is the classic understanding of enlightenment, which finds expression in many Eastern schools of thought, including Buddhist and Advaita Vedanta. In Cohen's book *Evolutionary Enlightenment*, for example, the word "personal" is used dozens of times throughout the text, but always with a negative and pejorative connotation. The personal is not to be embraced; it is to be transcended. "Leave your story behind" has become the clarion call of enlightenment teachings involving the Western adaptation of Eastern thought.

Gafni points out that the conflation of the *personal* with the conditioned *personality* is a confusion that needs to be corrected.[26] Unique Self Theory involves an essential distinction between the personal *before* realization (of non-dual and radically impersonal Emptiness or Godhead) and the personal that re-emerges *after* this realization. To confuse the personal before realization with the personal that manifests post-realization is a mistake of major consequence. We cannot surrender our person over to an impersonal process (such as cosmic evolution) without distinguishing which level of the personal is being abandoned. It is true that cosmic evolution (conceived as a panentheistic unfolding) is hierarchically beyond the pre-realized and conditioned personality (sometimes traditionally referred to as "ego"), but it does not efface the irreducible dignity of the post-realized Unique Self. In fact, the universal finds its expression only in and through an infinite variety of uniquely personal forms. This is a lesson that cannot be stressed enough, especially in a context where spiritual teachers are often preaching Emptiness, egolessness, and dissolution of the personal—all teachings wherein the particular is subsumed in the universal. When these kinds of ideas (about merging the self with a larger Self) are put in an evolutionary context, it is hard not to hear echoes of the tragedy and injustices that resulted from the enthusiasms of previous generations of evolutionary thinkers, from dialectical materialism to eugenics.

Importantly, Unique Self Theory does not play into the hyper-narcissistic tendencies of postmodern culture. This is a common criticism: that by emphasizing people's uniqueness it plays into their narcissism, and thus fans the flames of the current "crisis of narcissism" plaguing our most important institutions.[27] However, this criticism shows a misunderstanding of both narcissism and Unique Self Theory. According to most traditions in psychology (especially the self-psychology of Heinz Kohut and Harry Stack Sullivan), pathological narcissism is a sign of a *weak* ego structure—of a personality *not* convinced of its true uniqueness. Narcissism involves compensating for doubts about one's unique worth by emphasizing *separateness and specialness*, and thus setting up comparisons in which others are seen as less special. This can be thought of as a kind of defense mechanism, wherein a weakened and disorganized self-system does what it needs to do in order to preserve a sense of its own value. In its most extreme form the narcissist becomes unable to perceive themselves and the world accurately, as their need to see themselves as special distorts reality itself. Someone truly convinced of their uniqueness and intrinsic value would have no need to pathologically prove it to others. They would also have a greater capacity to recognize the uniqueness of others and to see the reality of their interconnections and interdependence. The cure for the narcissism that plagues our culture is, in fact, a deepening of considerations about uniqueness. Only then could there arise a new culture founded on the mutual-recognition of true uniqueness.[28]

Gafni's reclaiming of the personal is the ground of his non-dual humanism sourced deep in the lineage upon which he draws, specifically the work of the great scholar of Kabbalah, Mordechai Lainer of Izbica. The following passage from the Introduction to *Radical Kabbalah* engages this point and is worth quoting at length:

> It is in this sense that we can begin to understand Lainer's provocative idea that the Torah was given by a Moses who is merged with God—not in the voice of God, but in the voice of Moses.... Lainer uses the Zoharic phrase 'The *Shekhinah*[29] speaks through the voice of Moses' as a foundation for his position. This Zoharic phrase, describing the authorship of Deuteronomy, was understood in two very different ways. The theocentric understanding, reflected in most Hasidic works, is that Moses was so completely effaced that he became a kind of channel for the divine voice. For Lainer this is only the first instrumental level of enlightenment. The second possible understanding of the phrase 'the *Shekhinah* speaks through the voice of Moses,' corresponding to the higher level of enlightenment in Lainer's teaching, is almost the opposite: Moses is not effaced, but is rather so completely present that his voice and the voice of the *Shekhinah* become one. Moses' unique persona, his unique perspective, his voice and personality, incarnate the *Shekhinah*; through radical uniqueness, he participates in ontic unity with God.... The *Shekhinah* speaking comes through the *intensification of individuality*, rather than through its effacement. Because the human is a part of God, the principle of acosmism does not negate but rather empowers the individual. The divine voice finds expression in the voice of the unique soul, modeled by the prophet who manifests God's

> voice through the clear prism of his unique individuality. This is the core of Lainer's non-dual humanism.... Lainer argues, both explicitly and implicitly, that the unique individual is the portal through which comes the revelation of the unmediated divine will, the new Torah that can override the law of Sinai.... In various writings I have called this pivot in Lainer's thought 'sacred autobiography,' 'soul print' or 'unique self.'[30]

What is especially critical is that this capacity to "incarnate the *Shekhinah*" be understood not as a domain of the elite, but as an innate capacity available to every human being. Gafni overturns the dominant reading of Lainer's model, which has been mistakenly described as an attainment of elites. In fact Lainer was espousing what Gafni terms "the democratization of enlightenment." Again, from the Introduction to *Radical Kabbalah*:

> The goal of Lainer's teaching is no less than the full democratization of enlightenment. He implicitly identifies and distinguishes between two forms of enlightened consciousness. The first is what we might call the instrumental level. At this stage of realization, the person is an instrument, like a flute or shofar, played by the divine. Images describing this stage of illumination were replete in the Hasidic teachings and writings which constituted Lainer's intellectual framework. This is the level of utter surrender to the divine. As one internalizes this level and transcends it, one comes to another level, which Lainer associates with Temple energy and the Judah archetype. At this level, God does not move through the person as an external force animating and filling the person's voice, but rather God is incarnate within the person, who achieves a radical identity with the divine. Lainer makes clear that this enlightenment is a possibility for every member of the community. Every human being has the potential of Moses.[31]

This teaching principle of democratization is a pivotal focus in Gafni's more popular and accessible follow up to *Radical Kabbalah*, entitled *Your*

Unique Self. One of the defining characteristics of Gafni's work is that it seeks not only the evolution of the leading edge, but also the articulation of a world spirituality that can potentially become a shared spiritual language of the mainstream. This language revolves around the idea of "higher individuation beyond ego," tracing its roots to a lineage which places *sacred autobiography* at the center of the awakening realization. Again from *Radical Kabbalah*:[32]

> For Lainer, one who has become fully clarified becomes both the source of revelation and the incarnation of the *Shekhinah*.... Unlike most of the earlier sources, the kabbalist is not an empty vessel channeling the divine. Rather, the unique consciousness of the purified person, and even their unique unconscious, is divine. This implies that the *Shekhinah* that is one's essence speaks *naturally* from within the enlightened individual. For Lainer, the self of the mystic becomes so conscious as to become transparent to his divine self. Erotic merger with the *Shekhinah* yields not only the hermeneutics of sacred text, but the hermeneutics of sacred autobiography. In this way, Lainer extends the erotic motif beyond traditional hermeneutics and applies it to reading the 'text' of the person's soul print [unique self]. This allows the individual to recover the personal revelation of divine will which is addressed uniquely to him. This revelation comes through the unmediated embrace of the *Shekhinah*, which is antinomian in a way in that is clearly different than any previous sources. Lainer's incarnational *Shekhinah* theology is both empowering and lined with humanistic undertones."[33]

Or in a later passage:

> Sacred autobiography... is itself a sacred text. It is the book of life. This is Lainer's implicit reading of the old Kabbalistic teaching from Safed that every person has their own 'letter in the Torah.' Sacred autobiography both interacts with

> and, occasionally, even trumps sacred text, superseding one's obligation to the written canon. The initiate will understand that, far from giving easy license to one's desires, this post-conventional path requires extraordinary discipline. According to Lainer, one can only access this revelation through the identification and embrace of one's uniqueness. Lainer makes a strong distinction between the sense of specialness or uniqueness at an egoic level, which needs to be purified, and uniqueness at the enlightened level of Judah-consciousness, which is both the expression of and the path to full realization. This level of enlightenment may be achieved consistently or even just for a time in an individual's life. It is through the depths of one's unique individuality, one's soul print [unique self], rather than in the transcendence of individuality, that one hears the voice of the infinite God in the *lehishah*, the whisper of personal revelation.[34]

This notion of Unique Self has the potential to fundamentally change the way we think about enlightenment and thus reframes the nature of teacherly authority claimed by the spiritual teachers. Gafni's overarching point is that what is commonly referred to as enlightenment or awakening is available to every human being—not in some future incarnation, but now. This *democratization of enlightenment* is a core structure of classic Judeo-Christian thought, with some parallels in Eastern traditions such as Mahayana Buddhism. The widespread failure to understand this radical truth about the nature of enlightenment has kept it from being a legitimate modern belief and aspiration. Gafni seeks to redefine enlightenment in its most basic terms as *sanity*. Once you understand enlightenment as sanity, then the democratization of sanity (aka: enlightenment) becomes a self-evident requirement. What stands in the way is the incorrect conflation of uniqueness and separateness (or personal with personality, and both with ego) which motivates enlightenment teachers to reject uniqueness. This in turn motivates the mainstream population—who intuit personal uniqueness to be a critical source of human dignity—to reject enlightenment.

Ideals of enlightenment also shape the dynamics of teacherly authority involving spiritual teachers. If the goals and aspirations of spiritual practice and teaching are the shedding of what is unique and personal in favor of what is universal and collective, then certain kinds teacherly practice and authority structures will follow. The outcome tends to be one-size-fits-all dharma talks, groups of individuals engaging in identical practices, and a related homogenization of appearance, belief, and emotional disposition. According to this view, spiritual teachers are supposed to "kill your ego" and "shatter your story," the result being teacherly interventions and practices that can disregard essential individual differences, sometimes at great risk to an individual's psychological and physical integrity. Furthermore, if the outcome is for all individuals to attain the same insights and transformations, and if the spiritual teacher has (or claims to have had) these very revelations, then they seem to know everything needed in order to teach anyone. This is enlightenment pursued as a known outcome, with its transmission and teaching being akin to the *replication* of this single outcome. As one spiritual teacher entitled his book, *My Master is My Self*,[35] this encapsulates the traditional way of thinking about spiritual teaching, especially in Eastern traditions based on the model of the guru. This way of thinking about teaching and learning is remarkably similar to the forms of schooling critiqued in the Introduction and Chapter 1, where one-size-fits-all approaches were shown to ignore and even damage human dignity, screening out many valuable forms of learning and transformation. Recall the contrasting metaphors of *mind-as-computer* and *mind-as-ecosystem*, where the first would have all students treated as identical informational processors, and the second would have all students treated as unique and evolving. I will return to this parallel between traditional schooling and the postmodern spiritual marketplace. For now I simply note the pervasiveness (and familiarity) of a certain kind of educational configuration that is built around a false sense of the abstract individual who pursues an equally abstract, singular, and fixed learning outcome.

By contrast, Unique Self Theory suggests a way of pursuing enlightenment as an open-ended and individualized outcome, wherein the goal is not to shed the unique but to embrace it. Teacherly authority and practice are reconfigured accordingly. Instead of individuals all doing the same practices and being guided in the pursuit of similar (if not literally identical) experiences and transformations, individuals seek out practices that fit with their uniqueness, deepening and exploring it. The spiritual teacher's authority becomes bounded and context-specific, hinging upon their ability to diagnose the Unique Self trajectory of the individual. Unique Self Theory provides a framework for guiding individuals on a unique journey of awakening, which means that the teacher does not know the exact shape of the outcome, nor could a single teacher claim to be the one true guide on such a journey. This is radically different from the common idea that enlightenment means one thing for everyone and that one person can fully teach and embody it. Indeed, the highest truth of Unique Self Theory has to do with what is sometimes called *collective enlightenment*.[36] The truly "spiritual community" does not slide into cultish homogeneity, nor fracture into individualism, but rather weaves together into what Gafni calls a Unique Self Symphony. Collective enlightenment emerges naturally in a community of Unique Selves, a cooperative endeavor in which the free development of each is a condition for the free development of all. This is the ultimate educational environment, the ultimate learning society, and both a condition for and outcome of the integral paideia that is the focus of this book.

The importance of these contrasting views of enlightenment (and their implications for teacherly authority and educational practice) is brought home most vividly for me in two passages from Rabbi Lainer. Here Gafni explains the context for the passage, which makes reference to a section of the Talmud in which Moses takes the first census of the tribe while it wandered in the wilderness:

> The census of Israel in the desert is an affirmation of the radical uniqueness of every individual. *Mispar* [the Hebrew word for] 'number' is not a technical means of identification but rather a badge of each individual's metaphysical honor, the expression of their uniqueness. For Lainer, the census in the desert is not aimed at yielding population statistics, that is to say, the final number of the community; rather, it is focused on the act of numbering every individual as the revelation of their uniqueness. Lainer states: "The idea of 'lifting up of the

> head' (taking census) is in accordance with the Talmud (*b*Ber. 58a): 'One person's mind is not similar to another person's mind.' For God apportioned goodness and life to each one in particular, and no one is similar to anyone else. It is therefore written, 'Lift up the head.' That is, every person should be in the place belonging to [them]."[37]

Again, Gafni contextualizes another passage from Lainer on the same theme:

> Lainer moves from a language of providence… to a language of the mystique of participation. Uniqueness is rooted in an acosmic metaphysics in which the human being is not merely subject to divine providence but actually participates in divinity. The result of this ontology is the daring, yet obviously necessary, assertion made by Lainer that if one unique soul, *nefesh biferat*, were to be missing, then divinity itself would be lacking. Lainer interprets the phrase 'this shall be the number' (Hos. 2:1) as meaning that: "Everyone will be needed, for from all of the people of Israel, God's greatness can be seen. And if one person is missing… then 'the goblet would be lacking wine' (Cant. 7:2). Just as when the portrait of the king is drawn on many thousands of tiles—if one of them is lost, the portrait of the king would be lacking."[38]

This image brings to mind contemporary montages in which hundreds of thousands of photos are combined to make one face; the uniqueness of each face is unquestionably maintained in the close-up view, while the overall pattern of a single face is also distinctly clear from afar. This is a powerful yet simple encapsulation of the *acosmic humanism* that is the central scholarly contribution of Unique Self Theory. The theme is encapsulated in the mystical idea that each individual has a unique letter in the Torah. Each person is a unique word in an endless sentence spoken by God, whose illocutionary goal is total self-expression.

These kinds of theological and philosophical arguments for inviolable uniqueness and individual dignity pile up until a fundamentally new image of divinity and awakening dawns. It is not through the extinguishing of personality or the self that awakening unfolds. The goal of spiritual practice is not to merge one's personal uniqueness into some vast impersonal process. Instead, the goal of the religiosity argued for by Gafni is (in his nomenclature) to become "outrageously *sane,*" to be so *"fully human,"* so fully *yourself*, that you liberate the powers needed to actualize the stunning uniqueness of your life. In other words, the goal is to lift up your head and be counted, to affirm your irreducible individual dignity and be empowered to participate as only you can in the evolution of humanity.

Toward a New Language of Liberation and Social Emancipation

This is all very different from lowering your head to look at your navel in meditation. Why be counted when you are really *nobody*? Why work to build a world that affirms the dignity of each and every person's *illusory* self? The radical edge in Gafni's teachings expose the apolitical, apathetic, and defeatist underbelly of so much of Western Buddhism, where the teaching of meditation is combined with affluence and liberal values to create an insular and self-affirming escape from the obligations of uniqueness. Who is left to stand up for the dignity and rights of individuals when everyone is sitting down, counting their breaths, and spending a small fortune on retreats from the world? There is no better ideological lubricant to grease our decline into a global corporate dystopia than a form of religiosity that denigrates the individual, promotes quiescence, and calls for a personal disappearance into some larger structure or process.

As early as the 1970s, Habermas identified Zen Buddhism and yoga as "sedatives… orientations that channel outwardly directed protest into apolitical paths….[39] Decades later, the critical theorist Žižek would announce even more provocatively that:

> "Western Buddhism"… is establishing itself as the hegemonic ideology of global capitalism…. "Western Buddhism" presents itself as the remedy against the stressful tension of the capitalist dynamics, allowing us to uncouple and retain inner peace…

> it actually functions as its perfect ideological supplement.... Instead of trying to cope with the accelerating rhythm of technological progress and social changes, one should rather renounce the very endeavor to retain control over what goes on, rejecting it as the expression of the modern logic of domination—one should, instead, "let oneself go," drift along, while retaining an inner distance and indifference towards the mad dance of this accelerated process, a distance based on the insight that all this social and technological upheaval is ultimately just a non-substantial proliferation of semblances.... The "Western Buddhist" meditative stance is arguably the most efficient way, for us, to fully participate in the capitalist dynamic while retaining the appearance of mental sanity.[40]

The point here is not to critique Buddhism as a whole (some of my best friends are Buddhists), but rather to point out that the most rapidly spreading religion in the Western world (Buddhism) is not a form of spirituality that has been leading its adherents to perpetrate disruptive change in the name of social justice. There are exceptions, of course, and some forms of Buddhism provide essential psychological armature for revolutionaries. However, the last time religiously inspired social justice activism unfolded on a large scale in the United States it was a movement firmly rooted in the Judeo-Christian tradition, under the leadership of a reverend with a dream about the dignity of each individual, the inviolability of human rights regardless of race, and the unique expression of humanity represented by African Americans. Today our enthusiasms for Eastern spiritual imports are leading us away from a language of individual rights and democracy leveraged so eloquently by Reverend Dr. King, a language which has served as the most powerful catalyst of social change in history. This language of liberation that is our heritage is being replaced by a language of liberation that is predominantly about the qualities of our own minds and emotional states, including the remarkable idea that by sitting for an hour a day on our $90 buckwheat meditation cushion we are somehow helping to change the world. There is perhaps no more iconic representation of the new American postmodern spiritual landscape than a room full of homogenized white people sitting on sets of standardized cushions facing the wall.

In recent decades we have become increasingly homogenized and standardized, as individual lives have been forced into a matrix of techno-economic and political institutions of unprecedented reach and invasiveness. Counterintuitively, reported increases in individualism, narcissism, and entitlement reflect exactly these trends marking the twilight of the individual. The postmodern narcissist or entitled millennial are in fact suffering from radical doubt about their own self-worth and unbearable uncertainty about the value of their contributions to the world. As Kohut and other self-psychologists have taught us, the narcissistic personality is in fact an extremely fragile self-system, one almost totally dependent upon the affirmations of others.[41] Conspicuous displays of self through social media, self-aggrandizing, do-gooding, and demands for special treatment and attention—these are not signs of the self blown out of proportion, they are signs of a self desperate to be *seen*, a self needing to be *counted* among the worthy, needing to be *affirmed in its unique worth.*

The cure for the dysfunctions of postmodern identity formation is not a spiritual teaching that tells individuals to look through the illusions of their unique personal essence and beyond the unique time and place in which they live. In fact, the postmodern reader of spiritual books is already tenuously connected to their unique gifts (as opposed to the gifts the media leads them to wish they had) and the unique responsibilities of their time and place (as opposed to those directed toward a world represented through social media). Most spiritual books offer a weak balm for the stinging anonymity and depersonalization of mass-customized lifestyles and post-historical consciousness. These books tell us that our particular personalities and places are to be devalued in favor of some abstract universal (be it Evolution, Big Mind, or The Great Perfection), leaving the reader confirmed in their suspicion that their unique life has no special value.

As a way of bringing this point home and as a kind of poetic closing, it is worth quoting at length a teaching delivered by Gafni at Esalen Institute in 2012:

> Your Unique Self is your irreducibly unique perspective which

fosters your unique insight which creates your unique gift which engenders your unique responsibility to address the unique needs in your circle of intimacy and influence. Are you willing [as a seeker of enlightenment] to play a larger game? Let me state the core premise clearly. We live in a world of outrageous pain. The only response to outrageous pain is outrageous love. Why can we not access the outrageous love necessary to engage in the evolutionary healing and transformation of ourselves and our reality? Because we shut our hearts to the unbearable pain of the world. Not merely because, as the classic enlightenment teachers reprimand us, we are stuck in ego. Rather because the gap between our ability to feel and our ability to heal has become too great. It simply hurts too much. Through the virtues of the virtual media we are almost omniscient. We are aware today of a level of suffering that only God was aware of a hundred years ago. But unlike the classic vision of an omniscient but also omnipotent God, we are largely impotent to heal the suffering. Because the gap between our ability to feel and our ability to heal has become too great, we shut our hearts and turn inwards in varying mixtures of overt narcissism and more subtle spiritual materialism in the form of soothing meditations and various pseudo-realizations of oneness and enlightenment. This is in marked distinction to the realization of Unique Self that closes the gap between the ability to feel and the ability to heal…. We now come back to our core premise. We live in a world of outrageous pain. The only response to outrageous pain is outrageous love. What does an outrageous lover do? She commits outrageous acts of love. Which outrageous acts of love? Those acts of love that are a function of her Unique Self. In this way the enlightened Unique Self who is the incarnation of all that is, living in her as her and through her, intimately addresses the unique needs in her circle of intimacy and influence. In doing so she reclaims her potent power—the power of the *Shekhinah*—the power to heal and transform. The gap between the ability to feel and

> the ability to heal is closed. The heart opens once again and a sacred activism sourced in outrageous love perfumes all of reality.[42]

---

1. Habermas (2002, pp. 151-152).

2. See: Weber; Freud; Durkheim; Parsons; etc. And of course, many high-profile scholars still denigrate religion for comparable reasons. See: Dennett (2006).

3. Habermas (2009).

4. See: Wilber (2005). My definitions straddle several of his.

5. See: Paul Tillich's (1958) *Dynamics of Faith*. There are, of course, a number of scholars who have been critical of Tillich's views, and there is a history of definitional disputes from Durkheim, Weber, Freud, and Marx through Bruce Lincoln and Jonathan Z. Smith. I adopt the Tillich/Wilber view without argument, but I am aware of this complex conceptual terrain.

6. Habermas (2008); Wilber (2006); Taylor (1989); Nussbaum (2001).

7. This phrase is from Charles Taylor's (1989) *Sources of the Self.* In a series of other publications I have outlined comparable languages of evaluation, addressing issues in educational neuroscience, biotechnology, and developmental psychology, see: Stein et al. (2011); Stein (2010a); Stein & Heikkinen (2009). It should be noted that the work done in this chapter is mostly descriptive rather than prescriptive. The goal is to build a more robust way of characterizing religious/spiritual teacherly authority, which should reveal properties that bear on the normative worth of the enterprises in question. When it comes to building a language of evaluation, descriptive work unfolds so that richer and more explicit prescriptive work may follow.

8. This chapter would be called *A Preface to a Critique of Religious Education* were it published in another day, but here it is privileged to echo Wilber's (2005) *A Sociable God*, and Habermas' (1979) *Communication and the Evolution of Society*. Specifically, I will talk about *authority*, *justification*, and *legitimacy*, using them somewhat along the lines of Wilber's (1983) "Legitimacy, Authenticity, and Authority in the New Religions." In that paper Wilber's focus is mainly on *authenticity* and *depth*, or how religions get people to *transform vertically*, as it were. However, I will focus mainly on religious *authority*, its conferral, and related teacherly dynamics, a topic Wilber touches on explicitly and

insightfully (but briefly) in the paper just mentioned (Wilber, 1983).

9. Habermas (2002, p. 151).

10. Habermas (2008).

11. Habermas (2008, p. 131; 142).

12. See: Cremin's (1970; 1980; 1988) Pulitzer Prize-winning volumes on the history of American education, which read like a history of religious cultural movements, as Cremin himself notes.

13. Cremin (1970).

14. Cremin (1980); Richardson (1995).

15. This kind of claim has been made in lots of places, see: Habermas (2008); Wilber (1995). I would note that this shows us that these terms are not mutually exclusive (more modern does not equal less religious, etc).

16. Wilber (1983, p. 230; 238).

17. Habermas (1984; 1987).

18. Foucault (1972).

19. Authoritative versus authoritarian parenting styles being the most famous issue in this area.

20. Brandom (1994).

21. Adorno et al. (1950); Luhmann (2004).

22. Although see: Anthony, Ecker, & Wilber (1987).

23. Tomasello (1999).

24. Habermas (2002, p. 150).

25. Esbjörn-Hargens (2011); Engles, Fuhs & Gafni (forthcoming).

26. Gafni (2012a, Ch. 7).

27. Studies have shown that recent generations are more narcissistic than any in history. Many researchers and critics want to relate these findings to recent trends in education, law, and communications technologies, which have all contributed to the inflation of separateness, entitlement, and conspicuous displays of ego. See: de Zengotita (2006); Lasch (1979).

28. What *is* truly ironic is that a culture seemingly obsessed with individualism and self-display has so little room for truly unique forms of self-expression. Despite appearances, postmodern culture denigrates our sense of self and does not allow for the formation of self-reflectively unique personalities. This is because we are limited in how we can represent ourselves and others by communication patterns that are overwhelmingly superficial; the sound-bites, "tweets," and "status updates" that dominate the spaces in which we represent ourselves are antithetical to the kind of reflective and prolonged engagements that foster the recognition of uniqueness in self and other. Postmodern culture is focused on images, surfaces, and montage, as well as the compression of time and space into an ephemeral and ahistorical here and now. It can represent shallow forms of difference and often comes to overemphasize these, but it has no way to handle true depth and authentic expressions of uniqueness.

29. The term *Shekhinah* is one of the Hebrew names of God, connoting the Divine Presence in the world, often associated with the feminine or embodied existence of God.

30. Gafni (2012, pp. liii-liv).

31. Gafni (2012, p. lii).

32. I am taking so often from the Introduction because it is in essence a 60-page summary of the whole work, and beyond this I find that the main body of the text is too closely reasoned and tightly linked with primary sources to allow for an easy lifting of synoptic quotes. Also note that Gafni uses the terms "unique self" and "soul print" interchangeably.

33. Gafni (2012, p. lviii).

34. Gafni (2012, pp. lxii-lxiii).

35. Cohen (1995).

36. Stein & Gafni (forthcoming).

37. Gafni (2012, p. 7). I do not have space to explore the connections here between number, the census, and ancient forms of measurement and numerology mentioned in Chapter 3.

38. Gafni (2012, p. 22).

39. Habermas (1970, p. 27).

40. Žižek (2001, pp. 12-13).

41. Kohut (1971).

42. Gafni (2012b).

Chapter 6
Between Philosophy and Prophesy: Ken Wilber in Context

This essay follows from a request to elaborate on my contributions to a panel focused on critiques of Ken Wilber, held at the 2010 Integral Theory Conference. As I explain, the panel itself was interesting to me because it revealed the complexity of understanding Wilber's work, as well as the difficulty of revealing its value to those who have already dismissed it. Without some awareness of the various fields Wilber is drawing upon, as well as the rhetorical strategies and motivations guiding his writing, it can be hard to see the point of all these quadrants, levels, and other meta-theoretical distinctions being brought to the masses through books, videos, and websites.

Like the previous essay, this essay is also personal, as I know Ken Wilber to some degree and have worked with him on a few writing projects under the auspices of the Center for Integral Wisdom and Integral Institute. I've also exchanged emails with him on the difficulties of caregiving for a spouse. Ken's masterpiece, his book Grace and Grit, documents the spirituality and healing found in the life and death of his wife, Treya Killam Wilber. This is usually the first book I suggest people read when I introduce them to Wilber's work. It is also an important book in my own life, given the spirituality and healing found in the tragic illness of my wife, Meghan Byrnes, which I discussed briefly in the Preface. Grace and Grit transcends genres and boundaries and is profoundly readable and engaging, while also seeking to teach, inform, and be a platform for an emerging philosophy of human development, science, and religion.

The questions addressed in this essay related to the integral paideia have to do with the future of the "great man theory" as applied to public intellectuals. What is the ideal role of the writer and thinker in this age of multimedia spectacle and "edutainment"? Who should we listen to? On what grounds do we grant epistemic authority to others or claim it for ourselves? What are the questions worth discussing in our now planetary public culture, and in what ways should they be discussed?

Contextualizing Wilber's Work

> If we are going to take a step in the transition from civilization to planetization, we will need a map. Each of us carries within, an image of space and time, and this cognitive map tells us who we are, where we come from, and where we are going.... [This map is an] imaging of personal values and cultural forms.... A culture provides an individual with a mapping of time and space, but as the culture goes through a period of change and stressful transformation, the [map] becomes distorted.... In periods of intense cultural distortion, the [map] becomes so changed as to be almost obliterated. Then the individual becomes lost, profoundly lost in the most ontological sense of no longer knowing who or what he is, where he comes from, and where he is going. For some this can be a moment of terror, for others, a time of release. In a moment of silence in which the old forms fall away, there comes a new receptivity, a new centering inward, and in an instant there flashes onto the screen of consciousness a new re-*visioning* of the [map]. There in the receptive silences of meditation the new possibilities of time and space announce themselves, possibilities that lie beyond the descriptions of the old institutions of the old culture. This is the prophetic moment, the annunciation of a new myth, and the beginning of a new culture.
>
> —William Irwin Thompson[1]

In the summer of 2010, at the Integral Theory Conference (ITC) in the hills outside San Francisco, I sat on a panel dedicated to discussing criticisms of Ken Wilber's writings.[2] That day I said that his work is marked by three *laudable liabilities*. These aspects of his theorizing are problematic in that they render it controversial and unappealing to some, and yet they are also valuable, lending a certain intriguing power and validity to his work. The first laudable liability involves some particular theoretical issues having to do with Wilber's use of stage theories from developmental psychology. That topic involves some complex concerns about the *growth-to-goodness assumptions*, which I have already addressed in the Introduction. The second and third laudable liabilities are discussed here. Both of these aspects of Wilber's work have bearing on the future of education and specifically the role of the public intellectual as an educator in the postmodern public sphere.

In this essay I discuss the *engineered popularity* of Wilber's ideas, the second laudable liability I brought up at the ITC. For decades integral theory has been propagated through a variety of media, and was for a time aimed directly at the heart of popular culture. This has turned academics off, while turning on everyday people, non-experts, and intellectual renegades. I raise the question: what is the role of public intellectuals in today's society? Wilber's role as an intellectual in the public sphere is made more complex and controversial by the fact that he is often talking about overtly religious and spiritual topics. The third and final laudable liability I discuss in Wilber's work is its *soteriological orientation*. As I explain, "soteriology" is a term from theology that roughly means "reasoned discourse about salvation." Integral theory takes enlightenment and liberation seriously and offers them up as very real human potentials. Needless to say (and as discussed in the prior essay), this makes the task of being heard and respected harder in some circles.

The broader goal of this essay is to make sense of Wilber's work in terms of the historical era in which it exists. I believe this is the best way to frame a discussion of any problematic issues with any author and their corpus. An author should be understood, at least in part, against the backdrop of their times. When that author is a contemporary, this can have us looking at the present era as if through the eyes of a future historian of ideas. Positioning Wilber's work in the contemporary contexts of our current historical moment means characterizing the emergence of this work as a part of this "time of global transformation."[3]

Theorizing at the Edge of History

Popular philosophical movements are symptomatic of their times. In retrospect, historical moments are often best understood in terms of the ideas that thrived during such moments. Athenian Democracy and the Sophists and Socrates, Medieval Europe and the Church, The American and French Revolutions and the Enlightenment, the Industrial Revolution and Darwinism and Romanticism—no trick of critical historiography could explain away the catalytic *ideas* at the core of these civilizational eras. What ideas will be associated with the past 60 years, the era since the start of the so-called "American Century"? What have been the popular philosophies in the post-industrial social systems that emerged after World War II? This question is complicated by the dynamics of an era that witnessed explosive advances in informational technologies, enabling an unprecedented diffusion of ideas before a growing global public. It is too soon to tell, but the culture of late capitalism may very well be defined in terms of its *lack* of dominant comprehensive doctrines.[4] This has affected all aspects of life, from the media-saturated textures of our self-understandings to the economic policies that structure national geographies.

Today we are witnessing the end of the culture of late capitalism. As post-industrial societies reconfigure into the shape of tomorrow's planetary civilization, there are competing visions as to what the accompanying World Philosophies will be. There are, of course, the classic religious traditions with planetary intentions. East and West, the great traditions have been universalistic, seeking to unite all of humanity under one truth deemed true for all of humanity. These traditions experienced both invigoration and fragmentation during the postmodern decades, and have on the whole been overwhelmed by their own histories of blood, land, and ideological conquest. Nevertheless, the notion of a trans-traditional world spirituality that might transcend but include the great religions strikes me as a viable candidate for a world philosophy, with some traction in the public sphere and civil society.

Other "global noetic polities" will likely emerge as a part of the complex planetary organizations that will be built (and are already being built) to handle increasingly frequent large-scale humanitarian and ecological crises.[5] It is an open question as to whether these new post-national configurations will embody new political worldviews and socio-cultural practices, or if they will simply be bottling old ideological wine in new casks. It seems clearly preferable that institutions of global reach be guided by world-centric ideas and values. However, as organizations like the World Bank and the International Monetary Fund demonstrate, the rhetoric of economic globalism has already arrived and threatens to deliver us to a world of robust international interconnectedness and competition—but devoid of any universal values other than the bottom line.[6]

Globalization should not be confused with planetization; the latter is a term coined by Teilhard de Chardin, the former is a term coined by financiers. The Marxist-inspired image of an awakened humanity capable of retooling the channels built by global capitalism in the name of human dignity and justice is a powerful one. But it begs the question as to how human dignity and global justice should be conceived in the face of an indelible pluralism of cultural values and norms, let alone how such universalistic conceptions might be made available as a common point of reference in an emerging planetary public sphere.

I frame the following considerations about Wilber's integral theory as an example of a new species of planetary public philosophy. It is the kind of world philosophy around which some of tomorrow's planetary culture might congeal. I'm not suggesting that integral theory will become a hegemon. Rather, I think it is better to see Wilber's writings as a certain type of emergent cultural phenomenon, one with clear historical antecedents, but which also has new and distinctly twenty-first century characteristics that are beyond the postmodern mind.[7] Moreover, it is a public philosophy with global reach, widely translated and with copious audio and video offerings on the World Wide Web.

Below I first consider the *engineered popularity* of Wilber's ideas, the first laudable liability. The worry here is that the medium has become the message. In the context of new communications technologies and a radically commoditized media, the public sphere has become oversaturated with ostensibly urgent quasi-academic messages, and many people have grown skeptical of information flows driven by market mechanisms. But before retreating into scholasticism and academic elitism, recall that Kant was clear about the role of the cosmopolitan-comprehensivist philosopher, who would be a much needed servant of truth amidst the contestation in a democratic public sphere. Habermas, Emerson, Dewey, and a host of others have echoed this sentiment, as I have pointed out elsewhere.[8] In the context of a planetary digital media explosion, the issue of how to best *push* the message is complex, and hinges on what the message is.

With the exception of Wilber and Emerson, none of the aforementioned public intellectuals were religious adepts offering explicitly soteriological and eschatological messages. This is the second laudable liability I discuss below. Wilber's writings cannot be well-understood apart from their *soteriological orientation*. Integral theory is more than just a set of meta-theoretical orienting generalizations that can function to ensure the comprehensiveness of knowledge production processes and action orientations. In a very important way, Wilber's writings are mainly concerned with human liberation, awakening, and enlightenment in the fully religious sense of these terms. Reasoned discourse about these topics has been a ubiquitous part of human culture since ancient times and forms the core of the great religious traditions that began during the Axial Age. The transformative practices, rituals, and forms of life initiated by these traditions have a place at the core of Wilber's work. Yet in a cultural context where religious traditions are perceived in complex and contested ways—and religious believers are some of the most dynamic and dangerous ideologues and activists—the unabashed use of religious languages and practices by a highly educated subculture in the post-industrial West is cause for pause. At the edge of history, we must critically consider the World Philosophies to come.

Tomorrow's Public Intellectuals

> It helps to distinguish here between two types of public and publicity. In today's media society, the public sphere serves those who have gained celebrity as a stage on which to present themselves. Visibility is the real purpose of public appearances.

> The price that stars pay for this kind of presence in the mass media is the conflation of their private and public lives. The intention behind participation in political, literary, or scholarly debates or any other contribution to public discourse, by contrast, is quite different. Here reaching agreement on a particular topic or clarifying reasonable dissent takes priority over the self-presentation of the author. This public is not a space of viewers or listeners but an arena in which speakers and interlocutors exchange questions and answers. Rather than everyone else's gaze being focused on the celebrity, an exchange of opinions and reasons takes place.
>
> —Jürgen Habermas[9]

With the birth of the bourgeois public sphere in the seventeenth century came the emergence of the public intellectual (e.g., the academic, philosopher, or scientist) who gives voice to issues of broad interest using a public forum or form of media. The inclusiveness and reach of open public discourse has been increasing continually for the past several centuries.[10] There has been and continues to be *stratification*, both in terms of access and participation. But despite today's so-called "digital divide" which marks a real difference of educational opportunity between economic classes, when put in historical context our era is one that is hyper-communicative and media-saturated. This ever-expanding availability of "digital public space" has transformed the role of the public intellectual, who must now address a polycentric planetary culture.

A global book and newspaper consuming public followed in the wake of the world wars, as massive international publishing houses partnered with the first modern large-scale research universities.[11] Radios and televisions found their way into every home and the first global public moments were shared, experienced with rapt attention by a privileged few in the newly post-industrial West. Along the way, as the Beatles became bigger than Jesus, celebrities went cosmopolitan and thought leaders began to address a global public as communications technologies set the pace. The first global megalopolises began to transmit culture, with Los Angeles and New York churning out films, books, magazines, and mass-produced images—all products of the post-war "cultural industry" increasingly geared toward international dissemination. In the post-war decades, America emerged as the dominant exporter of cultural and intellectual trends, addressing the world as "a city upon the hill." The emergence of a truly global audience transfigured the shape of publicity and came to restructure the demands placed on the personalities populating the world stage, some of whom were philosophers.

Kant echoed the Stoics in arguing that philosophers ought to engage a cosmopolitan audience. Today this involves utilizing the affordances of global post-industrial entertainment-oriented communications technologies to address a planetary public. Dewey, Sartre, Russell, Habermas, and dozens of other public intellectuals began a trend toward explicitly addressing a planetary public in "real time" through whatever media was available. The industrial era climaxed with the engineering of computers and biotechnology, and these first meta-industrial economies have flourished as transnational enterprises. The digital media and Internet have radically transfigured the communicative affordances of the public sphere, affecting a kind of semantic centrifugal force, with public meaning spreading outward into expanding and splintering networks of complex information. These twenty-first century trends can work against the interests of a critical public philosophy.

> Internet use has led to an expansion and fragmentation of communications networks. Thus, although the Internet has a subversive effect on public spheres under authoritarian regimes, at the same time the horizontal and informal networking of communications diminishes the achievements of [industrial-democratic] public spheres. For the latter pool the attention of an anonymous and dispersed public within political communities for selected messages, so that the citizens can address the same critically filtered issues and contributions at the same time. The price for the welcome increase in egalitarianism due to the Internet is a decentering of the modes of access to [information]. In this medium, the contributions of intellectuals can no longer constitute a focal point.[12]

The effect Habermas is pointing out in this quote goes beyond recognizing the detriments of the informational shallows, the mediated and postmodern, and the now frequent observation that we are a distracted society overwhelmed by a commoditized media.[13] Habermas offers a deeper message about the structural transformations of the public sphere, as the structures of our communications technologies and media providers themselves are shifting from concentric hierarchical national networks to polycentric heterarchical international lattices.[14]

The use of the term *decentering* in the Habermas quote above is a nod to Piaget, who used it to refer to the process in epistemological development by which the child *puts their own perspective in perspective* as they are cognitively pushed out from the center of the universe.[15] Decentering is a process that leads toward decreasing narcissism and increasing objectivity and multipersectivalism. Habermas sees how the lattices of communications technologies that now encircle the planet have already started shifting patterns of cultural hegemony and influence, leading in the direction of increased cultural complexity and multiplicity.

The planetary culture that is emerging through the digital media is without governance (and arguably ungovernable). It is without a central nexus, and thus without a dominant historical narrative or vision of its own future. Social-media entertainment devices already figure prominently in childhood identity formation processes, and computers are replacing televisions and radios in many homes. Recent accelerations in the development and dissemination of communication and information technologies have set the lifeworld adrift, as traditions of cultural transmission are altered irreversibly. When photographs were first widely introduced they radically affected collective memory and education. Now hundreds of millions of people traffic in photos (and videos) that are digital and can be instantly shared almost anywhere in the world. Presidents do not give fireside chats for us to listen to by radio; Presidents use Twitter or stream weekly addresses via YouTube in multiple languages, self-consciously broadcasting to a global public. An emerging planetary culture is just beginning to take root within the informational infrastructures of global capitalism—this is the new frontier of education, democracy, and liberational agency. The public intellectual must now build a constituency through web-based communication networks. Affecting public opinion and will-formation requires working with decentralized media outlets and leveraging the new digital grassroots uprising made possible through of the blogosphere, social media, and other platforms. Organizing large-scale social change entails working to forge non-local noetic polities by communicatively linking up geographically diverse centers of local activity.[16]

In this light, Wilber's choreographed digital popularization appears as an undue cause for derision from critics, as well as an illegitimate reason for receiving premature dismissals from academics. The complex affordances of the media available to Wilber enabled the transformation of a writer-lecturer (in the tradition of Emerson and Watts) into a copiously conversant and articulate public philosopher. Wilber became strategic with the new media, linked into book publishing, web seminars, digital learning technologies, streaming video and audio content, and magazine appearances. This leaves him looking from afar like a self-styled cyber celebrity or New Age self-help profiteer, playing digital guru for power and money. But these kinds of criticisms beg the question as to what a twenty-first century planetary public philosophy can and should look like. Can we really anticipate what form intellectual currents will take as they begin circulating in the multimedia-rich planetary public sphere? In today's day and age, what is a public intellectual to do?

Wilber's initiatives with Integral Institute and its subsidiaries should be considered together with other contemporary projects guided by similar values, and of comparable scope and vision: Aurobindo's Auroville, Murphy's Esalen, Thompson's Lindisfarne, Mitchell's Institute of Noetic Sciences, and Gafni and company's Center for Integral Wisdom. This is an incomplete list of organizations founded under philosophical auspices for the express purpose of catalyzing our transformation into a planetary culture. Members of these groups have acted as intellectuals and educationists outside the academy, and serve public interests by engaging in discussions of topics vital to our collective sense of identity. The groups display varying amounts of web-based media dissemination, but all explicitly address a planetary public, and actively work to facilitate open public philosophical debates and inquiries into current events that range beyond both the monoculture of the national mainstream media and the fragmented cacophony of views on the Internet.

The kinds of "cultural ecosystems" that will facilitate the emergence of world-centric cultural agents will not resemble commoditized media entertainment or open platform info-egalitarianism. The public philosophies of the twenty-first century will not come from the academy, although they may transcend but include it. Instead, they will be predicated on the innovative use of planetary communication infrastructures, and thus they will be vulnerable to the limitations of these media. The *telos* of communicative rationality is comprehensive, universal, and cosmopolitan. Implicit in the structure of every speech act is an appeal for universal consensuses. This sets cultural evolution groping toward planetization.[17] During the course of the evolutionary drift there will likely be dozens of forms of new media aiming to instantiate the cosmopolitan community. Public intellectuals will need to work through these emerging channels despite their transience and the large probability that the medium will distort the message.

A great deal of wisdom about the evolution of cultures is contained in Marshall McLuhan's short and often repeated phrase, "the sloughed-off environment becomes a work of art in the new and invisible environment."[18] It points to a view of cultural evolution wherein a historical era is transcended when its taken-for-granted assumptions can be made explicit and displayed as an object. This is a process of shifting figure and ground and rendering visible what was once merely implicit. It is a process of "chunking," of summarizing the prior achievements of a culture so they can be viewed at a sweeping glance—a "miniaturization" of the prior cultural era. Examples abound of this kind of evolutionary cultural redux. For example, the great parks in our major industrial-era cities summarize the agrarian era's subduing of nature. The post-industrial era's recycling of abandoned factories into art studios, startup incubators, and co-working spaces is a re-visioning the industrial era's standardizations of space and time. The education hub network described in Chapter 1 is another example, insofar as it is an attempt to transcend and include post-industrial era schooling in new decentralized integral forms.

Wilber's theoretical imagination also provides an interesting case of evolutionary cultural redux. His writings are relentlessly synthetic and synoptic, making them somewhat akin to miniaturizations of broad cultural domains. They also explicate some of the implicit structures of knowledge production processes currently in use across a wide range of academic and non-academic contexts. These kinds of "brief histories of everything" are needed during times of cultural transformation because they rearticulate the self-understanding of the culture. As William Irwin Thompson explains:

> A historical curriculum is a miniaturization of one civilization and a transition to the next. The Irish monks of the Western European Dark Ages miniaturized the Greco-Roman civilization into a curriculum of the classics and thus established the foundation for what would become the high civilization of medieval Western Europe. Now it is necessary for us to miniaturize the industrial civilization we are leaving behind in preparation for the planetary civilization we are about to enter.[19]

So while the medium is often the message, some messages (like those that "chunk" whole prior eras) are able to transcend their medium. Wilber at his best offers a world philosophy ahead of its time, using today's media to intimate tomorrow's planetary culture. In the lifeword to come we will witness increasing cultural interanimation: Zen priests using Facebook to allocate capital toward web-based Dharma-focused enterprises; "meta-industrial villages" integrating education, local agriculture, and advanced green technology; and globalized entertainment industries marketing transnational trends.[20] Global capitalism will continue to increase the interconnectedness of mega-populated urban centers and the geopolitical landscape will fracture as it continues to stratify. This will be a world of terror and wonder. It will also be a world seen in terms of many different worldviews.

You could see all of these proliferating perspectives as competing worldviews and characterize it as a clash of civilizations.[21] But they can also be seen as worldviews in need of some kind of reconciliation. Wilber's meta-philosophical principle of *non-exclusion*, for example, privileges discourse about finding harmony and similarities between cultures, distilling their valuable complementarities. This is not to downgrade conflict and power, although some see it this way.[22] Instead, Wilber is articulating a more radically *decentered* view.

Remarks are warranted concerning the so-called New Atheists, a group of mainstream academics who have deployed rhetorically heavy-handed criticisms of religious culture, which they have broadcast loudly into the public sphere.[23] They map the cultural terrain in terms of a *conflict* between scientific worldviews and religious worldviews. In a planetary public sphere that is overwhelmingly religious, this kind of polarizing and culture warmongering is counterproductive. When I think about the demands placed on tomorrow's public philosophy as it courses through the communicative infrastructures of a globalized humanity, it seems that only comprehensive cosmopolitan philosophies will be fit to thrive in that cultural ecology. Importantly, these World Philosophies will need to be more than merely *tolerant* when it comes to religious cultures. Inter-religious dialogue and dialogues between science and religion must now be played out both in the global public sphere and as part of cooperative and reciprocal learning processes between cultures.

Questions about the media forms that might embody tomorrow's public philosophies have occupied us so far, but I will now turn to consider a crucial aspect of its content. Making sense of religion in the twenty-first century is a must for any viable world philosophy.

For God's Sake: Soteriological Knowledge-Constitutive Interests

> The interest [constitutive] of... the mind's attempt to reason about spirit, is *soteriological*—interest in salvation; an attempt to comprehend spirit in mental terms so as either to orient oneself toward the pull of a transcendental intuition or to help "picture" the spiritual realm for those minds not yet so *interested*. (The picture is always eventually paradoxical, as both Kant and Nagarjuna explained, but this neither hampers the human interest in the divine nor restricts the usefulness of mandalic reason...).
>
> —Ken Wilber[24]

Public intellectuals in America have put forth a variety of views about religious cultural practices and beliefs. On the whole they have been more religious than not, with historical currents in the American public sphere that have had a distinctively religious bent. The rhetorical tradition of the American Jeremiad has received some scholarly attention and is worth bringing up in connection with a discussion of Wilber's religious and spiritual writings.[25] This is a tradition of public intellectuals that stretches back through Emerson to Jonathan Edwards and the first Great Awakening. It includes figures like Martin Luther King Jr. and Abraham Lincoln, but it also includes dozens of Puritan, Protestant, and Unitarian preachers of lesser stature. Despite its name, the American Jeremiad is a literary trope that transcends both the Judeo-Christian tradition and US national borders, as Emerson most clearly demonstrated. In essence it is a call for moral renewal, which appeals to common religious or spiritual values and is both radically critical and spiritually ennobling. The central theme is that of a broken covenant with God that might be renewed; the central topic is the interface of the personality and the social system. It is a religious diagnosis of the present social condition (as an aspect of the human condition) and a religious prescription that typically involves some reformation of the personality.

The question of how far this tradition of teaching and preaching extends into postmodern times is an interesting one. There are undoubtedly still fiery religious leaders condemning social ills from coast to coast, from television evangelists and megachurches to small urban pulpits and suburban temples and congregations. The mainstream media pundits can be critical of society, but they typically do not dabble in religious topics and would never venture to suggest a religious reformation of the personality as the remedy. The most popular Oprah-style spiritual teachers who top the New York Times best-sellers list are not typically offering complex criticisms of the academic, social, and political landscape. So where has the American Jeremiad gone for the past 60 years?

Aside from the civil rights crusaders, certain public intellectuals and literary figures from the human potential movement and the early Vedanta Society (the Perennialists) come to mind. Aldous Huxley, Abraham Maslow, Rollo May, Jean Houston, Huston Smith, and William Irwin Thompson, for example, were all religiously oriented social critics writing in the post-war era. Reinhold Niebuhr and Paul Tillich are worth adding to this list, as are perhaps John Dewey and Margaret Mead, who brought the pragmatist tradition into the post-industrial public sphere with broad humanist sentiments. More contemporary lineage bearers would include Cornel West's prophetic pragmatism, Martha Nussbaum's capabilities approach to social justice, and Charles Taylor's ethics of authenticity. Positioning Wilber in this historical current is both accurate and hermeneutically helpful.[26]

Wilber has reflected on his own project along these lines, and has explicitly drawn attention to the type of post-secular constructs in which he traffics.[27] The quote that began this section comes toward the end of a book that is highly relevant to our purposes here. In *A Sociable God* (2005), Wilber articulates a broad and theoretical critical sociology of religion, in which he touches on the so-called "new religious movements" in particular. In the penultimate chapter, Wilber expands on Habermas' *Knowledge and Human Interests*, adding to the set of anthropological and deep-seated "knowledge-constitutive interests" detailed therein. Habermas is looking to reconstruct the anthropological structures of consciousness that were the evolutionary precursors and catalysts of our modern reflective discourses. He proposes that scientific discourse is constituted by an interest in gaining control over and explaining the workings of objectified natural processes. Hermeneutics is constituted by an interest in mutual understating and historical self-clarification. The therapeutic and critical discourses (e.g., psychoanalysis and critical theory) are constituted by an interest in liberating humanity from injustice and distorted interpersonal (and intrapersonal) relationships. This is Habermas' first pass at offering a pragmatist-inspired neo-Kantian splicing of epistemological structures (the "Big Three" by another name). Wilber was impressed enough to want to add a knowledge-constitutive interest of his own to the list.

Wilber proposes that a *soteriological knowledge-constitutive interest* should be added to Habermas' taxonomy.[28] This follows a clarification of the historical continuity of reflective religious discourse and the manner in which issues of social justice are transcended but included in considerations of religious salvation. The proposal is that religious discourse should be understood as being constituted by an anthropologically deep-seated interest in awakening to knowledge of God (Reality, Tao, Buddha-Nature, etc.), thus gaining freedom from the existential binds of the human condition. This involves posting a kind of primordial human interest in salvation and enlightenment in the fully religious meaning of these words. Wilber proposes that writers, speakers, and inquiry-oriented communities can be guided by an authentic interest in the religious transformation of the moral personality that results from knowledge of God. I believe that Wilber's broad project is best understood in terms of the soteriological knowledge-constitutive interest that guides it. As I have said, I think this is a double-edged sword—a laudable liability.

On the one hand, this kind of orientation makes Wilber a great deal more than the meta-theorist that many make him out to be. I have placed Wilber's work in the context of current debates about the role of meta-theoretical constructs in interdisciplinary knowledge production and philosophy.[29] But I have always been careful to point beyond the simple interpretation of his writings as a case of meta-theorizing. Some of Wilber's central concepts have explicit origins in spiritual practices and religious ideational frameworks, which makes his work part of an attempt to explicate what Habermas has referred to as the "untapped" semantic potentials of religious language. That is, beyond the task of building an overarching meta-theory unifying vast expanses of knowledge, Wilber has also taken up the task of synthesizing and updating certain aspects of the great religious traditions. This has implications that bear on our interpretation and criticism of Wilber's work. Writers that span a multiplicity of roles and discourses are hard to pin down because they offer arguments and texts that blend a variety of validity claims.

For example, in light of scientific research, Wilber argues that there are transformative effects that result from certain spiritual practices which can be verified through first-person phenomenological accounts and third-person scientific measures. He then goes on to claim that the full actualization of human potential and maturity entails the use of such practices to facilitate a reorganization of the personality around universal experiences and values.[30] This is a complex and, to my mind, fruitful argumentative strategy that blends the claims of science with the claims of religious experience and the soteriological imagination. Moreover, it marks his broad project as a certain type of trans-academic public intellectualism, one with historical precedence, as I have suggested. To really understand Wilber one should look back through the human potential movement to the nineteenth century New Thought synthesizers, to Emerson's Transcendentalism, and to the first American Jeremiads that enlivened the moral sentiments of the post-colonial public. For over a century there have been prophets working out their messages in the context of the reasonable pluralism of religious and scientific worldviews that characterize democratic cultures.[31]

But there are false prophets. Today one big concern is that we have a *marketplace* for spiritual ideas. We have prophets making profits. Book sales, retreats, pay-for-play web content, TV specials—religious and spiritual teachings sell, especially in America. The difference between authentic religious engagements and inauthentic ones is not easily seen. In the previous essay I have already discussed the type of authority exercised by spiritual and religious teachers and the various (and often treacherous) dynamics of such teacherly authority. Being a religious voice in the public sphere has always been an option in America, but the role of religious leaders, teachers, and writers has been transforming, at least since the late 1960s. Today's religious teachers constitute a multicultural, polyvocal, and dynamic group, especially in the context of new media.

Lately Habermas has taken up discussions about religion and the public sphere. He frames it, as I have here, in terms of broad planetary socio-political processes that have transformed the position of the reflective religious believer:

> In modern societies, religious doctrine has to accommodate itself to the unavoidable competition with other forms of faith, and other claims to truth.... Thus modern faith becomes reflexive. Only through self-criticism can it stabilize the inclusive attitude that it assumes within a universe of discourse *delimited* by secular knowledge and *shared* with other religions. This decentered background consciousness of the relativity of one's own standpoint... [is] characteristic of the modern form of religious faith.[32]

Where are the proponents of this reflexive religious faith in the burgeoning planetary public sphere? Wherever they are, I think that it is reasonable to count Wilber among them. As I have mentioned, the industrial-era sociologists who foresaw the decline of religion were mostly wrong. The trends they saw linking secularization, modernization, and democratization were gleaned from a partial sample and indicate only one path through industrialization and political modernization.[33] Ultimately, a plurality of religious voices and movements have come to inhabit the post-industrial world. Religion is not so much in decline as it is in transformation. Dissonances and harmonies will characterize the emerging reflective forms of world spirituality. There will be retreats into pre-reflective stances and reactionary traditionalism, as well as market-driven eclecticisms fueling the consumption of "happiness." There are some responsible voices touching deeply religious topics in the public sphere. It may be that some of the greatest public figures enabling the coming lurch toward planetization will embody the kind of religiosity that is worthy of coursing through our global communications infrastructures.

Twenty-First Century Wilber

I have reflected above on the popularity and publicness of Wilber's philosophy, positioning his work relative to the twenty-first century media forms that have become the inevitable accoutrements of today's public intellectual. The problem today is that all too often the medium is the message. A digital egalitarianism threatens to make all messages equal while transnational media conglomerates leave a reflective public suspicious. But these communications technologies with global reach and multimedia affordances also enable the emergence of near-total sensory immediacy and real-time participation. Humanity is moving toward transtextual (post-Gutenberg) forms of communication and culture, a polycentric and digitally intimate global public sphere. These new forms of communication present complex challenges and it remains an open question as to whether they also damage the scholarly integrity of those who wield them. Nevertheless, I believe that despite the risks there are good reasons for philosophers to consider themselves as having an obligation to address a cosmopolitan audience. On the whole doing so is a laudable liability. We need to navigate the tension involved between the desire to offer an educative public philosophy and the risk that through popularization it will be disfigured.

The same can be said of the second laudable liability discussed above. Wilber's relentless religiosity shines though all his work, and this should figure prominently in our interpretations and criticisms of it. It is both an asset and a liability for a public intellectual to be a religious figure. I follow Habermas in arguing that there are valuable untapped semantic potentials in religious languages, and I suggest that a large part of Wilber's work has been dedicated to rearticulating perennial religious ideas and forms of life. Religion is a twenty-first century flashpoint and figures prominently in most impending geopolitical crises. Moreover, the conflicts between religious and scientific worldviews have led to a variety of cultural polarizations, such that it is taken as highly improbable that one could be simultaneously a voice of reason and a voice for God (as Wilber is). Again, a sophisticated hermeneutics should recognize the complex mixture of validity claims implicated in Wilber's work. The concepts in play when taking up a soteriological orientation are unique, and are not best characterized as meta-theoretical or philosophical constructs.

Wilber is a popular public philosopher and a religious figure, for better and for worse. The dynamics of attraction and repulsion and the tendency to polarize audiences often characterizes great works of art,[34] and the theoretical imagination is also prone to powerfully affecting audiences. At the beginning of the twenty-first century it has become cliché in some circles to speak of the coming of a New Age, and rightly so. Many from my generation (born just on either side of 1980) dismiss Baby Boomers who come offering New Paradigms and East-West self-styled awakenings, all for sale on the spiritual marketplace. But I have seen Wilber's work cut through the cynicism and commodity-driven media forms that characterize the postmodern public sphere. I tried to make this clear on that panel at the ITC in 2010. Integral theory has certain laudable liabilities, just as we all do, as our greatest strengths are often closely allied with our greatest weaknesses.

---

1. Thompson (1977, pp. 13-14).

2. What transpired during that two-hour panel in California? I found myself having to explicitly bring up the need for a rigorous and historically sensitive *hermeneutics of respect*, as opposed to a parochial and pedantic *hermeneutics of suspicion*. We must read Wilber as we would read a signpost at the edge of history. The other panelists admitted to having not even read Wilber's books in their entirety.

3. Habermas (2006).

4. Habermas (1990); Jameson (1992).

5. See: Thompson (2004) on the idea of the *global noetic polity*.

6. Beck (2000).

7. Smith (1989).

8. Stein (2010).

9. Habermas (2008, pp. 11-12).

10. Habermas (1979; 1984).

11. Cremin (1988).

12. Habermas (2009, p. 53).

13. Carr (2011); de Zengotita (2006).

14. Benkler (2006).

15. Habermas (1979).

16. Harris, Moffitt, & Squires (2010).

17. Habermas (1979; 1998).

18. McLuhan (1964); Thompson (1998); de Zengotita (2006).

19. Thompson (2009, p. 11).

20. Thompson (2004).

21. Huntington (1998).

22. Edwards (2009).

23. See: Dennett (2006) or Dawkins (2008) for example.

24. Wilber (2005, pp. 144-145).

25. Bercovitch (1980).

26. Huxley (1963); Maslow (1971); May (1969); Smith (1989); Thompson (1971; 2004); Niebuhr (1960); Tillich (1959); Dewey (1960); West (1982); Taylor (1992).

27. Wilber (2000).

28. Wilber (2005).

29. Stein (2007; 2010).

30. Wilber (1995; 1999; 2000).

31. Cremin (1970).

32. Habermas (2002, p. 150).

33. Habermas (2001).

34. Nisenson (1993).

Bibliography

Adi Da Samraj. (2006). *Not-Two Is Peace: The Ordinary People's Way of Global Cooperative Order.* Middletown, CA: Is Peace 723.

Adorno, T. W., Frenkel-Brunswik, E., Levinson, D. J., & Sanford, R. N. (1950). *The Authoritarian Personality*. New York: Harper & Row.

Ahrne, G., & Brunsson, N. (2008). *Meta-organizations.* Northampton, MA: Edward Elgar Publishing.

Alder, K. (2003). *The Measure of All Things.* New York: Free Press.

Alexander, C. N., & Langer, E. J. (Eds.). (1990). *Higher Stages of Human Development: Perspectives on Adult Growth.* New York: Oxford University Press.

Angus, I. (2015, September). "When Did the Anthropocene Begin… and Why Does It Matter?" *Monthly Review, 67*(4), 1-11.

Angwin, J., Larson, J., Mattu, S., & Kirchner, L. (2016, May). "Machine Bias: There's Software Used Across the Country to Predict Future Criminals. And It's Biased Against Blacks." *ProPublica.org.*

Anthony, D., Ecker, B., & Wilber, K. (1987). *Spiritual Choices: The Problem of Recognizing Authentic Paths to Inner Transformation.* New York: Paragon House.

Apple, M. W. (2001). *Educating the "Right" Way: Markets, Standards, God, and Inequality.* New York: Routledge.

Apple, M. W. (2004). *Ideology and Curriculum.* New York: Routledge.

Apple, M. W. (2013). *Can Education Change Society?* New York: Routledge.

Armon, C. (1984). *Ideals of the Good Life: A Longitudinal/Cross-Sectional Study of Evaluative Reasoning in Children and Adults* (Unpublished Doctoral Dissertation). Harvard University, Cambridge.

Arnett, J. J. (2006). *Emerging Adulthood.* New York: Oxford University Press.

Arrow, K., Bowles, S., & Durlauf, S. (Eds.). (2000). *Meritocracy and Economic Inequality.* Princeton: Princeton University Press.

Baldwin, J. M. (1906). *Thought and Things: A Study of the Development and Meaning of Thought, or Genetic Logic* (Vols. 1-3). New York: Macmillan.

Basseches, M., & Mascolo, M. (2010). *Psychotherapy as a Developmental Process.* New York: Routledge.

Beck, U. (1992). *Risk Society: Towards a New Modernity.* London: SAGE Publications.

Beck, U. (2000). *What Is Globalization?* Cambridge, UK: Polity Press.

Beck, U. (2001). *Individualization: Institutionalized Individualism and Its Social and Political Consequences*. London: SAGE Publications.

Becker, G. S. (1964). *Human Capital: A Theoretical and Empirical Analysis, With Special Reference to Education.* Chicago: University of Chicago Press.

Benhabib, S. (1986). *Critique, Norm, and Utopia: A Study of the Foundations of Critical Theory.* New York: Columbia University Press.

Benkler, Y. (2006). *The Wealth of Networks: How Social Production Transforms Markets and Freedom.* New Haven: Yale University Press.

Bercovitch, S. (1980). *The American Jeremiad.* Madison: University of Wisconsin Press.

Bhaskar, R. (1986). *Scientific Realism and Human Emancipation.* New York: Verso.

Bhaskar, R. (1993). *Dialectic: The Pulse of Freedom.* New York: Verso.

Bhaskar, R. (2012). *The Philosophy of Metareality: Creativity, Love and Freedom.* New York: Routledge.

Bowles, S., & Gintis, H. (1976/2011). *Schooling in Capitalist America: Educational Reform and the Contradictions of Economic Life*. New York: Basic Books.

Bowles, S., & Gintis, H. (1986). *Democracy and Capitalism: Property, Community, and the Contradictions of Modern Social Thought.* New York: Basic Books.

Bowles, S., & Gintis, H. (1998). *Recasting Egalitarianism: New Rules for Communities, States, and Markets.* New York: Verso.

Brain, M. (2012). *Manna: Two Visions of Humanity's Future.* Cary, NC:

BYG Publishing.

Brandom, R. B. (1994). *Making It Explicit: Reasoning, Representing, and Discursive Commitment*. Cambridge: Harvard University Press.

Braun, J., Kahn, R., Froehlich, T., Auinger, P., & Lanphear, B. P. (2006). "Exposures to Environmental Toxicants and Attention Deficit Hyperactivity Disorder in U.S. Children." *Environmental Health Perspectives*, *114*(12), 1904-1909.

Brown, J. (1992). *The Definition of a Profession: The Authority of a Metaphor in the History of Intelligence Testing, 1890-1930*. Princeton: Princeton University Press.

Bruner, J. S. (1969). *The Process of Education*. Cambridge: Harvard University Press.

Brunsson, N., & Jacobsson, B. (2000). *A World of Standards*. New York: Oxford University Press.

Buck, J., & Villines, S. (2007). *We the People: Consenting to a Deeper Democracy: A Guide to Sociocratic Principles and Methods*. Washington, DC: Sociocracy.info Press.

Busch, L. (2011). *Standards: Recipes for Reality*. Cambridge: MIT Press.

Callahan, R. E. (1964). *Education and the Cult of Efficiency: A Study of the Social Forces That Have Shaped the Administration of the Public Schools*. Chicago: University of Chicago Press.

Campbell, D. T. (1975). "Assessing the Impact of Planned Social Change." In G. M. Lyons (Ed.), *Social Research and Public Policies: The Dartmouth/OECD Conference*, 3-45. Hanover, NH: Dartmouth College, Public Affairs Center.

Campbell, D. T. (1987). "Evolutionary Epistemology." In G. Radnitzky & W. W. Bartley (Eds.), *Evolutionary Epistemology, Rationality, and the Sociology of Knowledge*. La Salle, IL: Open Court Publishing Company.

Capra, F., & Luisi, P. L. (2014). *The Systems View of Life: A Unifying Vision*. New York: Cambridge University Press.

Carey, W. B. (2000). "What the Multimodal Treatment Study of Children With Attention-Deficit Hyperactivity Disorder Did and Did Not Say

About the Use of Methylphenidate for Attention Deficits." *Pediatrics, 105*, 863-864.

Carr, N. (2011). *The Shallows: What the Internet Is Doing to Our Brains*. New York: W. W. Norton & Company.

Carreira, J. (2009, November). "Napkin Drawing." Personal Communication, Cambridge.

Case, R. (1992). *The Mind's Staircase: Exploring the Conceptual Underpinnings of Children's Thought and Knowledge*. Hillsdale, NJ: Lawrence Erlbaum Associates.

Chamberlain, S., Robbins, T., & Sahakian, B. (2007). "The Neurobiology of Attention-Deficit/Hyperactivity Disorder." *Biological Psychiatry, 61*, 1317-1319.

Chapman, P. D. (1988). *Schools as Sorters: Lewis M. Terman, Applied Psychology, and the Intelligence Testing Movement, 1890-1930*. New York: New York University Press.

Chomsky, N. (1997, October). "What Makes the Mainstream Media Mainstream?" *Z Magazine*.

Chomsky, N. (2004). *Language and Politics*. Oakland: AK Press.

Churchland, P. M. (1996). *The Engine of Reason, the Seat of the Soul: A Philosophical Journey Into the Brain.* Cambridge: MIT Press.

Cohen, A. (1995). *My Master Is My Self: The Birth of a Spiritual Teacher*. Lenox, MA: Moksha Press.

Cohen, A. (2011). *Evolutionary Enlightenment: A New Path to Spiritual Awakening*. New York: SelectBooks.

Collins, A., & Halverson, R. (2009). *Rethinking Education in the Age of Technology: The Digital Revolution and Schooling in America*. New York: Teachers College Press.

Commons, M. L., Richards, F. A., & Armon, C. (Eds.). (1984). *Beyond Formal Operations*. New York: Praeger.

Commons, M. L., Trudeau, E. J., Stein, S. A., Richards, F. A., & Krause, S. R. (1998). "Hierarchical Complexity of Tasks Shows the Existence of Developmental Stages." *Developmental Review, 18*(3), 237-278.

Conrad, P. (2007). *The Medicalization of Society: On the Transformation of Human Conditions Into Treatable Disorders.* Baltimore: Johns Hopkins University Press.

Cremin, L. (1970). *American Education: The Colonial Experience, 1607-1783.* New York: Harper & Row.

Cremin, L. (1980). *American Education: The National Experience, 1783-1876.* New York: Harper & Row.

Cremin, L. (1988). *American Education: The Metropolitan Experience, 1876-1980.* New York: Harper & Row.

Darling-Hammond, L. (2010). *The Flat World and Education: How America's Commitment to Equity Will Determine Our Future.* New York: Teacher's College Press.

Dawkins, R. (2008). *The God Delusion.* New York: Mariner Books.

Dawson, T. L. (2002). "A Comparison of Three Developmental Stage Scoring Systems." *Journal of Applied Measurement, 3*(2), 146-189.

Dawson, T. L. (2003). "A Stage Is a Stage Is a Stage: A Direct Comparison of Two Scoring Systems." *Journal of Genetic Psychology, 164*(3), 335-364.

Dawson, T. L. (2004). "Assessing Intellectual Development: Three Approaches, One Sequence." *Journal of Adult Development, 11*(2), 71-85.

Dawson. T. L. (2015). "Anatomy of a DiscoTest." *Discotest.lectica.org.*

Dawson, T. L., & Gabrielian, S. (2003). "Developing Conceptions of Authority and Contract Across the Lifespan: Two Perspectives." *Developmental Review, 23*, 162-218.

Dawson, T. L., & Stein, Z. (2008). "Cycles of Research and Application in Education: Learning Pathways for Energy Concepts." *Mind, Brain, and Education, 2*, 89-102.

Dawson, T. L., & Stein, Z. (2011). "Virtuous Cycles of Learning: Redesigning Testing During the Digital Revolution." Originally presented at the Ettore Majorana Center for Scientific Culture. The International School of Mind, Brain, and Education, Sicily.

Dawson, T. L., Xie, Y., & Wilson, M. (2003). "Domain-General and Domain-Specific Developmental Assessments: Do They Measure the

Same Thing?" *Cognitive Development*, *18*, 61-78.

Dawson-Tunik, T. L. (2004). "A Good Education Is… The Development of Evaluative Thought Across the Life-Span." *Genetic, Social, and General Psychology Monographs*, *130*(1), 4-112.

de Zengotita, T. (2006). *Mediated: How the Media Shapes Your World and the Way You Live in It.* New York: Bloomsbury USA.

Dennett, D. (2006). *Breaking the Spell: Religion as a Natural Phenomenon.* New York: Penguin Books.

Despain, H. (Manuscript in preparation). *On the Higher Education: A Dialectal Critical Realist Philosophy of Education.* Northampton, MA.

Dewey, J. (1916). *Democracy and Education: An Introduction to the Philosophy of Education*. New York: Macmillan.

Dewey, J. (1922). *Human Nature and Conduct: An Introduction to Social Psychology.* New York: Henry Holt and Company.

Dewey, J. (1929). *The Sources of a Science of Education*. New York: Horace Liveright.

Dewey, J. (1960). *A Common Faith*. New Haven: Yale University Press.

Diamond, J. (1999). *Guns, Germs, and Steel: The Fates of Human Societies.* New York: W. W. Norton & Company.

Diller, L. H. (1999). *Running on Ritalin: A Physician Reflects on Children, Society, and Performance in a Pill.* New York: Bantam Books.

Diller, L. H. (2006). *The Last Normal Child: Essays on the Intersection of Kids, Culture, and Psychiatric Drugs.* Westport, CT: Praeger.

DiPerna, D. (2012). "Integral Religious Studies in a Developmental Context." *The Journal of Integral Theory and Practice*, 7(2), 1-18.

Divine, M. (2014, March). "World-Centric Warrior." Presentation to the Board of The Center for Integral Wisdom, Teleconference.

Duncan, O. D. (1984). *Notes on Social Measurement: Historical and Critical*. New York: Russell Sage Foundation.

Easterling, K. (2014). *Extrastatecraft: The Power of Infrastructure Space.* New York: Verso.

Edwards, M. (2008). "Every Today Was a Tomorrow: An Integral Method for Indexing the Social Mediation of Preferred Futures." *Futures*, *40*(2), 173-189.

Edwards, M. (2008a). "Where Is the Method to Our Integral Madness? An Outline for Integral Meta-Studies." *Journal of Integral Theory and Practice*, *3*(2), 165-194.

Edwards, M. (2009). *Organizational Transformation for Sustainability: An Integral Metatheory*. London: Routledge.

Eisenstein, C. (2011). *Sacred Economics: Money, Gift, and Society in the Age of Transition.* Berkeley, CA: Evolver Editions.

Eisenstein, C. (2012, May 28). "Permaculture and the Myth of Scarcity." *Charleseisenstein.net.*

Elgin, C. Z. (1996). *Considered Judgment.* Princeton: Princeton University Press.

Elliott, C. (2003). *Better Than Well: American Medicine Meets the American Dream.* New York: W. W. Norton & Company.

Engles, L., Fuhs, C., & Gafni, M. (Forthcoming). *Anatomy of a Smear*. Tucson, AZ: Integral Publishers.

Esbjörn-Hargens, S. (2010). "An Ontology of Climate Change: Integral Pluralism and the Enactment of Multiple Objects," *Journal of Integral Theory and Practice*, *5*(1), 143-174.

Esbjörn-Hargens, S. (2011). "Executive Editor's Note." *Journal of Integral Theory and Practice*, *6*(1).

Esbjörn-Hargens, S., & Zimmerman, M. E. (2009). *Integral Ecology: Uniting Multiple Perspectives on the Natural World.* Boston: Shambhala Publications.

Farber, P. L. (1998). *The Temptations of Evolutionary Ethics.* Los Angeles: University of California Press.

Feinberg, J. (1992). *Freedom and Fulfillment: Philosophical Essays*. Princeton: Princeton University Press.

Fischer, K. W. (1980). "A Theory of Cognitive Development: The Control and Construction of Hierarchies of Skills." *Psychological Review*, *87*(6), 477-531.

Fischer, K. W., & Bidell, T. R. (2006). "Dynamic Development of Action,

Thought, and Emotion." In R. M. Lerner & W. Damon (Eds.), *Handbook of Child Psychology: Theoretical Models of Human Development* (pp. 313-399). New York, Wiley.

Fischer, K. W., Hand, H. H., & Russell, S. (1984). "The Development of Abstractions in Adolescence and Adulthood." In M. L. Commons, F. A. Richards & C. Armon (Eds.), *Beyond Formal Operations: Late Adolescent and Adult Cognitive Development* (pp. 43-73). New York: Praeger.

Fischer, K. W., & Kennedy, B. (1997). "Tools for Analyzing the Many Shapes of Development: The Case of Self-in-Relationships in Korea." In E. Amsel & K. A. Renninger (Eds.), *Processes of Development* (pp. 117-152). Mahwah, NJ: Erlbaum.

Fiske, D. W., & Shweder, R. A. (Eds.). (1986). *Metatheory in Social Science: Pluralisms and Subjectives*. Chicago: University of Chicago Press.

Forman, M. (2010). *A Guide to Integral Psychotherapy: Complexity, Integration, and Spirituality in Practice.* Albany, NY: SUNY Press.

Foucault, M. (1972). *The Archaeology of Knowledge and the Discourse on Language*. New York: Pantheon Books.

Foucault, M. (1973). *The Birth of the Clinic: An Archaeology of Medical Perception.* New York: Pantheon Books.

Fowler, J. (1981). *Stages of Faith: The Psychology of Human Development and the Quest for Meaning*. San Francisco: Harper & Row.

Freeman, S. (2007). *Rawls*. New York: Routledge.

Fukuyama, F. (2002). *Our Posthuman Future: Consequences of the Biotechnology Revolution*. New York: Farrar, Straus & Giroux.

Fuller, R. B. (1971). *Education Automation: Comprehensive Learning for Emergent Humanity.* Zurich: Lars Muller Publishers.

Gafni, M. (2012). *Radical Kabbalah* (Books 1 & 2). Tucson, AZ: Integral Publishers.

Gafni, M. (2012a). *Your Unique Self: The Radical Path to Personal Enlightenment*. Tucson, AZ: Integral Publishers.

Gafni, M. (2012b, June). "Unique Self and the Self-Organizing Universe." Public lecture at Esalen Institute, Big Sur.

Gafni, M. (2015). *Self in Integral Evolutionary Mysticism: Two Models and Why They Matter*. Tucson, AZ: Integral Publishers.

Gafni, M., & Stein, Z. (Forthcoming). *The Universe: A Love Story*. Tucson, AZ: Integral Publishers.

Gardiner, H. W., & Kosmitzki, C. (2004). *Lives Across Cultures: Cross-Cultural Human Development*. New York: Allyn & Bacon.

Gatto, J. T. (2006). *The Underground History of American Education: An Intimate Investigation Into the Prison of Modern Schooling*. New York: Oxford Village Press.

Gebser, J. (1985). *The Ever Present Origin*. Athens, OH: Ohio University Press.

George, A. L., & Bennett, A. (2005). *Case Studies and Theory Development in the Social Sciences*. Cambridge: MIT Press.

George, S. (1977). *How the Other Half Dies: The Real Reasons for World Hunger*. Montclair, NJ: Allanheld, Osmun & Co.

George, S. (2010). *Whose Crisis, Whose Future? Towards a Greener, Fairer, Richer World*. Cambridge: Polity Press.

Gereffi, G., Garcia-Johnson, R., & Sasser, E. (2001). "The NGO-Industrial Complex." *Foreign Policy*, *125*, 56-65.

Gibbons, M., Limoges, C., Nowotny, H., Schwartzman, S., Scott, P., & Trow, M. (1994). *The New Production of Knowledge: The Dynamics of Science and Research in Contemporary Societies*. London: SAGE Publications.

Girard, R. (1989). *The Scapegoat*. Baltimore: John Hopkins University Press.

Goldhagen, D. J. (1996). *Hitler's Willing Executioners: Ordinary Germans and the Holocaust*. New York: Knopf.

Goldin, C., & Katz, L. F. (2008). *The Race Between Education and Technology*. Cambridge: Harvard University Press.

Gordon, D., Meyer, A., & Rose, D. (2016). *Universal Design for Learning: Theory and Practice*. Cambridge: CAST Professional Publishing.

Gould, S. J. (1996). *The Mismeasure of Man*. New York: W. W. Norton & Company.

Graeber, D. (2011). *Debt: The First 5,000 Years.* London: Melville House.
Graeber, D. (2015). *The Utopia of Rules: On Technology, Stupidity, and the Secret Joys of Bureaucracy.* London: Melville House.
Grassegger, H., & Krogerus, M. (2017, April). "The Data That Turned the World Upside Down." *Motherboard.vice.com.*
Greenhall, J. (2014, November). "The Coming Great Transition." *Medium.com.*
Greenhall, J. (2017, January). "Situational Assessment 2017: Trump Edition." *Medium.com.*
Habermas, J. (1970). *Toward a Rational Society: Student Protest, Science, and Politics.* Boston: Beacon Press.
Habermas, J. (1972). *Knowledge and Human Interests.* Boston: Beacon Press.
Habermas, J. (1975). *Legitimation Crisis.* Boston: Beacon Press.
Habermas, J. (1979). *Communication and the Evolution of Society.* Boston: Beacon press.
Habermas, J. (1984). *The Theory of Communicative Action, Vol. 1: Reason and the Rationalization of Society.* Boston: Beacon Press.
Habermas, J. (1987). *The Theory of Communicative Action, Vol. 2: Lifeworld and System: A Critique of Functionalist Reason.* Boston: Beacon Press.
Habermas, J. (1990). *The Philosophical Discourse of Modernity: Twelve Lectures.* Cambridge: MIT Press.
Habermas, J. (1993). "Lawrence Kohlberg and Neo-Aristotelianism." In J. Habermas, *Justification and Application: Remarks on Discourse Ethics* (pp. 113-133). Cambridge: MIT Press.
Habermas, J. (1996). *Between Facts and Norms: Contributions to a Discourse Theory of Law and Democracy.* Cambridge: MIT Press.
Habermas, J. (1998). *On the Pragmatics of Communication.* Cambridge: MIT Press.
Habermas, J. (1999). *The Inclusion of the Other: Studies in Political Theory.* Cambridge: MIT press.
Habermas, J. (2001). *The Postnational Constellation: Political Essays.* Cambridge: MIT Press.

Habermas, J. (2002). "A Conversation about God and the World." In J. Habermas, *Religion and Rationality: Essays on Reason, God, and Modernity*. Cambridge: MIT Press.

Habermas, J. (2003). *The Future of Human Nature*. Cambridge, UK: Polity Press.

Habermas, J. (2006). *Time of Transitions*. Cambridge: MIT Press.

Habermas, J. (2008). *Between Naturalism and Religion: Philosophical Essays*. Malden, MA: Polity Press.

Habermas, J. (2009). *Europe: The Faltering Project*. Cambridge, UK: Polity Press.

Hagopian, J. (Ed.). (2014). *More Than a Score: The New Uprising Against High-Stakes Testing*. Chicago: Haymarket Books.

Hamilton, M. (2008). *Integral City: Evolutionary Intelligences for the Human Hive*. B.C., Canada: New Society Publishers.

Harris, H. E., Moffitt, K. R., & Squires, C. R. (Eds.). (2010). *The Obama Effect: Multidisciplinary Renderings of the 2008 Campaign*. Albany: SUNY Press.

Harvey, D. (1990). *The Condition of Postmodernity: An Enquiry Into the Origins of Cultural Change*. New York: Blackwell Publishers Inc.

Harvey, D. (2005). *A Brief History of Neoliberalism*. New York: Oxford University Press.

Harvey, D. (2006). *Limits to Capital*. New York: Verso.

Harvey, D. (2009). *Social Justice and the City*. Athens, GA: University of Georgia Press.

Harvey, D. (2011). *The Enigma of Capital: And the Crises of Capitalism*. New York: Oxford University Press.

Harvey, D. (2013). *Rebel Cities: From the Right to the City to the Urban Revolution*. London: Verso.

Harvey, D. (2014). *Seventeen Contradictions and the End of Capitalism*. New York: Oxford University Press.

Harvey, D. (2016). *The Ways of the World*. New York: Oxford University Press.

Harvey, D. (2016a, March 28). "Senior Loeb Scholar Lecture." Harvard University Graduate School of Design, Cambridge.

Hawken, P., Lovins, A., & Lovins, L. H. (2010). *Natural Capitalism: Creating the Next Industrial Revolution.* London: Earthscan.

Healy, D. (1996). "Psychopharmacology in the New Medical State." In Healy, D., & Doogan, D. P. (Eds.), *Psychotropic Drug Development: Social, Economic and Pharmacological Aspects.* London: Chapman & Hall Medical.

Healy, D. (1997). *The Antidepressant Era.* Cambridge: Harvard University Press.

Healy, D. (2002). *The Creation of Psychopharmacology.* Cambridge: Harvard Education Press.

Hess, F. M., & Finn, C. E. (Eds.). (2007). *No Remedy Left Behind: Lessons From a Half-Decade of NCLB.* Washington, DC: AEI Press.

Hess, F. M., & Petrilli, M. J. (2006). *No Child Left Behind.* New York: Peter Lang.

Hill, J. D. (2009). *Beyond Blood Identities: Posthumanity in the Twenty-First Century.* Lanham, MD: Lexington Books.

Hirschi, J. S. (2015). *Ripe for Change: Garden-Based Learning in Schools.* Cambridge: Harvard Education Press.

Huntington, S. P. (1998). *The Clash of Civilizations and the Remaking of World Order.* New York: Simon & Schuster.

Hursh, D. (2008). *High-Stakes Testing and the Decline of Teaching and Learning.* New York: Rowman & Littlefield.

Huxley, A. (1945). *The Perennial Philosophy.* New York: Harper & Row.

Huxley, A. (1963). *Literature and Science.* New York: Harper & Row.

Hyman, S. (2002). "Ethical Issues in Psychopharmacology: Research and Practice." In S. J. Marcus (Ed.), *Neuroethics: Mapping the Field.* San Francisco: Dana Press.

Hyman, S. (2007). "Can Neuroscience Be Integrated Into the DSM-V?" *Nature Reviews Neuroscience, 8,* 725-732.

Illich, I. (1971). *Deschooling Society.* New York: Harper & Row.

Illich, I. (1976). *Medical Nemesis: The Expropriation of Health.* New York: Pantheon Books.

James, W. (1923). *The Varieties of Religious Experience: A Study in Human*

Nature. New York: Longmans, Green & Co.

James, W. (1950). *The Principles of Psychology* (Vols. 1-2). New York: Dover Publications.

Jameson, F. (1992). *Postmodernism, or, The Cultural Logic of Late Capitalism*. Durham, NC: Duke University Press.

Jaques, E. (1970). *Work, Creativity, and Social Justice*. London: Heinemann Educational.

Jaques, E. (1976). *A General Theory of Bureaucracy*. New York: Halsted Press.

Jensen, P. S., Hinshaw, S. P., Swanson, J. M., Greenhill, L. L., Conners, C. K., Arnold, L. E., ...Wigal, T. (2001). "Findings From the NIMH Multimodal Treatment Study of ADHD (MTA): Implications and Applications for Primary Care Providers." *Journal of Developmental & Behavioral Pediatrics*, *22*(1), 60-73.

Johnson, A. G. (2001). *Privilege, Power, and Difference*. Boston: McGraw-Hill.

Johnson, S. (2012). *Future Perfect: The Case for Progress in a Networked Age*. New York: Riverhead Books.

Jones, J. (2015). *Beyond Generosity: The Action Logics in Philanthropy* (Unpublished Doctoral Dissertation). University of San Diego, CA.

Kagan, J. (2009). *The Three Cultures: Natural Sciences, Social Sciences, and the Humanities in the 21st Century*. New York: Cambridge University Press.

Kamin, B. (2010). *Terror and Wonder: Architecture in a Tumultuous Age*. Chicago: University of Chicago Press.

Karier, C. (1986). *The Individual, Society, and Education: A History of American Educational Ideas*. Chicago: University of Illinois Press.

Kauffman, S. (1993). *The Origins of Order: Self-Organization and Selection in Evolution*. New York: Oxford University Press.

Kegan, R. (1982). *The Evolving Self: Problem and Process in Human Development*. Cambridge: Harvard University Press.

Kegan, R. (1994). *In Over Our Heads: The Mental Demands of Modern Life*. Cambridge: Harvard University Press.

King, P. M., & Kitchener, K. S. (1994). *Developing Reflective Judgment: Understanding and Promoting Intellectual Growth and Critical Thinking in Adolescents and Adults*. San Francisco: Jossey-Bass.

Kitchener, K. S., & Fischer, K. W. (1990). "A Skill Approach to the Development of Reflective Thinking." In D. Kuhn (Ed.), *Developmental Perspectives on Teaching and Learning Thinking Skills: Contributions to Human Development, Vol. 21* (pp. 48-62). Basel, Switzerland: Karger.

Klein, J. T. (2005). *Humanities, Culture, and Interdisciplinarity*. Albany: SUNY Press.

Kohlberg, L. (1981). *The Philosophy of Moral Development: Moral Stages and the Idea of Justice: Essays on Moral Development, Vol. 1*. San Francisco: Harper & Row.

Kohlberg, L. (1984). *The Psychology of Moral Development: The Nature and Validity of Moral Stages: Essays on Moral Development, Vol. 2*. San Francisco: Jossey Bass.

Kohut, H. (1971). *The Analysis of the Self: A Systematic Approach to the Psychoanalytic Treatment of Narcissistic Personality Disorders*. New York: International Universities Press.

Kozol, J. (2012). *Savage Inequalities: Children in America's Schools*. New York: Harper & Row.

Kuhn, T. (1962). *The Structure of Scientific Revolutions*. Chicago: University of Chicago Press.

Kula, W. (1986). *Measures and Men*. Princeton: Princeton University Press.

Lacan, J. (1977). *Écrits: A Selection* (A. Sheridan, Ed. and Trans.). New York: W. W. Norton & Company.

Lagemann, E. C. (2000). *An Elusive Science: The Troubling History of Educational Research*. Chicago: University of Chicago Press.

Lakoff, G., & Johnson, M. (1999). *Philosophy in the Flesh: The Embodied Mind and Its Challenge to Western Thought*. New York: Basic Books.

Lampland, M., & Star, S. L. (Eds.). (2009). *Standards and Their Stories: How Quantifying, Classifying, and Formalizing Practices Shape Everyday Life*. Ithaca: Cornell University Press.

Lasch, C. (1979). *The Culture of Narcissism: American Life in an Age of Diminishing Expectations*. New York: W. W. Norton & Company.

Laszlo, E. (2004). *Science and the Akashic Field: An Integral Theory of Everything*. Rochester, VT: Inner Traditions.

Lemann, N. (1999). *The Big Test: The Secret History of the American Meritocracy*. New York: Farrar, Straus & Giroux.

Lewin, K. (1936). *Principles of Topological Psychology* (F. Heider & G. M. Heider, Trans.). New York: McGraw-Hill.

Li, D., Sham, P. C., Owen, M. J., & He, L. (2006). "Meta-Analysis Shows Significant Association Between Dopamine System Genes and Attention Deficit Hyperactivity Disorder (ADHD)." *Human Molecular Genetics, 15*, 2276-2284.

Liebenau, J. (1987). *Medical Science and Medical Industry: The Formation of the American Pharmaceutical Industry*. London: Macmillan.

Loe, I. M., & Feldman, H. M. (2007). "Academic and Educational Outcomes of Children with ADHD." *Journal of Pediatric Psychology, 32*(6), 643-654.

Loevinger, J. (1976). *Ego Development: Conceptions and Theories*. San Francisco: Jossey-Bass.

Luhmann, N. (1995). *Social Systems*. Stanford: Stanford University Press.

Luhmann, N. (2004). *Law as a Social System*. New York: Oxford University Press.

Marx, K. (1844/1964). *Economic and Philosophic Manuscripts of 1844*. New York: International Publishers.

Marx, K. (1867/1977). *Capital: A Critique of Political Economy* (Vol. 1). New York: Vintage Books.

Mascolo, M. F., & Fischer, K. W. (2010). "The Dynamic Development of Thinking, Feeling, and Acting Over the Lifespan." In R. M. Lerner & W. F. Overton (Eds.), *The Handbook of Life-Span Development, Vol. 1: Cognition, Biology, and Methods*. Hoboken, NJ: Wiley.

Maslow, A. H. (1971). *The Farther Reaches of Human Nature*. New York: Arkana/Penguin Books.

May, R. (1969). *Love and Will*. New York: Norton.

McIntosh, S. (2007). *Integral Consciousness and the Future of Evolution: How the Integral Worldview Is Transforming Politics, Culture, and Spirituality*. St. Paul, MN: Paragon House.

McLuhan, M. (1964). *Understanding Media: The Extensions of Man.* New York: McGraw-Hill.

Mead, M. (1970). *Culture and Commitment: A Study of the Generation Gap.* New York: Doubleday.

Michell, J. (1972). *City of Revelation.* New York: Ballantine Books.

Moore, J. W. (2015). *Capitalism in the Web of Life: Ecology and the Accumulation of Capital.* New York: Verso.

Mumford, L. (1934). *Technics and Civilization.* New York: Harcourt, Brace and Co.

Mumford, L. (1967). *The Myth of the Machine, Vol. 1: Technics and Human Development.* New York: Harcourt, Brace and Co.

Mumford, L. (1970). *The Myth of the Machine, Vol. 2: Pentagon of Power.* New York: Harcourt, Brace and Co.

Murphy, M. (1992). *The Future of the Body: Explorations Into the Further Evolution of Human Nature*. New York: Tarcher.

Naam, R. (2013). *The Infinite Resource: The Power of Ideas on a Finite Planet.* Lebanon, NH: UPNE.

National Science Foundation (NSF). (2008). "Fostering Learning in the Networked World: The Cyberlearning Opportunity and Challenge." Arlington, VA: NSF Task Force on Cyberlearning.

Neil. M. (2015). "Authentic Assessment Inventory." *Fairtest.org.*

Nelkin, D., & Tancredi, L. (1989). *Dangerous Diagnostics: The Social Power of Biological Information*. New York: Basic Books.

Niebuhr, R. (1960). *Moral Man and Immoral Society: A Study in Ethics and Politics*. New York: Charles Scribner's Sons.

Nigg, J. T., Goldsmith, H. H., & Sachek, J. (2004). "Temperament and Attention Deficit Hyperactivity Disorder: The Development of a Multiple Pathway Model." *Journal of Clinical Child and Adolescent Psychology, 33*(1), 42-53.

Nisenson, E. (1993). *Ascension: John Coltrane and His Quest*. New York:

Da Capo Press.

Nussbaum, M. (2000). *Women and Human Development: The Capabilities Approach*. New York: Cambridge University Press.

Nussbaum, M. (2001). *Upheavals of Thought: The Intelligence of Emotions*. New York: Cambridge University Press.

Nussbaum, M. (2006). *Frontiers of Justice: Disability, Nationality, Species Membership*. Cambridge: Harvard University Press.

Olfman, S. (Ed.). (2006). *No Child Left Different*. Westport, CT: Praeger.

Overton, W. F. (2007). "A Coherent Metatheory for Dynamic Systems: Relational Organicism-Contextualism." *Human Development*, *50*, 154-159.

Parens, E., & Johnston, J. (2008). "Understanding the Agreements and Controversies Surrounding Childhood Psychopharmacology." *Child and Adolescent Psychiatry and Mental Health*, *2*, 5.

Parens, E., & Johnston, J. (2009). "Facts, Values, and Attention-Deficit Hyperactivity Disorder (ADHD): An Update on the Controversies." *Child and Adolescent Psychiatry and Mental Health*, *3*, 1.

Pariser, E. (2011). *The Filter Bubble: How the New Personalized Web Is Changing What We Read and How We Think*. New York: Penguin Books.

Pastor, P. N., & Reuben, C. A. (2008, July). "Diagnosed Attention Deficit Hyperactivity Disorder and Learning Disability: United States, 2004-2006." *National Center for Health Statistics: Vital Health Statistics*, *10*(237), 1-14.

Pavlov, I. P. (1927). *Conditioned Reflexes: An Investigation of the Physiological Activity of the Cerebral Cortex*. New York: Dover Publications.

Peirce, C. S. (1866). "The Logic of Science; or Induction and Hypothesis: Lowell Lectures of 1866." In Peirce Edition Project (Eds.), *Writings of Charles S. Peirce: A Chronological Edition* (Vol. 1). Bloomington, IN: Indiana University Press.

Peirce, C. S. (1933). "Book Two: Existential Graphs." In C. Hartshorne & P. Weiss (Eds.), *The Collected Papers of Charles S. Peirce* (Vol. 4).

Cambridge: Harvard University Press.
Pfaffenberger, A. H., Marko, P. W., & Combs, A. (2011). *The Postconventional Personality: Assessing, Researching, and Theorizing Higher Development.* Albany: SUNY.
Philipsen, D. (2015). *The Little Big Number: How GDP Came to Rule the World and What to Do About It.* Princeton: Princeton University Press.
Phillips, K. R. (2003). *Testing Controversy: A Rhetoric of Educational Reform.* Cresskill, NJ: Hampton Press.
Piaget, J. (1928). *Judgment and Reasoning in the Child.* London: Routledge and Kegan Paul.
Piaget, J. (1932). *The Moral Judgment of the Child.* New York: Harcourt, Brace.
Piaget, J. (1972). *The Principles of Genetic Epistemology.* London: Routledge and Kegan Paul.
Piketty, T. (2014). *Capital in the Twenty-First Century.* Cambridge: Harvard University Press.
Porter, T. M. (1996). *Trust in Numbers: The Pursuit of Objectivity in Science and Public Life*. Princeton: Princeton University Press.
Prigogine, I., & Stengers, I. (1984). *Order Out of Chaos*. New York: Bantam.
Purdy, J. (2015). *After Nature: A Politics for the Anthropocene*. Cambridge: Harvard University Press.
Quigley, C. (1961). *The Evolution of Civilizations: An Introduction to Historical Analysis.* New York: Macmillan.
Quigley, C. (1966). *Tragedy and Hope: A History of the World in Our Time.* New York: Macmillan.
Quigley, C. (1983). *Weapons Systems and Political Stability: A History.* Washington, DC: University Press of America.
Rasmussen, N. (2008). *On Speed: The Many Lives of Amphetamine*. New York: New York University Press.
Ravitch, D. (2010). *The Death and Life of the Great American School System: How Testing and Choice Are Undermining Education*. New York: Basic Books.
Ravitch, D. (2013). *Reign of Error: The Hoax of the Privatization Movement*

and the Danger to America's Public Schools. New York: Knopf.

Rawls, J. (1971). *A Theory of Justice*. Cambridge: Harvard University Press.

Rawls, J. (1996). *Political Liberalism*. New York: Columbia University Press.

Rawls, J. (1999). *Collected Papers*. Cambridge: Harvard University Press.

Rawls, J. (2001). *Justice as Fairness: A Restatement*. Cambridge: Harvard University Press.

Richardson. R. (1995). *Emerson: The Mind on Fire*. Berkley: University of California Press.

Ritzer, G. (1991). *Metatheorizing in Sociology*. Lexington, MA: Lexington Books.

Ritzer, G. (Ed.). (1992). *Metatheorizing*. Newbury Park, CA: Sage.

Robb, J. (2008). *Brave New War: The Next Stage of Terrorism and the End of Globalization*. Hoboken, NJ: John Wiley & Sons, Inc.

Rose, L. T., Rouhani, P., & Fischer, K. W. (2013). "The Science of the Individual." *Mind, Brain, and Education*, *7*(3), 152-158.

Rosenberg, S. W. (2002). *The Not So Common Sense: Differences in How People Judge Social and Political Life*. New Haven: Yale University Press.

Ross, W. D. (Ed.). (1921). *The Works of Aristotle, Volume X*. Oxford: Clarendon Press.

Sacks, P. (1999). *Standardized Minds: The High Price of America's Testing Culture and What We Can Do to Change It*. Cambridge: Perseus Press.

Safer, D. J., Zito, J. M., & Fine, E. M. (1996). "Increased Methylphenidate Usage for Attention Deficit Disorder in the 1990s." *Pediatrics*, *98*, 1084-1088.

Sahlberg, P. (2012). *Finnish Lessons: What Can the World Learn From Educational Change in Finland?* New York: Teachers College Press.

Saltman, K. (2016). *Scripted Bodies: Corporate Power, Smart Technologies, and the Undoing of Public Education*. New York: Routledge.

Samelson, F. (1990). "Was Early Mental Testing: a) Racist Inspired, b) Objective Science, c) A Technology for Democracy, d) The Origin of the Multiple Choice Exams, e) None of the Above?" In M. Sokal (Ed.), *Psychological Testing in American Society, 1890-1930* (pp. 113-128). New Brunswick: Rutgers University Press.

Santens, S. (2015, May 27). "The Basic Affordability of Basic Income." *Huffingtonpost.com.*

Sax, L., & Kautz, K. J. (2003). "Who First Suggests the Diagnosis of Attention-Deficit/Hyperactivity Disorder?" *Annals of Family Medicine*, *1*(3), 171-174.

Scheffler, R. M., Hinshaw, S. P., Modrek, S., & Levine, P. (2007). "The Global Market for ADHD Medications." *Health Affairs*, *26*(2), 450-457.

Schneider, H., & Eisenberg, D. (2006). "Who Receives a Diagnosis of Attention-Deficit/Hyperactivity Disorder in the United States Elementary School Population?" *Pediatrics*, *117*(4), e601-e609.

Scholz, T., & Schneider, N. (Eds.). (2017). *Ours to Hack and to Own: The Rise of Platform Cooperativism, A New Vision for the Future of Work and a Fairer Internet.* Portland: OR Books.

Scott, J. C. (1998). *Seeing Like a State: How Certain Schemes to Improve the Human Condition Have Failed.* New Haven: Yale University Press.

Searle, J. R. (1995). *The Construction of Social Reality.* New York: Free Press.

Seba, T. (2014). *Clean Disruption of Energy and Transportation: How Silicon Valley Will Make Oil, Nuclear, Natural Gas, Coal, Electric Utilities and Conventional Cars Obsolete by 2030.* Silicon Valley, CA: Clean Planet Ventures.

Seidman, L. J., Valera, E. M., & Makris, N. (2005). "Structural Brain Imaging of Attention-Deficit/Hyperactivity Disorder." *Biological Psychiatry*, *57*(11), 1263-1272.

Sen, A. (1982). *Choice, Welfare, and Measurement.* Cambridge: Harvard University Press.

Sen, A. (2000). "Merit and Justice." In K. Arrow, S. Bowles, & S. Durlauf (Eds.), *Meritocracy and Economic Inequality* (pp. 5-16). Princeton: Princeton University Press.

Siegler, R. S. (1981). "Developmental Sequences Within and Between Concepts." *Monographs of the Society for Research in Child Development*, *46*(2), 84.

Singh, I. (2008). "Beyond Polemics: Science and Ethics of ADHD." *Nature Reviews Neuroscience*, *9*(12), 957-964.

Singh, I., & Rose, N. (2009). "Biomarkers in Psychiatry." *Nature*, *460*(7252), 202-207.

Skinner, B. F. (1938). *The Behavior of Organisms: An Experimental Analysis*. New York: D. Appleton-Century Co.

Smith, H. (1989). *Beyond the Postmodern Mind: The Place of Meaning in a Global Civilization.* Wheaton, IL: Theosophical Publishing House.

Sonuga-Barke, E. J. S. (2005). "Causal Models of Attention-Deficit/Hyperactivity Disorder: From Common Simple Deficits to Multiple Developmental Pathways." *Biological Psychiatry*, *57*(11), 1231-1238.

Spring, J. H. (1989). *The Sorting Machine Revisited: National Educational Policy Since 1945*. New York: Longman.

Spring, J. H. (2010). *American Education*. New York: McGraw-Hill.

Stecher, B., Vernez, G., & Steinberg, P. (2010). *Reauthorizing No Child Left Behind: Facts and Recommendations*. Santa Monica, CA: RAND Corporation.

Steffen, W., Broadgate, W., Deutsch, L., Gaffney, O., & Ludwig, C. (2015). "The Trajectory of the Anthropocene: The Great Acceleration." *The Anthropocene Review*, *2*(1), 81-98.

Stein. Z. (2007). "Modeling the Demands of Interdisciplinarity: Toward a Framework for Evaluating Interdisciplinary Endeavors." *Integral Review*, *4*, 91-107.

Stein, Z. (2009). "Educational Crises and the Scramble for Usable Knowledge." *Integral Review*, *5*(2), 355.

Stein, Z. (2009a). "Resetting the Stage: Introducing a Special Section About Learning Sequences and Developmental Theory." *Mind, Brain, and Education, 3*(2), 94-95.

Stein, Z. (2010). "On the Normative Function of Metatheoretical Endeavors." *Integral Review*, *6*(3), 5-22.

Stein, Z. (2010a). "On the Difference Between Designing Children and Raising Them: Ethics and the Use of Educationally Oriented Biotechnology." *Mind, Brain, and Education*, *4*(2), 53-67.

Stein, Z. (2013). "Ethics and the New Education: Psychopharmacology, Psychometrics, and the Future of Human Capital." *Journal of Integral Theory and Practice*, *8*(3-4), 146-162.

Stein, Z. (2014). "On the Use of the Term Integral." *Journal of Integral Theory and Practice*, *9*(2), 104-114.

Stein, Z. (2015). "Beyond Nature and Humanity: Reflections on the Emergence and Purposes of Metatheories." In R. Bhaskar, S. Esbjörn-Hargens, N. Hedlund, & M. Hartwig (Eds.), *Metatheory for the Twenty-First Century: Critical Realism and Integral Theory in Dialogue*. New York: Routledge.

Stein, Z. (2016). *Social Justice and Educational Measurement: John Rawls, the History of Testing, and the Future of Education*. New York: Routledge.

Stein, Z. (Forthcoming). "On Realizing the Possibilities of Emancipatory Metatheory: Beyond the Cognitive Maturity Fallacy, Toward an Education Revolution." In R. Bhaskar, S. Esbjörn-Hargens, N. Hedlund, & M. Hartwig (Eds.), *Metatheory for the Anthropocene: Emancipatory Praxis for Planetary Flourishing*. London: Routledge.

Stein, Z. (Manuscript in preparation). *Recreating Humanity: A Thought Experiment in the Philosophy of Education*.

Stein, Z., Dawson, T. L., & Fischer, K. W. (2010). "Redesigning Testing: Operationalizing the New Science of Learning." In M. S. Khine & I. M. Saleh (Eds.), *The New Science of Learning: Cognition, Computers and Collaboration in Education* (pp. 207-224). New York: Springer Press.

Stein, Z., della Chiesa, B., Hinton, C., & Fischer, K. W. (2011). "Ethical Issues in Educational Neuroscience: Raising Children in a Brave New World." In J. Illes & B. Sahakian (Eds.), *Oxford Handbook of Neuroethics*. Oxford: Oxford University Press.

Stein, Z., & Gafni, M. (Forthcoming). *Towards a New Politics of Evolutionary Love*. Tucson, AZ: Integral Publishers.

Stein, Z., & Heikkinen, K. (2009). "Metrics, Models, and Measurement in Developmental Psychology." *Integral Review*, *5*(1), 4-24.

Stiglitz, J. E., & Greenwald, B. C. (2014). *Creating a Learning Society: A New Approach to Growth, Development, and Social Progress.* New York: Columbia University Press.

Sullivan, H. S. (1984). *Personal Psychopathology.* New York: W. W. Norton & Company.

Swanson, J. M., Kinsbourne, M., Nigg, J., Lanphear, B., Stefanatos, G. A., Volkow, N., ... Wadhwa, P. D. (2007). "Etiologic Subtypes of Attention-Deficit/Hyperactivity Disorder: Brain Imaging, Molecular Genetic and Environmental Factors and the Dopamine Hypothesis." *Neuropsychological Review*, *17*(1), 39-59.

Swanson, J. M., Sergeant, J. A., Taylor E., Sonuga-Barke, E. J., Jensen, P. S., & Cantwell, D. P. (1998). "Attention-Deficit Hyperactivity Disorder and Hyperkinetic Disorder." *Lancet*, *351*(9100), 429-433.

Tavernor, R. (2007). *Smoot's Ear: The Measure of Humanity.* New Haven: Yale University Press.

Taylor, C. (1989). *Sources of the Self: The Making of the Modern Identity.* Cambridge: Harvard University Press.

Taylor, C. (1992). *The Ethics of Authenticity.* Cambridge: Harvard University Press.

Taylor, F. W. (1911). *The Principles of Scientific Management.* New York: Harper & Brothers.

Thompson, W. I. (1971). *At the Edge of History: Speculations on the Transformation of Culture*. New York: Harper & Row.

Thompson, W. I. (1977). *Darkness and Scattered Light*. New York: Anchor Books.

Thompson, W. I. (1998). *Coming Into Being: Artifacts and Texts in the Evolution of Consciousness*. New York: Palgrave Macmillan.

Thompson, W. I. (2004). *Self and Society: Studies in the Evolution of Culture*. Charlottesville, VA: Imprint Academic.

Thompson, W. I. (2009). *Transforming History: A New Curriculum for a Planetary Culture*. Great Barrington, MA: Lindisfarne Books.

Tillich, P. (1958). *Dynamics of Faith.* New York: Harper & Brothers.

Tillich, P. (1959). *Theology of Culture.* Oxford: Oxford University Press.

Toch, T. (2006). "Margins of Error: The Education Testing Industry in the No Child Left Behind Era." Washington, D.C.: Education Sector.

Tomasello, M. (1999). *The Cultural Origins of Human Cognition.* Cambridge: Harvard University Press.

Twist, L. (2003). *The Soul of Money: Reclaiming the Wealth of Our Inner Resources.* New York: W. W. Norton & Company.

United Nations. (1989, November 20). Convention on the Rights of the Child. United Nations, New York.

van Geert, P. (1994). *Dynamic Systems of Development: Change Between Complexity and Chaos.* New York: Harvester Wheatsheaf.

Wallerstein, I. (1974). *The Modern World System: Capitalist Agriculture and the Origins of the European World-Economy in the Sixteenth Century.* New York: Academic Press.

Wallerstein, I. (2003). "Intellectuals in an Age of Transition." In W. A. Dunaway (Ed.), *Emerging Issues in the 21st Century World-System, Vol. 2: New Theoretical Directions for the 21st Century World-System* (pp. 14-29). Westport, CT: Praeger.

Wallerstein, I. (2006). *World-Systems Analysis: An Introduction.* Durham, NC: Duke University Press.

Ward, P. D., & Brownlee, D. (2000). *Rare Earth: Why Complex Life Is Uncommon in the Universe.* New York: Copernicus Books.

Watson, M. W., & Fischer, K. W. (1980). "Development of Social Roles in Elicited and Spontaneous Behavior During the Preschool Years." *Developmental Psychology, 16*(5), 484-494.

Weber, B. H., & Depew, D. J. (Eds.). (2007). *Evolution and Learning: The Baldwin Effect Reconsidered.* Cambridge: MIT Press.

Werner, H. (1957). "The Concept of Development From a Comparative and Organismic Point of View." In D. B. Harris (Ed.), *The Concept of Development: An Issue in the Study of Human Behavior.* Minneapolis: University of Minnesota Press.

West, C. (1982). *Prophesy, Deliverance! An Afro-American Revolutionary*

Christianity. Philadelphia: Westminster John Knox Press.

Whitaker, R. (2015). *Anatomy of an Epidemic: Magic Bullets, Psychiatric Drugs, and the Astonishing Rise of Mental Illness in America.* New York: Random House.

White, M. (2016). *The End of Protest: A New Playbook for Revolution.* Toronto, ON: Knopf Canada.

Wilber, K. (1983). "Legitimacy, Authenticity, and Authority in the New Religions." In K. Wilber, *Eye to Eye: The Quest for the New Paradigm.* In K. Wilber, *The Collected Works of Ken Wilber* (Vol. 3). Boston: Shambhala Publications.

Wilber, K. (1995). *Sex, Ecology, Spirituality: The Spirit of Evolution.* Boston: Shambhala Publications.

Wilber, K. (1999). *One Taste: Daily Reflections on Integral Spirituality.* Boston: Shambhala Publications.

Wilber, K. (2000). *Integral Psychology: Consciousness, Spirit, Psychology, Therapy.* Boston: Shambhala Publications.

Wilber, K. (2001). *Grace and Grit: Spirituality and Healing in the Life and Death of Treya Killam Wilber.* Boston: Shambhala Publications.

Wilber, K. (2005). *A Sociable God: Toward a New Understanding of Religion.* Boston: Shambhala Publications.

Wilber, K. (2006). *Integral Spirituality.* Boston: Shambhala Publications.

Wilber, K., Engler, J., & Brown, D. P. (1986). *Transformations of Consciousness: Conventional and Contemplative Perspectives on Development.* Boston: Shambhala Publications.

Wilson, E. O. (1975). *Sociobiology: The New Synthesis.* Cambridge: Harvard University Press.

Wolfram, S. (2002). *A New Kind of Science.* Chicago: Wolfram Media.

Zito, J. M., & Safer, D. J. (2005). "Recent Child Phamacoepidemiological Findings." *Journal of Child and Adolescent Psychopharmacology, 15*(1), 5-9.

Žižek, S. (2001). *On Belief.* New York: Routledge.

CPSIA information can be obtained
at www.ICGtesting.com
Printed in the USA
LVHW021937010421
683194LV00001B/6